The Egyptian Pyramids

The Egyptian Pyramids

A Comprehensive, Illustrated Reference

by

J.P. Lepre

McFarland & Company, Inc., Publishers
Jefferson, North Carolina, and London

British Library Cataloguing-in-Publication data are available

Library of Congress Cataloguing-in-Publication Data

Lepre, J.P.
The Egyptian pyramids : a comprehensive, illustrated reference /
J.P. Lepre.
p. cm.
[Includes index.]
Includes bibliographical references. ∞
ISBN 0-89950-461-2 (lib. bdg. : 55# alk. paper)
1. Pyramids — Egypt.   2. Egypt — Antiquities.   3. Pharaohs.
I. Title.
DT63.L47   1990
932 — dc20   89-43623
                                        CIP

Manufactured in the United States of America

McFarland & Company, Inc., Publishers
Box 611, Jefferson, North Carolina 28640

To my devoted parents,
Joseph and Elena

Preface

This reference to the early pyramid pharaohs and their celebrated monuments is the result of a 15-year study involving, among other research, three trips to Egypt, where I resided for nearly one year, investigating these monuments firsthand on a daily basis. Through this exploration and accompanying research, I have been able to compile this reference, emphasizing improved organization of previously scattered material, new illustrations, and original discussion based on the most up-to-date information available. I hope that with these emphases, the rudiments of a previously clouded subject will be brought into a clearer light.

Among the devices used to present this composite information is a chronological listing of the 42 pyramid pharaohs, which concisely reports available facts about each pharaoh, his pyramid, and his pyramid complex in a quick-reference format, in order to save the reader much rummaging through the text. More detailed discussion of the various pyramids may be found within the Dynasties Sections.

Illustrations here published for the first time include a diagram of the subsidiary pyramid of the Dynasty III Bent Pyramid of King Sneferu, at Dahshur; a diagram of the curious, sarcophagus-shaped Dynasty IV tomb of Queen Khentkawes, at Giza; and a three-dimensional diagram of the Dynasty XII Pyramid of Amenemhat III, at Hawara. Also, there are new illustrations of the Great Pyramid of King Khufu, at Giza. These include drawings of the oft-mentioned, mysteriously contrived "crosses" located in the east and west walls of the Grand Gallery; the controversial "raised boss" and "granite leaf" in the antechamber; the popular granite sarcophagus in the burial chamber, illustrating its ingenious assembly; the unorthodox, tri-shaped southern air channel in that same chamber; newly discovered red ocher construction lines and symbols in the east and west walls of the Queen's Chamber horizontal passageway; and a detailed rendition of the Subterranean Chamber.

This book began as a manuscript compilation for my own reference, providing me with quick access to crucial information while in the field. I sought to accumulate a mass of data so that the manuscript would represent the most detailed compendium possible of well-organized primary and secondary facts. The result, I found, was a volume of information useful both to the serious researcher and to the beginning student. It touches upon all aspects of Egyptian pyramids, including archaeological, historical, and

Egyptological schools of thought, and stresses the tomb theory of pyramid building. Even now, in this finished form, it represents an ongoing project which will eventually require a lifetime of work. Many more pyramid sites need to be examined, and much more data harvested. This does not mean that a sizeable amount of information has not been accumulated, but that it will always need to be sifted and focused more clearly, in conjunction with fresh data.

There is so much work yet to be done in dealing with these ancient edifices. The various pieces of the fractured puzzle, so many of them missing for so long, need to be brought to the fore and recorded. Mountains of work confront the Egyptologist specializing in pyramids.

It is my hope that this book will inspire an enlightened understanding of the principal features of study concerning Egyptian pyramids, and make the user more aware of how, why and by whom these mysterious monuments were built. I hope that both scholar and layman alike may benefit from the information contained herein.

This book is intended as an aid in familiarizing the reader, in an orderly arrangement, with the early pyramid pharaohs and their celebrated monuments. It represents a compendium of the more substantial and pertinent facts gleaned from the detailed works of Egyptologists Grinsell, Weigall, Edwards, Petrie, Lauer and other great authorities on Egyptian pyramids, interspersed with my own accumulated material. I am especially indebted to Sir Arthur Weigall, on whose comprehensive study of the early kings much of the information regarding the pyramid-pharaoh commentaries was based, and to Sir Alan Gardiner, for his indispensable and monumental treatise on hieroglyphic grammar.

In the preparation of this manuscript I am further indebted to Joyce A. Mayer for assisting with portions of the typing, Kimberly A. Mayer for drawing several of the diagrams, Peter Stuart of Australia for several of his photographs of the Great Pyramid, and to my publisher, McFarland & Company, for their superlative editing of the text. Also, a debt of a less direct kind, but one which is perhaps the most profound, is to my brother Anthony, who helped defray the cost of my journeys to Egypt and allowed me opportunities and leisure for research, without which this book could not have been written.

J.P.L.

Contents

Contents

VI.   Dynasties V–XI (The Decline)   153

Dynasty V   153

Dynasty VI   176

Dynasty VII   189

Dynasty VIII   191

Dynasty IX   191

Contents   xii

Introduction

For centuries the Egyptian pyramids have fascinated scholar and layman alike, fostering numerous theories and a great deal of speculation on their origin and purpose. Some have proposed that they were the burial tombs of the pharaohs; others, that they were used as granaries, water pumps, geodetic markers, astronomical observatories, initiation places for a secret priesthood and scores of other structures almost too numerous to mention. Some even suggest they were built by visitors from other planets or galaxies. Upon a thorough examination of the various pyramid sites, though, it becomes obvious that these monuments were in fact the burial tombs of the Old and Middle Kingdom pharaohs. All of the other fanciful hypotheses have failed to convince the serious researcher because they are inconsistent with the fundamental archaeological evidence. Theory must be supported by fact or lose credibility. Everyone has at some time formulated an idea, or a host of ideas, regarding a particular subject; but can those ideas be supported by the evidence? The mass of evidence supporting the theory that the Egyptian pyramids were the depositories for the mummies of deceased pharaohs is irrefutable, and should not be casually ignored by interested parties who wish to express their own views on the subject. If the reports of archaeological evidence that supports this tomb theory were researched beforehand, the number of fantastic theories regarding these edifices would surely be considerably reduced.

The Egyptian pyramids are all built along the west bank of the Nile — not a single one is on the east bank — for a distance of 600 miles from north to south; from Athribis, several miles north of famed Giza, to Elaphantine, at the first cataract.

I have listed the number of pyramids as 100, but in reality the 99th and 100th "pyramids" are the two sarcophagus-shaped tombs of the Pharaoh Shepseskaf and his sister, Queen Khentkawes, both of Dynasty IV. Because of their long association with and proximity to the pyramids, they are recorded by me as "pyramids" number 11 (Khentkawes) and 60 (Shepseskaf).

Few people are aware of the existence of so many Egyptian pyramids. Most individuals, when questioned, will answer that there are anywhere from two or three to a dozen or so pyramids in Egypt. Even researchers who appear to be familiar with the subject usually number anywhere from 70 to 80 pyramids, with only a few citing as many as 90. This does not necessarily reflect poorly on their own particular knowledge of other aspects of pyramid study, but merely suggests an oversight in adequately summoning together all of the piecemeal information to arrive at the correct number.

Too many books and documentaries on the subject of Egyptian pyramids continue to attest that the first pyramid ever built in Egypt was the famed Step Pyramid of King Djoser from Dynasty III. In truth, Djoser's pyramid represented the first *large* pyramid ever built, with a baseline of 411' by 358' (being of an unusual rectangular shape). Yet ten much smaller step pyramids (lengths approximately 60' to 75') actually preceded Djoser's monument, a fact seldom, if ever, mentioned.

The scale of Djoser's tomb at Sakkara was quite large, and immensity remained the rule for subsequent pyramids. Massive indeed were the two pyramids of Snefru, the last pharaoh of the Third Dynasty, at Dahshur; but the competition for size reached its zenith in the Great Pyramid of Khufu, first pharaoh of the Fourth Dynasty, at Giza.

During this illustrious period of pyramid building, not only were the principal monuments extremely large, but their interior designs were somewhat complex. Post-Khufu, the Pharaoh Khafra had a pyramid almost as large, but with a simpler interior plan. In post–Khafra times, not only did pyramids dramatically decrease in size, but simultaneously they became oversimplified in their internal schemes, reaching a point where the last major pyramid of the Fifth Dynasty and the first six major pyramids of the Sixth Dynasty were all built on the same simple "copy-cat" design.

Not until the Twelfth Dynasty — after an absence of nearly all pyramid building since the Seventh Dynasty — was there a pyramid revival of a sort. Here the monuments became much larger and more complicated internally, although never again achieving the size and sophistication of the Great Pyramid.

Today, most of the pyramid sites are abandoned and in ruins, a cheerless situation that might persist forever — or nearly so. With its resources and economy strained, the Egyptian government has had little choice but to let the majority of its national monuments fall into a severe state of disrepair. With other economies of the world also struggling, archaeological expeditions to Egypt are on the wane, and the attention given to the pyramids and other landmarks has thus declined. If the excavation work on the pyramids were to be intensified and updated, many more of the centuries-old questions might probably be answered — questions such as, Why were the majority of pyramids abruptly abandoned in the midst of their construction? Where are the remains of most of the 42 pyramid pharaohs, given that the present remains are so few in number? What is the true purpose of the satellite or subsidiary pyramids?

Although we may appear to know very much about the Egyptian pyramids if we devote ourselves to lengthy studies of particular aspects of the subject, this knowledge is, at the most, superficial. For we surmise how the ancient builders may have manipulated huge blocks of stone, but we do not understand the specifics; we can assume that the pharaoh was mummified in a solution of natron and other ingredients, but we do not know the exact formula; we can conjecture that officiating priests conducted funerary offices in the mortuary and valley temples, but we cannot reconstruct the ceremonies.

We do not know how the ancients set certain stones into their final resting places while working in close quarters; nor why some of the subsidiary pyramids contained "burial chambers" that were too small for a burial; nor whether the casing stones were placed into position working from the bottom of the monument up or from the top down; nor how many priests were assigned to the funerary temples; nor exactly what the function of each one was.

We are very much in the dark about many facets of the pyramid age, the principal reason being that so many of the pyramid sites have been so long neglected. If they were ever to be properly excavated, these areas could reveal untold knowledge of this great era in Egyptian history.

Chronology:
Dynasties of Ancient Egypt

Dynasty		Date (B.C.)	Years
–	Predynastic Period	3800–3408	392
	Early Dynastic Period		
1		3407–3144	519
2		3143–2888	
	Old Kingdom		
3		2887–2790	
4		2789–2716	434
5		2715–2588	
6		2587–2453	
	1st Intermediate Period		
7		2452–2378	
8		2377–2272	340
9–11		2271–2112	
	Middle Kingdom		
12		2111–1899	366
13–14		1898–1745	
	2nd Intermediate Period		
15		1744–1728	163
16–17		1727–1581	
	New Kingdom		
18		1580–1351	
19		1350–1201	
20		1200–1086	
21		1085–951	867
22		950–818	
23		817–731	
24		730–713	
	Post Kingdom		
25		712–664	186
26		663–526	
	Persian Rule		
27–30		525–333	192
	Greek Rule		
31–46		332–31	301
	Roman Rule		
–		30 B.C.–A.D. 364	334

I. The First Kings of Egypt

Egypt at the dawn of history was divided into seven distinct kingdoms or spheres of influence: the Hornet Kingdom of Lower Egypt; the Reed Kingdom of Memphis and Heracleopolis; the Hawk Kingdom (of Nekhen); the Thinis (Theni) Kingdom; the Set Kingdom; the Kingdom of On (Heliopolis); and the Hawk Kingdom (of Ro and Ket).

The Hornet Kingdom extended from the Mediterranean shores to the apex of the Nile Delta. The Turin Papyrus has been assigned to this period, which originated about 5507 B.C.

There are no extant records of these early kings other than certain fragments of their names taken from several of the more reliable annals. This does not mean to imply, however, that their civilization was not a sophisticated one. Even at that early stage of history the Delta region included busy river traffic, rich fields, countless villages, cities and a maritime trade with Asia. The hieroglyphic script was known to exist in Egypt long before the reign of Menes, the first pharaoh of the First Dynasty, and it is not unlikely that it was being developed at the time of the Hornet Kingdom. The center of government could have been at either Sais or Buto, or perhaps they enjoyed the status of co-capitals.

The title of these early kings was *Bya,* meaning "Bee" or "Hornet." Later the temple of Sais was referred to as "The House of the Bya."

The famous Red Crown of Lower Egypt is said to have originated with these hornet kings, for their royal treasury was called the "Red House." The association of one of the co-capitals, Buto, with the Pharaonic symbol of royalty, the cobra, should be noted. The cobra was the symbol of Buto's patron goddess, Utho (Uto).

The people of this Hornet Kingdom were of mixed race, and there is some speculation that at least some of them may have been of Mesopotamian origin, while there was a strong Libyan element residing in the capital of Sais itself.

The Reed Kingdom also enjoyed dual capitals; one at Heracleopolis and the other at Memphis. Manetho mentions 30 kings who ruled over the latter city 1,790 years before Menes. The Turin Papyrus partially supports this contention, recording 19 premenite kings from Memphis. Also recorded by Manetho is the date of this kingdom's foundation, set at about 5197 B.C.

Of the twin capitals of Heracleopolis and Memphis, the former (also known earlier as Eheninsi) was most probably the original. Its sovereign was called Insi, meaning "the reed," and it was from him that the tall, white crown of Egypt was first made known. The royal treasury of this kingdom was referred to as the "White House," and the kingdom's symbolic color was also white.

After Menes had fully united Upper and Lower Egypt, the Insi (Reed Kingdom) title was coupled with the

1

Bya (Hornet Kingdom) to form the afterwards famous and enduring Insi-Bya (Reed and Hornet) title.

It appears that some time after the establishment of this kingdom the influence of Heracleopolis waned and the newly built city of Memphis became the full-time royal residence. The southern border of the Reed Kingdom seems to have penetrated as far as Asyut and Denderah, butting against the kingdom of the Hawk kings, while its northern borders were contact points with the previously mentioned Hornet Kingdom.

It seems as if the people of this Reed Kingdom had originally come from the more northern parts of the Delta and could actually have comprised a nomadic element from the Hornet Kingdom, having made their way further south in those great river-going vessels so often depicted in drawings found in Lower Egypt.

The Hawk Kingdom ruled from Hieraconpolis (Nekhen), appropriately called "the City of the Hawks." It lay near to Edfu, between Aswan and Luxor. Chronologically, it preceded Menes, but the names of its rulers are not recorded on any of the annals; the facts of the dynasty are quite obscure.

The title of these kings was written with the sign of a hawk situated above a sort of temple enclosure or tomb facade, or more probably, that of the royal palace itself. These monarchs were called *Hur* (or Her, Hor, Har), meaning "the Hawk," and their original sphere of influence was most likely confined to the "Hawk-province" that included Edfu and Hieraconpolis.

The original inhabitants of the Hawk Kingdom are said to have migrated north from the land of Pount (Punt), on the Red Sea coast. In that sense, Pount is often referred to as the "Land of the Gods." In olden times there was an important caravan route from Pount to certain points in Egypt, and the conquering Hawk-people may have entered the Nile Valley via this passage.

The Theni Kingdom was comprised of 10 monarchs who held control over the city of Theni (Thinis or This) for 650 years. The capital lay between Asyut and Luxor. Although we have the names of the last four of these kings, the first six are lost.

On the majority of their monuments these monarchs employ the title of the Hawk. It seems, then, that this branch of rulers succeeded the original dynasty of Hawk-kings of Hieraconpolis (Nekhen). Actually, each of these kings, although ruling from Theni (Thinis), was crowned at Nekhen, yet each seems to have had a second (Theni) name other than that of the Hawk.

The foundation of this kingdom took place circa 3757 B.C. (just 350 years before Menes), probably the date of the fall of the Hawks of Nekhen Kingdom.

The Set Kingdom worshipped the god Set (originally in the form of a wild pig) at Shashotpe, the capital of the Set province. From the Book of the Dead we learn of Set's transformation into a black pig, and Plutarch tells us that later Egyptians had the custom of yearly sacrificing a pig to this god.

The Set people, although primarily situated at their capital city of Shashotpe, were apparently scattered throughout all of Egypt. Legends place them in the town of Sesesu in the Fayum, where the god Set was said to have been born; in the marshes of the Delta; and at a city called Avaris, also in the Delta. They also resided between Luxor and Aswan, specifically at El Kab and Esneh, and on the banks of the Nile in the Eleventh Province; but they eventually settled in greater numbers at Ombos, where they erected a great temple to Set. Here can be found vast cemeteries dating to the period prior to Dynasty I.

Plutarch tells us that these Set people were men of red hair, and this may be a reference to some Libyan factions who are known for this trait.

The On (Heliopolis) Kingdom was located at the head of a great caravan trail to Sinai, Suez and Arabia. The name On seems to represent some sort of a pillar or obelisk, while the word Heliopolis was interpreted as "the City of the Sun."

On is also read An or In, but the former is the more accepted spelling. On was referred to as "Pillar City."

The inhabitants of this kingdom worshipped Re (Ra), the sun-god, whose symbol was a small pyramidion called a *Benben* or simply *Ben.*

Besides this capital city of On, there were two other like-named cities in Egypt, one just south of Thebes (Luxor), and the second close to modern Denderah.

The Hawk Kingdom (of Ro and Ket) was located just west of the twin cities of Theni (Thinis) and Abydos (Ebod) in Upper Egypt. At this site tombs of the several monarchs immediately preceding Menes were discovered, being brick-lined pits of considerable size. Here were found inscriptions reading "Ro," above which was the sign of the hawk, and a chronicle of one of these monarchs, who actually had the personal name Ro.

The royal residence was at Theni, near where this king was buried, but the older capital of the original Hawks, Nekhen, was more than likely the center of the kingdom. The southern boundary of these people appears to have been at Gebel Sil-

sileh, and the northern boundary met with the southern boundary of the Reed-king of Heracleopolis.

The monarch who followed Ro was called Ket (Ke), and his name was likewise written with the symbol of the hawk above it. His tomb was discovered close to that of Ro, being also a large, brick-lined pit. Ket's name was also found written alongside that of another monarch who was known as "the Scorpion." It is surmised, then, that Ket and the Scorpion ultimately may have shared a joint rule, such co-regencies being popular in various phases of Egyptian history.

Following the reign of Ket was the king known as the Scorpion (3450–3425 B.C.), and following him, the famous Narmer (3425–3407 B.C.) of the "Narmer Palette." After Narmer comes Menes (Mene), the illustrious unifier of Upper and Lower Egypt, and the first pharaoh of the first officially numbered and labeled dynasty, Dynasty I.

(Here the author would like to rectify the widespread misconception that the last predynastic Hawk-Pharaoh, Narmer, and the first dynastic Pharaoh, Menes, were somehow one and the same person. That these men were two separate personages is clear from their sculpted portraits: Narmer is depicted as thin-faced — not only on the noted "Narmer Palette," but also in a second sculpting executed some 25 years later in honor of his Jubilee Ceremony — whereas Menes is depicted as having much fuller and wider [possibly Negroid] facial features. Further evidence that Narmer and Menes were two different pharaohs lies in the famous "Ivory Plaque of Menes" [DeMorgan, *Recherches,* 1897, reproduced in Budge, *History,* I, 178], which shows that the Hawk-name of Menes was not Narmer, but Ohe.)

Thus the foundation of early Egypt was laid. From these vital beginnings, the first two dynasties developed inspiration and organization, which ultimately produced the resources and energetic drive required to support the early period of the great Third and Fourth Dynasty pyramid building age and beyond.

The beginnings of that great pyramid age, being of the Old Kingdom, lie close to the days of the predynastic kingdoms, through whose existence all of Egypt was eventually shaped. One must examine these roots of pharaonic evolution to better understand the wondrous era of pyramid building which followed not very long thereafter. With this knowledge in hand, a certain calculated insight into the pharaohs, and a more well-rounded view of pyramids as a whole, can be appreciated. The heritage of Khufu and Khafra, and of all other great pyramid-pharaohs, originated in the blood of the predynastic kings, the forefathers of a great and wondrous line of pharaohs who ruled Egypt for over 3,000 years.

II. The Mastaba:
Precursor to the Pyramid

The mastaba (pronounced más-ta-ba and not mas-tá-ba) preceded the pyramid as the standard burial tomb of the pharaohs, and was also used by other ancient Egyptian royalty, priests and upper middle class. It was in fact the most popular form of tomb ever utilized in Egypt. Even during the pyramid building age the mastaba did not cease to exist as a form of burial tomb, but actually increased in popularity, so that many more were constructed on an even larger and more complex scale. Indeed, even after the period of pyramid building had long passed, the mastaba still maintained its popularity. In modern times, too, the low, rectangular shape of this structure is still the preferred tomb design of the Egyptians, with the fundamental difference lying, not in shape, but in the modern version's diminutive size.

Although one hundred pyramids are known to have been built in Egypt by the pharaohs of old, the number of mastabas is far greater, estimated in the thousands. At the site of the Great Pyramid alone, at Giza, nearly 200 of these early tombs were erected.

In predynastic times, and in the very early dynasties, mastabas were built of mud-brick; but soon thereafter many of them began to be built of stone blocks, with the substructures being hewn out of the solid rock. The principal purpose of these tombs was to house and protect the body of the deceased. The impor-

tance of the tombs to the ancient Egyptians is evident when one considers that, while the mastabas were built of stone, the houses of the villagers—and even the palaces of the pharaohs themselves—were built of mud-brick. The erection and durability of the tomb, then, took precedence over residential, governmental and commercial installations. Even the majority of military garrisons were constructed of mud-brick rather than stone.

Prior to the first mastabas of predynastic times, small pits dug into the desert sands were utilized to bury the dead. After interment, the pit was merely filled in again with sand. In the stage of tomb development immediately following this era, a noticeable, oval mound of dirt was usually fashioned at the surface, constituting an official marker of a sort. This change was subsequently followed by another, wherein a layer of mud-bricks was placed over the mound of sand. Thus a clear evolutionary pattern is evident in early Egyptian burial practices.

The premastaba pit gradually increased in size and was eventually roofed with rough cedar beams, which undoubtedly acted as a protective device against the machinations of thieves; for even in earliest times, the Egyptian dead were buried with certain of their valuables. In some cases the beams were split and narrowed so as to form planks of a sort with which to line the walls of the pit. Said pit, initially of oval shape,

5

Ancient Egyptian Royal Tomb Development

Period	Type	Approach from	via
Predynastic	Pit — oval or rectangular	Above	Pit itself
Dynasties 1 & 2 on	Mastaba (rectangular)	Above or side	Shaft or stairway
Dynasty 3 on	Pyramid	Side or ground	Ramp or stairway
Dynasties 4, 5 & 6	Rock-hewn	Above or side	Passage in cliffs
End of Dynasty 6	House-shaped	Above	Shaft
Dynasty 11	Pyramid-temples	Side	Passage in cliffs

evolved into rectangular form, which eventually inspired the shape of a rectangular mastaba superstructure. With the advent of the above-ground mastaba, the burial pit was afforded a greater degree of protection. It was not long before the pit chamber was hewn out of the rock substrata, rather than being dug out of the sand; first as an open trench roofed with wooden beams, and then hollowed out of the rock completely, so that the roof, too, was of solid rock.

Although the ancient Egyptians referred to their burial markers as tombs, it was latter-day Arabs who first adopted the name mastaba, evidently because those structures resembled a rectangular bench of that name which is a customary fixture of Egyptian homes and coffee-shops.

Not long after the first predynastic mastabas were built in Egypt, and at a very early period of the First Dynasty, the subterranean burial section evolved into a more complex system containing several compart-ments, with the body of the deceased usually occupying the central chamber. Above these several chambers, and built into the mastaba superstructure itself, were numerous smaller storage compartments. These were utilized for supplies of food, water, wine, incense and other paraphernalia necessary for the use and well-being of the deceased in the after-life. In time, the once-small mastaba reached large-scale proportions. This can be appreciated by the photo cross-section, page 8 of the 280'-long mastaba of Thethi Kheneri, the last pharaoh of the Second Dynasty. Ultimately, the mastaba-type tomb underwent a substantial change in plan and evolved into true pyramid form. This evolution is indicated by the schematic diagram on page 9. But the mastaba contributed more than outward form to the pyramid; indeed, the fundamental elements of the later pyramid complexes were borrowed from the earlier mastaba tombs. Completely

Rows of mastabas. (G. Perrot and C. Chipiez)

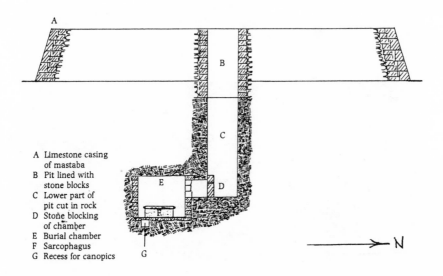

A Limestone casing
  of mastaba
B Pit lined with
  stone blocks
C Lower part of
  pit cut in rock
D Stone blocking
  of chamber
E Burial chamber
F Sarcophagus
G Recess for canopics

Bottom: *Cross-section diagram of a mastaba.* (G. Perrot and C. Chipiez)

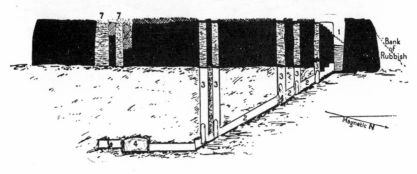

1. Descending *stairways*
2. *Passages* descending underground
3. *Plug-blocks* and *shafts*
4. Large walled *chamber*

5. Gallery stored with *grain* in
   sacks
6. Chambers for *offerings*
7. *Wells* for offerings

———————➤ N

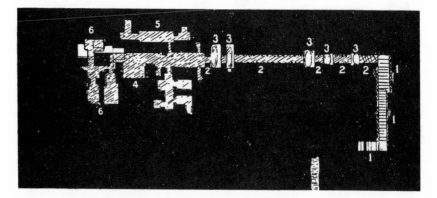

From top: *Photo; cross-section; second plan (with same legend as cross-section) of the mastaba of Thethi Kheneri.* (J. GARSTANG)

MASTABA
EARLY DYN. I

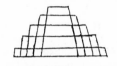

MASTABA-STEP PYRAMID
LATE DYN. I
DYN. II

PYRAMID-MASTABA TYPE

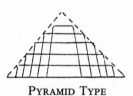

STEP PYRAMID
EARLY DYN. III

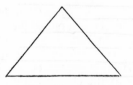

PYRAMID TYPE

TRUE PYRAMID
LATE DYN. III

From mastaba to true pyramid.
(J.P. LEPRE)

surrounding some of the larger mastabas was a protective wall of mud-brick, the predecessor to the great 30'-high stone walls of the more famous pyramid dynasties. In the pyramid era, large mortuary temples were constructed just east of the pyramid's midsection, with said temples containing an inner sanctuary and altar, and facing the pyramid; the mastabas were also equipped with an altar situated to the east. In the case of the mastabas, however, the altar, rather than being separated from the superstructure by a short distance and contained within a massive temple, was actually designed as an integral part of the mastaba itself. Here the altar was set against the east side of the mastaba, facing a "false door" (where the spirit of the deceased was free to exit the tomb and re-enter at will) cut into its stonework at that point.

Also, the presence of small boat pits (to accommodate the "funerary ships" of the deceased) lined with mud-bricks at some mastaba sites are analogous to the much larger and more extensive stone boat pits of the more advanced pyramid complexes.

While the mastaba tomb was flat-topped, as compared with the triangular-shaped pyramids, and while its facing angle was 53 degrees, as compared to 49 to 52 degrees for a typical pyramid, nevertheless the recessed-panel design of the mastaba found its counterpart in the design of the temenos wall of the pyramid complex. The best example of this architectural association is evident in the pyramid complex of the Pharaoh Djoser at Sakkara. (See page 33.)

Parent pyramids were usually accompanied by subsidiary or satellite models; so, too, smaller mastabas were usually built adjacent to much larger ones. As with the pyramids, the mastabas were aligned to the four compass points.

The large mastabas of Dynasties I and II contained scores of individual storage compartments, a pattern which was similarly manifested in three of the earliest large pyramids: those of Djoser and Djoser-Tati at Sakkara, and Khaba at Zawaiyet el-Aryan.

Some of the mastabas (like the pyramids) possessed entrances situated at their north sides, while access to most mastabas was gained through a vertical shaft cut through the roof. As with the pyramids, these apertures were usually sealed with plug stones and portcullis arrangements immediately after the burial. Although the portcullises of the pyramid tombs were of vertical, horizontal or oblique design, those contained within mastabas were almost always vertical.

The more advanced mastabas of the Third Dynasty transferred the position of the storage chambers from the superstructure to the subterranean sections. With burial, secondary and storage chambers now being all on the same level, the subterranean plan of the mastaba constituted a labyrinth of a sort, even including at times a central hall complete with rows of stone columns and various stairwells. As many as 80 rooms were found within some of these mastabas.

Although some of the larger mastabas were constructed almost entirely of stone, a good number of them still consisted of a core of rubble and sand faced with stone slabs. While the evolutionary account indicates that the earlier mastabas were being built of mud-brick and the later ones of stone, this particular pattern is not to be taken literally in all cases; for even in the time of the building of the Great Pyramid, mud-brick structures of all kinds—including numerous mastabas—were still being fashioned alongside those of stone. The chosen medium very much depended on the financial status of each individual tomb owner. Actually, it was not at all unusual for even a pharaoh's financial capability to be strained to the limit; so that the less costly mud-brick was sometimes employed rather than the preferred limestone. A noteworthy example of this reversion existed within the pyramid complex of King Menkara of the Fourth Dynasty; for here, although this pharaoh's main pyramid and at least one of his three subsidiary pyramids were ambitiously sheathed in costly rose granite, his valley temple was finished in mud-brick. Interestingly, though, even in mastabas built and faced with mud-brick, the burial chamber itself was almost always endowed with high quality white limestone facing.

As the great era of pyramid building can be attributed to the late Third and early Fourth Dynasties, so too can the great era of mastaba building.

Among the large stone mastabas, an innovation during this period was the elimination of the north sloping corridor found in the earlier mastaba types, leaving the vertical roof shaft as the sole entrance into the monument. Other innovations, particularly of the Fourth Dynasty, were the presence of a statue (a ka or double) of the deceased in one of the subterranean chambers (the *serdab*) and the presence of idyllic scenes of everyday life painted or carved on several of the chamber walls. (e.g. the deceased hunting, fishing, boating, or being offered food, water and wine by his household servants).

It must be noted that, although such scenes as were found on the walls of mastaba tomb chambers were also found on the causeway walls of pyramid complexes during this period, they were absent on the walls of pyramid burial chambers. Concerning these pyramid chamber walls, only the hieroglyphic texts now popularly known as "The Book of the Dead" were ever inscribed or painted thereon (beginning with King Unas, last pharaoh of the Fifth Dynasty).

The innovation of wall painting was hereafter followed through by the subsequent dynasties of ancient Egypt, where this particular funerary practice became quite popular.

III. The Pyramid Complex

With the evolution from mastaba to pyramid, we have the development of the Pyramid-Complex, which consisted of ten elements:

1) Main Pyramid
2) Satellite Pyramid(s)
3) Mortuary Temple
4) Valley Temple
5) Offering Shrine
6) Mastaba(s)
7) Funerary Ship(s) & Pit(s)
8) Causeway
9) Temenos Wall
10) Canal

With the death of the pharaoh, his corpse was taken from his palace at Memphis, and up the Nile on a *funerary ship*. The ship entered an artificial *canal* which led to the *valley temple* situated on the West Bank of the river.

It should be noted that aside from the parent pyramid, the valley and mortuary temples have probably inspired the most speculation about their functions in the complex. Each no doubt had its own purpose in the funerary rites, just as each part of the rites ministered to some part of the man (who, according to ancient Egyptian beliefs, consisted of his *ab* [heart], *ba* [soul], *ka* [double], *khaibet* [shadow], *khat* [body], *khu* [spirit], *ren* [name], *sahu* [spiritual body], and *sekhem* [power]). Although the specifics of these rites remain a mystery, enough information has been accumulated regarding embalming and mummification to offer a general picture of what may have been involved.

We do know that, prior to the embalming procedure, the pharaoh was ritually washed during a purification ceremony, a procedure symbolic of the regeneration of his now lifeless body. The liturgy manifested at this time emphasizes that the monarch is not of human parentage, has escaped death and shall be transformed to everlasting life, departing in the West and shining anew in the East, thus becoming an imperishable star. Later during the course of lengthy ceremony, mention is made of the pharaoh's senses being restored, with the opening of his eyes, ears, nose and mouth, and his body members being symbolically reassembled. The chief instruments employed here were the ceremonial chisel and adze. These incantations and physical acts were believed to constitute the crux of the embalming process.

Exactly in what order the elements of ceremony occurred is not precisely known, but the following steps are believed to have taken place:

1). The brain was drawn through the nostrils with a hooklike instrument.

2). The lungs, liver, intestines and stomach were removed through an incision made in the abdomen, and were permanently stored in four canopic urns or vases. (The heart was left untouched.)

3). The open cavity was filled with frankincense and myrrh and sprinkled with palm-wine.

4). The incision was sewn up and the corpse placed in a solution, of

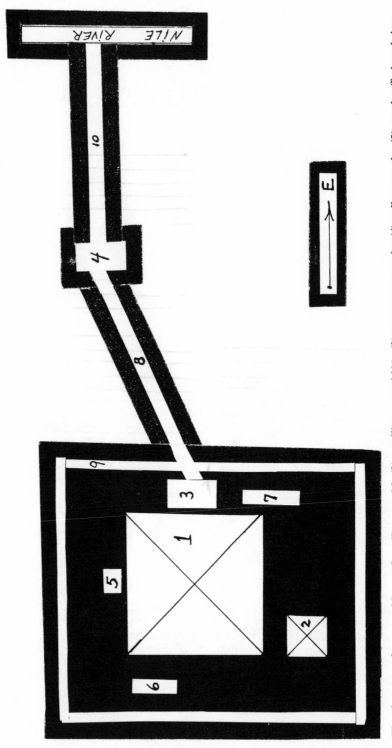

The elements of a pyramid complex: (1) pyramid; (2) satellite pyramid(s); (3) mortuary temple; (4) valley temple; (5) north offering shrine; (6) mastaba(s); (7) funerary ship(s); in pit(s); (8) causeway; (9) temenos wall; (10) canal. (J.P. LEPRE)

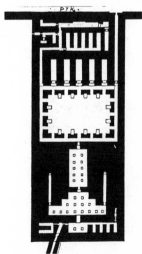

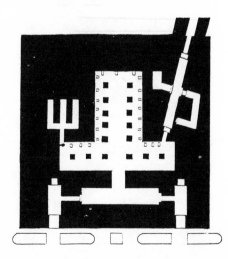

Top: *Painted limestone relief, mortuary temple of Userkaf.* (L. BORCHARDT)
Bottom left: *Plan of Khafra's mortuary temple.* Bottom right: *Plan of Khafra's valley temple.* (A. FAKHRY).

Top: *Causeway, Pyramid of Huni, Maidum.* (MUSEUM OF FINE ARTS, BOSTON)
Bottom: *Gateway of temenos wall.* (G. PERROT AND C. CHIPIEZ)

which the chief constituent was natron. Bitumen was also used.

5). After an undetermined amount of time, the soaked corpse was lifted from the natron solution, placed on a stone slab or table, and mummified. For this process, strips of flaxen cloth were employed, having first been soaked in resin or smeared with a gum. Sometimes amulets, scarabs, statuettes of gods and various other mystic charms were wrapped inside the bandages to impart a degree of power to the deceased. In this manner, should the practical benefits of the wrappings fail in their purpose, the element of magic would ensure the protection of the mummy. In some instances, the fingers and toes of the mummy were bandaged independently, and sometimes a portrait mask in the image of the pharaoh was placed over the face of the mummy prior to its being inserted into the coffin. A ceremonial false beard was sometimes attached to the chin.

Finally, the finished mummy was inserted into a wooden coffin, often fashioned from cedar. Usually there were three of these coffins, with one being set into the other. They may or may not have been inscribed with hieroglyphics.

The initial funerary rites were probably carried out at the valley temple, after which the body was taken up a *causeway,* from ¼ to 1 mile long, extending westward, and to the *mortuary temple,* which was at the end of the causeway and adjacent to the parent pyramid. It would appear that the majority of the funerary ceremonies were carried out here rather than in the valley temple, for the mortuary was usually the larger of the two and contained more storerooms. A standard mortuary temple usually had the following features:

1. Entrances, front and rear.
2. Court, with
3. pillars, in colonnades;
4. altar (offering table); 2nd
5. drainage channel.
6. Vestibules, several (for storage of vessels and offerings).
7. Serdabs, usually five (for housing KA statues of pharaoh).
8. Sanctuary, inner, with
9. false door, and
10. altar (offering table).
11. Roof, over entire building.
12. Staircase to roof.
13. Patio on roof.

Among the ceremonies conducted in the mortuary temple were daily prayers, incantations, and offerings. The offerings were placed on a main altar ideally situated in the inner sanctuary. Such a sanctuary consisted of the altar itself, a "false door" facing west, and two stela inscribed with the pharaoh's royal titles.

After an undetermined period of time, the mummy, now enclosed in its mummy-case, and attended by a lavish funerary cortege, was brought into the *pyramid,* and placed in a stone sarcophagus within the burial chamber. Long after the pharaoh was interred, ritual ceremonies and offerings were carried out by the priests. Although the content of these liturgies varied, their main thrust was to emphasize the greatness of the deceased pharaoh, and how well he deserved to carry on his life in the spirit world.

Usually a *satellite pyramid* was built to the south or east of the parent pyramid. Some parent pyramids were surrounded by several such pilot pyramids.

There is much speculation as to the purpose of the satellite pyramids. Clearly at least some were the burial tombs for the pharaoh's favorite queens and princesses, as can be attested by the several sarcophagi and some fragmentary female mummy remains found therein; but there is also the hypothesis that others were not intended for burials, but were built for the Ka, or double, of the deceased pharaoh.

The Spirit of the pharaoh used the medium of a statue in the likeness of the pharaoh, and food offerings regularly placed before this statue, to perpetuate its own existence in the heavenly realm which lay beyond. For this reason, it was necessary for the pyramid priests to make daily offerings to the Ka statue and to insure its safety. If anything were to happen to the Ka statue, then the spirit of the deceased pharaoh would never gain entrance into the heavenly realm. In accordance with this belief, the ancient Egyptians thought it meet to fashion several statues of each king, insuring the survival of at least one of these models to successfully house the pharaoh's spirit. This is why the valley temple of Khafra at Giza, was found to contain no fewer than 23 life-size statues of that king.

This author rejects the idea that certain pyramids were built as Ka pyramids for two reasons; first, because Ka statues of the pharaoh have never been found in any of these satellite pyramids (where we would expect them to be, were they "Ka" pyramids); and secondly, because certain references in the hieroglyphic texts suggest that the pharaoh and his Ka "shared" the same burial pyramid, and did not have a separate housing. In *The Pyramids of Egypt* (p. 35), Dr. I.E.S. Edwards states that "the dead king and his Ka are often mentioned in the Pyramid Texts as being *together...in the tomb,* where the Ka shares its benefits with the owner." L. Grinsell, in *Egyptian Pyramids* (p. 88), quotes one of the Pyramid Texts: "Offer this

pyramid and this temple (the mortuary) to K (Pharaoh) *and* to his Ka." (not one or the other, in separate dwellings, but in unison). And A. Moret, in his *Nile and Egyptian Civilization* (pp. 174-175), states that the Heliopolitan Texts also tell us that the pharaoh (his mummy or body) shared the pyramid with his Ka. At one point the texts read: "O Tum, put thy two arms behind King N...behind this pyramid...that the *Ka* of King N may be in it, forever.... Let no evil come here to the *body* forever."

Thus it seems that the satellite pyramids were most likely intended solely for burial of the pharaoh's queens and princesses. However, it must be realized that although the above information is, in a certain respect, somewhat convincing, we cannot at this time claim to understand very much about the true purpose of the satellite pyramids. Only further investigation will better define the situation.

Besides the satellites, pyramid complexes usually featured several *mastabas,* built close to the main pyramid, which served as tombs for the pharaoh's family, members of royalty, and the priestly class.

After the sealing of the pyramid, the pharaoh's funerary ship was lowered into a huge 100'- to 200'-long *boat pit* situated quite close to the monument. This pit was then covered over with huge limestone slabs.

From this point on, offerings to the pharaoh were made at a small *shrine* on the north side of the pyramid and, primarily, in the inner sanctuary of the mortuary temple.

The entire complex was finally enclosed by a 30'-high limestone *temenos wall,* so that all of the several parts became a whole — hence, the pyramid complex.

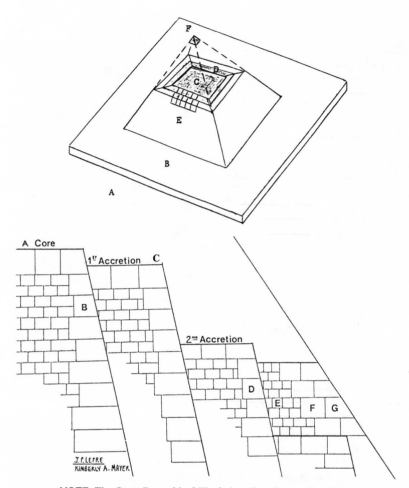

NOTE: The Great Pyramid of Khufu has 19 such accretion layers.

Top: *The structure of a pyramid. A = rock foundation; B = platform; C = core; D = backing stones; E = casing stones; F = pyramidion. A-E are of white limestone; F is black granite or basalt.* (J.P. LEPRE) **Bottom:** *Pyramid superstructure. Blocks: A = core; B = core facing; C = accretion; D = accretion facing; E = fill-in; F = backing; G = casing. A and C are made of small and large blocks; E is made of small blocks; remaining layers and large blocks.*

THE FUNCTION OF THE PYRAMID

The chief element of the ten comprising the pyramid complex was, of course, the parent pyramid. While the 1929 *Encyclopaedia Britannica* gives a practical description of a pyramid as "a building bounded by a polygonal base and plane triangular sides which meet in an apex," an ancient Egyptian hieroglyphic inscription describes it more spiritually as "the Pharaoh's House of a million years." Quite simply, the main function of the pyramid was to house and protect the mummy and possessions of the deceased pharaoh against tomb robbers and the ravages of time.

The entrance to the pyramid was usually located at the north of the monument, either at a point on its face, or at ground level, close to the base. This entrance, only 4' high by 4' wide, was bridged by several huge gable slabs of limestone which, along with the entrance aperture, were ultimately covered over completely by the casing or sheathing stones of the monument.

From the entrance, a descending passageway 100–300' long cut into the natural rock foundation on which the pyramid stood. At its bottom, it leveled off for a short distance, and then terminated in a subterranean burial chamber.

The majority of pyramids, with minor variations, obey this basic plan. There are, however, pyramids which have the burial chamber located in the superstructure — sometimes just above ground level, and at other times at a considerable height.

Anterior to the burial chamber, either in the horizontal corridor immediately preceding it, or in the lowermost section of the descending passage, were from 1 to 3 one-ton portcullis blocking slabs of granite or quartzite. In reality, these slabs were not much of a deterrent to the determined tomb robber, but they did act as a means of buying time for the keepers of the pyramid making their rounds of inspection. The more conscientious and alert the guardians, the more beneficial were the portcullis blocking systems, the breaking through of which, though certain, nevertheless required a good number

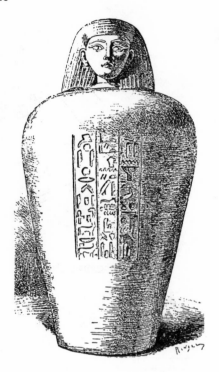

Canopic jar. (G. MASPERO)

of laborious hours on the part of the thief.

At the west end of the burial chamber stood the stone chest or sarcophagus containing the mummy of the deceased pharaoh. The one-ton lid of this chest was sealed to the three-ton chest by a resinous glue and by the ingenious use of granite pinions and beveled edges, presenting yet another deterrent for the ambitious tomb plunderer. Within the chest, a wooden coffin enclosed the royal mummy and its solid gold funerary mask.

Besides the pharaoh's assorted possessions, there were also in the burial chamber a stone slab or offering table and a small stone box containing four canopic jars. The four jars held several of the entrails of the deceased king—his liver, lungs, stomach and intestines.

After the pharaoh had been placed in his sarcophagus, the sarcophagus sealed, and offerings made, the funerary party exited from the burial chamber and the portcullis blocking stones were lowered.

Beyond this, the length of the descending passageway was then sealed with 20 to 40 huge three-ton plug stones. The outside entrance casing stone, cut and fitted to precision, was then sealed shut, thus rendering it indistinguishable from the thousands of other stones which sheathed the edifice. With this final measure, the interment of the pharaoh was complete.

It should be noted that the plan just explained had several variables. For example, the plan might have ranged from a pyramid with one horizontal portcullis blocking stone at the lower end of the descending passage, to a pyramid with three vertical portcullis blocking stones, housed in a sizeable antechamber in the horizontal passage preceding the burial chamber. It also might have varied from a pyramid having a descending passage, a short subterranean horizontal passage and a burial chamber to a pyramid with a descending passage and a *series* of twisting and turning subterranean horizontal (and vertical) passages leading to a burial chamber.

Therefore, although we can generalize about pyramid plans, each pyramid, most especially some of the more sophisticated, represents a variation on a theme or, in some instances, an entirely new theme or plan.

With these variations in mind, we now introduce the reader to the listing of the pyramid pharaohs.

IV. The 42 Pyramid Pharaohs

The word "pharaoh" is the Hebrew form of the Egyptian *per aa,* corrupted to *peroe,* and originally meaning "the great house," in the sense of the pharaoh being "the great hereditary proprietor," as he was legal heir to all the property in Egypt, and his subjects were merely tenants of the land they worked.

This listing begins with the pharaohs of Dynasty III, who saw the first pyramids built, and extends through Dynasty XIII. It includes notes on non-pyramid dynasties and pharaohs within this range and is followed by a brief discussion of other possible pyramid pharaohs and other pyramid ages.

Where possible, the listing for each pharaoh includes:

1. A pharaoh information capsule and comments on his reign.

2. A portrait of the pharaoh and a reproduction of his cartouche.

3. A photo of his pyramid.

4. A cross-sectional diagram of his pyramid.

5. A plan diagram of his pyramid.

6. Photos or sketches of pyramid interior and pyramid complex.

7. A pyramid information capsule.

8. A pyramid complex information capsule.

9. Satellite pyramid(s) information capsule(s).

10. Satellite pyramid(s) diagram(s).

Unfortunately, not all of this material is available for all pharaohs. For example, of the 42 pyramid pharaohs, portraits could be found for only two-thirds. For some pyramids, neither a cross-sectional diagram, plan diagram, nor photo of the monument exists.

For the names of the pharaohs of the non-pyramid Dynasties I and II, see Appendix A, page 291.

The names and genealogies of the pharaohs are taken from the "King Lists," recorded lists of the pharaohs from Dynasties I–XII citing their hieroglyphic names, length of their reigns, etc. Very few of these lists have survived and are available to us. The six that have been preserved, on which our chronology is based, are (1) The Abydos List, from an inscription on a temple wall of the Nineteenth Dynasty; (2) The Sakkara List, from an inscription on a tomb wall of the Nineteenth Dynasty; (3) The Palermo Stone List, from an inscription carved into diorite fragments, dated from the Fifth Dynasty; (4) Petrie's "Fragmented List," inscriptions carved into and painted on sundry objects of the Third–Thirteenth Dynasties; (5) Manetho's List, inscriptions painted on a papyrus scroll, from 3 B.C.; and (6) The Turin Papyrus List, inscriptions on a papyrus scroll of the Seventeenth Dynasty. Of these lists, numbers 1 through 5 ennumerate the pharaohs of Dynasties I–V, while number 6 lists pharaohs of Dynasties I–XII.

The "Pyramid Texts" referred to in

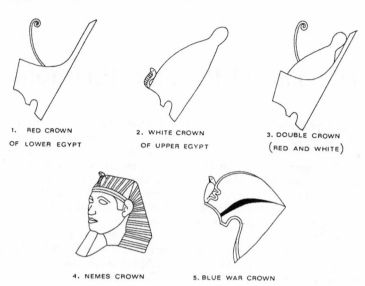

1. RED CROWN OF LOWER EGYPT

2. WHITE CROWN OF UPPER EGYPT

3. DOUBLE CROWN (RED AND WHITE)

4. NEMES CROWN

5. BLUE WAR CROWN

The royal crowns of the pharaohs.
(J.P. LEPRE / K. MAYER)

this work constitute hieroglyphic funerary inscriptions written on the walls of the burial chambers of 10* of the 100 pyramids. These inscriptions consisted of a series of incantations which sought to insure the pharaoh's successful journey to the heavens, where he would carry on his life for eternity.

These incantations were written on the walls of Old Kingdom pyramids, on coffins during the Middle Kingdom (and known as the "Coffin Texts"); and on papyrus scrolls in the New Kingdom (and known as the "Book of Coming Forth by Day").

All of these texts, along with sundry other texts and inscriptions, together constitute what is popularly

*Pyramids having Pyramid Texts: Unas, Dynasty V; Teti, Dynasty VI; Pepy I, Dynasty VI; Iput I (Pepy's queen), Dynasty VI; Merenre I, Dynasty VI; Pepy II, Dynasty VI; Iput II, Neit, and Udjebten (Pepy II's queens), Dynasty VI; and Iby, Dynasty VII.

known as the "Egyptian Book of the Dead."

As earlier indicated, the listing for each pharaoh contains that pharaoh's *cartouche*. A cartouche is the hieroglyphic name of a pharaoh enclosed in a royal name case or cartridge. It was oval in shape and was used only by the pharaohs.

The origin of the royal cartouche is explained for us in Vol. I, p. 285, of *The Cambridge Ancient History*. It there states that "under the IIIrd Dynasty Khasekhem (Sekhemkhet) places his personal name, Besh, within what looks like a signet ring with a broad bezel, but is in reality a representation of a cylinder-seal rolling over a flat piece of clay or wax.... Soon this circular ring altered its shape, lengthening in order to accommodate conveniently the signs of the royal name; and under Snefru we find it has assumed its final shape as the familiar 'cartouche' within which at first only the personal name was contained."

But for the presence of the cartouches of Cleopatra and Ptolemy in the Rosetta Stone, that famous stele — and, indeed, the whole of the ancient Egyptian language — may never have been deciphered.

In a number of cases, the cartouche given in this book for each pharaoh may not, in exact translation, match the pharaoh's popular name as it appears in the caption. This discrepancy indicates, not a failing of the book's accuracy, but the modification of original name forms by the passage of time.

The information capsule on each pharaoh also includes, where available, the *titulary,* or five royal names, of that pharaoh. These names were assumed on the day of accession to the throne, and included (1) the *Horus, Horus-Ra,* Hawk, or personal name; (2) the Vulture-and-Cobra, or Two Ladies, name; (3) the Golden Horus, Hawk-of-Nubi, or Set name; (4) the Reed-and-Hornet, or Lord of the Two Crowns, name (*prenomen*); and (5) the Son-of-the-Sun-God, or Ra, name (*nomen*).

The reader will notice that the names of certain pharaohs or places are sometimes spelled differently; for example: Sneferu is also spelled Snefru, and Dashshur is also spelled Dashur or Dahshur. This is illustrative of the variations of interpretation of some words, rather than spelling errors in the text. (For more on this subject, see pages 298-300.)

The 42 pyramid pharaohs, listed chronologically by reign, are:

Pharaoh	Dyn.
1	Beby	III
2	Djoser	III
3	Djoser-tati	III
4	Khaba	III
5	Eke	III
6	Huni	III

	Pharaoh	Dyn.
7	Sneferu	III
8	Khufu	IV
9	Rededef	IV
10	Khafra	IV
11	Menkara	IV
12	Userkaf	V
13	Sahure	V
14	Neferefre	V
15	Sisires	V
16	Neferirkare	V
17	Neuserre	V
18	Menkeuhor	V
19	Djedkare-Isesi	V
20	Unas	V
21	Teti	VI
22	Ity	VI
23	Pepy I	VI
24	Merenre I	VI
25	Pepy II	VI
26	Merenre II	VI
27	Khui	VI
28	Merikari	VI
29	Neferkere	VII
30	Iby	VII
31	Akhtoy IV	IX
32	Amenemhat I	XII
33	Senusert I	XII
34	Amenemhat II	XII
35	Senusert II	XII
36	Senusert III	XII
37	Amenemhat III	XII
38	Amenemhat IV	XII
39	Sebek-Neferu-Ra	XII
40	Ameny	XIII
41	Ay	XIII
42	Khendjer II	XIII

The same group listed alphabetically reads as follows:

	Pharaoh	Dyn.
1	Akhtoy IV	IX
2	Amenemhat I	XII
3	Amenemhat II	XII
4	Amenemhat III	XII
5	Amenemhat IV	XII

6	Ameny	XIII	29	Neuserre	V
7	Ay	XIII	30	Pepy I	VI
8	Beby	III	31	Pepy II	VI
9	Djedkare-Isesi	V	32	Rededef	IV
10	Djoser	III	33	Sahure	V
11	Djoser-tati	III	34	Sebek-Neferu-Ra	XII
12	Eke	III	35	Senusert I	XII
13	Huni	III	36	Senusert II	XII
14	Iby	VII	37	Senusert III	XII
15	Ity	VI	38	Siseres	V
16	Khaba	III	39	Sneferu	III
17	Khafra	IV	40	Teti	VI
18	Khendjer II	XIII	41	Unas	V
19	Khufu	IV	42	Userkaf	V
20	Khui	VI			
21	Menkara	IV			
22	Menkeuhor	V			
23	Merenre I	VI			
24	Merenre II	VI			
25	Merikare	VI			
26	Neferefre	V			
27	Neferirkare	V			
28	Neferkere	VII			

The chronology of the pyramid rulers is not continuous because there were three non-pyramid dynasties (VIII, X, and XI), and within the pyramid dynasties, non-pyramid rulers.

V. Dynasties III–IV/ (Heyday of Pyramid Building)

DYNASTY III

• *Duration:* 98 years (2887–2790 B.C.). *Pharaohs:* 1. Beby. 2. Djoser. 3. Djoser-Tati. 4. Khaba. 5. Eke. 6. Huni. 7. Sneferu.

Although the heyday of pyramid building is generally thought to have occurred, for the most part, in Dynasties III and IV, the surge for pyramids did not demonstrably begin with the first king of the Third Dynasty, Beby, but with the well-known and ambitious "Step Pyramid" of the second king, Djoser. Also, it did not continue through to the last (seventh) king of the Fourth Dynasty, Imhotep, but rather with the fifth king of that dynasty, Menkara.

Keeping this in mind, we now move on to the bulk of our material, beginning with the Third Dynasty.

PHARAOH 1: BEBY.
Position in dynasty: First. *Portrait:* yes (page 29). *Length of reign:* 19 years. *Dates of reign:* 2887–2869 B.C. *Mummy:* not found. *Sarcophagus:* not found. *Burial chamber:* not found. *Treasure:* not found. *Hawk name:* ?. *Vulture-and-Cobra name:* ?. *Set or Hawk-of-Nubi name:* ?. *Reed-and-Hornet name:* Nebka (Nebkara) (Possessing the Spirit of the Sun-God). *Son-of-the-Sun-God (Ra) name:* none. *Other names:* Nebkara Bebi; Nebke; Nebkere Beby; Nubka I; Necherophe; Necherochi; Sa-Nekht.

The new dynasty begun by Beby was, according to Herodotus, of Memphite origin; and Beby was the son of his predecessor, Kheneri, his mother being the northern princess, Nemaethapi. This pharaoh's name is inscribed on the rocks in the Sinai Desert, at Wady Maghara, which implies that the copper mines there were worked by his men.

Although Manetho gives Beby a reign of 28 years, the Turin Papyrus gives him 19 years, with the latter being correct. On the Palermo Stone the annals of the first five years of his reign were recorded, with the beginning of the building of his royal palace, "the Refreshment of the Gods," occurring in the fourth year. During his reign, there was a revolt of the Libyans, but this revolt was quickly suppressed.

Although the first pharaoh credited with building a pyramid was Beby's successor, Djoser (of the famous "Step Pyramid" at Sakkara), there are ten step pyramids whose ownership cannot be ascertained that appear to be earlier models than Djoser's monument. These are the pyramids at Athribis, Abu Roash, Seila, Zawaiyet El Amwat, Abydos, Ombos, Nagada, El Kola, Edfu, and Elephantine (pyramids no. 1, 2, 89, 93, 95–100). All ten of these pyramids are devoid of a pyramid complex.

The principal reasons for the popularity of Djoser's pyramid, compared to these seldom-mentioned ten, are that Djoser's edifice is of stone, whereas the others are almost certainly all of brick, and that Djoser's is a much larger monument.

Now, as Beby was the first king of the Third Dynasty, preceding Djoser, and as these pyramids are smaller and of cruder construction than Djoser's massive monument, it is not unreasonable to assign at least one of these pyramids to him. Actually, Beby may be responsible for building several of these edifices. Perhaps Djoser built the remaining ones, before attempting his more ambitious project at Sakkara.

This area is open to much speculation, and only future investigation will reveal the actual owners of these early monuments. And although it is unlikely that Beby built all ten of these pyramids, we include them in his portfolio for lack of a better arrangement.

Pyramid: Beby? *Name:* Pyramid Athribis. *Number:* 1. *Exterior photos:* no. *Interior photos:* no. *Cross-sectional diagram:* no. *Plan diagram:* no. *Pyramid field:* Athribis. *Field number:* I. *Length:* ?. *Height:* ?. *Angle:* ?. *Type:* step? *Materials:* brick. *Location of entrance:* ?. *Portcullises:* ?. *Chambers:* one?. *Comments:* No record of investigation for this pyramid.

Pyramid: Beby? *Name:* Northern Pyramid of Abu Roash. *Number:* 2. *Exterior photos:* no. *Interior photos:* no. *Cross-sectional diagram:* no. *Plan diagram:* no. *Pyramid field:* Abu Roash. *Field number:* II. *Length:* approx. 75 ft.?. *Height:* 55 ft. (in 1842); superstructure now razed. *Angle:* ?. *Type:* step?. *Materials:* brick. *Location of entrance:* ?. *Portcullises:* ?. *Chambers:* one. *Comments:* No record of investigations for this pyramid.

Pyramid: Beby? *Name:* Pyramid Seila. *Number:* 89. *Exterior photos:* no. *Interior photos:* no. *Cross-*

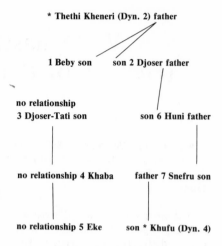

Dynasty III Genealogy

sectional diagram: no. *Plan diagram:* no. *Pyramid field:* Seila. *Field number:* XII. *Length:* 71 ft. *Height:* approx. 53 ft.? (now 5 ft.). *Angle:* 53 degrees?. *Type:* step. *Materials:* limestone. *Location of entrance:* ?. *Portcullises:* ?. *Chambers:* one?. *Comments:* This pyramid is as yet unexplored.

Pyramid: Beby? *Name:* Pyramid Zawaiyet El Amwat. *Number:* 93. *Exterior photos:* no. *Interior photos:* no. *Cross-sectional diagram:* no. *Plan diagram:* no. *Pyramid field:* Zawaiyet El Amwat. *Field number:* XV. *Length:* approx. 60 ft. *Height:* ?. *Angle:* 53 degrees?. *Type:* step. *Materials:* limestone. *Location of entrance:* ?. *Portcullises:* ?. *Chambers:* one?. *Comments:* Besides the entrance, the descending passage and burial chamber, nothing has yet been found, although pyramid has been investigated.

Pyramid: Beby? *Name:* Pyramid Sinki (Abydos). *Number:* 95. *Exterior photos:* no. *Interior photos:* no. *Cross-sectional diagram:* no. *Plan diagram:* no. *Pyramid field:* Abydos. *Field number:* XVII. *Length:* ?. *Height:* ?. *Angle:* ?. *Type:*

Pharaoh Beby and his cartouche.
(HEAD: LOUVRE MUSEUM)

step?. *Materials:* brick?. *Location of entrance:* ?. *Portcullises:* ?. *Chambers:* No chambers yet discovered. *Comments:* No record of investigation for this pyramid.
    Pyramid: Beby? *Name:* Pyramid Ombos. *Number:* 96. *Exterior photos:* no. *Interior photos:* no. *Cross-sectional diagram:* no. *Plan diagram:* no. *Pyramid field:* Ombos. *Field number:* XVIII. *Length:* ?. *Height:* ?. *Angle:* 53 degrees. *Type:*

step. *Materials:* brick?. *Location of entrance:* ?. *Portcullises:* ?. *Chambers:* one?. *Comments:* No record of investigation for this pyramid.
    Pyramid: Beby? *Name:* Pyramid Nagada. *Number:* 97. *Exterior photos:* no. *Interior photos:* no. *Cross-sectional diagram:* no. *Plan diagram:* no. *Pyramid field:* Nagada. *Field number:* XIX. *Length:* approx. 60 ft. *Height:* ?. *Angle:* 68 degrees?. *Type:* step (4 levels). *Materials:* limestone core. *Location of entrance:* none—no shaft leading to burial chamber. *Portcullises:* ?. *Chambers:* one—a "pit" only. *Comments:* This pyramid has defied all attempts of investigators to find an entrance and descending passage. Burial chamber (pit) found empty by Petrie.
    Pyramid: Beby? *Name:* Pyramid El Kola. *Number:* 98. *Exterior photos:* no (sketch only). *Interior photos:* no. *Cross-sectional diagram:* no. *Plan diagram:* yes. *Pyramid field:* El Kola. *Field number:* XX. *Length:* 61 ft. *Height:* approx. 28 ft. *Angle:* 53 degrees?. *Type:* step (3 levels). *Materials:* limestone core; mud and white plaster casing. *Location of entrance:* ?. *Portcullises:* ?. *Chambers:* ?. *Comments:* Although investigated, entrance, descending passage and burial chamber not yet found. Pyramid oriented N–E, S–W, S–E, N–W instead of N, S, E, W as are all other pyramids.
    Pyramid: Beby? *Name:* Pyramid Edfu. *Number:* 99. *Exterior photos:* no. *Interior photos:* no. *Cross-sectional diagram:* no. *Plan diagram:* no. *Pyramid field:* Edfu. *Field number:* XXI. *Length:* ?. *Height:* ?. *Angle:* ?. *Type:* step?. *Materials:* brick?. *Location of entrance:* ?. *Portcullises:* ?. *Chambers:* No chambers yet discovered. *Comments:* No record of investigation for this pyramid.

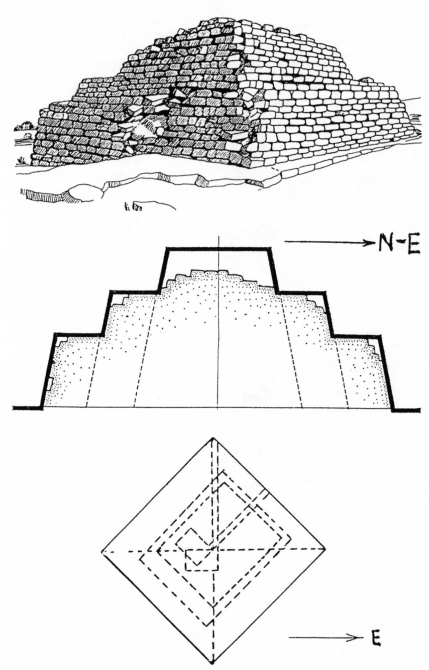

Top: *Pyramid El Kula (of Beby?).* **Center:** *Cross-section.* (J. Stienon) **Bottom:** *Plan, showing unorthodox orientation.* (J.P. Lepre)

Pharaoh Djoser and his cartouche. (STATUE: EGYPTIAN MUSEUM, CAIRO)

Pyramid: Beby? *Name:* Pyramid Elephantine. *Number:* 100. *Exterior photos:* no. *Interior photos:* no. *Cross-sectional diagram:* no. *Plan diagram:* no. *Pyramid field:* Elephantine. *Field number:* XXII. *Length:* ?. *Height:* ?. *Angle:* ?. *Type:* step?. *Materials:* brick?. *Location of entrance:* ?. *Portcullises:* ?. *Chambers:* No chambers yet discovered. *Comments:* No record of investigation for this pyramid.

There are no pyramid complexes for any of the ten pyramids assigned to Beby.

PHARAOH 2: DJOSER.
Position in dynasty: Second. *Portrait:* yes. *Length of reign:* 19 years. *Dates of reign:* 2868–2850 B.C. *Mummy:* possibly a mummified foot only. *Sarcophagus:* none. *Burial chamber:* yes?. *Treasure:* not found. *Hawk name:* Neterkhet (God in the Flesh). *Vulture-and-Cobra name:* ?. *Set or Hawk-of-Nubi name:* Re-Nubi. *Reed-and-Hornet name:* Tcher (Djoser). *Son-of-the-Sun-God (Ra) name:* none. *Other names:* Retho; Thoser; Zoser.

Djoser, "The Holy," is most famous for his Step Pyramid at Sakkara. The Turin Papyrus assigns him a reign of 19 years, while Manetho lists it as 29 years. The Turin Papyrus, however, is the more authoritative source. Although Manetho's records are somewhat reliable on some accounts, they are more often so corrupt and incorrect that they should be disregarded entirely. He is often guilty of adding hundreds of years to Egyptian chronology, so as to make the record appear more ancient.

Besides the fact that Djoser constructed the first large step pyramid, he is also noted for the labors of Imhotep (Iemhotpe), his chief priest,

physician, scribe, philosopher and architect.

An inscription on the rocks of Sehel Island, at the First Cataract, tells of a terrible famine that occurred in the eighteenth year of Djoser's reign and of the weakening effect that it had on the people and government.

At Philae, in a Ptolemaic inscription, King Djoser was remembered as having been a wise and powerful administrator. Another such inscription describes how, under Djoser, a tax was levied on water drawn from the Nile.

Although a mummified foot was found in the burial chamber of this pharaoh's pyramid, there is an indication that another structure, a huge, 300' long by 150' wide mastaba was built by him at Bet Khallaf in Upper Egypt. The question then arises as to which of these tombs was the actual burial crypt of this great pharaoh.

The presence of the mummified foot in the Step Pyramid indicates that he may very well have been interred in that tomb (although we cannot be absolutely certain that this is his foot), yet it appears as if this pyramid may only have been a cenotaph or dummy tomb, one clue being the absence of a portcullis arrangement in the corridor system (although a single portcullis plug was inserted in the roof of the burial chamber).

With the mastaba at Bet Khallaf, though, we have on the one hand the absence of any mummified parts whatsoever, but on the other hand the presence of five great portcullis blocking stones in the entrance shaft, indicating that this was a true burial crypt.

Although no sarcophagus was found in this king's supposed burial chamber within the pyramid, two

Top: *Pyramid of Djoser, North Sakkara.* (A. MARIETTE) **Bottom:** *Step pyramid complex of Djoser, North Sakkara.* (RECONSTRUCTED MODEL BY J.P. LAUER; PHOTO BY J.P. LAUER)

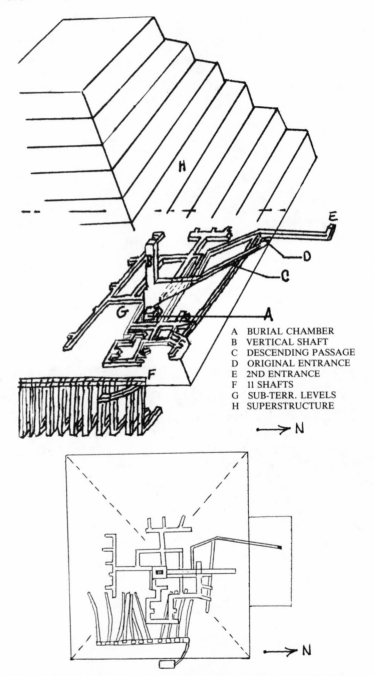

A   BURIAL CHAMBER
B   VERTICAL SHAFT
C   DESCENDING PASSAGE
D   ORIGINAL ENTRANCE
E   2ND ENTRANCE
F   11 SHAFTS
G   SUB-TERR. LEVELS
H   SUPERSTRUCTURE

Top: *Pyramid of Djoser: Three-dimensional diagram.* (J.P. LEPRE) **Bottom:**
Pyramid of Djoser: Plan. (AUTHOR'S IMPROVEMENT ON J.P. LAUER)

alabaster sarcophagi were in fact found in two of the subterranean galleries. Judging from their small size, they were probably meant to contain the mummies of children or young women. Also found in the galleries were several limestone pedestals for yet other sarcophagi. Considering the above findings and the extent of the subterranean portions of this pyramid, it appears as if a communal burial, involving perhaps a dozen or more of the royalty, took place or was at least planned for this monument. A communal burial of this nature is extremely rare, as most pyramids contained the single burial of the pharaoh, and on odd occasions, a second interment.

Pyramid: Djoser. *Name:* Step Pyramid Sakkara. *Number:* 40. *Exterior photos:* yes. *Interior photos:* yes. *Cross-sectional diagram:* yes. *Plan diagram:* yes. *Pyramid field:* North Sakkara. *Field number:* VI. *Lengths:* rectangle 411 ft. E–W; 358 ft. N–S. *Height:* 204 ft. *Angle:* 53 degrees?. *Type:* step (6 levels). *Materials:* limestone. *Location of entrance:* north—ground level. *Portcullises:* one—burial chamber roof. *Chambers:* several. *Comments:* Pyramid volume = 22 million cubic ft. Pyramid Architect—Imhotep (vizier, physician, philosopher, chief scribe, chief priest).

Pyramid Complex: Djoser. *Main pyramid:* yes. *Satellite pyramid(s):*

Cartouche of Pharaoh Khaba.

no. *Mortuary temple:* yes. *Valley temple:* not found. *Offering shrine:* yes. *Mastaba(s):* yes—several. *Ship(s):* no. *Ship pit(s):* no. *Causeway:* not found. *Temenos wall:* yes. *Canal:* destroyed.

PHARAOH 3: DJOSER-TATI.
Position in dynasty: Third. *Portrait:* yes.* *Length of reign:* 6 years. *Dates of reign:* 2849–2844 B.C. *Mummy:* not found. *Sarcophagus:* alabaster. *Burial chamber:* yes?. *Treasure:* a fraction found. *Hawk name:* ?. *Vulture-and-Cobra name:* ?. *Set or Hawk-of-Nubi name:* ?. *Reed-and-Hornet name:* Tati; Teta; Djoser-Tati. *Son-of-the-Sun-God (Ra) name:* none. *Other names:* Besh; Sekhem-Khet; Thosertati; Tosertasi.

This son of the previous pharaoh, the Great Djoser, chose to erect his monument to the immediate west of his father's controversial Step Pyramid, and he seems to have tried to duplicate the latter with identical measurements, temenos wall, etc.

When this "Buried" Pyramid was first discovered and entered in 1954,

*Several authors have dated the statue shown on page 37 (Cairo Museum) as late Second Dynasty (example: I. Woldering, in *The Art of Ancient Egypt*), with the hieroglyphic cartouche (king's name) reading Ka-sekhem. Surprisingly, though, a perusal of the composite king list painstakingly assembled by Sir Arthur Weigall in his *History of the Pharaohs* (Volume I) finds no such king of that name from the late Second Dynasty. The last three pharaohs of that era are listed as Neferkesokar, Huthefi and Thethi Kheneri. On the other hand, the third king of the Third Dynasty, Djoser-Tati, was also known as Sekhem-khet. It seems more likely, then, that this statue of "Ka-sekhem" is actually that of Sekhem-khet (Khet-sekhem/Ka-sekhem). For this reason, I have tentatively assigned this statue to Sekhem-khet (Djoser-Tati), the third pharaoh of the Third Dynasty, as I feel the name association is conclusive.

expectations of finding a pharaonic mummy ran high when the team, led by M. Ghoneim, encountered a sealed, alabaster sarcophagus in the burial chamber. The sarcophagus proved empty; it seems likely, though, that this pharaoh may once have been interred in this pyramid, as a cache of gold jewelry was found buried beneath sand and debris in one of the subterranean corridors — evidently the remnants of the rich burial of this great king.

Djoser-Tati is mentioned in both the Sakkara and Turin Papyrus king lists. The latter indicates that he reigned for six years, and no contemporary objects of his tenure are known. He appears to have been, like his father, a benevolent pharaoh, for there was still a priestly service commemorating his memory in the Twenty-sixth Dynasty.

Pyramid: Djoser-Tati. *Name:* "Buried Pyramid." *Number:* 38. *Exterior photos:* yes. *Interior photos:* yes. *Cross-sectional diagram:* yes. *Plan diagram:* yes. *Pyramid field:* North Sakkara. *Field number:* VI. *Length:* 400 ft. *Height:* approx. 210 ft. *Angle:* 53 degrees?. *Type:* step (7 levels) (14 accretions). *Materials:* limestone. *Location of entrance:* north — ground level. *Portcullises:* no. *Chambers:* one — also 120 storerooms.

Pyramid Complex: Djoser-Tati. *Main pyramid:* yes. *Satellite pyramid(s):* no. *Mortuary temple:* no. *Valley temple:* no. *Offering shrine:* no. *Mastaba(s):* ?. *Ship(s):* no. *Ship pit(s):* no. *Causeway:* no. *Temenos wall:* yes. *Canal:* destroyed.

PHARAOH 4: KHABA.
Position in dynasty: Fourth. *Portrait:* no. *Length of reign:* 1 year. *Dates of reign:* 2844–2843 B.C.? *Mummy:* not found. *Sarcophagus:*

no. *Burial chamber:* yes?. *Treasure:* not found. *Hawk name:* ?. *Vulture-and-Cobra name:* ?. *Set or Hawk-of-Nubi name:* ?. *Reed-and-Hornet name:* Khaba?. *Son-of-the-Sun-God (Ra) name:* none.

Almost nothing is known of this obscure pharaoh. We have assigned the "Layer" Pyramid to him, solely because of the presence of his hieroglyphic name on a number of bowls found in nearby tombs. He is not mentioned in any of the early king lists, but this omission may be due to the fact that his reign was of exceptionally short duration (one year, perhaps two). Evidence of the brevity of his reign is the condition of his pyramid, which was left in an unfinished state. The subterranean sections, for example, most especially the burial chamber, have been left looking more like a quarry than a finished crypt.

The step pyramid of King Khaba has long been termed the "Layer Pyramid." But the specifics of the connotation of this term have been neglected by most authors. Indeed, up till now no drawings exemplifying this phenomenon had been published, thus leaving the curious reader in the dark as to the true meaning of the word "layer." For all of the pyramids were built in *horizontal* layers, but such layers are not implied when referring to the Pyramid of Khaba. Here we are speaking of *vertical* layers — or near vertical, as the stones of this pyramid were set on an angle or inclined inwards. However, so as not to confuse the reader on this account, we shall let schematic drawings explain the situation for us (page 40).

Pyramid: Khaba. *Name:* "Layer Pyramid." *Number:* 17. *Exterior photos:* yes. *Interior photos:* no. *Cross-sectional diagram:* yes. *Plan*

Pharaoh Djoser-Tati and his cartouche. (STATUE: CAIRO MUSEUM)

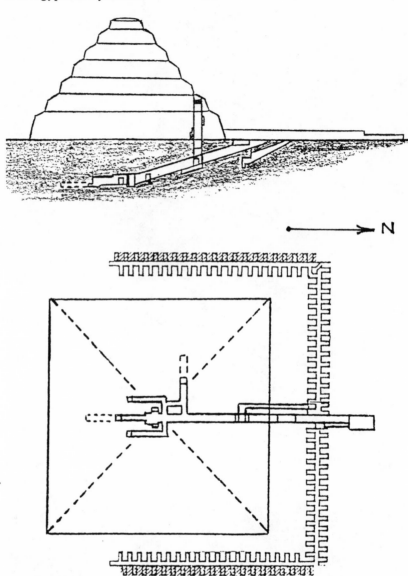

Djoser-Tati's "Buried Pyramid," North Sakkara. **Top:** *Cross-section.* **Bottom:**
Plan. (J.P. LEPRE)

diagram: yes. *Pyramid field:*
Zawaiyet El Aryan. *Field number:*
IV. *Length:* 275 ft. *Height:* approx.
145 ft. (now 25 ft.). *Angle:* 53
degrees. *Type:* step. *Materials:*
limestone. *Location of entrance:*
north – ground level. *Portcullises:*
no. *Chambers:* one. (also 32
storerooms).

Pyramid Complex: Khaba. *Main
pyramid:* yes. *Satellite pyramid(s):*
no. *Mortuary temple:* no. *Valley*

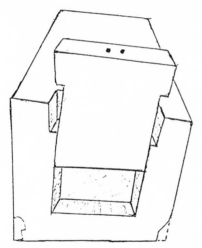 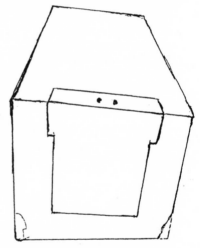

*The alabaster sarcophagus of Djoser-Tati. The raised portion at the left end
is a unique sliding panel in the open position (see diagrams below photo).*
(PHOTO: J.P. LAUER. DRAWINGS: J.P. LEPRE)

temple: no. *Offering shrine:* no.
Mastaba(s): yes — several. *Ship(s):*
no. *Ship pit(s):* no. *Causeway:* no.
Temenos wall: no. *Canal:* no.

PHARAOH 5: EKE.
Position in dynasty: Fifth. *Por-*

trait: yes. *Length of reign:* 6 years.
Dates of reign: 2843–2838 B.C.
Mummy: not found. *Sarcophagus:*
granite, oval. *Burial chamber:* ?.
Treasure: not found. *Hawk name:*
Nebka. *Vulture-and-Cobra name:*
Eke. *Set or Hawk-of-Nubi name:* ?.

Reed-and-Hornet name: Nebkara (Nebka). *Son-of-the-Sun-God (Ra) name:* none. *Other names:* Ache; Nebkara; Nebkere; Nefer-ka-ra; Nubka; Sethes.

The "Unfinished" Pyramid of this great pharaoh is one of the more impressive examples of the grand scale on which Egyptian architects were building, even at that early date.

Realizing that any description that I could give of this edifice would probably fall short of Baikie's wonderful commentary on the monument, I herewith insert said commentary for the reader's perusal.

"Though it is only the sketch for the finished work, it is perhaps, for that very reason, almost more impressive than a finished pyramid might have been.

"Nebkere, (Nebka), (Eke), began the work for his great tomb by sinking through the limestone rock of the plateau a huge oblong pit, 73′ deep, 82′ long and 46′ wide. The sides of this gigantic shaft are of sheer rock, and it was destined to form the chamber, or perhaps, the series of chambers, of the completed pyramid. He next drove down to the foot of the shaft, a sloping stairway of the most superb character, 360′ long and 28′ wide, down which the massive blocks of granite and other material for the completion of the great chamber could be brought with ease and comfort. Down the stairway he then brought a quantity of great granite blocks for the pavement of the burial chamber. The average block weighs about nine tons; while the great block, which was destined to form the centre of the pavement, weighs at least 45 tons. Into the centre of this sumptuous pavement, he sank a fine sarcophagus, also of

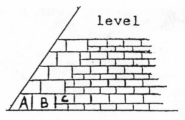

level

A - casing stones
B - backing stones
C - fill-in stones

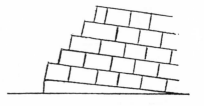

inclined

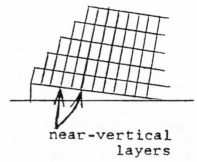

inclined

near-vertical
layers

Methods of laying stones.
(J.P. LEPRE)

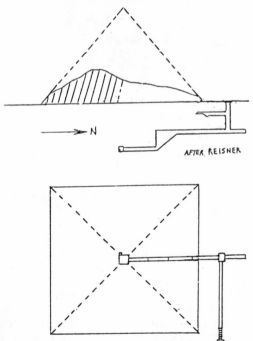

AFTER REISNER

Top: *"Layer Pyramid" of Khaba, Zawaiyet el-Aryan.* Center: *Cross-section.*
Bottom: *Plan.* (J.P. LEPRE)

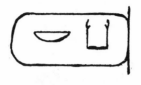

Pharaoh Eke and his cartouche. (PHOTO OF HEAD: J. VANDIER)

red granite, of an oval form, quite different from the type of sarcophagus used by the succeeding dynasty. It had a lid of red granite, and the workmanship of both sarcophagus and lid was of a high order.

"... There are many finished pyramids and tombs which are of far less significance than the unfinished pyramid of Zawyet el-'Aryan. Here we are really at the very beginning of pyramid-building, with only a few years between us and the first attempt at a pyramid which Zoser (Djoser) and his wise man, Imhotep, reared a

few miles south of us at Saqqara (Sakkara); yet, there is no hesitation, or fumbling after an ideal only imperfectly seen as yet. The architect has seen, with perfect clearness, what he intended to do, and has done it as if he had the labour of Titans at his command....

"Maspero has written of the 'almost brutal strength' of Nebkere's work; but 'brutal' is a totally wrong word to use of work which shows such careful thinking out, and such skillful adaptation of means to a foreseen end as this. The brute was left far behind in the past before

Nebkere and his architects planned this astonishing tomb."

In spite of Baikie's enthusiasm for the main pyramid, the pyramid complex of Eke has been little explored. Among the numerous writings by the various pyramid authors, no mention is ever made of the mortuary temple, valley temple, or causeway. Grinsell mentions the possibility of their existence, but states that these elements have never been found.

In my investigation of that site in 1987, however — and quite to my surprise — I viewed what were the obvious remains of a razed temple situated at the southeast corner of the pyramid. Its groundplan was quite large, and the scattered remnants of fractured pink granite columns could clearly be discerned lying here and there across the span of an ancient pavement. It was, without doubt, the remains of the Mortuary temple of that pyramid.

The absence of any account of this temple seems surprising until one considers its location. It is situated on a modern military base — and not only within the perimeter of military jurisdiction, as are the two pyramids of King Sneferu at Dahshur, but situated adjacent to a central army complex, containing soldier's barracks, truck depots and administration offices. It is primarily for this reason that the immediate site of the Pyramid of Eke is strictly off-limits to most researchers. Even the archaeological teams that do have government influence are confronted with substantial obstacles within the military bureaucracy regarding access to this pyramid site.

It also seems that the few archaeological organizations that might eventually gain permission to examine this location, if they were so inclined, simply choose not to do so. The majority of Egyptologists no doubt believe that explorer Alessandro Barsanti misjudged in assuming that the Pyramid of Eke is worthy of further serious attention. The result of this general lack of interest, coupled with the impediment of military red tape, is that few, if any researchers have examined this site since Barsanti's death in 1917; therefore, the established consensus inaccurately maintains that Eke's pyramid is devoid of any architectural complements, such as a mortuary or valley temple.

Yet the ruined temple is there for all to see, and, interestingly, illustrates the fact that at least in this particular case, the mortuary temple was begun — and perhaps brought to completion — prior to the completion of the pyramid itself. In general, it has been assumed that the pyramid was constructed first, and then the adjoining temples.

Beyond the existence of the mortuary temple just noted, the scant remains of a causeway, leading from the mortuary temple and directed northeast to a distance of approximately 1,000′, are also discernible. Although the beginning of this causeway, where it connects with the mortuary temple pavement, is evident to the discerning eye, the remainder of its length is buried, first under a modern asphalt road, and then under the surrounding desert plateau. Yet at the point 1,000′ distant from the mortuary temple is a low-rising tell of a sort, with a few limestone blocks and numerous limestone fragments scattered about. This tell rises at the edge of a slight hillock where another asphalt road passes beneath it. By all indications, then, this was the site of Eke's valley temple.

The downward slope of the terrain from the site of the mortuary temple to the assumed site of the valley temple is also noticeable. It is not unreasonable to assume, from the particular lay of the land, that the entire lower area likely met with the level of the Nile—or an adjacent canal thereof—at the time of the Third Dynasty, while the mortuary temple, built on higher ground, would have been situated far enough above the water table to have made its construction and that of the pyramid itself a practical undertaking.

Although the mysteries involved in the building and sealing of the pyramids are in themselves enough to tax the calculative resources of the inquisitive mind, the dedicated investigator is further confronted with the accumulated data and opinions which have been formulated concerning these sites. Here, for example, we do in fact have the presence of a mortuary temple, causeway and valley temple—however scant the remains of the latter may be—but we also have an official record that states otherwise.

In this unusual case involving the pyramid complex of Eke, the taboo of this site as set by the military is not to be underestimated, for only with great difficulty and a long lapse of precious time was the author finally able to gain access into the compound, and only for a limited time at that. Hopefully we will soon be allowed enough time at the site at least to trace the ground plan of the mortuary temple. Having inquired about the role of the army at the Zawaiyet el-Aryan pyramids, I was informed by a very old villager from Abu Sir that the military had occupied this location ever since his childhood; and this presence has been instrumental in thwarting the efforts of countless pyramid investigators since shortly after the notable excavation by Barsanti. Such are the

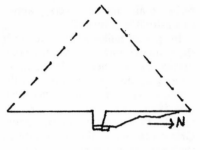

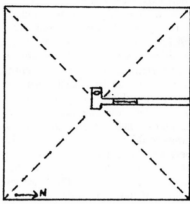

Pyramid of Eke, Zawaiyet el-Aryan. **Top:** *Cross-section.* **Bottom:** *Plan.* (AUTHOR'S IMPROVEMENTS ON A. BARSANTI.)

difficulties one inevitably confronts in dealing with some of the pyramid sites.

Pyramid: Eke. *Name:* "Unfinished Pyramid." *Number:* 16. *Exterior photos:* yes. *Interior photos:* no interior—constitutes an open pit. *Cross-sectional diagram:* yes. *Plan diagram:* yes. *Pyramid field:* Zawaiyet el-Aryan. *Field number:* IV. *Length:* rectangle 590 ft. E–W; 650 ft. N–S. *Height:* approx. 330 ft. *Angle:* 53 degrees. *Type:* step. *Materials:* limestone. *Location of entrance:* north. *Portcullises:* no. *Chambers:* one. *Comments:* Volume of pyramid, had it been completed, would have been 35 million cubic feet.

Pyramid of Eke, Zawaiyet el-Aryan. **Top left:** *Portion of Great Trench.* (J.P. LAUER) **Top right:** *The rock-cut subterranean pit, showing granite sarcophagus lid.* (J. CAPART) **Bottom:** *The rock-cut pit, showing lower half of 350' staircase.* (J.P. LAUER)

Pyramid Complex: Eke. *Main pyramid:* yes. *Satellite pyramid(s):* no. *Mortuary temple:* yes. *Valley temple:* yes. *Offering shrine:* no. *Mastaba(s):* no. *Ship(s):* no. *Ship pit(s):* no. *Causeway:* yes. *Temenos wall:* yes. *Canal:* destroyed.

PHARAOH 6: HUNI.

Position in dynasty: Sixth. *Portrait:* yes.* *Length of reign:* 24 years. *Dates of reign:* 2837–2814 B.C. *Mummy:* possibly found at Bet Khalaf in large mastaba. *Sarcophagus:* no. *Burial chamber:* yes?. *Treasure:* not found. *Hawk name:* Huni. *Vulture-and-Cobra name:* ?. *Set or Hawk-of-Nubi name:* ?. *Reed-and-Hornet name:* Huni. *Son-of-the-Sun-God (Ra) name:* none. *Other names:* Neferhere; Neferkere; Keneferre; Kerphere.

This pharaoh is credited with building two great monuments: his pyramid at Maidum and a huge mastaba at Bet Khallef in Upper Egypt. Although fragments of a wooden coffin were found inside his pyramid, his skeleton and the pulverized remains of yet another coffin were found in the burial chamber at Bet Khallef.

The presence of two coffins, in two tombs, for one pharaoh may perhaps be explained by the possibility that the coffin found in the Maidum pyramid was that of Huni's successor and son, King Sneferu. For although Sneferu is credited with building the two great pyramids at Dahshur, both of these monuments are devoid of sarcophagi, and neither gives any evidence of a burial having taken place there. Moreover, although Huni commenced work on the Maidum pyramid, it is not certain whether he actually completed it; it may well have been brought to completion by the illustrious Sneferu, favoring the hypothesis that he, and not Huni, may have been buried here.

The name Huni is represented as the king's Hawk-name in his mastaba at Bet Khallef, and as his Reed-and-Hornet name in the Sakkara List, Prisse Papyrus and the Turin Papyrus, with the latter ascribing to him a reign of 24 years. Curiously, however, there are few remains of this era, but for the pyramid, mastaba and a rock inscription at Sinai noted by Gardiner and Peet. This inscription indicates that Huni worked the copper mines there, as did his predecessors. In a book of maxims written during this king's tenure, it is noted that upon Huni's death, "King Sneferu became the new pharaoh."

Pyramid Complex: Huni. *Main pyramid:* yes. *Satellite pyramid(s):* yes

---

*While some authors describe the head shown on page 47 as that of "a late Third Dynasty king," others more assertively identify it as "King Huni?, late Third Dynasty." As if often the case, several of the heads of the kings of this particular era are completely absent. Therefore, there is all the more difficulty in placing questionable heads within the consecutive arrangement. Yet with this particular era, we already have the head of the pharaoh preceding Huni (King Eke), and the head of Huni's successor (King Sneferu), who is the last pharaoh of the Third Dynasty. Thus, if this particular head is indeed of a "late Third Dynasty King," then who else could it possibly be but Huni? Not only this, but the resemblance of this head to that of King Khufu (who was Huni's grandson, and who ruled shortly after Huni) is remarkable, so that a direct familial resemblance is obvious. In light of the points just cited, I have no reservations in ascribing this head to King Huni until there is submission of evidence to the contrary.

Pharaoh Huni and his cartouche.
(HEAD: BROOKLYN MUSEUM)

(one — no. 88). *Mortuary temple:* yes — well preserved. *Valley temple:* yes — in ruins. *Offering shrine:* no. *Mastaba(s):* yes — several. *Ship(s):* no. *Ship pit(s):* no. *Causeway:* yes — two (mortuary, well-preserved; construction, buried). *Temenos wall:* yes. *Canal:* destroyed.

Satellite Pyramid: Huni. *Name:* Pyramid Queen?. *Number:* 88. *Exterior photos:* no. *Interior photos:* no. *Cross-sectional diagram:* no. *Plan diagram:* no. *Pyramid field:* Maidum. *Field number:* XI. *Length:* approx. 130 ft. *Height:* approx. 80 ft. (now razed). *Angle:* ?. *Type:* limestone?. *Materials:* brick. *Location of entrance:* ?. *Portcullises:* ?. *Chambers:* one?. *Comments:* No record of investigation for this pyramid.

PHARAOH 7: SNEFERU.
Position in dynasty: Seventh (last). *Portrait:* yes. *Length of reign:* 24 years. *Dates of reign:* 2813–2790 B.C. *Mummy:* not found. *Sarcophagus:* none. *Burial chamber:* yes?. *Treasure:* not found. *Hawk name:* Nebmaet (Lord in Truth). *Vulture-and-Cobra name:* Nebmaet. *Set or Hawk-of-Nubi name:* Sneferu. *Reed-and-Hornet name:* Sneferu (The Gladdener). *Son-of-the-Sun-God (Ra) name:* none. *Other names:* Sephur; Sneferu; Snefru; Snephur; Snofru.

Although sometimes regarded as the first pharaoh of the Fourth Dynasty, most scholars prefer to refer to Sneferu as the last king of the Third Dynasty. It is quite likely that he was the son of his predecessor, Huni, and certain that he was father to his successor, Khufu.

Sneferu was perhaps the most ambitious of all pyramid pharaohs, as he is credited, not only with building the two great pyramids and the satellite at Dahshur, but also with having completed the pyramid at Maidum; and if we assign to him one-half of the work on the Maidum monument, then he was responsible for the erection of 116 million cubic feet of masonry in three edifices alone (disregarding the Dahshur satellite). Khufu's Great Pyramid, the largest *single* structure, comprises 94 million cubic feet of masonry. It is interesting to note the size of the monument Sneferu could have built had he put all of his effort into one pyramid, rather than three.

Sneferu, "The Gladdener," was the king's Reed-and-Hornet name, but Lepsius notes that both his Vulture-and-Cobra and Hawk names were Nebmaet, "Lord in Truth." (Lepsius, *Denkmaler,* II, 2).

Pyramid of Huni, Maidum. (J. BREASTED)

A new pharaonic title first appears in this dynasty in the royal titulary, the Hur-nubi, or "Golden Horus" name. Weigall points out that the term does not imply a golden hawk, but that *nubi,* "golden," is more correctly a representation of the city Ombos (Nubi), "the Golden City," and that Horus was worshipped there. Thus Hur-nubi is to be read "Horus of Nubi" (Ombos), and not "the Golden Horus."

Like the rulers preceding him, Sneferu also worked the copper mines at Sinai. With three large pyramids accredited to his reign, copper cutting tools would have been used extensively. Later hieroglyphic inscriptions speak of the vast scope of operations carried out at these mines by Sneferu.

The two most illustrious royal princes of this reign were buried at the site of the Maidum Pyramid ascribed to Sneferu, one of these being a son of the king, Ra-hotep (Re-hotpe). Magnificent lifelike statues of him and his wife, Lady Nofret (Cairo Museum), exhibit the high artistic achievement of this early period, with the statue of Nofret regarded as one of the greatest accomplishments of ancient Egyptian sculpture.

Snofrunofreher and Kenofre, two other royal princes, were buried close to the pyramids at Dahshur.

Several scarabs and stone bowls bearing Sneferu's name have been found throughout Egypt, and a priestly administration set up for ministrations to his spirit extended to Dynasties IV, V, XIII, XVIII and XXVII. Even in Ptolemaic times, worship of Sneferu had survived.

An interesting story relating to Sneferu in the Westcar Papyrus tells of how he was relieved from a bout of depression by his chief wise-man fetching 20 pretty, young maidens to row him about in a pleasure boat equipped with gold and ebony paddles. Although the origin of the story could well be based on nothing more

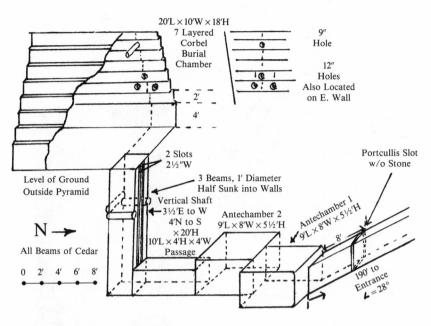

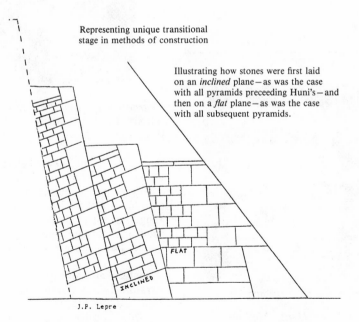

Pyramid of Huni, Maidum. **Top:** *Three-dimensional diagram.* **Bottom:** *Drawing showing transitional stages of construction.* (J.P. LEPRE)

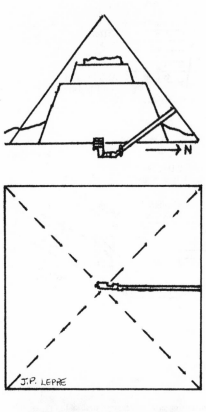

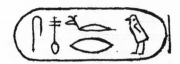

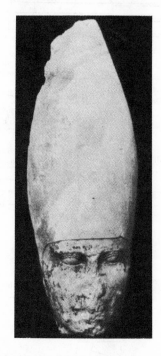

Pharaoh Sneferu and his cartouche.
(HEAD: EGYPTIAN MUSEUM, CAIRO;
PHOTO BY A. FAKHRY)

than a fairy tale, nevertheless, if it were true, it would not be inconsistent with the fabulous wealth attributed to the kings of the Old Kingdom, where many of the objects used for the pharaoh's pleasure would have been fashioned from gold.

Sneferu and the First Five True Pyramids. King Sneferu is credited with building the three pyramids at Dahshur and having completed the one built by his father King Huni, at Maidum. Sneferu must surely have also had a hand in the construction

Pyramid of Huni, Maidum. **Top:** *Cross-section.* **Center:** *Plan.* (J.P. LEPRE) **Bottom:** *Plan of mortuary temple.* (W.M.F. PETRIE)

or completion of the satellite pyramid of the Maidum parent pyramid. His son, Khufu, is credited with building four pyramids, but particularly the Great One, which directly relates to the above-mentioned monuments at Dahshur and Maidum. (Actually, the satellite pyramid at Maidum can, for the time being, be excluded in any attempt to describe and compare the internal arrangements of these several monuments, as there are no records which exist of its interior plan.)

King Sneferu's reign encompassed the majority of the evolutionary period of the true pyramid, a period beginning with Huni's pyramid at Maidum and reaching its zenith with Khufu's great monument. A brief study of the five pyramids built within that period not only traces the evolutionary process, but possibly provides clues to the whereabouts of Sneferu's mummy and sarcophagus, never found to this day. The five pyramids for our study are the Pyramid of Huni, Maidum; the Southern ("Bent") Pyramid of Sneferu at Dahshur; the satellite pyramid of the Bent Pyramid; the Northern ("Red") Pyramid of Sneferu, also at Dahshur; and the Great Pyramid of Khufu, at Giza.

Huni's pyramid at Maidum represents the first pyramid which was finished as a true pyramid; with sheer, sloping sides rather than the step-pattern of all previous pyramids.*

This monument, like so many of the mastabas and step pyramids which preceded it, was quite simple in design, consisting of a descending passageway entering from the north, a portcullis block at its lower end, two subterranean antechambers and a burial chamber. Although the plan was simple enough, an important innovation had taken place, for the burial chamber was — for the very first time — built in the superstructure, and not the substructure, of the pyramid. With the Maidum Pyramid, then, the evolution is not only from step pyramid to true pyramid, but also from burial chambers located in the rock substrata to a burial chamber built into the superstructure. (The chamber is, however, situated low in that superstructure, its floor at ground level.)

The next pyramid to be built was entirely the undertaking of Sneferu: his Southern Pyramid at Dahshur, otherwise known as the Bent, Blunted or Rhomboidal Pyramid due to its angle of inclination cutting in dramatically at its halfway mark. This monument is especially interesting when discussing the evolution of pyramid building, for here quite a complex internal design has been fostered; there is not only an entrance from the north, but a second one entering from the west — an unprecedented phenomenon for an Old Kingdom pyramid. Also, its antechamber and lower chamber — both subterranean — are dramatically

---

*The Bent Pyramid is not, in the strictest sense of the word, a *true* pyramid, due to its dramatic change in angle. Yet I feel comfortable in referring to it as a true pyramid because, except for the obvious deviation of its sloping sides, it is a true pyramid in every other sense of the word. At any rate, a step pyramid it is not, so that it is more reasonable to place it in the true pyramid category. Additionally, it was no doubt begun as a true pyramid and was meant to be finished as such, were it not for the serious structural problems which became evident when the monument was built up to its approximate halfway mark. It was the presence of these structural defects that prompted the builders suddenly to change its angle of inclination.

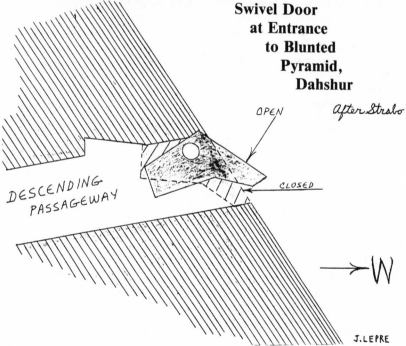

**Swivel Door
at Entrance
to Blunted
Pyramid,
Dahshur**

OPEN   *after Strabo*

DESCENDING
PASSAGEWAY

CLOSED

⟶ W

J. LEPRE

Bent (Rhomboidal) Pyramid of Sneferu, Dahshur. **Top:** *1906 photo.* (K. OPPEL) **Bottom:** *Drawing shows swivel door at entrance.* (J.P. LEPRE)

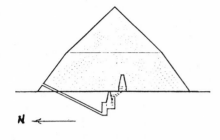

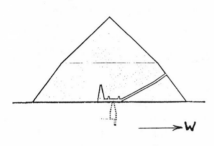

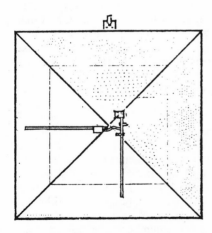

Bent Pyramid of Sneferu, Dahshur.
Top: *Cross-section 1.* **Center:** *Cross-section 2.* **Bottom:** *Plan* (H. VYSE AND J. PERRING)

increased in size, with the employment of corbel architecture very impressive here.

As in its predecessor, the Pyramid of Maidum, there is also a principal chamber in the Bent Pyramid, located above the first two and in the superstructure, with its floorline similarly situated at ground level.

A further innovation within the Bent Pyramid is the fact that the portcullis blocking system in the western corridor is more sophisticated than any portcullis system previously devised; it consists of very large twin blocks which operate diagonally, rather than horizontally or vertically.

The discovery of two other filled-in cavities or chambers in this pyramid further testifies to its innovative complexity. It is apparent that with the interior design of the Bent Pyramid the architect was groping and experimenting, taking maximum advantage of the huge volume of the monument (50 million cubic feet), the largest pyramid constructed to that date.

It would seem from this picture that the next pyramid in line would be even more complex. The next major pyramid is Sneferu's Northern (Red) Pyramid at Dahshur, approximately one mile north of the Bent Pyramid. Prior to constructing this colossus, however, Sneferu built a small subsidiary pyramid to accompany the Bent Pyramid. This satellite pyramid lay immediately south of the parent pyramid. Although only a fraction of the size of the main monument, it nevertheless displayed similar complexity in its internal design, not only with its burial chamber situated in the superstructure, but with a long, ascending — rather than descending — passageway as well. This rising corridor — oriented to the west, and not the usual north — indicates that Sneferu's architect was now entertaining the idea of multiple chambers and corridors to be built in the superstructure of the next major monument, with a further deemphasis of the previously popular underground chamber-corridor system.

With grand expectations the eager student of pyramid evolution now looks to the next large monument for a further complication of design. But here, with the Red Pyramid of Sneferu at Dahshur, the interior plan seems to take a surprising turn, regressing to a simpler design than its main predecessor, the Bent Pyramid. On the one hand, the plan of the Red Pyramid of Dahshur is not that simple, having two antechambers and a principal chamber. All three are built entirely in the superstructure, although they are close to ground level. In this sense, the arrangement of the interior of the Red Pyramid acknowledges the innovations of its three forerunners. Yet on the other hand, there is no ascending corridor — western or otherwise — no western or second entrance, and no unique portcullis system, though these three innovations had just preceded the building of this pyramid. It is as if the evolutionary rhythm skips a beat, at this point in the development process.

The Great Pyramid, which was the next one in line, is indeed complex, more so than any which had preceded or followed it. This complexity was to be expected, thanks to the creative developments which occurred with the Maidum Pyramid and the two south Dahshur pyramids. But complexity was to be expected, in some way or other, in the Red Pyramid at Dahshur as well. That the plan of the Red Pyramid reverts nearly to the simplicity of the Pyramid of Maidum — which preceded it by two pyramids — is difficult to comprehend or accept. Following the bold changes in design in both the Bent Pyramid and its small satellite pyramid, it is inconceivable that the next pyramid in line would have been given such an elementary design.

It is more than likely that the Red Pyramid did in fact obey a more complex plan for its internal arrangement, as would have been in keeping with the chain of development up to that point in time, and that this pyramid does in fact contain other well-hidden chambers or passageways that would establish it as the true link between its great predecessor, the Bent Pyramid at Dahshur, and its great successor, the Pyramid of Khufu at Giza.

For the above reasons the Red Pyramid remains one of the chief pyramids that may possibly contain secret chambers, not the least of which may be the true burial chamber of King Sneferu himself.

What a twist of fate, then, that the Red Pyramid is one of the least-explored pyramids in Egypt, the main reasons being that it is located on an off-limits army base, and that most Egyptologists have erroneously accepted the hypothesis that its present design is its final design, and that there is little likelihood that other, hidden chambers will ever be found there.

Aside from the clues present in the evolutionary development of these first five true pyramids, there is further evidence that the mummy of King Sneferu may still be deposited within the Red Pyramid. An interesting point is that although two of Sneferu's sons and other family members are buried near the Maidum pyramid, and most of the priestly class are buried in a graveyard adjacent to the Bent Pyramid, Sneferu's youngest

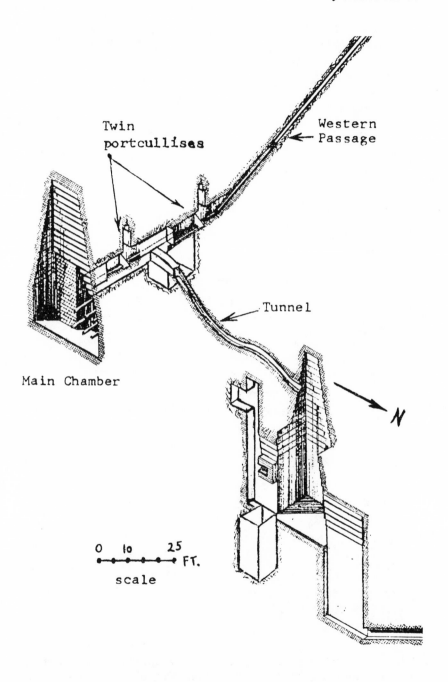

Twin
portcullises

Western
Passage

Tunnel

Main Chamber

0 10 25 FT.
scale

N

Bent Pyramid of Sneferu, Dahshur: Three-dimensional interior diagram.
(Author's Improvement on A. Fakhry)

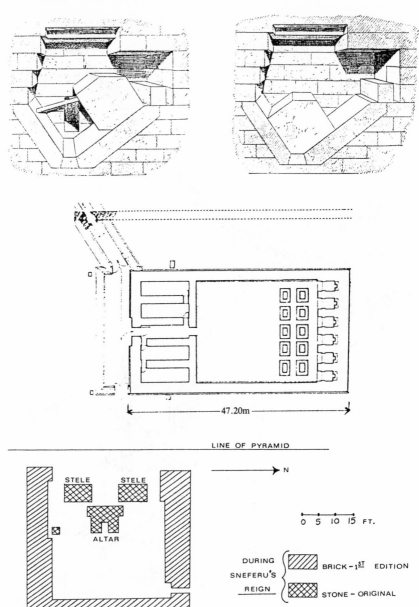

Bent Pyramid of Sneferu, Dahshur. **Top:** *Drawings show open (left) and closed positions of oblique five-ton portcullis block in horizontal passageway.* (G. PERROT AND C. CHIPIEZ) **Center:** *Valley temple Plan.* (G. MASPERO) **Bottom:** *Plan of mortuary temple.* (J.P. LEPRE/K. MAYER)

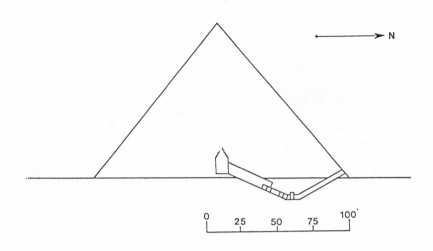

Satellite pyramid of Bent Pyramid Complex, South Dahshur (cross-section).
(J.P. Lepre/ K. Mayer)

children — among whom was Sneferu's eldest surviving son, Kano-
fer — are buried in mastabas to the
southeast of the Red Pyramid.

It would seem from this arrangement that Sneferu's older children,
having died first, were buried close to
the Maidum Pyramid because this
was initially planned to be Sneferu's
tomb. But then Sneferu built a larger
pyramid to the north (the Bent Pyramid), and afterwards yet another,
even larger pyramid further north
(the Red Pyramid), and his younger
children were interred in mastabas
adjacent to the Red Pyramid. Might
these interments suggest that the Red
Pyramid was to be Sneferu's final
place of rest? It is unlikely that this
pharaoh would have constructed a
third major pyramid, the largest up
till then in Egypt, if he did not intend
to be buried there.

An interesting pattern of building
pyramids and of burying the dead
during the period of Sneferu and
Khufu reveals itself in the geo-

graphical sites of pyramids and their
adjacent graveyards. The five main
pyramids in the Sneferu-Khufu series
are built from south to north. The
first pyramid, that of Maidum, is the
farthest south of the five, and the last
of the five is that of Khufu at Giza,
the farthest north. So too with the
scheme of Sneferu's gravesites,
whose capsulated form also displays
a movement from south to north. Insofar as the pyramids are concerned,
the movement northward continues
on with the next major pyramid in
the chronology, that of Khufu's son
and successor, Rededef, who built
his monument several miles north of
Giza, at Abu Roash. It is not until
the raising of the next great pyramid
by Rededef's successor, King
Khafra, that this pattern of moving
from south to north is broken, with
that pyramid being built south of
Rededef's monument.

Finally, some greater complexity of design, if it existed in the
Red Pyramid, would have been an

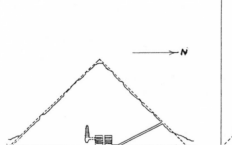

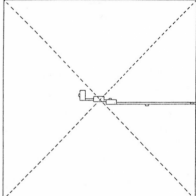

Top: *Northern (Red) Pyramid of Sneferu, Dahshur.* **Bottom left:** *Cross-section,* **Bottom right:** *Plan.* (A. FAKHRY)

additional incentive for the Red Pyramid rather than the Bent Pyramid being chosen as the final resting place for Sneferu. Again we must wonder if the Red Pyramid's design is as simple as it appears. . . or is it so much more complex than its predecessors that the innovative new sections have thus far remained undetected? It seems likely that the complexity of the Red Pyramid has yet to be dis-

covered, but that does not mean the complexity does not exist.

During the building of the first five true pyramids progressive innovations were being made, so much so that it was inevitable that both the Red Pyramid and the Great Pyramid would be conceived on a complex internal plan. For example, even if the chambers and passages of the Great Pyramid which were found high in the superstructure had not been discovered in the ninth century A.D. by the Caliph Al Mamoun, the development of pyramids up to that point would undoubtedly have indicated that such chambers did in fact exist.

The upper chambers and passages within the Great Pyramid were discovered, not by protracted detective work, but by sheer luck. Anyone having any knowledge of the history of the Great Pyramid knows that the chances of Al Mamoun breaking into the First Ascending Passage after the original entrance had been long covered over with rubble were extraordinarily remote. If not for that lucky stroke, we may well have surmised that additional chambers and passages were located in that pyramid's superstructure, but we also may never have discovered them.

With the Red Pyramid of Dahshur, the stroke of luck has not occurred, and may never occur. It will require full-time investigative effort to be able someday to deduce where the hidden chambers or passages lie in this edifice—chambers and passages that I am certain exist.

Pyramid: Sneferu ("Bent," "Blunted" or "Rhomboidal"). *Name:* Sneferu Gleams. *Number:* 71. *Exterior photos:* yes. *Interior photos:* yes. *Cross-sectional diagram:* yes. *Plan diagram:* yes. *Pyramid field:* Dahshur. *Field number:* VIII. *Length:* 620 ft. *Height:* 335 ft. *Angle:* two—upper, 43 degrees, 21 minutes; lower, 54 degrees, 31 minutes. *Type:* true. *Materials:* limestone. *Location of entrance:* two—north face and west face. *Portcullises:* two—oblique. *Chambers:* two. *Comments:* Volume = 50 million cu. ft.

Pyramid Complex: Sneferu (Bent Pyramid). *Main pyramid:* yes. *Satellite pyramid(s):* yes—one

pyramid no. 72). *Mortuary temple:* yes. *Valley temple:* yes. *Offering shrine:* no. *Mastaba(s):* yes—several. *Ship(s):* no. *Ship pit(s):* no. *Causeway:* yes. *Temenos wall:* yes. *Canal:* destroyed.

Satellite Pyramid: Sneferu. *Name:* Pyramid Queen Hetepheres. *Number:* 72. *Exterior photos:* yes. *Interior photos:* no. *Cross-sectional diagram:* yes. *Plan diagram:* no. *Pyramid field:* Dahshur. *Field number:* VIII. *Length:* 181 ft. *Height:* 107 ft. (now 67 ft.). *Angle:* 50 degrees, 11 minutes. *Type:* true. *Materials:* limestone. *Location of entrance:* north face. *Portcullises:* yes—1 vertical (plus 4 plugs). *Chambers:* one. *Comments:* This pyramid has a north offering shrine, and two stela and an altar on its east side.

Pyramid: Sneferu (Red Pyramid). *Name:* Sneferu Appears. *Number:* 66. *Exterior photos:* yes. *Interior photos:* yes. *Cross-sectional diagram:* yes. *Plan diagram:* yes. *Pyramid field:* Dahshur. *Field number:* VIII. *Length:* 720 ft. *Height:* 320 ft. *Angle:* 43 degrees, 36 minutes. *Type:* true. *Materials:* limestone. *Location of entrance:* north face. *Portcullises:* none. *Chambers:* three. *Comments:* Volume = 57 million cu. ft.

Pyramid Complex: Sneferu (Red Pyramid). *Main pyramid:* yes. *Satellite pyramid(s):* no. *Mortuary temple:* yes—destroyed. *Valley temple:* yes—remnants. *Offering shrine:* no. *Mastaba(s):* yes—several. *Ship(s):* no. *Ship pit(s):* no. *Causeway:* yes—three—1 funerary, 2 construction. *Temenos wall:* no. *Canal:* destroyed.

DYNASTY IV

• *Duration:* **74 years (2789–2716** B.C.). *Pharaohs:* **1. Khufu. 2.**

Northern (Red) Pyramid of Sneferu, Dahshur, showing 50'-high corbeled chamber. (A. FAKHRY)

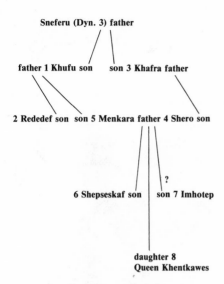

Sneferu (Dyn. 3) father

father 1 Khufu son   son 3 Khafra father

2 Rededef son   son 5 Menkara father 4 Shero son

6 Shepseskaf son   son 7 Imhotep

?

daughter 8
Queen Khentkawes

Dynasty IV Genealogy

Rededef. 3. Khafra. 4 Shero (no pyramid). 5. Menkara. 6. Shepseskaf (mastaba). 7. Imhotep (no pyramid).

PHARAOH 8: KHUFU.
Position in dynasty: First. *Portrait:* yes. *Length of reign:* 23 years. *Dates of reign:* 2789–2767 B.C. *Mummy:* not found. *Sarcophagus:* red granite. *Burial chamber:* yes?. *Treasure:* not found. *Hawk name:* Metheru (The Energetic). *Vulture-and-Cobra name:* Metheru. *Set or Hawk-of-Nubi name:* Khufu (He Protects). *Reed-and-Hornet name:* Khufu. *Son-of-the-Sun-God (Ra) name:* none. *Other names:* Chembres; Chemististes; Chemmis; Cheop; Cheops; Comastes; Khembes; Khemmes; Kheop; Kheops; Kheuf; Khnem-Kheuf; Khnum-Kheuf; Khuf; Khufu; Khufui; Khufwey; Kouf; Koufou; Nem-Shufu; Noh-Suphis; Saoph; Saophis; Sen-Suphis; Shofo; Shure; Shufu; Soris; Suph; Suphis; Surid; Xufu. *Principal Queens (Wives):* Henutsen; Mertityotes; Senit. *Principal Princesses (Daugh-*

ters): Honitsonu; Hotpheres; Meritsenkhes; Nofrehotpes.

Although this pharaoh's Reed-and-Hornet and Hawk-of-Nubi names were both Khufu, "He Protects," he is more characteristically represented by his Hawk and Vulture-and-Cobra name, Metheru, "The Energetic." How befitting a name for the grand pharaoh who built the Great Pyramid.

Both Herodotus and Manetho speak of Khufu as an arrogant and tyrannical ruler who caused the temples of the gods to be closed so that he could more expediently construct his colossal monument.

Although the three-inch-high ivory statuette (found by Petrie at Abydos [Ebod], now in the Cairo Museum), is the only true likeness that we have of Khufu, his stylized image is cut into a rock cliff in the Wady Maghara, in Sinai. Here he is depicted smiting a Bedouin chieftain.

At the First Cataract, on the island of Sehel, his name is inscribed upon a rock; near Tell-el-Amarna, there is a tablet of his; on the island of Elephantine, an inscription records the name of an official of his reign; and at Tidel (in the northwest Delta) and Zagazig (Bubastis), several stones from his temples have been found. Other records of his rule are few, but the names of four of his daughters are written in hieroglyphic texts as Henutsen, Nofrehotpes, Hotpheres and Meritenkhes (Meritsenkh). Two of Khufu's wives, Mertityotes and Senit, are also mentioned.

Khufu was perhaps the most powerful pharaoh ever to rule Egypt, the accomplishment of building the Great Pyramid being the testament to the might and discipline of a grand civilization at its zenith.

This impressive monument was

Pharaoh Khufu and his cartouche. (STATUETTE: CAIRO MUSEUM) *Of this three-inch-high ivory statuette of Khufu, G. Maspero wrote: "The work is of extraordinary delicacy and finish; for even when magnified it does not suggest any imperfection or clumsiness, but might have belonged to a life-sized statue. The proportion of the head is slightly exaggerated; as, indeed, is always the case in minute work; but the character and expression are as well handled as they might be on any other scale, and are full of power and vigor. The idea which it conveys to us of the personality of Khufu agrees with his historical position. We see the energy, the commanding air, the indomitable will, and the firm ability of the man who stamped for ever the character of the Egyptian monarchy and outdid all time in the scale of his works. No other Egyptian king that we know resembled this head; and it stands apart in portraiture...."*

When this statuette of Khufu was discovered at Abydos by Petrie in 1909, it was headless. Yet due to the observation that the fracture appeared to be fresh, Petrie had his workers meticulously sift through the surrounding rubble for three full weeks before they finally found it. It was not quite ¾ of an inch high.

composed of 2½ million blocks of stone, each weighing an average of 2½ tons, and comprising conglomerately over 6 million tons; it encompassed an area of 13½ acres in a 3,000′ base perimeter, and displaced a volume of 94 million cubic feet of solid masonry.

Despite the length of the following essay describing the Great Pyramid, only the most basic information is supplied. The pyramid is so very complex that to make mention of all or most of its characteristics would necessarily involve a far lengthier discourse on the subject, one which would undoubtedly comprise volumes of written material. This should suffice, though, to supply the curious reader with a better-than-fair understanding of the fundamental plan of this colossal edifice, the secrets of which have eluded serious scholars and researchers for scores of centuries.

"The fact that such an erection was possible," said James Baikie in 1917, "reveals the power and the

Top: *Great Pyramid of Khufu, Giza.* (J. AND M. EDGAR) **Bottom:** *The Pyramids of Giza.* (PHOTO BY R. HAWTHORNE, ORIENTAL MUSEUM OF CHICAGO)

unquestioned authority of the man who could thus bend the resources of a whole nation to the construction of a monument whose sole use was to add to his own personal glory, while it is also a tribute to the wonderful skill with which the labor of the nation was organized and made available for a single purpose. No building, ancient or modern, is so widely known, or has commanded such an amount of interest and attention, as Khufu's gigantic mausoleum. . . .

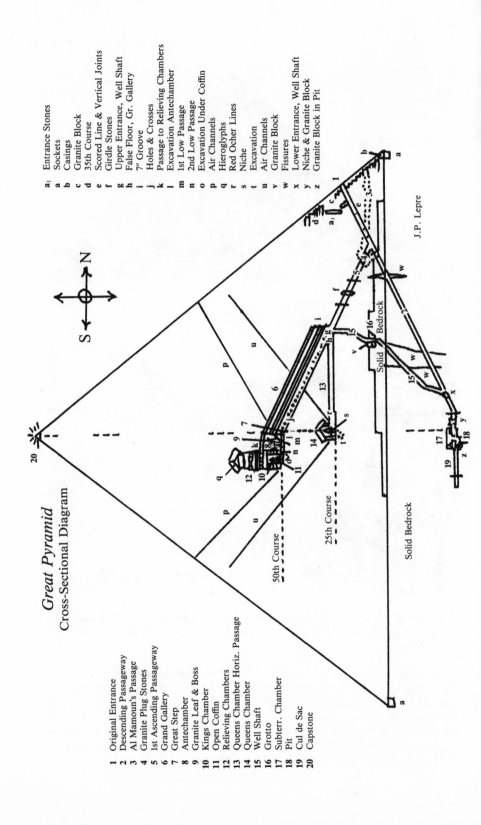

Great Pyramid
Cross-Sectional Diagram

1 Original Entrance
2 Descending Passageway
3 Al Mamoun's Passage
4 Granite Plug Stones
5 1st Ascending Passageway
6 Grand Gallery
7 Great Step
8 Antechamber
9 Granite Leaf & Boss
10 Kings Chamber
11 Open Coffin
12 Relieving Chambers
13 Queens Chamber Horiz. Passage
14 Queens Chamber
15 Well Shaft
16 Grotto
17 Subterr. Chamber
18 Pit
19 Cul de Sac
20 Capstone

a₁ Entrance Stones
a Sockets
b Casings
c Granite Block
d 35th Course
e Scored Line & Vertical Joints
f Girdle Stones
g Upper Entrance, Well Shaft
h False Floor, Gr. Gallery
i 7" Groove
j Holes & Crosses
k Passage to Relieving Chambers
l Excavation Antechamber
m 1st Low Passage
n 2nd Low Passage
o Excavation Under Coffin
p Air Channels
q Hieroglyphs
r Red Ocher Lines
s Niche
t Excavation
u Air Channels
v Granite Block
w Fissures
x Lower Entrance, Well Shaft
y Niche & Granite Block
z Granite Block in Pit

J.P. Lepre

S ← ⊕ → N

50th Course
25th Course
Solid Bedrock
Solid Bedrock
Bedrock

"The size of this vast monument is not, however, its only claim to notice. The fineness of the workmanship, the skill with which the building has been planned and oriented, and the precision of its levels, are all most extraordinary—'equal to optician's work of the present day,' says Petrie, 'but on a scale of acres instead of feet or yards.'"

One very unusual feature of the Great Pyramid is a concavity of the core that makes the monument an eight-sided figure, rather than four-sided like every other Egyptian pyramid. This is to say, that its four sides are hollowed in or indented along their center lines, from base to peak. This concavity divides each of the apparent four sides in half, creating a very special and unusual eight-sided pyramid; and it is executed to such an extraordinary degree of precision as to enter the realm of the uncanny. For, viewed from any ground position or distance, this concavity is quite invisible to the naked eye. The hollowing-in can be noticed only from the air, and only at certain times of the day. This explains why virtually every available photograph of the Great Pyramid does not show the hollowing-in phenemenon, and why the concavity was never discovered until the age of aviation. It was discovered quite by accident in 1940, when a British Air Force pilot, P. Groves, was flying over the pyramid. He happened to notice the concavity and captured it in the now-famous photograph.

VIEW FROM THE OUTSIDE AND APPROACH. The normal approach to the Giza plateau is from the northeast, via Cairo's Street of the Pyramids. There, on the summit of that promontory, stands the 4,500-year-old Great Pyramid of Khufu, the first pharaoh of the Fourth Dynasty.

The pyramid, when seen from a distance, does not appear inordinately large, due to the background of the barren Sahara. As one reaches the end of the Street of the Pyramids, however, and begins to ascend the grade to its north face, the colossal size of the monument begins to assert itself. At the top of the grade, with the pyramid now in full view just 200' away, one is held in awe.

Six million tons of solid masonry built on a solid rock foundation, with weathered, yellow stone and truncated summit—this is the starkness with which one is confronted.

As the visitor walks across the flat and spacious limestone pavement and draws closer to the monument, the bottom course of the two hundred and ten (which once culminated in a pyramidion caping the edifice) stands out among the other courses, in that it is white, not yellow, in color. The predominant yellow, nummulitic limestone comprises the core of the building. The white finish or cover stones still seen on the bottom course once sheathed the entire pyramid, but were subsequently stripped from the monument for latter-day building projects in Cairo and at other pyramid fields. These casing stones, of which only a few remain at the first course of masonry, were originally fitted together with such unerring precision that the jointing between them was barely discernible to the naked eye, resembling hairlines rather than joints of masonry.

Two million, three hundred thousand individual stones comprised the Great Pyramid; the majority were of the yellow, core limestone, quarried from the immediate pyramid site itself, while the remaining 144,000 casings, of white, unblemished limestone, were cut from the Tura and Masara quarries on the east bank of the Nile on the outskirts of modern Cairo. It is said that the monument

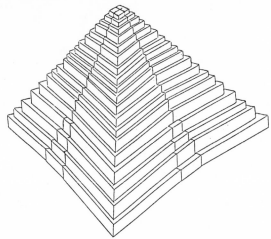

Great Pyramid of Khufu, Giza. **Top:** *Aerial photo by P. Groves, showing unique hollowing-in of core masonry that makes the pyramid into an eight-sided figure. (Pyramid Khufu at top rear; Pyramid Khafra in foreground.)* (E. RAYMOND CAPT) **Bottom:** *Drawing of hollowing-in, showing 19 accretion layers.* (J.P. LEPRE)

in its pristine state was an all-white surface of smooth, close-fitting casing stones which glistened in the sun.

There is much controversy as to whether the ediface's pyramidion or capstone was ever set into place. Some authors point out that the triangulation of the monument itself was flawed and therefore could not properly receive the pre-cut capstone,

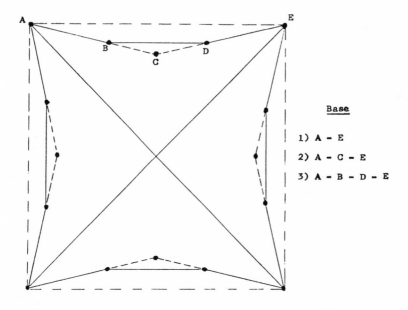

Various base lines of Great Pyramid, the result of the hollowing-in of the core masonry.

while others argue that the crowning pyramidion was blemished or fractured, and was never set into place because it was rejected by the builders.

Yet, on the other hand, there is the opposing theory that the capstone of this edifice was in fact set into place, but that it was removed during the time when the bulk of the casing stones were extracted from the site. In support of this line of reasoning is the fact that, when Herodotus the Greek historian described the exterior of this pyramid as still having each of its white sheathing stones intact, he does not mention the absence of the pyramidion—a point which, one would think, he would hardly have omitted, were it missing at the time.

If the capstone was actually set into place by the pyramid builders, and then subsequently removed from its unique position at the apex of the monument, it would no doubt have been hurled down to the ground with the other extracted stones. But at that point, what exactly would have been its fate? For the casing stones themselves were all square-cut and represented rectangular blocks that would have been ideal for further building purposes, but the pyramidion was in fact the only odd-shaped stone of the 144,000; it was triangular and comprised nothing more than a miniature pyramid of a sort. It would have no practical use as a common building block, its only purpose being to cap a pyramidal structure.

Its fate, however, may well be traced to the bottom of the 200' escarpment upon which the pyramid itself is built. (The vast majority of Egyptian pyramids are not situated on such a high plateau, but are constructed on flat terrain.) The capstone of the Great Pyramid may well have been rolled or dragged along the foundation surface of its north side, and then tossed off the edge of the high escarpment. Giving credence to this supposition, the base of the plateau at this point is straddled with large mounds of rock debris intermingled and covered over with desert sand. Surely these mounds represent the thousands of fractured or discarded pieces of casing stones which had accumulated at the base of the pyramid when the stripping work was being conducted — pieces that were rolled, dragged or carried to the edge of the precipice and then tossed over in order to facilitate the dismantling process.

Not only the pyramidion, but whole sections of casing blocks — and perhaps even some remnants of the mortuary temple or north offering shrine — could possibly be found here. Even today, fragments of hewn and squared blocks can be seen protruding from these huge mounds

located at the base of the escarpment.

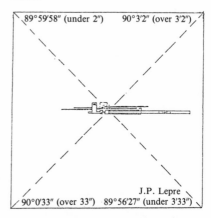

Pyramid Khufu, Giza: Plan.
(J.P. LEPRE)

Furthermore, it is not at all unreasonable to assume that even fragments of statues of the Pharaoh Khufu may be buried beneath these

*Casing blocks at base of Pyramid Khufu. Joints, otherwise indiscernible, indicated by charcoal lines. *Note pavement on which blocks are set.*

Great Pyramid Khufu

(Measurements of 19 accretion courses)

Accretion	Precise Course	Approximate Course	Ratio
1)	* 19	20	5
2)	25	25	10
3)	* 35	35	10
4)	* 44	45	15
5)	59	60	10
6)	* 67	70	5
7)	74	75	10
8)	84	85	5
9)	* 90	90	10
10)	98	100	10
11)	* 108	110	10
12)	118	120	10
13)	130	130	15
14)	144	145	5
15)	150	150	15
16)	164	165	15
17)	180	180	15
18)	196	195	10
19)	204	205	

Top of Core   206

Bottom of Capstone 209

Top of Capstone   210
(Apex of Pyramid)

       * Easily discernible to
        the naked eye from a distance.

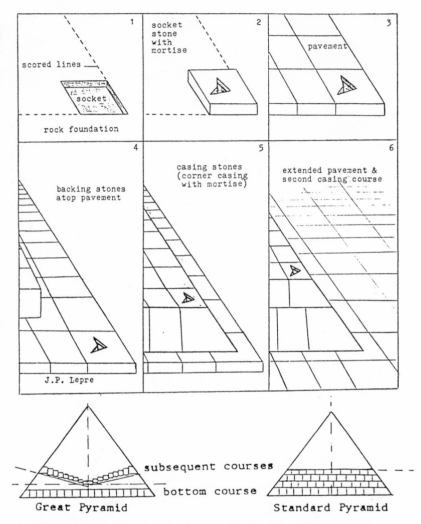

Great Pyramid of Khufu, Giza. **Top:** *Illustration of a socket and socket stones, one of four sets located at this pyramid's four corners. The phenomenon of such socket stones is unique to the Great Pyramid. Whereas the four socket sets lock the four corners into place, each corner casing has a mortise hollow at its top surface and a tenon protrusion at its bottom, further locking the four arris edges together.* **Bottom:** *Packing blocks. "In each horizontal row of blocks a gentle grading was carried out, by which the blocks at the edge were very slightly higher than those in the middle of the face. In this way, the corners of each layer of packing blocks were slightly lifted, making the whole layer slightly concave towards the apex. This method provided an additional inward thrust which further counteracted any tendency of lateral forces to develop."* Mendelssohn, **Riddle of the Pyramids,** *p. 122. (Diagram exaggerated to illustrate point.)* (J.P. Lepre)

piles of rubble. To find such fragments would be a remarkable discovery indeed, as the only known statue of this energetic king is the three-inch-high ivory statuette found by Petrie at Abydos.

The casing stones are without parallel, having been so perfectly cut and squared that their corners were found to be true 90-degree angles to within 1/100 of an inch. This is remarkable indeed, considering the fact that some of them weighed up to 15 tons and were over 8' in length. Today there are only 138 of these peerless stones remaining at the base of the pyramid: 18 on the north face; 20 on the south; 15 on the east; and 85 on the west. Most of them are very badly fractured, and only seven of them are fairly well intact. The average size of the ones situated at the lowest or first course of masonry is 5' long by 5' high by 6' deep.

A final word regarding the capstone, and the refutation of the theory that it was never set into place because it was rejected by the builders; why couldn't these builders, at that stage in the construction process—which represented the very end of a 20-year, full-time project—not have fashioned another, more acceptable, pyramidion? Surely the effort would have been insignificant compared to what was already expended on such a colossal edifice. With the resources and workforce which were then available, it does not seem at all consistent that the architect would have been thwarted in this final effort to crown the pyramid and bring his work to its full culmination.

ENTRANCES. As one draws nearer to the pyramid and is dwarfed beneath its imposing bulk, an entrance of a sort can be discerned. It is located midway across the monument and 35' up from ground level, at the thirteenth course of masonry. One has to ascend the edifice step-fashion to see the actual aperture which gives access to the interior of the pyramid, but the entrance's massive portal stones can be seen clearly from the distance. While the actual aperture or doorway is a mere 4' high by 3½' wide—as is the passageway that enters into the pyramid at that point—each gable stone, of which there are four visible to the naked eye, is a 10'-long, 15-ton monolith. Together they form an inverted V above the entrance aperture. The striking configuration of these entrance stones seems symbolic of the grandeur which lies beyond, a sort of introduction to a high order of things.

The 3½' by 4' aperture is the original entrance to the pyramid, and the only one planned by the builders as far as we know. There is a second entrance, on the sixth course of masonry, but it is rather a forced, cavernous access, carved out with a fire and vinegar application by the Caliph Al Mamoun in the ninth century A.D. It leads to the junction of the descending and ascending passage systems and is roughly 5' wide by 8' high.

Al Mamoun forced this passage in order to gain entrance into the inner reaches of the pyramid. He was obliged to utilize this tactic because by his time, the original entrance had become camouflaged, owing to the great number of extracted casing blocks which had accumulated at that section of the north face of the monument.

This man penetrated the pyramid in this crude fashion hoping to discover the secret chamber of the Pharaoh Khufu. Although he was the first explorer actually to reach the burial chamber, when he arrived there he found no treasure whatsoever. The

Great Pyramid entrance. (**Left,** G. RAWLINSON; **right,** J.P. LEPRE)

chamber was empty, but for a solitary, empty sarcophagus.

As to the original entrance to the pyramid, the Greek geographer Strabo (circa 63 B.C.–A.D. 24) describes a swivel door of stone that was presumably once in place. It was supposed to have been designed with rounded, side protrusions which fit into hollows or sockets cut into the doorway, and by this means could be opened or closed at will by priests in charge of maintenance.

Today, however, all traces of this movable stone are gone, and the entrance is covered over by a weathered steel grating, locked shut by an old, rusted lock. All access into the building is now conducted via Al Mamoun's forced passage.

Although we have no visible evidence that such a door existed, Strabo's story has a ring of truth to it. For at the Bent Pyramid of Khufu's father, Sneferu, at Dahshur, there are to be found at its western entrance, two access stones set into the north and south walls containing distinct sockets, the bold remnants of a swivel-door mechanism. (See diagram, page 52.) Indications of similar sockets were discovered at the Third Dynasty pyramid of Khufu's grandfather Huni, at Maidum.

DESCENDING PASSAGE. The original 4' high x 3½' wide entrance gives rise to a 350'-long descending passage of similar height and width. It is composed of limestone throughout, and cuts through the masonry of the pyramid for the first 50' of its length, and then through the solid bedrock of the pyramid plateau for its remaining distance of 300'. Descending at an angle of approximately 26 degrees, it terminates in a subterranean chamber nearly 100' below ground level.

Height and Width of Passageways of the Great Pyramid

	Passageway	Height	Width
1	Descending Passageway	47¾″	42″
2	1st Ascending Passage – at north end	47¼″	38½″
3	1st Ascending Passage – at midway point	48″	41½″
4	1st Ascending Passage – at south end	53″	42″
5	1st Low Passage to King's Chamber	44″	41½″
6	2nd Low Passage to King's Chamber	43½″	41½″
7	Queen's Chamber Horizontal Passage	47″	41½″
8	Horizontal Passage to Subterranean Chamber	45¾″	35″
9	Cul De Sac – at Subterranean Chamber	30″	30″
10	Cul De Sac – at midway point	27″	27″
11	Cul De Sac – at furthermost end	30″	30″
12	Well Shaft	36″	36″

Note: This table indicates how exploration of a pyramid can be an awkward procedure.

This shaft, most of which is hewn through the solid bedrock, is but ⅟₅₀ of an inch off square along the course of its entire length. Using little more than copper and stone cutting tools, the ancient builders could be said to have thus achieved the extraordinary. Yet the floor of the passageway, though once as smooth as its walls and ceiling, has been very much broken up by ambitious explorers, and is quite uneven as a result. This presents an inconvenience to the visitor, but has been somewhat compensated for in modern times by the placing of wooden ramps with footholds by the Egyptian government.

The hundreds of wall joints located in this corridor are perfectly aligned to the passage itself. This is to say, that the passage slopes downward, and the wall joints are perpendicular to its floor line. Yet, curiously, at a point 35′ from the original entrance there are, on either wall side, two joints which rise vertically — the only such ones in the entire passage. Also, close to these two joints, on both walls, is a single chiseled line running, like the majority of joints, perpendicular to the passageway. Yet these are not joints proper, comprising a "seam" between two wall stones, but lines that are actually inscribed into the stones at these points.

The late professor P. Smyth, who spent three months investigating this pyramid in 1865, stated that these lines were "drawn by a powerful hand, and with a hard tool." Their exact

Pyramid Khufu: Descending Passageway. (J.P. Lepre)

purpose is a matter of speculation, but they could be a sign for the existence of a secret chamber, as a similar incongruent line further down the corridor and located in the floor, did in fact point to the chambers and passages in the superstructure of the monument. This particular line — a joint set opposite to the other floor joints — was discovered by Smyth in his inspection of the descending corridor. He correctly referred to it as "a sign in the floor for the wise." For here, at that point immediately above the unorthodox joint, lay the lower end of the pyramid's ascending passage which gave access to the upper reaches of the monument.

This lower end of the passage was originally sealed or camouflaged by a removable ceiling stone which was indistinguishable from the other stones comprising the lengthy descending passageway. This specially cut stone is referred to as the "prism stone," as it is thus shaped. It was held into place by small protrusions at its sides which were received by hollows cut into the ceiling at the point where it meets with the upper-

most corners of the east and west wall sections of the corridor. The prism stone has since disappeared, but the shallow hollows can still be seen to this day. With the prism stone thus removed, the lower end of a five-ton plug stone is now clearly visible, still there after having been set into place nearly 4,500 years ago.

The removal of this prism stone occurred quite by accident when Al Mamoun's passage was being tunneled in this direction. Before this time, however, it served its purpose of concealing the ascending passage system and in keeping secret the upper portions of the pyramid from curious explorers. As a result, Greek and Roman tourists frequently visited the subterranean chamber via the descending passage without being aware of the ascending passageway and the burial chamber itself.

If these visitors to the pyramid had been somewhat more inquisitive, perhaps they might have discovered the curious floor jointing that was spoken of by Professor Smyth, and the King's Chamber could well have been discovered 1,000 years or more before the penetration of the ninth century A.D. Smyth is to be commended for this observation, for his discovery could not have been an easy one; not only are the floor joints of this corridor extremely fine, but at the time of his investigation this floor, for its entire length, was so full of debris and rubble that it had become increasingly difficult to move from one end of it to the other. It was only after much painstaking excavation that Smyth was able to clear out the greater portion of the debris and thereby make his observations. Furthermore, he had to manage all of this by primitive lamplight.

Located at various points in the descending passageway are sections of three large fissures, evidently the results of earthquake activity. The middle of these fissures is so wide as to admit the body of a grown man, and must have been filled in at one time by the original builders. If this were ever the case, though, the blocks have now been removed. The speculation that they were once shored up is based on the fact that they present visual eyesores along a stretch of wall that has otherwise been finely cut and smoothed. Perhaps subsequent earthquakes widened the ancient crevices and dislodged some of the packing blocks, from which point on curious excavators extracted the blocks in search for hidden cross-passages. Where the fissures do occur, they encompass the entirety of walls, floor and ceiling.

The length of the descending corridor levels off at its bottommost section for approximately 18′, where it passes through a small recess or niche cut into the corridor's west wall. This niche was most likely planned to be an antechamber, wherein several portcullis blocking stones were to have been housed, thus preventing access into the large subterranean chamber which lay beyond. Such a system was common in both pyramid and mastaba-type tombs. Yet the builders ceased working on this niche when they abandoned the idea of using the subterranean chamber to contain the mummy of the pharaoh. Another burial chamber was begun in the superstructure of the monument, and this previously planned antechamber left unfinished. Said antechamber measures about 6′ long by 6′ wide by 4′ high.

FIRST ASCENDING PASSAGE. Retracing our footsteps back up the descending passageway almost to the position of the "scored lines," we arrive at the junction of this corridor and the first ascending passage. Here, as has been previously mentioned, can be seen the lower end of a granite plug stone which completely bars access to the ascending corridor. In order to enter that upper corridor one must pass through a short cavity in the west wall which leads to the terminus of Al Mamoun's Passage and thence to the lower end of said upper corridor.

The granite plug stone at the lower end is but one of three such stones, each 5′ long and weighing approximately seven tons. The lowermost and middle of the three are completely intact, but the southern end of the uppermost block is somewhat fractured, the result of Al Mamoun having broken into the ascending passage at that point. All three are butted one against the other and present a formidable obstacle for anyone who may have wanted to enter the upper reaches of the pyramid from the descending corridor.

These plug stones fit into the passageway so tightly that many authors have concluded they were built *in situ* at the time of the construction of the corridor. An enlightening observation, however,

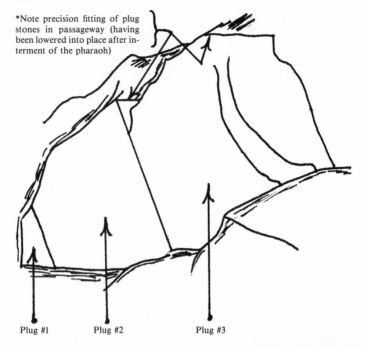

*Note precision fitting of plug stones in passageway (having been lowered into place after interment of the pharaoh)

Plug #1   Plug #2   Plug #3

Great Pyramid of Khufu, Giza: The three granite plug stones at lower end of first ascending passageway. Drawing at top shows precision fitting. (**Top:** J.P. LEPRE. **Bottom:** J. AND M. EDGAR)

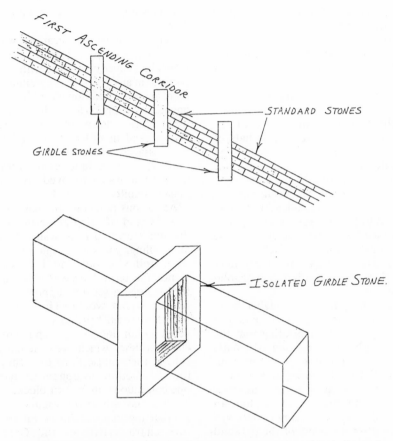

Great Pyramid of Khufu, Giza: Unique girdle stones. (J.P. Lepre)

contradicts this line of reasoning and suggests that the plug blocks were in fact lowered into place from the upper reaches of the pyramid. For with all of the other corridors within this monument the height and width, once set at one end, are carried entirely through the corridor to its furthermost end with a striking degree of accuracy. Yet with this passage, the height and width at its uppermost end are 53″ and 42″ respectively; at its midway section 48″ and 41½″; and at its termination point 47¼″ and 38½″. Thus the height and width of the corridor, over its total distance of 129′, gradually narrow by 5¾″ and 3½″. This funnel shape is good evidence that the corridor was tapered to better receive the plug stones, which were not built *in situ,* but were slid down the passageway from above.

When one considers the tremendous size and weight of these blocks, the distance that they had to travel in their descent, and the precision with which they would have had to have been slid into place—allowing for near-zero tolerance at their final place of rest, without their having been jammed—it is truly staggering to comprehend.

A further observation which

supports the theory that the plug stones were slid into place afterwards is Petrie's account of how the wall stones of the first ascending corridor were laid. He indicates that these layers of wall blocks were set horizontally for the first half of the length of the passageway, but were inclined to the rising angle of the passageway for the second half of its length. This phenomenon indicates that, for the lower end of the passage — where the plug stones were set — the passage was being built up as if there were no indication that an ascending passage system was planned for the pyramid at this phase of construction. The fact that the wall stones were laid level here displays a mere continuation of solid masonry.

But then, at a much higher level, the wall stones begin to be laid at a 26-degree angle, indicating that the builders had now initiated a dramatic change of direction; they here conceived of incorporating an ascending passage system into their ultimate plan. The suggestion is that an ascending system was not conceived until after the plane of the pyramid had reached a point of construction well above the level where the plug stones were ultimately set. If that ascending system — and the plug stones therein — was an afterthought, that fact should eliminate any notion that those blocking stones may have been built in situ.

Another characteristic of this limestone corridor is the presence of its so-called "girdle stones." The customary manner in which the ancient Egyptians constructed narrow, low-lying passages was to simply place stone upon stone in each of the wall sections, and to stagger them as much as possible. The ceiling stones would merely be set across these wall sections, in much the same way that a lintel would be placed over a doorway.

Yet in this corridor, because it was situated high in the superstructure — which had never been done with any corridor in any other large pyramid — there arose the additional problem of having to support a much greater weight thrust down from the levels above. And in order to strengthen the passageway against this excess burden, a very unique architectural innovation was employed by the master architect.

At various points in this passageway, instead of using numerous individual stones to form walls, floor and ceiling, massive, single stones were hollowed out and inserted. Hence the term "girdle stones," as they insured a greater support than regular stones would. There were four of these full "girdle stones" staggered within this passage, and three "half-girdles," which were actually split at their midsections to form a top and a bottom portion rather than one continuous, unbroken block.

This assembly represents yet another ingenious architectural feature characteristic of the Great Pyramid alone, and which serves as additional proof of this pyramid's individuality and superiority to all others.

Also located in this passage are several small inset stones situated in the east and west wall sections. Their presence is somewhat puzzling, but one is tempted to conclude that they somehow must have been used in conjunction with the lowering of the granite plug stones. Perhaps they were in some way employed to facilitate the manipulation of these blocks, acting as chocks to control the sliding process. All of this is pure speculation, though, and their specific purpose still remains a mystery.

The first ascending passage—most especially the ceiling—is very much exfoliated from the passage of time. But even in its fractured, soot-covered state, and under extremely poor lighting conditions, one can readily discern the smoothness and straightness of its few intact wall sections. With the aid of a modern, wooden ramp equipped with hand rails polished smooth by the use of hundreds of tourists who visit this pyramid daily, one ascends this narrow corridor to its terminus, where it opens into the stately Grand Gallery.

GRAND GALLERY. Majestic, exalted and noble are a few of the words which spring to the mind of men and women who view the Grand Gallery. "The glory of the workmen who built the Great Pyramid". . . say Perrot and Chipiez, in their *Ancient Egyptian Art,* "is the masonry of the Grand Gallery. . . . The faces of the blocks of limestone of which the walls are composed have been dressed with such care that it is not surpassed even by the most perfect example of Hellenic architecture on the Acropolis at Athens."

This magnificent gallery stretches upward for 153' at an impressive 26-degree angle and presents an eerie, looming effect, due to the gradual cutting in of its seven-layered corbel walls. Each layer overlaps the one beneath it by 3", resulting in the gallery's 7' floor width being gradually reduced to 3½' at its 28'-high ceiling which is composed of 40 stones (not 36, as is reported by many authors). Resultingly, the walls are not perpendicular, as most walls are, but close in on themselves in dramatic fashion. The overall appearance is that of a long, exalted tunnel of a sort.

Although the gallery is very much blanketed by soot deposits from torches having been passed through here for over 1,000 years, and is further darkened by lack of adequate lighting, in its original, pristine state it was quite white, having been constructed of unblemished limestone blocks from the Tura and Masara quarries. The contrast between the original (the smooth, polished white stones) and the altered (the fractured, darkened stones) is extraordinary. Nevertheless, this passage continues to instill in the visitor a strong sense of the majesty of the ancient pyramid age.

The position of this gallery is such that it connects, at its lower extremity, with the upper (southern) end of the first ascending passageway; the north end of the queen's chamber horizontal passageway; and the upper entrance of the well shaft. At its upper extremity, it connects with the horizontal passage which leads to the antechamber.

There is nothing quite like this gallery in any of the other pyramids in Egypt. Its predecessor is the upward sloping corridor of the subsidiary pyramid of Sneferu's Bent Pyramid at Dahshur, but that corridor is built on a much smaller scale and does not employ corbel architecture.

Technically speaking, the Grand Gallery should not be in the Great Pyramid. Most of the passageways in both this pyramid and others conformed to an orthodox and predetermined height and width ratio, approximately 4' high by 4' wide. In a few pyramids these dimensions were sometimes increased by anywhere from one to two feet, as was the case with the horizontal passage leading to the burial chamber in the Pyramid of King Khafra, also located at Giza.

In all other pyramids the corridor systems merely represented an avenue through which to transport the mummy and coffin of the king, along

Great Pyramid of Khufu, Giza: Grand Gallery. (J. AND M. EDGAR)

with other miscellaneous funerary equipment, from the outside of the monument to the burial chamber; they were simply access routes. To have constructed them at a much greater height and width than was necessary for the transport of said funerary equipment would have created a more difficult task for the workers whose job it was afterwards to seal off these corridors with plug stones or portcullis slabs of limestone, granite, quartzite or basalt. The amount of labor involved would be dramatically reduced by cutting out or building up a small rather than a large channel or corridor.

Photograph of Grand Gallery. (J.P. Lepre)

The Grand Gallery, on the other hand, was so high, and so elaborately contrived, that one wonders whether it served a dual purpose. The first, expected purpose would be to allow the transport of the deceased pharaoh and his funerary equipment from the lower to the upper reaches of the pyramid; any other reason, however, is speculative.

I am of the opinion that the architect, realizing he was about to begin construction in a unique area—so very high in the superstructure of the pyramid—decided to seize upon the opportunity not only to allow passage of the deceased pharaoh from a lower point to a higher one, but to display his talents on a grandiose scale never before equaled. As the Great Pyramid represented the apogee of pyramid building and design, so the Grand

Gallery represented the apogee of architectural achievement within the pyramid itself.

In a somewhat different vein, several authors point to the possibility that the gallery possessed a high spiritual symbolism. Perhaps this theory is not far from the truth; it very well could have been symbolic of all that the ancient builders had been trying to achieve up to that period of the Old Kingdom. The two theories may of course be related.

J. Seiss, author of *The Great Pyramid, a Miracle in Stone,* wrote of this passageway: "The Grand Gallery in this edifice, so sublime in height, so abrupt in beginning and termination, so different from all the other passages before or beyond it, so elaborately and peculiarly contrived and finished in every part, is absolutely incomprehensible on the tomb theory or on any other, save that of a high astronomical, historical, and spiritual symbolism, having nothing whatever to do with the entombment of an Egyptian despot."

While I disagree with the astronomical and historical connotations of Seiss' statement, and about his dissociation of the tomb theory with this gallery, I do feel that a high symbolism was intended by the architect when he so perfectly fashioned this extraordinary corridor in the very center of the pyramid's massive superstructure.

There are unique features within this gallery that deserve comment, features which for centuries have perplexed researchers, several of whom have formulated theories to explain these individual puzzles, but whose theories upon close scrutiny warrant serious criticism. One of the main problems is that theories have been formulated without a clear understanding of all of the pieces of the puzzles.

For instance, L. Borchardt gives his version of how a sort of wooden scaffolding might have been erected by the builders within the gallery to facilitate the lowering of the granite plug stones from the gallery into the first ascending passage. But he fails to adequately describe the unique architectural features within the gallery upon which the scaffolding would actually have been built, or how they would have lowered the stones. As a result, the theory is neither practical nor workable, and the system proposed by him cannot be executed with any degree of accuracy or success. Remarking on Borchardt's theory, I.E.S. Edwards states that it is "open to some clear objections" and is "not convincing."

This is not to say that Borchardt is being singled out for undue criticism. It is evident from his well-executed diagrams and other noteworthy achievements that he is a first-rate scholar of the Egyptian pyramids. This is only an indication that no author on the pyramids — Borchardt and myself included — has yet given an adequate rendition of the way in which all of the peculiarities of the Grand Gallery come together in a working order to explain the purpose of the gallery in its relationship to the pyramid as a whole.

In light of this apparent void in understanding the gallery, I feel that an in-depth description of some of its curious architectural features should first be undertaken before any theories attempting to explain their use can be formed.

Among the interesting architectural features of the Grand Gallery are two grooves cut into the east and west walls. These grooves are 7″ high, 1″ deep, and run the entire length of the Gallery, precisely 5″ up from the third overlapping corbel sections of the walls. Hundreds of rough chisel marks are staggered along the top edges of these grooves.

Egyptologists have long stated that a wooden platform was once set into the grooves, traversing the span of the Gallery. They say that this platform was used to keep the three granite plug stones, now lodged at the bottom of the first ascending passageway, in a position above the funeral cortege, as this cortege would have had to pass through the Gallery unhindered in order to gain access to the burial chamber. Yet this theory is untenable because the three plug stones were no more than a total of 15′ in length, whereas the gallery is 150′ long. Surely, a 150′ platform was not necessary to hold 15′ of stone.

It is still certain, however, that something did traverse the Gallery;

and it is interesting to note that it did so throughout its entire length, except for the area immediately above the Great Step. At this point there are no chisel marks. Everywhere that these marks are present, they are located above the grooves. It seems then, that access to the area above the platform was just above the Great Step, and that intruders climbed through this opening to the top of the platform. From this location they chiseled downwards, in order to break into the grooves and thus remove whatever was lodged within. This was definitely a more convenient and workable position than an approach from below.

But from this description, the question naturally arises: What exactly was it that would have traversed the Gallery throughout its entire length, except for the area immediately above the Great Step? And another question also presents itself: If the material traversing the Gallery were wood or stone, why would late intruders (intruders I say, for the chisel marks are extremely rough and the resulting breakage uneven) have taken the pains to extract this material throughout the full length of the Gallery? The material must have been of some value (more than plain wood or stone) for intruders to have wanted to extract it. Could it have been cedar panels inlaid with gold? It is a well-known fact that King Sneferu, the father of Khufu, used cedar from Lebanon in various building projects, notably in the main chamber of his Bent Pyramid at Dahshur; and Sneferu's father (Khufu's grandfather), Huni, also employed cedar beams inside his corbel burial chamber in the Pyramid of Maidum.

Another of the Gallery's architectural oddities is the series of 50 cavities filled with inset stones along

its lower wall sections. It has been surmised that these, in conjunction with the 7″ grooves in the mid-wall sections and the 54 holes cut into the east and west ramps, acting with a beam and rope system, to aid the builders in lowering the 3 seven-ton blocking stones into the first ascending passageway.

In regard to the series of inset stones located along the Gallery's east and west lower-wall sections, the author noticed that all the inset stones on the east wall, except for one (vertical) set, were in a slightly slanted position from true vertical; and that all of the others on the west wall, except for one (slanted) set, were in a true vertical position. The twenty-sixth set on the east wall is on the vertical, and the thirteenth set on the west wall is slanted.

This discrepancy between the east and west wall sections is slight; however, it is readily noticeable upon close scrutiny and measurement. If a rope and beam system did once traverse the Gallery, the east and west wall sections may have been set up in this manner in order to insure the proper torque or adjustment for control of the manipulation of the heavy plug stones. The exact method employed, still remains a mystery.

As to the so-called Flag Stones which comprise inverted L-shapes, they are, in reality, inverted L-shaped cavities filled in with mortar. Yet this is not mortar in the typical sense of the word, but an incredibly solid and durable type which is certainly as strong as the surrounding limestone. It is indeed the very same cement which was used extensively by the original builders throughout the external portions of the monument to obtain a more solidified bond between the huge blocks of coarse, nummulitic limestone.

It appears as if the smaller cavities within which the cement was placed may originally have been cut at their 45-degree angles to allow ropes to pass behind the beams without interference. This theory is, of course, highly speculative, but it does seem to fit in with the general scheme of things and cannot be disregarded.

After the pharaoh's mummy, wooden coffin, and heavy funerary furniture were hauled up the Gallery, the ropes were pulled out and the beams were dismantled, the large wall cavities filled in with the inset stones, and the smaller, angled cavities filled in with cement. At this point, probably, the diagonal grooves were cut into the surface of the inset stones and the adjacent wall sections. These grooves were nearly two inches deep. Sections of the beamwork may then have been put back into place and, again working with the ropes, now used to lower the granite plug stones down the corridor to their final resting place at the lower end of the first ascending passageway. This time, however, the ropes passed through the 2″-deep diagonal grooves located behind the beams, as the much smaller, 45-degree wall cavities had now been filled in. Beyond this, with the first ascending passage now sealed off, the workers exited via the vertical well shaft.

Diagrams of these architectural features are at right.

There are 40 ceiling stones in the Grand Gallery. They measure approximately as follows in length (measurements in inches — from north to south):

1. 42; 2. 50; 3. 37; 4. 52; 5. 39; 6. 48; 7. 50; 8. 50; 9. 40; 10. 50; 11. 50; 12. 50; 13. 37; 14. 48; 15. 50; 16. 50; 17. 50; 18. 42; 19. 28; 20. 38; 21. 50; 22. 36; 23. 50; 24. 30; 25. 45; 26. 50; 27. 50; 28. 40; 29. 50; 30. 50; 31. 50; 32.

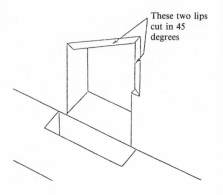

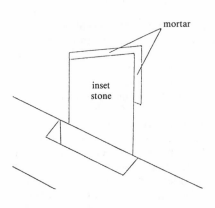

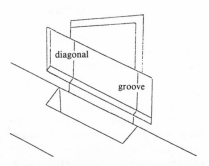

Great Pyramid of Khufu, Giza: Grand Gallery. **Top:** *Example of cavity, west wall.* **Center:** *Inset stone and mortar fill-in.* **Bottom:** *Diagonal groove cut into inset stone and extending into wall.* (J.P. LEPRE)

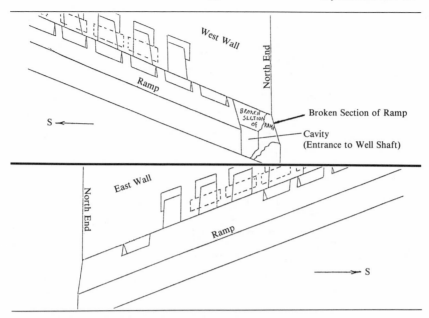

Great Pyramid of Khufu, Giza: Missing wall insets, diagonals and holes in ramps. (J.P. LEPRE)

50; 33. 50; 34. 48; 35. 45; 36. 50; 37. 50; 38. 35; 39. 40; 40. 12. All stones are 42″ wide.

All told, then, we have 1 stone that measures 12″ long; 1, 28″; 1, 30″; 1, 35″; 1, 36″; 2, 37″; 1, 38″; 1, 39″; 3, 40″; 2, 42″; 2, 45″; 3, 48″; 20, 50″; and 1, 52″. The total length of the Gallery at the ceiling is 1,782″, or 148½′; at the floorline, 1,182″, or 157′.

At the top of the Grand Gallery, at its southernmost end, rises the Great Step. This "step" is actually a high platform, for it does not rise a mere 8-10″ — as the average step would — but is, rather, a 3′-high, 7′-wide, 5′-deep block of squared limestone. Once the step or platform is surmounted, the viewer can then stand and turn to look down the long gallery — a position so advantageous that this abrupt rise almost appears to have been built for just that purpose. From this locale, one can take the time to truly appreciate the awe

that the architect was doubtless seeking to inspire in the curious observer. Here, as in no other place in the pyramid, one is cast in a position to concentrate on the most glorious achievement of the ancient builders. From this unique vantage point the streamlined architectural perfection of design can be fully comprehended.

In Dynasties I and II the Egyptian engineer was experimenting and familiarizing himself with the basic techniques for building in stone. In Dynasty III he was beginning to perfect these techniques on a much larger scale, but he was still groping. In Dynasty IV he truly grasped the secrets of configuration and design, and marshalled all of the resources available to him to forever make his mark in stone. Not before or since has such a hall been so simply yet exquisitely designed and executed. The degree of excellence which has long been associated with ancient Egyptian

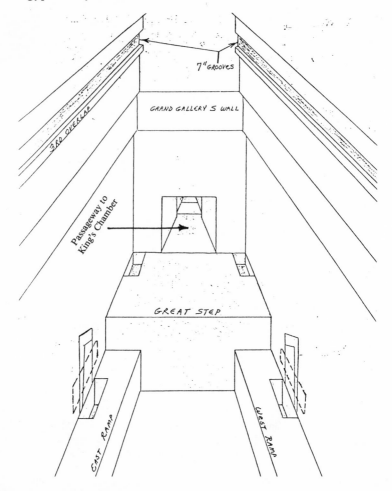

*Great Pyramid of Khufu, Giza; Grand Gallery, showing Great Step and 7"
grooves in east and west walls.* (J.P. LEPRE)

civilization has been forever locked
in the measurements and jointing of
this superb gallery, and it can best be
appreciated from the top of the
Great Step, so ingeniously situated
by the master architect.

ANTECHAMBER. At the top of
the Grand Gallery, situated immediately behind the Great Step
in the lowermost section of the
gallery's south wall, is a 44"-high by
42"-wide aperture which gives rise
to a short underpass leading to a
petite apartment known as the antechamber.

This chamber, which once housed
3 two-ton granite portcullis slabs
used to block entrance to the burial
chamber that lies just beyond, measures 10' long by 4' wide by 12½'
high. The three blocking slabs have
long since disappeared, probably
broken asunder by the first defilers of
the pyramid to reach this upper
level, and then by subsequent vandals and souvenir seekers.

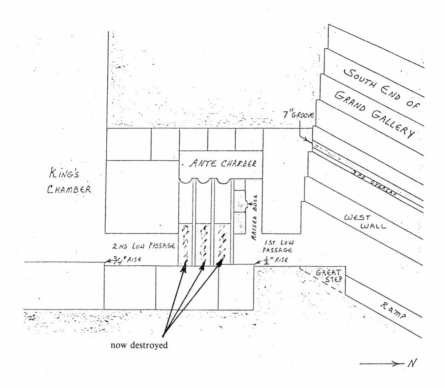

Great Pyramid of Khufu, Giza: Antechamber. (J.P. Lepre)

We can presume that these blocks once existed, though, from the presence of large grooves cut into the east and west walls of the chamber, grooves into which these slabs were most likely set so that they could be lowered at will after the pharaoh's mummy was deposited within the burial chamber.

To support this assumption, there are also much smaller grooves (3½" wide) cut into the chamber's south wall, evidently to allow the four ropes that were used to lower the portcullises into place to slide downwards without jamming between the southernmost of these slabs and the south wall of the chamber.

The three missing slabs were to have acted in conjunction with two half-ton granite counterweights which are still housed in their original positions, set into ledges in the east and west walls.

Each of the large grooves in the east and west walls of the antechamber is over 3" deep and 21½" wide. They rise up 105" from the floor, at which height they form ledges or wainscots.

These grooves, along with those in the chamber's south wall, the three portcullis slabs, the counterweights and the system of ropes, were all supposed to have worked in conjunction with semi-hollows fashioned into the upper sections of the wainscots to allow for the lowering of the slabs. Rollers were thought to have traversed the chamber, having been set into the semi-hollows of the wainscots. This initiates the popular theory of a roller system for the manipulation of said slabs.

Yet although the several parts come together rather cohesively, there is a very serious flaw in this hypothesis—a missing piece of the puzzle—which contradicts the supposed validity of the theory. For while the semi-hollows supposed to have received the wooden rollers are indeed present at the top of west wainscot, they are missing on the east wainscot. The ledge of this east wainscot is entirely flat and therefore could not have received the edges of the rollers said to have spanned the width of the chamber. Not only this, but the west wainscot is nearly 9″ higher than the ledge of the east wainscot.

These facts seem to negate the only logical theory for the interaction of the various components of this strange little compartment. For how could rollers be used when one side of those rollers would have had no semi-hollows within which to be set, and they would furthermore be tilted to such a degree as to make the manipulation of the portcullis slabs a quite impossible task? Why the master architect designed the elements of this chamber in such a contradictory manner presents a unique and puzzling problem for all serious pyramid scholars.

This small apartment is also odd in that, whereas it is comprised primarily of slabs of rose granite, it is also interspersed with several blocks of limestone. This strange mixture is certainly atypical of ancient Egyptian masonry techniques, representing the only example of its kind that this author is aware of. In this pyramid alone, the descending passageway is entirely of limestone, as are the first ascending passage, the Queen's Chamber horizontal

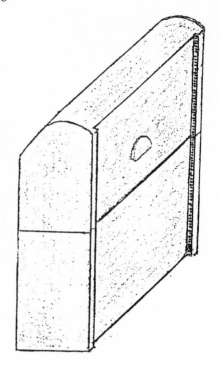

Great Pyramid of Khufu, Giza: Double counterweights of portcullis system in Antechamber, showing projecting boss. (J.P. LEPRE)

passage, the Queen's Chamber and the Subterranean chamber. Also, the King's Chamber is entirely of granite, and not a single block of limestone is to be found there.

The relieving chambers that lie immediately above the King's Chamber are likewise built of granite throughout, except that the peaked ceiling and the walls of the highest of these chambers are constructed of limestone. This exception, however, is an understandable and practical tactic used by the builders to allow the tremendous weight of the superstructure pressing down from above to be more evenly dispersed.

Yet in the antechamber there does

not appear to be any logical reason for the uneven distribution of the blocks of granite and limestone. The architect may very well have had a rational motive in this peculiar design, but it has yet to be explained by any modern investigator.

Yet another curiosity about the antechamber is that, at a point in its floorline just north of the counterweight blocks, its granite floor level rises ¼ inch until it reaches the entrance to the King's Chamber, where it then rises ¾ of an inch. These rises are not attributed to any roughness in the floor itself—for that floor is very finely leveled and smooth—but to a deliberate adjustment by the architect.

Aside from the several idiosyncrasies within the antechamber, certainly the strangest feature by far is a chiseled protrusion in the approximate center of the topmost of the granite counterweights. Shaped something like a protractor, it juts out from the face of the block by a full inch at its lowest, horizontal level, to zero degrees tolerance at its highest, arched level.

This three-dimensional symbol—or "raised boss," as it is called—at first glance may not appear that unusual. Yet when one considers its unique position within the chamber, it warrants a much closer inspection. The boss projects at eye level into a cramped space, only 18″ from front (where the boss is) to back. Standing quite confined in this space, the visitor contemplates the carving scant inches away from his or her face. Why should this 5″-wide by 4″-high object—so cunningly carved—be positioned in such a closed space in such a way?

Scholars have tried to dismiss this controversial symbol by simply passing it off as one of those rough construction bosses or protuberances which the ancient Egyptian builders did in fact employ on many of their construction stones. But this particular protrusion does not extend out far enough to be of service as a typical boss, and is not quite the same shape as the typical boss—although nearly so; for the typical boss, although also protractor-shaped, has a higher angle of curve. Additionally, the horizontal, bottom lip of the standard construction boss is flat, so as to more readily receive a bar or a rope and minimize slippage. Yet the bottom edge of this particular protrusion is slanted, and would simply not function in the manner that a rough boss would.

The granite leaf from which the boss is fashioned is also pecularly shaped. For it is not a simple rectangular shape, but has 1″ rebates at either end of its boss-side. These ridges or rebates running vertically along the opposite sides of this slab make it 16½″ wide at its outside edges, while its bulk remains at 15½″.

Another "mysterious" feature of the Great Pyramid mentioned by numerous authors is the presence of four granite fragments or blocks of stone, three of which are located inside the pyramid and one outside. The three on the inside are to be seen (a) at the very bottom of the descending passageway, within the small, adjacent niche; (b) on the ledge in the pit of the subterranean chamber; and (c) in the grotto. The block outside the pyramid is located just beyond the point of the original entrance, on the thirteenth course of masonry.

Scholars concerned with the archaeological or "tombic theory" of the monument refer to these four stones, but as yet have declined to speculate on their origin. These stones are not set into the masonry, but are loosely set on portions of limestone. Hence the so-called "mystery," as they are in areas where there is no other granite.

Proponents of the occult, on the other hand, make quite a stir about these four granite fragments and have conjured up fanciful theories as to their meaning. But while there are no doubt a number of unsolved mysteries with which the Great Pyramid can be credited, this is certainly not one of them. We may never be able to deduce how forty-ton stones were delicately maneuvered into their final resting places or the true purpose of the 7" grooves that run the length of the Grand Gallery walls, but the mystery of the four granite fragments appears to be easy enough to solve with a little application.

First, the fragments must be scrutinized and their specific measurements taken; then we must attempt to match these measurements with any granite stones which were once built into the pyramid, but have since been misplaced or broken loose. In obeying these simple rules the author has noted that although the Great Pyramid is, for the most part, of limestone throughout, there are in fact two chief areas within the monument which are constructed of granite: the antechamber and the King's Chamber.

Examining the former, it is obvious that — as has been mentioned earlier — the three granite portcullis slabs are now missing, presumably having been broken up by tomb robbers wishing to gain entrance into the burial chamber. Insofar as the King's (Burial) Chamber is concerned, the two-ton granite lid of the sarcophagus is missing, as well as two large floor stones. Actually, four large floor stones were once extracted from this chamber by plunderers who then burrowed under the pavement looking for Khufu's treasure,

but only two of these are now missing, with the other two now resting on the still-intact section of the floor.

Having measured the four mysterious granite fragments, and having matched them with the dimensions of the missing sarcophagus lid and floor stones, I have discerned that the lid is too narrow and the floor stones much too bulky to fit the measurements of the four fragments. The dimensions of the sarcophagus lid are calculated to have been 7' 5½" long by 3' 2½" wide by 10–12" thick; those of the floor stones were 58" long by 21" wide by 18" deep, and 33" long by 31" wide by 28" deep.

On examining the antechamber, however, it soon became evident that this room could very well have been the origin of the fragments. The measurements of the three missing portcullis slabs were each 48½" wide by 48½" high by 21" thick; this is specifically determined by the width of the chamber where the slabs were to have been set into place, the width of the grooves located in the side walls, and the height of the passage leading from the antechamber to the King's Chamber. It appears obvious that the fragments are well accounted for; for the sizes of those four mysterious fragments are: 38" long by 21" thick by 29" high; 18" long by 21" thick by 18" high; 30" long by 21" thick by 12" high; and 18" long by 21" thick by 17" high.

The important factor to note here is that the thickness of each of these stones is a consistent 21", the exact thickness of the portcullis slabs that would have fit into the 21½" wide grooves in the antechamber, allowing for ¼" tolerance to either side. The height and width of the several fragments are not critical, because there is a much greater allowance here. It is to be remembered that the four mysterious stones are fragments only. The width of each of these portcullis stones was originally 48½″; any of the listed widths of the granite fragments could easily fit into this range. The same is true of the heights.

The principal fact that supports all of the above information and measurements, though, is something of a different, yet directly related, nature: the fact that three of the four mysterious fragments have 3½″ holes bored into them. This is highly significant because the three missing portcullis slabs from the antechamber would also have been drilled in this manner. It was necessary for the tops of the portcullis slabs to contain drill holes in order to receive the ropes required for the lowering of the blocks after the interment of the pharaoh in the King's Chamber. Not only this, but the diameter of these holes is wonderfully dictated by the very channels in the south wall of the antechamber through which these ropes would also have to pass in order to facilitate the lowering of the block lying adjacent to that wall — in both cases the width being 3½″. If additional proof of the origin of the fragments is necessary, let it be noted that in the case of the granite fragment now located outside the monument, just outside the original entrance, there are three holes, and not one, drilled into the block, and they are exactly 6½″ apart — the precise distance between the vertical channels cut into the south wall of the antechamber. The block from the pit has two such holes.

Thus, the so-called "Mystery of the four Granite Blocks" is now irrefutably solved, and the fanciful speculation regarding their origin can finally be laid to rest.

It should be mentioned in passing that there are two additional sources of granite fragments at the Great

Pyramid: the pyramidion and the three plug stones at the lower end of the first ascending passage. Yet even if it had not been proven beyond any doubt that the four mysterious fragments had actually come from the remnants of the three portcullis slabs in the antechamber, these two other sources could not in any way be associated with the mysterious fragments. The pyramidion can be ruled out because of its unique triangular shape — which is not at all like the fragments in question — and the granite plug stones because the only missing section from them would not have three squared surfaces comprising a perfect 21″ cut, nor 3½″ bored holes.

Furthermore, the section that would have come from the upper granite plug stone — the only one of the three which is in any way fractured — would have represented a true fragmented piece. For even though the four mysterious stones are popularly called the granite "fragments," they are, in reality, *blocks* of fractured stone, or *squared* "fragments."

The reader is no doubt curious as to how these four granite stones ever managed to come to rest at such disparate locations both inside and outside of the pyramid. Although the monument is now under the strict supervision of government officials, with an iron gate and padlock regulating the flow of tourists into the building via Al Mamoun's Passage, that security has come about only recently — and Al Mamoun's Passage was forged in A.D. 820. Thus, for over a thousand years the interior of the edifice was considered fair game for treasure seekers, vandals, despoilers and the like. It is likely that at some time during this lengthy period, fragments of the portcullis blocks, which had first been broken up by Al

Mamoun's men, became the objects of revelry for groups of delinquents who needed to let out their frustrations at not having found anything of value in their search of the pyramid.

It is not very difficult to visualize how groups of such men could have rolled the two granite fragments now found in the pit of the subterranean chamber and the niche preceding it from the antechamber, down the Grand Gallery, first ascending corridor and descending passage to the above-mentioned locations. Admittedly, the locations of the third and fourth granite fragments do present something more of a problem. For the block located just outside of the original entrance of the pyramid, after having been playfully rolled down the Grand Gallery and first ascending passage, would then have to be pushed up—and with great labor I might add—that 50'-section of the descending passage which runs from the terminus of Al Mamoun's Passage where it breaks into the west wall of that descending passage, to the aperture of the original entrance. Why vandals would have devoted so much effort to positioning this granite block at that point may at first seem puzzling. Yet if one considers the pitch and fervor of the moment, and the great enthusiasm which usually accompanies such acts of frenzy and impetuousness, the resulting behavior is quite comprehensible.

With the repositioning of the fourth and final stone the reasoning of such actions can likewise be understood. But here, the method employed is even more unusual. This fragment was first rolled down the Grand Gallery, as were the other granite fragments. From here it was lowered down the well shaft and placed inside the grotto. But it could not have been rolled down the well

shaft, which is vertical at its upper end; rather it had to be lowered, having been first fastened with a rope—an activity which must have presented no small difficulty.

KING'S CHAMBER. Continuing on beyond the antechamber, one must pass through another squat granite passage—this time 8' long—before reaching the celebrated King's Chamber. This is indeed a chamber fit for a king, being a spacious 19'1" high by 34'4" long by 17'2" wide, and built of durable rose granite throughout, finely cut and polished. It is comprised of nine monolithic beams spanning its ceiling, the largest stones in the Great Pyramid, each weighing an average of 50 tons; 101 wall stones; and 21 floorstones. The overhead beams, which traverse the chamber from north to south, actually extend beyond the walls upon which they are set by 5' on either side, so that each is 27' long.

The chamber, situated on the fiftieth course of masonry, is entirely empty but for a lidless sarcophagus of rose granite situated at its far west end, instilling in the viewer a detached and somber feeling. This stone chest, which may once have housed the mummy of the great Pharaoh Khufu, bears the scars and chippings of hordes of visitors and souvenir-seekers; its once-straight edges are rounded down, and its southeast corner is very much fractured.

Sir William Flinders Petrie was the first to notice traces of saw marks running along its sides and the telltale signs of a powerful drill having been bored into the base of its hollow interior. It was hewn from a single block of granite and weighs approximately 3¾ tons. The lid, which is now missing, is calculated to have weighed over two tons. Traces of angled grooves and three pinion

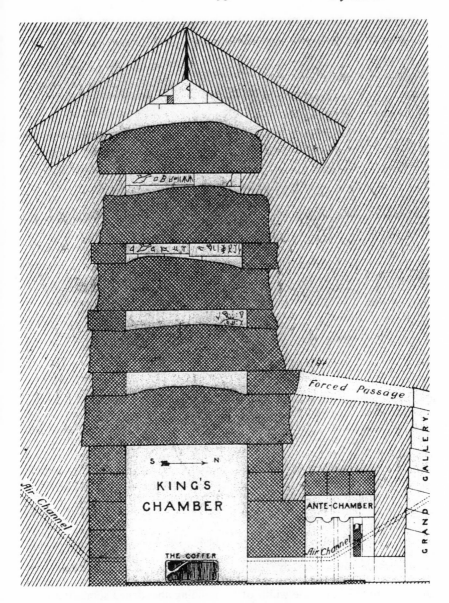

Great Pyramid of Khufu, Giza: Burial (King's) Chamber. (J. AND M. EDGAR)

holes used, along with a resinous glue, for the fastening of the lid are still barely discernible at the top edges of the sarcophagus.

There is some speculation as to whether this sarcophagus was set into the King's Chamber as the chamber was being built up, with the walls and roof of the chamber being set into place afterwards, or hauled through the original entrance and then up the various corridors to this

Great Pyramid of Khufu, Giza: Sarcophagus Chamber. (J. CAPART)

location sometime after the chamber had been completed and prior to the burial of the pharaoh.

This uncertainty is easily resolved. The height and width of the sarcophagus are, respectively, 42″ by 39″, whereas the height and width of the first ascending passage at its lower end — where lay the granite plug blocks, and through which the sarcophagus would necessarily have to pass were it brought in afterwards — are 47¼″ by 38½″ respectively. Since the width of the chest is a full ½″ over the width of the lowermost section of the first ascending passageway, the sarcophagus must have been set into its final position as the burial chamber was being built up.

Further evidence to support this arrangement is the discovery of a finished alabaster sarcophagus inside the Unfinished Pyramid of Sekhem-Khet (Djoser-Tati) at Sakkara. This chest was obviously in place before the pyramid was completed.

That this was the procedure commonly used by the pyramid builders for the positioning of sarcophagi is once more indicated by the example of the Pyramid of Eke (Nebka) at Zawaiyet el-Aryan, just south of Giza. The oval granite sarcophagus discovered there, which was built into the floor, was set into place very early in the construction, and the building abandoned soon after.

Both the north and south walls of the King's Chamber contain air vents — a phenomenon not to be found in any other pyramid. They are channeled horizontally through the granite wall blocks, and then, after a distance of approximately 6′, turn upwards to pass through the mass of the pyramid's masonry, debouching at the 101st course of the monument's outside faces.

The north channel is rectangular in form, being 5″ high by 7″ wide, while the south air channel has a stranger configuration. Within the chamber itself it is dome-shaped, representing a quite wide 18″ by 24″ opening. After a few feet it maintains this basic dome-shape, but is now reduced to a 12″ by 18″ aperture which, after a few feet more, narrows to approximately 8″ by 12″. It maintains these dimensions as it passes through the pyramid's masonry to the 101st outside course, but takes two sharp bends in the process. In the first of these turns it changes its shape from dome to oval, and in the second turn (or its third line of travel), from oval to rectangular or oblong. This is a very strange design, to say the least, one which is classically demonstrative of the architect's propensity to dramatically shift design when it is least expected.

To add to this idiosyncrasy is the fact that, at the first turn or bend, this air channel changes its direction, inclining to the south-southwest from true south; it then alters its direction once more, further southsouthwest, at its second turn. The entire direction and configuration is so bizarre that it has thus far defied any logical explanation.

In contrast, the north air channel of the King's Chamber maintains its basic rectangular shape throughout its long journey to the exterior of the edifice. Yet it, too, changes its direction during the course of its travel, and takes, not two, but four distinct bends or turns. For although its basic upward angle is not altered, it deviates, first to the north-northwest, then back to north, then to the northnortheast, finally returning to true north. Thus it curves in a semi-circu-

lar pattern, and then returns to its original direction.

The reader may wonder how so many turns in such small channels could possibly be sighted by the author or any other viewer; certainly the apertures spoken of are much too tiny to admit a man — or even a very small child, for that matter. But recall that the beginning 6′ section of the southern air channel measures 18″ by 24″ at its commencement inside the burial chamber and 12″ by 18″ where it reaches its first bend. In the confines of this space it is possible for a small to medium-size person to crawl forth, and by stretching, to view the two sharp bends which the channel then takes.

In respect to the northern air duct, it is of course not possible to be afforded such a view from the interior of the burial chamber, as the 5″ by 7″ duct cannot admit the body of a viewer, and even if it could, no one would sight four turns of the duct from a single vantage point.

Fortunately for the interested observer — though sadly for the pyramid — although the first 8′ of this channel has remained perfectly intact, the distance of the next 30′ or so has been excavated by inquisitive explorers who broke through to this section and tunneled northward, following the direction of the channel. They did not begin their excavation where the air channel commences, in the King's Chamber, but broke into the west wall of the short passage leading to that chamber, where an iron grating has now been placed by the Egyptian government to ward off further observation. Within this cavernous tunnel, one can immediately see the first, second and third bends which the air duct takes in this confined area. By stretching one's self at the northern, more narrow end of this tunnel, the fourth

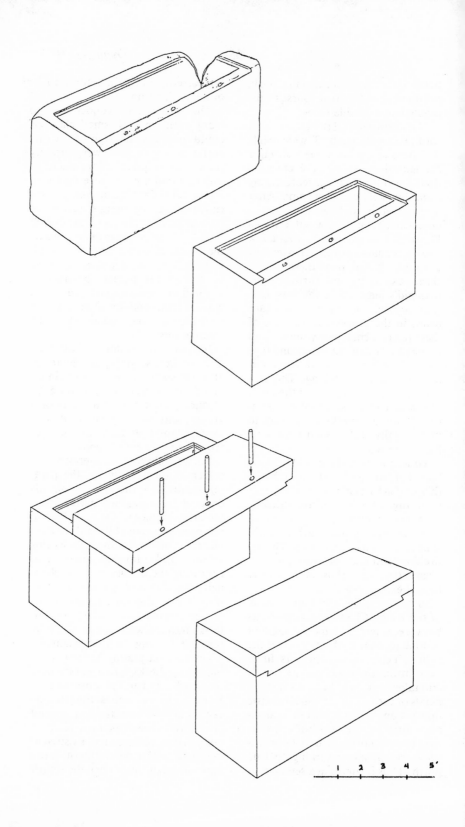

bend in the channel can also be seen. Were it not for this fortuitous but barbarous quarrying we would never have been made aware of the interesting features of this northern air vent.

While the unorthodox curve in the southern air vent is puzzling, in the northern air channel the direction is even more eccentric, with that channel turning once again to its original direction. One's initial reaction to this deviation is that this duct was shifted and then brought back shortly thereafter in order to avoid something in that area of the King's Chamber north wall. Could we then deduce that there may be a cavity or a passage of a sort in that location that the architect wished to keep secret? This is, of course, pure speculation. Only one thing is certain: that the architect had a purpose in diverting and then redirecting this channel.

The southern air shaft, being 175' long, rises at a 45-degree angle; while the northern shaft, being 235' in length, ascends at an angle of 31 degrees.

Both succeed in admitting a flow of fresh air into the chamber, a much-needed respite from the otherwise stagnant supply, although the north vent does not execute its task as well, being severed for a short distance within the excavated section just spoken of. The popular story exists that the presence of these two ventilation shafts keeps the King's Chamber at a constant temperature— day and night, winter and summer— of 68 degrees Fahrenheit, which is considered to be ideal for human habitation. Yet upon using a Fahrenheit thermometer in both the

daytime and the nighttime sessions which I spent in this chamber during the autumn, winter and spring seasons, I found that temperatures often fluctuated within the range of 70 to 80 degrees. Perhaps if the northern air channel were not fractured (as it has been from postpharaonic days) the chamber might well retain the ideal temperature. It would be interesting to record the results if the channel were someday to be repaired.

Many writers have referred to the air channels as mysterious phenomena, pointing out that the Pharaoh Khufu would have no need for air once he was dead. This being stated, few other explanations are ever given, for such is the "mysterious" nature of these channels.

However, it should be further considered that, although the deceased Pharaoh Khufu certainly did not require air for breathing, the members of his funeral cortege did—family, close friends and associates, aristocrats, high priests, etc. Many people had to pass through this very confined area.

Therefore, it is not unreasonable to deduce that the two air shafts in the burial chamber were fashioned for just this purpose. Understandably, the number of people attending and enacting ceremonies on so pompous and significant an occasion would not be small, and a chamber containing little air—and stagnant at that—would not be at all favorable to these dignitaries, chiefmost of whom would have been the heir to the throne, the now-reigning Pharaoh Rededef (Djedefre).

During the age of the pharaohs the burial party would have had to

Opposite: *Sarcophagus, Great Pyramid of Khufu, Giza.* Top left: *Present condition.* Top right: *Lidless.* Bottom left: *Open position.* Bottom right: *Sealed position.* (J.P. LEPRE)

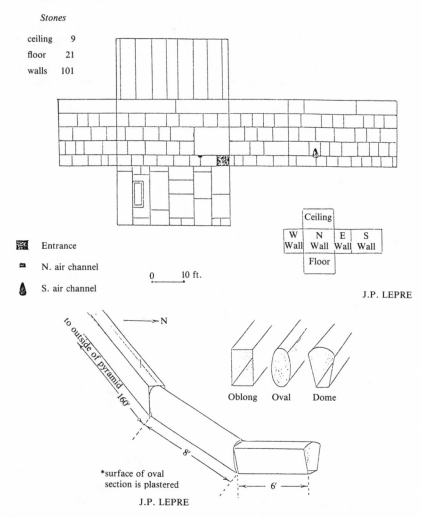

Stones

ceiling	9
floor	21
walls	101

▓ Entrance

⌑ N. air channel

◊ S. air channel

0   10 ft.

J.P. LEPRE

Oblong   Oval   Dome

*surface of oval
section is plastered

J.P. LEPRE

Great Pyramid of Khufu, Giza: King's Chamber. **Top:** *Drawing shows walls, floor and ceiling of chamber opened out on plane of north wall. Could the four small stones laid in two pairs along the south wall be cover stones for the four canopic chests of King Khufu? Such is the position assumed for many such chests—against the chamber's south wall.* **Bottom:** *South air channel of chamber. Drawing shows how it is comprised of three different shapes.* (J.P. Lepre)

illuminate the dark burial chamber with air-consuming torchlight. This factor, acting in conjunction with the number of people involved and the length of the ceremonies, would further tax the already scant air supply to the point where dramatic innovations were required.

That the burial chamber, without these channels, would not have provided sufficient enough air to allow the members of the funerary party to

Wall joint

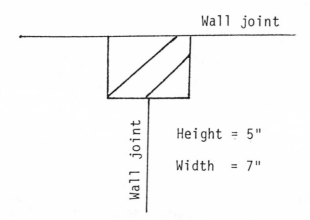

Height = 5"

Width = 7"

Wall joint

Great Pyramid of Khufu, Giza: **Top:** *Drawing showing wall joint.* **Bottom:** *King's Chamber, north air channel. Note superior jointing.* (J.P. LEPRE)

comfortably enact their ceremonies, is proven by the following facts:

1) That the burial chamber is 350′ distant from the pyramid's only fresh air supply at its entrance—which is twice or thrice the distance from burial chamber to entrance found in all other pyramids.

2) That the burial chamber is located upward, in the superstructure of the monument, whereas nearly all pyramids have their burial chambers downward, in the sub-

structure, or in a few rare cases, at ground level (entered from the substructure). Because hot air rises, the burial chamber in the Pyramid of Khufu receives warmer air, whereas the subterranean burial chambers of other pyramids receive cooler air. The subterranean chambers of all pyramids, being hewn from the rock substrata, can be likened to wine cellars. Within the Great Pyramid itself, although the final resting place of Khufu appears to have been the

King's Chamber, the subterranean chamber is always 10 to 20 degrees cooler than the chambers situated in the superstructure.

I have noticed that on many occasions inside the King's Chamber, when a good number of people were present, there were several complaints about the stagnant air — and this with one air duct functioning and the other partially so. Without these shafts it is certain that breathing in that chamber would be quite difficult. (On the other hand, many visitors first entering the subterranean chamber remark on the pleasantness of the air.)

A number of Egyptologists refer to the north air channel in the Great Pyramid as the representation of the pharaoh's association with Alpha Draconis, which was the pole star during the reign of King Khufu. They note, as further evidence of the connection between stars and pharaoh, that the constellations of Orion and Sirius would pass over the air channel at fixed intervals. Yet it would appear that there is a much stronger affiliation with astrology here than with science.

First, the assumption put forth by this school is that the north air shaft is directed in a straight line toward the pole star of 4,500 years ago, Alpha Draconis. Yet it has already been illustrated that the north air channel of the Great Pyramid does not ascend in a straight-forward manner, but rises in a series of twists and turns. A deduction that that channel would have pointed to the pole star of that era at its final passage through the monument would be based on extreme speculation.

It was not expedient for the north air shaft of Khufu's pyramid to be aligned with Alpha Draconis, but it was expedient for that air channel to

supply fresh air for the funerary cortege.

If there were any association to be made between the pharaoh and the north pole star, that association could surely have been brought about through the use of the Great Pyramid's descending passageway. It would not have been necessary for that passage to have been directly connected with the burial chamber.

Some scholars have claimed that the burial chamber of King Khafra's pyramid at Giza displays signs of two air channels having been begun in its north and south walls. These two cavities cut into these walls for 1' and are approximately 1' high by 8" wide.

Upon serious reflection, however, one sees that these cavities could not have represented air shafts. For if air shafts were in fact contemplated for this pyramid, they would have had to have been fashioned as they were in the burial chamber of Khufu's pyramid — not hewn out of an existing block which had already been set into the chamber, but cut out beforehand. The air vents had to be hollowed out as the monument was being built up gradually; they were much too small to have been hewn through solid stone. Therefore, the so-called beginnings for the air channels in the Pyramid of Khafra are likely nothing more than small cavities fashioned by the original builders to receive beams or logs which spanned the chamber. The exact purpose for such beams is presently unknown, but similar cavities are also to be found in the pyramids of Menkara (Giza), Huni (Maidum) and Sneferu (Dahshur). The burial chambers of Huni's and Sneferu's pyramids still have logs set into their shallow cavities, traversing said chambers.

As further evidence that the small cavities in the walls of the burial chamber of Khafra were never

[1 = 8 ft.,   7 in. = 103 in.]
width 2 = 17 ft.,   2 in. = 206 in.
short wall diagonal 3 = 25 ft.,   9 in. = 309 in.
long wall or floor length 4 = 34 ft.,   4 in. = 412 in.
central diagonal 5 = 42 ft., 11 in. = 515 in.

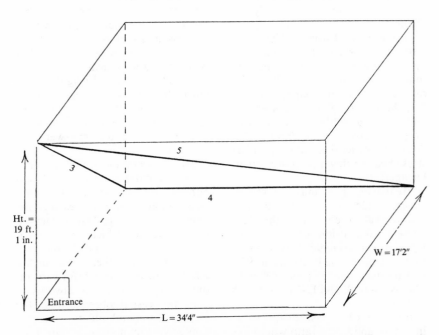

Great Pyramid of Khufu, Giza: Diagram showing manifestation of Pythagorean Triangle in basic dimensions. (J.P. LEPRE)

intended to be air ducts, recall that Khafra's burial chamber was subterranean and would not have been in critical need of a fresh supply of air as was the burial chamber located so high in the superstructure of the Great Pyramid.

Returning to the masonry of the King's Chamber, one notes that of the 21 stones comprising the burial chamber floor — most of which are of a formidable size — two have been lifted from their original positions and set on top of some of the other still-intact floorstones. These two stones were removed long ago so that

tomb robbers could tunnel through the softer limestone beneath in search of possible treasure which they surmised might lie under the floor of the chamber in the immediate area of the sarcophagus. Two other floorstones were also once removed, but no longer exist, evidently having been broken asunder by vandals.

As a result, a huge chasm of a sort has been dug out here to a depth of some 30 feet. Its width varies greatly, but it more or less forms a cavernous excavation approximately 6-10' wide. It would appear, though, that the frantic search brought little or no reward for the zealous mischiefmakers. Today, the two extracted floor stones still lie on the King's Chamber floor, but the pit itself is crudely covered over with an iron grating, upon which planks of hard wood are haphazardly fashioned.

Of the 101 wall stones which fashion the four walls of this chamber, one is different from the others in that it comprises two, rather than one, courses of masonry. It is, by far, the largest of the wall stones — and understandably so, as it is positioned directly over the entrance. No doubt it was set there to support the stress bearing down on that particular aperture.

Measuring this massive stone, which is 124″ long by 93″ high, I found that it contained the fundamental dimensions of the 3-4-5 or Pythagorean Triangle. This is to say, that its length is 124″, its height 93″, and its diagonal 155″; and 93″ is to 124″ as 3 is to 4, and 124″ is to 155″ as 4 is to 5.

If one were to measure every stone in the pyramid, this ratio would undoubtedly be repeated on many occasions. Yet here we are not dealing with the average stone, but with one that stands out conspicuously. This may be nothing more than a coincidence, but that coincidence has now been noted.

A further coincidence, if it can be termed such, is the fact that this 3-4-5 sequence is similarly manifested within the basic dimensions of the King's Chamber itself. For as the length of this chamber is 34′4″, its width 17′2″ and its height 19′1″, so its short (east or west) wall diagonal is 25′9″, and its long central diagonal (which cuts directly through the chamber obliquely) is 42′11″. In simpler terms we have:

$$3 = 25′9″ = 309″$$
$$4 = 34′4″ = 412″$$
$$5 = 42′11″ = 515″$$

Thus, 309″ is to 412″ is to 515″ as 3 is to 4 is to 5.

This, too, may be nothing more than a coincidence. But one must be reminded, that with these measurements, we are not dealing with a careless array of infinite combinations of random measurements, but with the basic dimensions (simply, the length, width and height) of the chief chamber within the pyramid, the one for which all other parts of the monument — and the monument itself, for that matter — were fashioned.

The presentation of this evidence for the manifestation of the Pythagorean Triangle should not be construed in any way as a breach of the scientific or archaeological method of investigation which I have ceaselessly strived to maintain throughout this work, but rather, as a further addition to that straightforward inquiry. For it should be obvious to even the casual observer that the ancient Egyptian builders — and particularly, the master architect of the Great Pyramid — had profound knowledge of certain fundamental principals of both geometry and mathematics. If that were not so, this great monument could never have been so perfectly aligned and oriented.

We often speak of the awesome progress of recent centuries, but in another respect, the ancient builders had a more profound knowledge in areas that we have only begun to touch upon. That something was lost from the time of the pyramid building age up this present era is certain; otherwise, why is it that not a single modern scholar — whether associated with the field of physics, engineering, archaeology, Egyptology, mathematics, geometry or scores of others—can conclusively state exactly how the mighty pyramids were built?

The 3-4-5 Pythagorean Triangle was not supposed to have been discovered or brought to the attention of the scientific community until the formulation of the Pythagorean Theorem by Pythagoras, the Greek mathematician of 497 B.C. Yet Napoleon's chief savant, Jomard, in his description of the Egyptian pyramids in 1829 informs us that Pythagoras was taught his geometric theorems by the Egyptians of his era, whose ancestors first mastered that discipline. It is also a known fact that the ancient Egyptian builders had specific knowledge of the Pi and Phi formulae (3.14159 and 1.618) and that they ingeniously incorporated these proofs into the exterior dimensions of the Great Pyramid (see page 127). These formulae are said to have come through Archimedes, the Greek mathematician of Syracuse (circa 287–212 B.C.), and Leonardo da Vinci (A.D. 1452–1519).

Most of the nearly 300 joints in the King's Chamber are so tight as not to admit the breadth of a hair. Only four are in any way open, and three of those represent three of the sides of a square, four-sided wall block. This is to say, that one of the wall blocks located on the west wall of the chamber, at its lowest course, has three open joints surrounding it. Its right side joint is open $\frac{1}{4}''$; its left side, $\frac{1}{8}''$; and its top joint, $\frac{1}{16}''$. It is worth noting that whenever a passageway enters or exits from a chamber in any of the pyramids, the aperture is usually situated at a lower righthand or lefthand corner of the chamber. The block in this particular instance is in just such a position, occupying the lower lefthand corner of the west wall of the King's Chamber. The base or bottom edge of the block

rests directly on the floor of the chamber, with a tight joint.

It appears very significant indeed that the only stone in the entire chamber with three open joints should occupy the unique position of that of a lower course corner stone. Is it possible this stone could be moved if enough pressure were applied to it from the interior of the King's Chamber? Again, it is the only stone in the entire chamber with open joints on three sides, and one which is located in the exact spot where another entrance or passage is likely to be set. The original builders, who were for some strange reason fond of plastering certain joints throughout the pyramid, used this method on the three open joints surrounding this particular stone. The plaster application on this lower corner stone, having aroused my curiosity, was partially removed from certain areas by my using a sharp pen knife. When I noted the open joints which had been hidden by that mass of plaster—a phenomenon first cited by me in 1978—the idea of a possible western entrance came to mind.

That there may be a second, western entrance at this point in the King's Chamber is not such an improbable idea as it may seem. For in the Bent Pyramid of Khufu's father Sneferu, at Dahshur, there is a western entrance as well as the standard one on the north side. It is not at all unreasonable to assume that Khufu may have duplicated the design of his father's pyramid in his own monument insofar as an auxiliary, western entrance is concerned.

The reader will probably ask why the plastered sections spoken of have not warranted the attention of numerous other pyramid investigators throughout the centuries. The answer is that these plastered areas are not the only ones which exist within the King's Chamber. A number of other joints are plastered over, most of them located very close to the above-mentioned ones. Thus most people viewing the west wall do not pay particular attention to that section of plaster which actually camouflages the three open joints. I personally believe that the pyramid builders plastered over the additional joints — which are all perfectly tight — to divert anyone from singling out the block of stone in the lower lefthand corner.

Another reason why such close scrutiny of this or any other part of the King's Chamber is not always feasible is the very poor lighting conditions with which one has to contend. The use of a weak or mediocre flashlight does little to aid one's vision in such a dark and shadowy compartment. It is not unreasonable to guess that many people who visit this chamber come ill-prepared and are actually without a flashlight of any kind, assuming that such a world-famous monument will be very well lit and accommodating to the inquisitive tourist and explorer alike. In truth, a very powerful flashlight is indispensible for examining, not only the King's Chamber, but all of the Great Pyramid.

Any serious investigator of any phenomenon ideally needs to conduct that investigation under the most serene and private conditions possible. Yet I have personally witnessed such interested parties striving to accomplish their task in the midst of hordes of excited and often boisterous tourists. Judging from the records of the ticket office located on Pyramid Hill, anywhere from 5,000 to 8,000 tourists visit this edifice during any given week. With such constant distractions imposed on the serious scholar by the often unruly crowds, very little close and

uninterrupted examination of the interior of the pyramid is likely.

No one who has ever experienced this dilemma will argue with the assertion that the only time in which anyone with serious intent can investigate the pyramid completely unimpeded is late at night and in the early morning hours, when the iron gate leading into the edifice is locked shut by the gatekeeper and the bats which have their nest in the relieving chambers located above the King's Chamber are the only inhabitants.

A nighttime investigation of the monument, however, is not easily accomplished. Very few of the many who wish to explore the Great Pyramid in the late night or early morning hours are ever given this permission by suspicious government inspectors whose purpose it is to protect the building from those who seek to probe and explore to their hearts' content. I was fortunate in this respect, having met the right officials.

In 1986 a French expedition detected several small, hidden cavities behind sections of the west wall of the horizontal passage leading to the Queen's Chamber. They were allowed to bore a single hole into that wall, which verified the existence of a hollow filled with sand, obviously the original design of the builders. Yet to this day, the Egyptian government has refused this team permission to break through that wall in order to investigate first-hand the sand-filled cavity. Such is the opposition one meets when one's investigation seeks to expand beyond pure observation to the actual excavation of the walls or other solid portions of the pyramid; and rightfully so. For too long too many explorers have had a free hand in digging up Egypt piecemeal, often acting on misguided and whimsical theories at the expense of that nation's precious monuments.

As to the discovery of the sand-cavities by the French expedition in 1986, this detection was accomplished by the employment of a microgravi-meter, a sonar-like device. In my own investigation of the Queen's Chamber horizontal passage in 1978 I detected the presence of these cavities — or something that I felt was present in that section of the corridor — by an entirely different method. As no thorough investiga-tion of that corridor had ever been conducted, I attempted to map out the entirety of walls, floor and ceiling of that corridor, marking each and every joint of masonry. I found a total of 130 blocks of stone compris-ing this passageway, with the major-ity of them (122) being either of the same relative size or oriented in the same direction.

Yet eight of the 130 stones did not obey this basic rule. Two of them, al-though of the same general dimen-sions as the majority of other blocks in the corridor, were floor stones which represented the area of a single block, with a joint separating them which ran in the opposite direction of the joints of the other floorstones. This is the very same situation which exists in the descending passage floor and which pointed to the fact that the secret ascending passage system rose above that area of the descending passage. The reader may recall that P. Smyth termed this idiosyncrasy "a sign in the floor for the wise."

Immediately beyond these two stones lie six other blocks which are different from the others in the passageway in that they are much larger in size, being double the length of the average stone. Not only this, four of the six are exactly parallel to one another, two situated on the east wall and two on the west wall.

To further emphasize the position of these blocks in the passageway they are inscribed with red-ocher construction symbols. These sym-bols and straight red-ocher lines, which run nearly the entire length of the corridor on the east and west walls, were discovered by me while I was mapping out the jointing of the passageway. Both the symbols and the horizontal lines are very faint and hardly discernible to the naked eye, but they are there and can be seen by anyone with good vision and the aid of a powerful flashlight. The jointing of the stones in this corridor is similarly difficult to discern, the joints being extremely fine and the stone being damaged by natural ex-foliation and the buildup of salt encrustations so common to this sec-tion of the pyramid and to the Queen's Chamber.

Knowing full well that the Egyp-tian government would deny me per-mission to excavate in this area — as they did the French team — I chose to retain this information until such time as I could present it to the general public through a published account such as this.

Though I have deviated from my account of the possibility of a west-ern entrance originating at the west wall of the King's Chamber, I felt that the particulars of the Queen's Chamber horizontal passage were relevant to that issue.

Concluding my description of the characteristics of the King's Chamber, I remind the reader that a fourth open joint had been noted in describing the masonry of that chamber. This single joint is a full inch wide but is almost impossible to discern, being located in the highest wall course, at a distance of 15'8" to 19'1" from the floor. It is a vertical corner joint at the northeast end of the chamber. Unfortunately, I have never had the time or opportunity to investigate it from a ladder, having had so many other important sections of the pyramid which required more immediate attention. This open joint should nevertheless be probed in the near future, presenting as it does such a stark exception to the rule in a chamber containing so many close-fitting stones.

RELIEVING CHAMBERS. There are five relieving chambers located immediately above the King's Chamber. These are not burial chambers, but specifically designed support systems used to relieve the King's Chamber ceiling from the tremendous amount of weight pressing down on it from above. (See diagram of King's Chamber, page 93.)

These compartments, working in conjunction with the walls of the King's Chamber, form a most ingenious method of dealing with the serious problem of weight distribution. For if this special system were not used, it is certain that the magnificent King's Chamber would long ago have collapsed under the pressure of the superincumbent weight.

To begin with, the walls of the King's Chamber were built independently of its floor, so that if undue pressure were put on these walls from above, they would not be crushed between that weight from above and the solidness of the granite floor beneath them but would slide down past the floor and compress the softer surrounding limestone, which would "give" first. Thus, these walls would grow shorter, and the King's Chamber would remain intact.

Yet more than this safeguard was required, as the wall system of the King's Chamber had its limitations

and could not, in itself, relieve all of the stress from the ceiling. This is where the relieving chambers come into play.

As there would have been a great weight bearing down on the King's Chamber ceiling, the master architect had these five support chambers built in such a manner that each had the weight bearing down upon it redirected to the walls and not the ceilings. This was accomplished by constructing the uppermost relieving chamber with a gable (pointed) roof of limestone, so that the weight imposed upon it from above would be channeled downward and to the sides. This weight would then be distributed to the relieving chambers beneath. Such a system resulted in the pressure being shifted to the walls, and not the ceilings, of these several compartments, said pressure traveling downward through their wall courses until reaching the walls of the King's Chamber.

The entrance which leads to the five relieving chambers is located 22' above the level of the Great Step, in the east wall of the Grand Gallery where it joins with the south wall at the ceiling. To reach the first relieving chamber from this 32" high by 27" wide aperture one must pass through a 24' long corridor. This corridor is roughly cut but is very much squared and leveled, its accuracy of direction attesting to the fact that it was an original, intregal part of the design of the architect and not a plunderer's tunnel.

This passageway was purposely left open by the builders so that the guardian priests could periodically

Opposite: Great Pyramid of Khufu, Giza: Relieving chambers. **Top:** *Campbell's Chamber, the uppermost of the five relieving chambers.* **Center:** *Lady Arbuthnot's Chamber. Notice the curious grooves in floor stones, and the architect's red-ocher construction line and triangular symbol.* **Bottom:** *Nelson's Chamber (looking west).* (J.P. LEPRE)

inspect the first relieving chamber for any signs of structural damage that may have befallen the tops of the ceiling stones of the King's Chamber, which lay immediately above, and the first relieving compartment itself.

This first compartment, called Davison's Chamber, is, like the other four chambers which rise above it, of the very same length and width as the King's Chamber. It is 3' high, although this height is not at all uniform. The only unusual feature about this compartment is a large excavation on its south side.

Beyond this lowermost chamber, the other four, situated above it, were never meant to be viewed or to be an open, working part of the overall design. They were discovered by Colonel Howard Vyse, who having inspected this first compartment, surmised that another chamber might well be situated above it.

On February 14, 1837, Vyse employed his work crew to use dynamite in order to blast their way upward from this first compartment. This labor created a new passage which revealed the existence of four more relieving chambers.

After a period of six weeks, and after having reached the fourth of the newfound chambers — or the fifth of the group — Vyse discontinued dynamiting. For it was clear from the design of this last compartment, which had a peaked rather than a flat roof, that nothing more lay beyond. Not only was the roof of this chamber — which was dubbed Campbell's Chamber — pointed, but it was a full 7' high, as compared with the 3'-high ceilings of the compartments below.

The second chamber up, called (General) Wellington's, displayed a rough-cut construction boss on its north wall and some traces of red-ocher quarrymen's hieroglyphics. Construction bosses, which were used in some way to aid with the manipulation of heavy stone blocks, were usually removed afterwards if that stone was placed in the area of a finished chamber or passageway. But here the boss was kept intact because this chamber was to be forever sealed from view.

Hieroglyphs were in fact discovered in all four of the relieving chambers penetrated by Vyse, but they were workmen's markings, painted on at the quarries. This assertion is supported by the facts that: (1) they were of the crude, not decorative type; (2) these upper apartments were construction cavities only; and (3) some of these hieroglyphics were actually set upside down. With the markings already on them, the blocks were set into place according to how their weight and dimensions were to be oriented, and not so that the hieroglyphs would be easily readable for anyone viewing the chamber afterwards. The readings of some of these signs were actually cut off from view where the blocks were set into place behind other cross stones. Many of them had the various names of the construction gangs written on them — titles such as: "The crew, the White Crown of Khnum-Khuf (Khufu) is powerful"; or "The crew, Khufu excites love."

These mentions of the Pharaoh Khufu are the only real historical testament to the assumption that Khufu was the builder of the Great Pyramid. His hieroglyphic name is mentioned many times on the walls of tombs and mastabas which riddle the Giza graveyard complex, those having been the burial places of his family, dignitaries and priests. But the hieroglyphics which grace the relieving chambers are the only ones bearing his name that were ever found in or on the pyramid itself.

The third of the relieving chambers, dubbed (Admiral) Nelson's Chamber, displays two construction bosses on its south wall, along with some of the better-preserved of the hieroglyphics.

Lady Arbuthnot's is the fourth of the relieving chambers and contains some interesting red-ocher straight geometric lines, as well as hieroglyphics. There are also two large construction bosses located on the north wall which are set side by side to within a few inches of each other—a very strange appearance in such a barren compartment. It is the only time that I have ever seen "twin bosses" carved from one stone.

This chamber's side walls, unlike those of the three chambers beneath, are of limestone rather than granite, a building technique used to address the weight pressing down from above. There is a very high central floorstone here, approximately 27' by 7' by 5'. It may quite possibly constitute the largest single stone of the entire pyramid; Edgar calculated its weight at 70 tons.

There are three intriguing floorstones present in this compartment, having grooves or furrows running across them breadthwise. The grooves resemble certain of the trenches located at the north base of the Pyramid of Khafra, Khufu's brother—trenches which are said to have been carved for leveling the plateau by using trapped water. There is evidence of a similar furrows at the north side of the Great Pyramid, but in a single instance only.

The fifth or uppermost of the relieving compartments, called (Colonel) Campbell's Chamber, is in many ways the most interesting of the five. It has the narrowest entrance of all those in the pyramid, a petite 20″ by 20″, which will certainly not admit a large-size man. Its walls and peaked ceiling are of limestone, to facilitate the architect's plan for dealing with the superincumbent pressure, but its monolithic floorstones are of rose granite.

There are a number of hieroglyphics painted on the ceiling, a few of which give the name of King Khufu, and one in particular which records that this stage in the construction of the monument was reached during the seventeenth year of his reign.

There are also straight geometric red-ocher lines criss-crossing one another on the sides of some of the massive floorstones; these lines intersect at the exact center of these stones, seeming to indicate that they were used as guidelines for leveling and centering them within the chamber. On one of these stones, where these lines cross, is a quaint little pyramidal or triangular symbol finely painted in black.

Of the seven huge floorstones in this chamber, four of them have odd-looking basins carved into them at their ends. These basins or bowls are roughly square, a strange phenomenon indeed.

It is in this uppermost chamber that the numerous bats which have adopted the Great Pyramid as their permanent home have set up their nests. They are to be seen clinging from the pointed ceiling here, but do not appear to occupy any other part of the pyramid's interior, although I have twice seen a single bat flying through the Grand Gallery.

There is a vertical cleft of a sort, approximately 1½″ wide, located on the east wall of this chamber. It appears to be from 10–15' long. At the end of this fissure there appears to be a bend of a sort, possibly giving rise to a small cavity or hidden apartment. All of this is difficult to discern, since there is no lighting whatsoever in any of these relieving chambers, and one cannot successfully shine a flashlight down such a long and narrow opening. I am certain, however, that the innermost area of the crevice is where the bats are more fully congregated, as I have seen numbers of them clinging to its side walls. At any rate, this most isolated sector of the pyramid should be more thoroughly investigated in the near future, as I am certain that it has not yet revealed all of its well-kept secrets.

THE QUEEN'S CHAMBER. The Queen's Chamber is the second of the main chambers of the pyramid and is situated high in the superstructure at the twenty-fifth course of masonry. It is a good-sized chamber, measuring 19' long by 17' wide by 15' high. The jointing of the limestone blocks comprising this chamber is so nearly perfect that many of them are practically invisible to the naked eye. Therefore, one receives the mistaken impression that the chamber is carved out of a solid piece of rock rather than built of many individual blocks fitted together. This absolutely perfect jointing is even more astonishing when one considers that the monument is close to 5,000 years old and has experienced numerous earthquakes throughout the centuries.

This chamber was given the title Queen's Chamber, not because the queen of the pharaoh was interred here, but because of the shape of its roof, which is pointed or gabled. It is the custom of modern Arabs to bury their women in such chambers, whereas the men are buried in chambers with flat ceilings.

The most obvious feature of this chamber is a huge niche cut into the east wall. This niche is 5' wide at its bottom and rises 15' in five corbel sections.

This chamber is thought to be the "serdab" chamber of King Khufu. It was not at all unusual in pyramid building to have a chamber with such a niche, separate from the burial chamber, containing a very large statue in the likeness of the pharaoh. Then again, others believe that this room was supposed to be the burial chamber of the king, but that it was abandoned before it was finished when the architect decided to build another burial chamber (the King's Chamber) higher in the superstructure. This could very well be the case, as this chamber was obviously left unfinished. This is evidenced by the extreme roughness of the floor; the fact that its air channels were never completed; the fact that this room was permanently sealed off from the Grand Gallery by a camouflaging "false floor" at the lower end of the Gallery; and by the presence of red-ocher construction lines in the passageway leading to it. It was only under close scrutiny that the author first noticed the presence of these lines and of certain geometrical symbols connected with them.

These red-ocher lines are ⅛" thick, finely painted and leveled, and are situated approximately 22" up from the floor, and thereby 20" down from the ceiling of this horizontal passageway. The corridor is 150' long and these lines originally ran almost this entire length, but are now visible through only portions of this distance. In some areas the paint has either worn off or been obscured by the accumulation of grime. There are, nevertheless, at intervals, sections of the lines that are distinguishable to the searching eye. Another reason for these lines not having been detected earlier is that the corridor leading to the Queen's Chamber is devoid of any lighting. Pre-twentieth century explorers relied on torches and kerosene lamps; modern investigators have had only flashlights.

These red-ocher lines are construction lines. Similar ones are found in other pyramids and tombs where the building process was unfinished. They were used as a rough guide in the positioning and leveling of the various stones. Where construction was completed, these lines were erased and the finished product polished and made ready for the burial of the pharaoh, as the lines would have presented an eyesore. There are instances, though, where a certain area was completed, but was never polished or brought to perfection because it was merely an architectural support section (the relieving chambers are an example). The Queen's Chamber and the corridor approaching it are not architectural supports, so we can assume they were simply left unfinished.

Like the King's Chamber of the Great Pyramid, the Queen's Chamber is supplied with dual air ducts. The north channel is 240′ long, while the south channel is somewhat longer, being 250′ in length. Both ascend through the masonry of the monument at 38-degree angles. Unlike the vents leading out from the King's Chamber, these channels terminate just 20′ short of the exterior.

These vents are also different from those in the King's Chamber in that they do not begin their ascent in the chamber proper, but 5″ in from the north and south wall stones of that chamber. A 5″ veneer of the wall stones through which these channels were to have entered the Queen's Chamber was left intact by the architect, camouflaging the channels from the sight of anyone who might happen to be in the chamber. This veneer was discovered and removed by Mr. Waynman Dixon in 1872.

Much ado has been made about these air ducts and the fact that they were sealed off inside the Queen's Chamber and cut to within 20′ of debouching at approximately the ninetieth masonry course. The furor is understandable, for this is one of the greatest mysteries of the Great Pyramid. Why the architect would have expended so much time and labor to cut two channels through the pyramid's masonry, each for at least 240′, only to leave both of their ends sealed off is a question to strain one's mental faculties. My proposed solution to this enigma follows.

The subterranean chamber of the Great Pyramid was the original burial chamber planned for the Pharaoh Khufu. While that crypt was being excavated, however, the architect decided to build a more suitable and unorthodox burial chamber high in the superstructure of the monument; this was the Queen's Chamber. As progress was being made on the construction of this second apartment, work on the subterranean chamber was abandoned, resulting in its present unfinished condition.

The architect, realizing that the new Queen's Chamber would be in need of ventilating shafts for the funerary cortege, adopted this unprecedented feature. Yet soon after the walls of this chamber had begun to be built up—when they had reached the point exactly where the air vents were supposed to have been initiated—the architect envisioned a third and final burial chamber even higher up in the masonry; this would be the King's Chamber.

If, however, the Pharaoh Khufu should die while the Queen's Chamber was totally abandoned and the King's Chamber not yet completed, there would not be a finished burial chamber for him to occupy within the pyramid. To say that such an

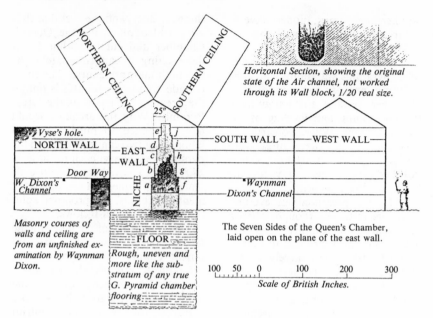

Horizontal Section, showing the original
state of the Air channel, not worked
through its Wall block, 1/20 real size.

Masonry courses of
walls and ceiling are
from an unfinished ex-
amination by Waynman
Dixon.

Rough, uneven and
more like the sub-
stratum of any true
G. Pyramid chamber
flooring

The Seven Sides of the Queen's Chamber,
laid open on the plane of the east wall.

100   50   0   100   200   300

Scale of British Inches.

Queen's Chamber (open on plane of east wall). (P. SMYTH)

occurrence would place the master architect in a somewhat embarrassing
position would be an understatement.

Therefore, construction on the
Queen's Chamber was not abandoned, for it was to serve as an auxiliary chamber should a catastrophe
occur. The air channels of that chamber would be hewn in expectation of
a dramatic turn of events, for they
would not commence within the
chamber itself, but within 5″ of the
north and south wall sections. If the
King's Chamber were completed as
planned, then the funerary party
would have no use for the Queen's
Chamber, nor, consequently, for the
air channels of that chamber; that
chamber would then be utilized as a
special compartment for a Ka statue
of the King. That it served this
ultimate purpose after the work on
the King's Chamber had been completed is evidenced by the huge four-
tiered statue niche which was even-

tually cut into the east wall of the
Queen's Chamber.

If, by chance, the pharaoh died
before the King's Chamber was finished, it would have been easy
enough for the workmen to break
through the 5″ veneers of stone in the
north and south walls of the Queen's
Chamber, altering it from a Ka
chamber to a burial chamber adequately furnished with air vents for
the comfort of the funeral cortege.

If the King's Chamber were to be
used, it would not have sufficed
merely to complete the basic chamber; the relieving chambers had to be
finished as well. They were as integral
a part of that burial complex as the
sarcophagus itself. Without these
support chambers the King's Chamber might well have collapsed under
the tremendous weight bearing down
from above. For this reason, these
upper relieving chambers needed to
be completed before the King's

Chamber could be pronounced structurally fit for the burial of the pharaoh.

That the air shafts leading from the Queen's Chamber were not discontinued in their ascent through the pyramid's masonry until they reached this exact level of the monument — the very peak of the gabled ceiling beams of Campbell's Chamber, 215' above ground level — is in keeping with the theory that construction on the Queen's Chamber continued, for safety's sake, until the King's Chamber was finished. At this level, the Queen's Chamber air vents were cut short in their ascension because (a) the King's Chamber complex had now been completed; and (b) to have needlessly continued them on from here (just 20' shy of the exterior of the edifice) would have drawn unnecessary attention to the monument from anyone viewing it from the outside. The outside apertures of the King's Chamber air vents could similarly have drawn attention to the pyramid, but the presence of these apertures was unavoidable. If apertures were present for the Queen's Chamber air vents, the attention would have been even greater, especially in light of the fact that they would have been positioned 11 courses lower, at the ninetieth masonry level.

The astute reader may question the lack of a stone sarcophagus in the Queen's Chamber if it were prepared to be an alternative burial chamber for the pharaoh were the King's Chamber not to be completed in time.

Possibly the best answer to this valid question is that because the Queen's Chamber was planned as a mere alternative burial compartment, the architect did not deem it necessary to set the sarcophagus into place as the chamber was being built up. As demonstrated in the pyramids

of Kings Khafra, Eke, Djoser-Tati, Khufu (King's Chamber) and others, the sarcophagi were in fact placed within the burial chambers beforehand. Yet in this situation, the Queen's Chamber was a tentative receptacle, and would not necessarily have warranted the placing of a sarcophagus within it as the chamber was being built up. This line of reasoning has further merit when one considers the fact that, if that sarcophagus were slightly larger than the dimensions of the corridor approaching the burial chamber — in this case, the Queen's Chamber horizontal passage — then that sarcophagus could not have been removed should the architect choose to do so.

In light of this situation it is likely that a sarcophagus was never set into this chamber at all, and would only have been inserted at a much later date if a turn of events had so required.

There is also the likelihood that a sarcophagus was set into this chamber and later removed by the builders when the completion of the King's Chamber above was guaranteed. In this instance that sarcophagus would have been cut slightly narrower that the corridor preceding the Queen's Chamber.

Yet another possibility is that a sarcophagus may have been initially set into the Queen's Chamber as that chamber was being constructed, that it was left there, empty — by the builders, and then broken up by tomb robbers who took pleasure in vandalizing the pyramid. As the King's Chamber, being fashioned from granite, contained a granite sarcophagus, so the Queen's Chamber, being fashioned from limestone, may have housed a limestone sarcophagus. A limestone sarcophagus, being much softer than a granite one, could easily have met with destruction at the hands of despoilers. In support of this theory, the finely cut limestone blocks which once comprised this chamber's floor are also now missing, presumably having been similarly violated.

SUBTERRANEAN CHAMBER. Immediately beyond the petite niche situated at the bottommost, level section of the descending passage, lies the subterranean chamber, which is entirely of limestone, having been cut out of the solid bedrock. Upon entering this spacious chamber, which is 55' long by 30' wide by 12' high, there is an 18" drop in the floor level, a design undoubtedly implemented to receive a paved floor of finely cut limestone blocks, floorstones which were never set into place.

The chamber is extremely rough-hewn, to a degree that has prompted pyramid explorers to dub it "The Chamber of Chaos." Chamber of Chaos it is, being as if a mad-man, rather than a master architect, had his hand at fashioning it. Everything — ceiling, walls, floors (plural here, for the floor rises and falls at different pitches and levels) is totally disproportionate; there are whole chunks of limestone haphazardly cut here and there, and numerous protrusions in many sections, giving this chamber a very distorted look.

In a section of the floor a dozen or so feet from the doorway, halfway between north and south walls, is a square-cut shaft, measuring 8' by 8' by 15' deep, whose bottom is filled with loose rubble and debris. At one point excavators had removed the filling and discovered that the original depth of the shaft was not quite 60'. Said shaft is not cut parallel with the four walls of the chamber, but runs diagonally to that configuration.

Approximately 10' down from the top of the shaft a ledge of a sort is fashioned; upon it a large block of squared granite is lodged.

This shaft is probably the least likely place within the entire pyramid where one would think to look for the secret chamber of the Pharaoh Khufu. The subterranean chamber is so utterly crude in its design, that this pit — as it has been so ignominiously referred to — by its lowly position within this chamber, would seem to be representative of all that is insignificant or unworthy of attention. Yet in this respect, it is beneficial to note that the tomb of Khufu's mother, Queen Hetepheres, was found, quite by accident, at the bottom of a similar, inconspicuous shaft near to the northeast corner of the great pyramid. Even though her chamber may have represented nothing more than a cenotaph, or dummy tomb — as it was found to be devoid of a mummy when first penetrated in the twentieth century — a lesson might be drawn from this discovery. Actually, further excavation of the shaft in the subterranean chamber was indefinitely cancelled because the workmen employed for this investigation had difficulty breathing in the stale air. To my knowledge, no other excavations have been conducted on this curious shaft since the probing by P. Smyth in 1865.

The previously mentioned granite block which rests on the ledge of the pit is finely hewn and polished and has two large drill holes, 3½" in diameter, running through it. This is one of the four "mysterious" granite fragments discussed on pages 89–92.

The odd configuration of this disheveled subterranean chamber does not end here. At the lower end of the south wall — where it adjoins the east wall — there is an entrance to a very small passageway (30" high by 30" wide) which rises 7" above the floor of the chamber, and which continues

← S

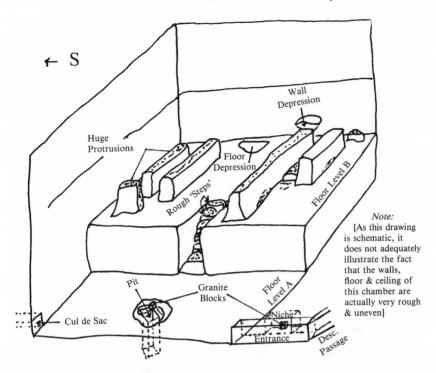

Huge
Protrusions

Wall
Depression

Floor
Depression

Floor Level B

Rough 'Steps'

Note:
[As this drawing
is schematic, it
does not adequately
illustrate the fact
that the walls,
floor & ceiling of
this chamber are
actually very rough
& uneven]

Pit

Granite
Blocks

Floor
Level A

Cul de Sac

Niche

Entrance

Desc.
Passage

Great Pyramid of Khufu, Giza: Subterranean chamber (Chamber of Chaos).
(DIAGRAM, J.P. LEPRE. PHOTO, J.P. LEPRE)

south in snakelike fashion for 53′,
terminating at that point in a
cul-de-sac.

This tortuous passage at first
glance appears to be a latter-day excavation by tomb plunderers, but

upon a more thorough inspection it
can clearly be noted that the cutting
through of the natural rock is anything but crude, and displays the indelible mark of the ancient quarriers. For
although the passageway is zig-zag in

its orientation, the chiseling of the stone is of too fine a quality for any ordinary despoiler. Why the original architect would have attempted to sink a shaft straight down, and a horizontal passageway due south, both into the solid bedrock and apparently leading to nowhere, is somewhat perplexing.

Cut into the ceiling of the chamber is a 4'-square impression, approximately 6" deep at its eastern end and tapering to zero degree tolerance at its western end. This may very well have represented the initial stages of an ascending passage which was to have inclined upwards at this location. As with the various other architectural features present in this chamber, it too was haphazardly abandoned by the builders, a further testimony to an ambitious conception having met with a premature conclusion. With this chamber now discarded, a new one was conceived high in the pyramid's superstructure.

WELL SHAFT. The well shaft in the Great Pyramid is a 200'-long, rough-cut passageway that connects the junction of the lower end of the Grand Gallery, upper end of the first ascending passage and north end of the Queen's Chamber horizontal passage with the bottom end of the descending passageway.

It follows five different directions through its tortuous, shadowy path; two vertical and three oblique, as it passes, first through the masonry of the pyramid, and then through the solid bedrock. It is approximately 28" square throughout and is lined at intervals with rough footholes, apparently fashioned there by the pyramid builders.

This shaft is the area of the pyramid least frequented by visitors and explorers alike. Devoid of artificial or natural lighting, with steep and vertical turns throughout, it presents a very real element of danger to even the most adept of climbers.

Its uppermost, vertical, section is composed of the pyramid's core masonry blocks, and is fairly well squared and level. Beyond this 25'-long shaft the passage turns obliquely to the south, where it is hewn through the masonry in a very rough fashion, having been dug out after the blocks of stone comprising this area had already been set into place. Here it travels for 35' until it once again begins to run vertically.

This next vertical section, only 10' in length, is composed of coarse but leveled courses, along side of which entrance to a small cavity dubbed "the grotto" can be gained. This section of the well shaft is at the precise level where the pyramid's core masonry meets with the level of the natural bedrock upon which the monument is built. This level, though, is not on the same plane as that upon which the pyramid's base perimeter is set, but is a full 25' higher, representing a natural outcrop or rise in the central region of the pyramid plateau.

From here on the well shaft travels a few more feet vertically, where it now begins to cut into the solid rock foundation, after which it once more turns obliquely for a straight, long run of 100', still passing through the bedrock of the plateau. Two large fissures can clearly be seen running through the uppermost area of this portion of the shaft, the remnants of past earthquake activity.

A final 30' oblique section, turning further south, completes the length of the well shaft, where it terminates at the bottom of the descending passageway.

This shaft acted as an escape route for the workers whose job it was to lower the granite plug stones from the Grand Gallery down the first

ascending corridor after the interment of the pharaoh, thereby sealing
off the upper reaches of the pyramid.
Once exiting the shaft at the bottom
of the descending passageway, they
sealed that aperture with a block of
limestone which would have been indistinguishable from the other stones
comprising the west wall of that corridor. Perhaps that camouflaging
stone was movable and allowed the
high priests to enter and leave the
shaft at will, but perhaps not. This
question may never be resolved, as
the stone with which the aperture was
once sealed has now disappeared.
We know that it was there as recently
as Roman times, for these people are
recorded to have visited the subterranean chamber without ever having
an inkling that the pyramid contained chambers in its superstructure. It was removed by the Caliph
Al Mamoun in the ninth century A.D.

The well shaft was dug out from
the top down. This is indicated by the
fact that its bottom end penetrates a
few feet below its lowermost doorway. If it had been hewn from the
bottom up, this bottom section
would surely have been level with its
doorway at that point.

Actually, the well shaft was not
conceived of by the pyramid's
architect until the pyramid's
superstructure had reached the level
of the halfway mark of the first
ascending passageway. It is for this
reason that the topmost, vertical section of the well shaft is built up
evenly of blocks set there for that
purpose, whereas the oblique section
immediately below that vertical pass
is roughly hewn and irregular.

THE GROTTO. Aside from a small
ten-course section of roughly hewn
and squared limestone blocks comprising its crude entrance, the grotto
of the Great Pyramid, situated just
below the monument's ground level,

constitutes what appears to be the
hollowing-out of a once-smaller,
natural pocket of earth at the center
of the pyramid plateau. Unusual as it
may seem, being uniquely located in
the very middle of an otherwise solid
rock foundation, no other explanation can be given.

Even more curious than the presence of this earthen cavity is the fact
that its ceiling is composed, not of
packed earth as would be expected,
but of gravel packed in damp, caked
sand. Whereas the earthen walls of
this cavity are relatively hard to the
touch, the ceiling of small stones is so
loosely packed that one has only to
reach up and dig in with one's fingers
in order to extract whole handfuls of
this material. M. Edgar collaborates
this observation by stating that this
ceiling "crumbles when touched."
This is a very unusual configuration,
and one which would lead us to believe that perhaps the ceiling might
represent an impromptu fill-in by the
builders.

The ceiling is also unusually damp
to the point where there is actually a
perceptible coating — like a light
frost — over the pebbles themselves.
This unusual composition naturally
tempts one to speculate about the existence of a nearby water source. Yet
a water source — and especially one
so very cool — does not seem likely in
the middle of a solid rock foundation
at the edge of a barren section of
desert.

A probing of the ceiling of the
grotto would appear to be in order,
but it might prove to be a hazardous
venture, due to its loose condition
and to the immense weight of the
core of the pyramid bearing down on
it from above. Oddly enough, Pliny,
the roman scholar, writing about the
Great Pyramid in A.D. 79, makes
mention of a "water-well" being
located within the monument. Could

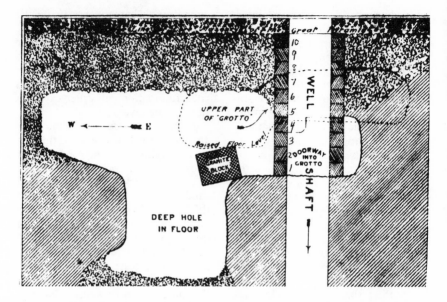

Great Pyramid of Khufu, Giz̲a: The Grotto. (J. AND M. EDGAR)

there once have been a supply of water running through this section, with the remnants of some underground reservoir still trickling in to dampen the ceiling of the Grotto?

Located in the center of the Grotto is a single block of granite with a 3½″ drill hole bored through it; its dimensions are 21″ by 18″ by 17″. The question of how this squared block of stone ever managed to be placed here, in such a remote area of the pyramid, is one of speculation and is addressed in that section of the text dealing with the four "mysterious granite fragments" (see pages 89–92).

The shape of the grotto is unorthodox, displaying several levels. Only at its center is it high enough for the average man to barely stand erect. It curves or bends in its configuration, and forms a rough L-pattern.

Although seemingly insignificant when compared to the other, much more commanding, apartments of the Great Pyramid, the grotto never-theless had a special purpose which we are not presently familiar with. A more thorough investigation of this cavity should be undertaken in the near future, as it represents that area of the pyramid which, more than any other, has been so neglected by nearly all researchers and explorers. As proof of this, although so many authors have mentioned the grotto in passing within the context of their treatises on the subject of the Great Pyramid, very few have actually had the opportunity to visit it for themselves.

KHUFU'S MORTUARY TEMPLE. This wonderful temple, now completely destroyed, was totally unlike any of the mortuary temples which preceded or followed it. Its plan is so utterly simple and yet so very elegant, that it is obvious that, here too, as with the Great Pyramid, a master architect had his hand in its design and execution.

This once-beautiful temple, 170′ long by 130′ wide, was highlighted by

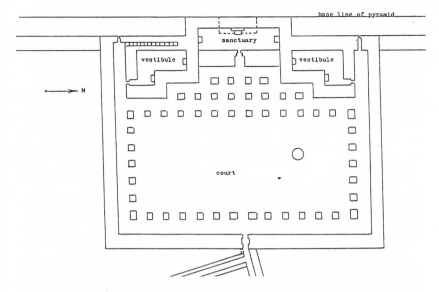

Great Pyramid of Khufu, Giza: Plan of Mortuary Temple. (J.P. LEPRE)

a spacious, oblong court surrounded by 50 square granite columns. West of this open court were two large vestibules, a large inner sanctuary and a staircase leading to a patio on the roof.

The color combination of this building was quite impressive, having rose granite columns, a black basalt floor and white limestone walls. The symmetry of the temple, in the unique orientation of both its columns and wall sections, bears witness to an order and superiority of design not to be found in any other Egyptian temple.

KHUFU'S MISSING VALLEY TEMPLE. Although the valley temple of Khufu is now missing, speculation as to its original site is sorely lacking. Every author who has ever written about that valley temple has unreservedly placed that site approximately ¼ of a mile to the northeast of the Great Pyramid, dismissing its absence on the supposition that its razed remains are now buried under the modern village of Nazlet el Samman, otherwise known as the Village of the Sphinx.

The reasons for this unanimous agreement as to the valley temple's position within the Great Pyramid complex are as follows:

1) From the Great Pyramid's mortuary temple, situated on the immediate east side of the pyramid, the apparent remnants of a causeway stretch from that point to the northeast.

2) That apparent causeway, after a distance of approximately ¹⁄₁₆ of a mile, terminates at the edge of a high escarpment or hill; and that hill, being of solid rock throughout, is completely absent of any traces of a valley temple.

3) That distance of ¹⁄₁₆ of a mile was considered to be much too close to the Great Pyramid and to its mortuary temple to have accommodated a valley temple.

4) The natural inclination of the scholar is then to address that area

which lay an additional ⅛ of a mile or so beyond the escarpment, continuing on in the direction of the northeast, or in the direction in which the causeway is stretching.

5) Thus the scholar concludes or deduces, from all of the above evidence and speculation, that the missing valley temple of the Pharaoh Khufu is located somewhere at the ¼ mile mark, or within a reasonable distance thereof.

Upon a thorough inspection of that calculated site, we find no traces of a valley temple, but a dozen or so ramshackle houses which constitute a section of the outer perimeter of Nazlet el Samman Village.

With this knowledge being attained, and with the further knowledge that the Egyptian Government forbids any excavations at this site so that the rights and property of the present-day residents might be respected, the matter of the location of Khufu's valley temple seems irrefutably settled, and no additional speculation as to another possible location for its existence is warranted.

To endeavor to prove invalid this widespread and well-accepted theory based on evidence which may be present at the locations of the Great Pyramid's mortuary temple, causeway section, extension of that causeway section, or present-day village homes occupying the proposed site of the lost valley temple, would probably prove fruitless; for without getting into the subject of the immediate terrain and its several characteristics, it will suffice to say that such a line of reasoning, based on the meager evidence which is available on this account, would be too complex and speculative to make a lasting impression or to succeed in changing the minds of all those who presently accept and support the orthodox theory thus far stated.

It would seem, therefore, that the issue of the location of the ruined valley temple of Khufu is firmly and forever settled. I, too, like so many others, once accepted this theory — at least in part. Unfortunately, though, the acceptance of this train of thought only succeeds in closing one's mind to the possibility of the village area not being the actual site of the missing valley temple, and of another, more obvious, location being the true site thereof.

By this time the reader suspects that I am leading up to suggesting an alternative location for the missing valley temple — a location based on concrete evidence. Rather than state the proposed location forthright, however, I will follow the exact line of reasoning that ultimately led me to believe in the existence of this second site, and then specifically mention the site; I will then support this suggestion with certain unique characteristics present at that location.

The standard placement for both valley and mortuary temples, which were intregal elements of pyramid complexes, was always to the east of the pyramid. Only a few rare examples constitute the exception to this rule, namely, the pyramid sites of pharaohs Djoser, Dynasty III; Rededef (Djedefre), Dynasty IV; and Userkaf, Dynasty V.

In the first instance, the alteration in plan was due to the fact that Djoser chose to incorporate into his pyramid complex and expansive arrangement of symbolic buildings — a deviation from the typical pyramid complex up till that time, and never thereafter duplicated — for which the east side of the pyramid was the ideal location. Thus, in this unparalleled instance, Djoser's mortuary temple was erected at the north side of the pyramid.

In the second instance, although Rededef's mortuary temple was placed, as usual, immediately to the east of his pyramid, the valley temple could not possibly occupy its customary position ¼ to ½ mile further eastward, because at a distance not quite ⅟₁₆ of a mile in that direction there existed the precipice of the high promontory upon which the pyramid was built. To have constructed a causeway which would have extended far beyond the precipice, to the customary site of a proposed valley temple, would have involved shoring up the promontory at that point — a tremendous strain on the resources and manpower available to the pharaoh at that time.

Therefore, purely because of geographical considerations, the valley temple of Rededef — and subsequently the long causeway connecting it with the pyramid — was constructed to the north. The remains of that mile-long causeway can still be seen today.

In the third instance, the mortuary temple of King Userkaf was built to the immediate south of his pyramid, rather than to the east; this was attributed to the fact that the area due east of that pyramid rose steeply, ruling out the feasibility of that temple being built there. According to C.M. Firth, the excavator of the complex, the east side of the pyramid also lacked adequate space to successfully construct the mortuary temple.

In all three instances, then, it can be seen that geographical considerations were responsible for the altering of the mortuary and valley temple plans.

Now with the Pyramid of Khufu, geographical considerations are also to be taken into account. The area immediately east of the edifice was composed of solid rock, and there the spacious mortuary temple was

built. As was explained earlier, that rock foundation extends eastward where, after a short stretch, it terminates at a cliffside.

It is at this point that the popular theory of the valley temple being located even further east begins to show serious defects. For we have here an example which bears a close affinity to the repositioning of Rededef's valley temple. Not only were both sites stricken with the problem of having a cliff situated just east of their pyramids, but these pyramid complexes were built back-to-back, so to speak, as Rededef was Khufu's son and heir-apparent and ruled immediately after Khufu.

If the problem of building a shored-up causeway was remedied by Rededef through the reorientation of his valley temple to another side of his pyramid, then why couldn't Khufu have done the same? For although it is easy enough to speculate that Khufu's valley temple is located northeast of his pyramid, it would not have been an easy task to have shored up the escarpment at that section of Pyramid Hill. It would have been a formidable task indeed, and one which, more than likely, would have been avoided by Khufu's architect as it was by Rededef's. Then again, it is not at all that improbable that the very same architect served both of these pharaohs. In that case, why would he embark on two different approaches when confronted with essentially the same problem?

Another question which can hardly be dismissed is, if the true position of the lost valley temple is actually within the prescribed area of the perimeter of Nazlet el Samman Village, and if the extension of the causeway leading northeast from the Great Pyramid was laboriously shored up — as it would have to be, were the temple situated to the northeast — then where are the remnants of that extended causeway? For even if that causeway had been afterwards broken up by latter-day builders who sought to utilize the finely squared and polished blocks with which it was undoubtedly paved for their own building projects at other temple or pyramid sites, or in modern-day Cairo, then surely, a core mound of some sort would still be discernible. But that section of Pyramid Hill displays no such mound or packing of the surface. Rather, the cliffside falls off abruptly, giving no indication that it was ever shored up or reinforced.

Reflecting once again on the geographical considerations which were given the other pyramid sites, and taking into account the geographical characteristics just noted for the Khufu complex, let us now shift our attention from the east of the Great Pyramid to other alternative sites for the possible construction of the lost valley temple.

Building the valley temple to the north of the pyramid would meet with an even greater obstruction than was present at its east side. For here is a continuation of the promontory, which rises at an even loftier height than that section situated to the east.

That the valley temple may have been located to the west of the pyramid is incomprehensible, due to the presence in that area of hundreds of mastabas of Khufu's priests and dignitaries. Not only this, but to direct the valley temple toward the west would have been to direct it too far in the opposite direction from the valley itself, from which the term "valley temple" is derived.

To the south of the pyramid lie several very large mastabas belonging to Khufu's close family members. Additionally, beyond these mastabas, the route that the pyramid's

causeway would now have to follow — were the valley temple directed to the south — would, after a short distance, lead to another abrupt drop in the level of the ground; not so much so as to the east or north, but nevertheless, to a considerable degree.

It would seem now, with all four of the compass points being covered, and with obstacles being present in each of these directions, that we are at a loss as to being able to find an alternative site for the Great Pyramid's valley temple.

Upon further reflection, though, a way appears to be opened up for us. For between the east cliff and the gradual — yet formidable — drop to the south, there is a large tract of gradually sloping ground which is directed, from an area close to the southeast corner of the pyramid, down to the edge of the valley below. It is oriented southeast, and is in fact the only route which one can take — by foot, camel, horse or automobile — if one wishes to ascend or descend Pyramid Hill. That it would be the only feasible place to have oriented a causeway leading from the pyramid and its mortuary temple to a valley temple site is quite obvious. This is further emphasized by the stream of both tourists and Arabs alike who ply this route daily to gain access to Pyramid Hill from the village below, or vice-versa. In this respect this grade is well paved with asphalt to accommodate the heavy flow of constant traffic.

So then, it would seem after all that there would have been a more suitable direction for the causeway of the Great Pyramid where it might be connected with a distant valley temple which preferably lay to the east, northeast or southeast.

If, for the sake of curiosity, we now follow that sloping road down to the bottom of Pyramid Hill, assuming that it might once have represented the true causeway of the Great Pyramid which led to the distant valley temple, exactly what is it we find there—besides modern souvenir shops and hawkers selling their wares?

Amazingly, we find at that site where the valley temple would be expected—approximately ¼ of a mile to the southeast, and at the base of the sloping hill—a huge limestone temple! For here is located the so-called Temple of the Sphinx. And why is it thus referred to? Because it stands immediately in front of the Great Sphinx of Giza.

This temple, once lined with granite, is flanked on the west by the Sphinx and on the south by the valley temple of Khafra, and has long been associated with both of these monuments, but only because they are in such close proximity to one another. For other than this close geographical association, no other relationship between the three structures has ever been drawn. There is much speculation in this respect, but no proof.

Every author who has ever referred to the Temple of the Sphinx, being at a loss for concrete evidence, automatically assumes that it was built by Khafra, based solely on the fact of its being adjacent to Khafra's valley temple.

Khafra's valley temple can surely be ascribed to him, his larger-than-life diorite statue having been found within a deep pit in the floor by A. Mariette. This likeness of King Khafra, considered to be one of the finest examples of ancient Egyptian statuary extant, is now in the Cairo Museum, Tahrir Square. Khafra's valley temple can also be attributed to him, since his pyramid causeway leads directly into it. The Great Sphinx statue, too, is credited to

Khafra because of the striking resemblance it bears to his numerous portraits.

Yet no statues of King Khafra or of any other monarch have ever been found in the Temple of the Sphinx. The building is likewise devoid of any inscriptions or hieroglyphics.

It is a well-known fact among pyramid scholars that no mortuary or valley temple complex belonging to one pharaoh exactly resembles those belonging to other pharaohs. Pyramids, although many had unique characteristics all their own, obeyed many of the same basic rules of design. Yet each valley and mortuary temple complex was uniquely set apart from the rest. It would appear that the chief architects of these several monuments, being compelled more or less to follow traditional patterns when building the various pyramids, enjoyed a greater freedom when it came to the planning and construction of the mortuary and valley temples; and thus the more widespread individuality of patterns evident therein.

Yet although one pharaoh's complex was of a different design than that of another, the mortuary and valley temples which belonged to a single pharaoh, and which were integral parts of one particular complex—even though those two temples were designed on slightly different plans—basically resembled, and were in fact meant to complement one another. This phenomenon is ideally illustrated by comparing the popular diagrams of the mortuary and valley temples of King Khafra (page 15). For here one can readily appreciate the different aspects of each design—dictated by the disparate purpose which each temple obviously represented—and the resemblance as well. This is further evidence that that particular valley temple belonged to the Khafra mortuary temple and pyramid complex.

Let us now examine a plan diagram of the mortuary temple of Khufu and compare it to a plan diagram of the so-called Temple of the Sphinx. And when we do just that, lo and behold, we find a very compatible match!

To say that these two temples are closely akin in design would be an understatement. Rather than choosing to explain and define the various similarities step by step, I would suggest that the interested reader examine these diagrams for himself or herself (pages 119 and 125). There can be no doubt that said diagrams speak for themselves.

The reader may now question why such an obvious comparison had not been revealed before this time. Is it not often that the obvious eludes us—whether in the field of Egyptology, or sociology, or anthropology or everyday life in general? For nearly 15 years I have been involved in this particular field of study. Many times have I inspected both the Temple of the Sphinx and the barren foundation of the mortuary temple of Khufu, examining their diagrams and scores of others besides. Yet it was not until recently that I hit upon the concept that perhaps the Temple of the Sphinx was the actual valley temple of Khufu. The field of Egyptology is so very complicated and so all encompassing that it is often difficult to tune into something which is in essence so utterly simple and easy to understand. The mind of the curious and interested Egyptologist is many times being pulled in several different directions at once. With the hieroglyphs alone, there is a mountain of work, and enough of a complexity therein to occupy one's thoughts for a lifetime. In my own

situation regarding Khufu's missing valley temple, I never really contemplated trying to associate it with the Temple of the Sphinx or with any other nearby temple, having promptly accepted the opinion of so many scholars that it was hopelessly buried under the village of Nazlet el Samman; but upon reinspecting the site in 1987, I began to seriously question the validity of that popular concept.

That the diagrams of the mortuary temple of Khufu and the Temple of the Sphinx bear striking similarities seems to me no mere coincidence. Other scholars may question this association, but I personally fail to see where there would be any validity behind such a denial. Until now researchers have been perplexed as to why King Khafra would be endowed with two separate valley temples, and, choosing not to grasp such an unorthodox concept, they have assigned this second temple to the Sphinx statue itself. Yet the giant Sphinx is none other than the image of Khafra; so the association is once more denied by utter logic.

That the brothers King Khafra and King Khufu built two grand pyramids back to back on the wide Giza plateau is a fact of history. In my opinion, so were their individual valley temples adjacently placed, a further testimony to their close affinity in death as well as life.

Will the remnants of the true causeway of the Pharaoh Khufu yet be discovered under the present asphalt pavement that veils the sloping road leading up to the Pyramid Plateau and down to the mysterious valley temple? That is something to be left to future investigation. The present stretch of the wide, barren hilltop, which so many have for so long described as the original causeway of Khufu, needs also to be reexamined,

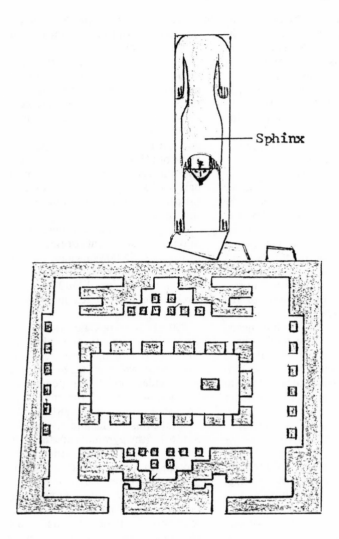

Sphinx

0'   120'

N

Mortuary "Temple of the Sphinx," Giza. (G. Perrot and C. Chipiez)

for in truth, it represents nothing more than a natural stretch of the plateau and, for the several reasons described in this essay, might never have been a true causeway.

It may have been a causeway, in the sense that it led to a small, symbolical valley temple which the builders could have erected at the cliff's edge. But it is doubtful that it led to the true valley temple.

As some of what I have been attesting to is hypothetical only, a valley temple of Khufu could possibly be unearthed in that area of Nazlet el Samman where scholars have insisted that it has been all along. Yet, even if such an event were to someday take place, then we still have the striking similarities between Khufu's mortuary temple and the Temple of the Sphinx to contend with. Surely the same architect created both projects, his indelible signature having been secured in the floor plans of these buildings, plans which were so diligently retraced and made available to us by Egyptologists U. Holscher (Temple of the Sphinx) and J.P. Lauer (Khufu's mortuary temple).

PI INCORPORATED INTO THE GREAT PYRAMID. If one takes the original height of the Great Pyramid (485.5') and treats it as the radius of an imaginary circle, then multiplies this height by 2, the figure 971' is obtained, which is the diameter of said circle. If this diameter is then multiplied by Pi (3.14) the circumference of this circle (3,048.96') is obtained.

The second step is to take the length of one of the Pyramid's sides at the base, which is 762.24' and multiply it by 4. The product is 3,048.96', or the perimeter of the base.

One can readily see how the figures from the two calculations match. For the circumference of the circle equals the perimeter of the square base.

Therefore, we have the complementary squaring of the circle and circling of the square!

The reader may think the symmetry of these fundamental measurements a coincidence. Yet this is more than a coincidence when one considers that in order to obtain such an equivalence, the angle of the Pyramid must be the perfect and specific angle of 51° 51' 14.3". Only a pyramid with this special angle, or ratio of its base to its height (the 7/11 or 11/7 ratio), will circle its square and square its circle.

The Pi formula, although built into the measurements of this monument nearly 5,000 years ago, was not discovered (or rediscovered, as the case may be) until 300 B.C. by Archimedes, the Greek mathematician of Syracuse.

PHI INCORPORATED INTO THE GREAT PYRAMID. If one takes the length of one of the pyramid's sides at the base, which is 762.24 feet, and then divides it in half (at the point of the hollowing-in of the masonry), one obtains the figure 381.12'. We now take this 381.12' and divide it into 616.7'. (the pyramids apothem, or length of one of its sides from ground to peak). This calculation gives us the figure 1.618, or Phi.

RESTORATION AND UPKEEP. Although it would be nearly impossible to restore this pyramid to its former splendor, there are however, many refurbishing projects which can be undertaken to partially rejuvenate some of the more important areas of the monument.

Most of the damage has occurred at the outside of the edifice due to the removal of almost all the protective casing blocks. These blocks were designed to protect the internal layers from the natural forces of wind, rain, sand and humidity. Although these exquisite casing

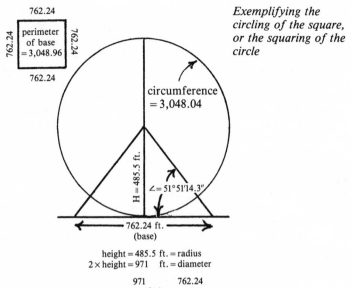

*Exemplifying the
circling of the square,
or the squaring of the
circle*

762.24

perimeter
of base
= 3,048.96

762.24

762.24

762.24

circumference
= 3,048.04

H = 485.5 ft.

∠ = 51°51′14.3″

762.24 ft.
(base)

height = 485.5 ft. = radius
2 × height = 971 ft. = diameter

$$\begin{array}{cc} 971 & 762.24 \\ \times 3.14\ (\pi) & \times 4 \end{array}$$

(circumference of circle) 3,048.94 = 3,048.96 = (perimeter of base)

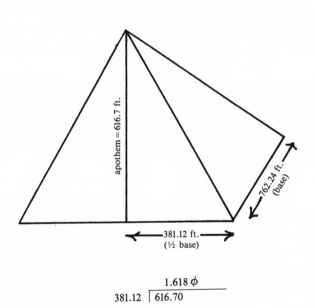

apothem = 616.7 ft.

762.24 ft.
(base)

381.12 ft.
(½ base)

$$381.12\ \overline{)\ \begin{array}{l} 1.618\ \phi \\ 616.70 \end{array}}$$

Pi (top) and phi ratios incorporated into the Great Pyramid of Khufu, Giza.
(J.P. Lepre)

stones can never be replaced, the exterior of the building could, at least, be given a thorough cleaning. There are numerous stone chippings and large piles of accumulated debris and desert sand covering the Pyramid which only succeed in giving it an overall dilapidated appearance.

The interior of the monument is also in need of extensive repair. And as the true glory of this Pyramid is in these internal arrangements, a little work in certain key areas would certainly reap wonderful rewards. The magnificent Grand Gallery, for example, needs to be sand blasted. Built of pure white limestone, it is now browned and blackened, the result of the cumulative soot deposited over the ages from torches and candles. The King's Chamber, too, and its marvelous stone sarcophagus, the granite of both once being of a pink-red, inspiring color, are now nearly black, as are all other parts of the monument.

The original entrance is blocked by an iron door which is padlocked shut, obliging visitors to gain access to the interior of the Pyramid via the cavernous passageway carved by the Arab Caliph Al Mamoun. This original entrance could easily be opened, making a visit to the Pyramid much more enjoyable to the tourist.

Also, the visitors should be made aware in their tour of the building, of the wonderful and profound qualities of this edifice by guides especially trained for this purpose. At present, this is not the case. The old guides should be retrained and new guides hired, as there are hundreds of tourists visiting the Pyramid daily,

and very few guides to assist them.

Finally, there are certain sections within the Pyramid which are off-limits to tourists and to most investigators. The author feels that the entire monument should be made available to those seeking to explore it. The author would also like to see some sort of "Pyramid Foundation" established. This foundation would work in conjunction with the Egyptian Government to partially restore and maintain this first built and last remaining of the Seven Wonders of the Ancient World.*

CURRENT BOOKS ON "PYRAMID POWER." Today there are many books in circulation having to do with "Pyramid Power." All of these books are directly or indirectly the result of numerous investigations and information which has recently come to light regarding the Great Pyramid. Each of these books speak of this monument and various pyramid-shaped models as having the secret power to sharpen razor blades, enhance meditation, preserve food and drink, increase life expectancy and fertility, stimulate the senses, heal and provide many other benefits.

The author may not believe that this power emanates from the Great Pyramid or pyramid-type structures, but neither does he deny the existence of such a power. At any rate, it must be emphasized that this power is not the main issue regarding this edifice. For if such a power does exist, it is of minimal importance in the study and understanding of far deeper properties attributed to this miracle of stone masonry. This does not mean to say that the author is critical of such

*The Seven Wonders of the Ancient World: 1. The Great Pyramid of Giza (Egypt); 2. The Lighthouse of Alexandria (Egypt); 3. The Colossus of Rhodes (Greece); 4. The Statue of the Olympian Zeus (Greece); 5. The Mausoleum of Halicarnassus (Asia Minor); 6. The Temple of Diana at Ephesus (Asia Minor); 7. The Hanging Gardens of Babylon (Iraq).

Giza Complex. (P. SMYTH)

literature on the subject, but that he would have the reader be aware that there is much more to the nature of this pyramid than these books present to the public. Surely, the study of this monument should not be treated so one-sidedly.

Pyramid: Khufu. *Name:* Luminous Horizon. *Number:* 5. *Exterior photos:* yes. *Interior photos:* yes. *Cross-sectional diagram:* yes. *Plan diagram:* yes. *Pyramid field:* Giza. *Field number:* III. *Length:* 763 ft.

Height: 485 ft. *Angle:* 51 degrees, 51 minutes. *Type:* True. *Materials:* limestone. *Location of entrance:* north face. *Portcullises:* three vertical, red granite. *Chambers:* five.

Pyramid Complex: Khufu. *Main pyramid:* yes. *Satellite pyramid(s):* yes — three (nos. 6, 7 & 8). *Mortuary temple:* yes — fragments. *Valley temple:* not found?. *Offering shrine:* no — destroyed. *Mastaba(s):* yes — scores. *Ship(s):* yes — one (142 ft. long). *Ship pit(s):* yes — six. *Causeway:* yes —

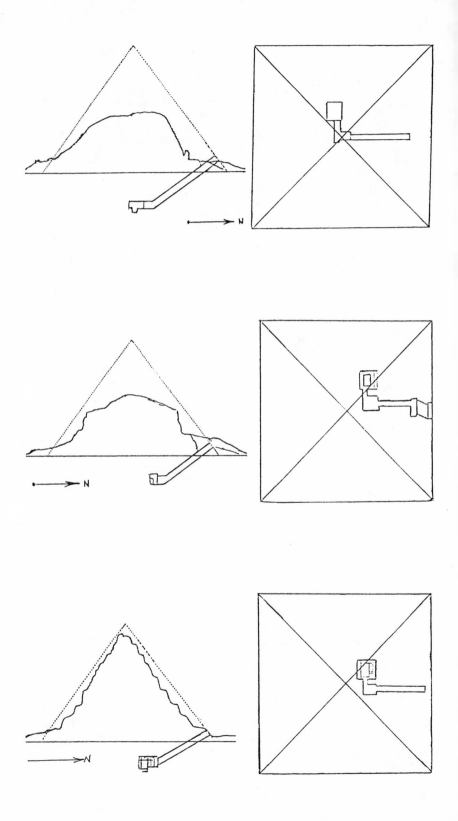

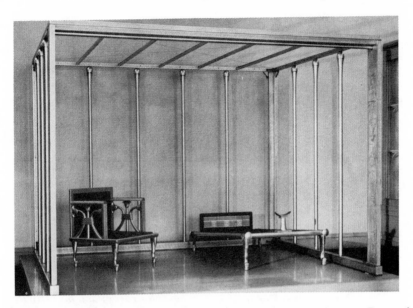

Funerary furniture of Queen Hetepheres. (Museum of Fine Arts, Boston)

fragments. *Temenos wall:* destroyed. *Canal:* destroyed.

North Satellite Pyramid: Khufu. *Name:* Pyramid Queen Mertityotes. *Number:* 6. *Exterior photos:* yes. *Interior photos:* no. *Cross-sectional diagram:* yes. *Plan diagram:* yes. *Pyramid field:* Giza. *Field number:* III. *Length:* 140 ft. *Height:* approx. 90 ft. (now 20 ft.) *Angle:* 51 degrees. *Type:* true. *Materials:* limestone. *Location of entrance:* north face. *Portcullises:* no. *Chambers:* two. *Comments:* This pyramid has a small mortuary temple on its east side, and a boat pit on its south side.

Central Satellite Pyramid: Khufu. *Name:* Pyramid Princess Hotpheres. *Number:* 7. *Exterior photos:* yes. *Interior photos:* no. *Cross-sectional diagram:* yes. *Plan diagram:* yes. *Pyramid field:* Giza. *Field number:*

III. *Length:* 145 ft. *Height:* approx. 95 ft. (now 30 ft.) *Angle:* 52 degrees. *Type:* true. *Materials:* limestone. *Location of entrance:* north face. *Portcullises:* no. *Chambers:* two. *Comments:* This pyramid has a small mortuary temple on its east side.

South Satellite Pyramid: Khufu. *Name:* Pyramid Queen Henutsen. *Number:* 8. *Exterior photos:* yes. *Interior photos:* no. *Cross-sectional diagram:* yes. *Plan diagram:* yes. *Pyramid field:* Giza. *Field number:* III. *Length:* 143 ft. *Height:* approx. 93 ft. (now 35 ft.) *Angle:* 51 degrees. *Type:* true. *Materials:* limestone. *Location of entrance:* north face. *Portcullises:* no. *Chambers:* two. *Comments:* This pyramid has a small mortuary temple on its east side, and a boat pit on its south side.

Opposite: *Satellite pyramids of Khufu, Giza.* **Top:** *Northern satellite, cross-section (left) and plan.* **Center:** *Middle satellite, cross-section (left) and plan.* **Bottom:** *Southern satellite, cross-section (left) and plan.* (Author's Improvements on H. Vyse and J. Perring)

QUEEN: HETEPHERES.
Although not a pharaoh, it seems appropriate to here make mention of this honored queen, mother of Khufu and wife of Sneferu. While neither a pyramid nor a mastaba, the unmarked tomb of this famous lady brought much excitement to the archaeological community when it was first penetrated in 1925. It was discovered beneath a 100′ vertical shaft situated near to the northeast corner of the Great Pyramid.

The burial chamber contained her sealed alabaster sarcophagus, but it was found to be empty when opened. This chamber did, however, yield a rich assortment of the queen's personal articles, several of which were of gold, including a beautiful gold-cased armchair and bed frame.

Of this furniture, Dr. I.E.S. Edwards has remarked: "No description can do justice to the artistic excellence and technical perfection of the equipment of Hetepheres; in comparison with its exquisite simplicity of design, much of the tomb furniture used in later periods seems tawdry."

PHARAOH 9: REDEDEF.
Position in dynasty: Second. *Portrait:* yes. *Length of reign:* 8 years. *Dates of reign:* 2766–2759 B.C. *Mummy:* not found. *Sarcophagus:* none?*. *Burial chamber:* none. *Treasure:* not found. *Hawk name:* Kheper (Creator). *Vulture-and-Cobra name:* ?. *Set or Hawk-of-Nubi name:* ?. *Reed-and-Hornet name:* Tet-f-ra (Djedefre) (The Sun-God Establishes Him). *Son-of-the-Sun-God (Ra) name:* none. *Other names:* Radafra; Ragosis; Ratoise; Ratoises.

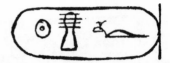

Pharaoh Rededef and his cartouche.

The son of Khufu, and supposed renegade heir to the throne, this king declined to build his pyramid beside his father's great colossus at Giza, and chose a lonely site two miles to the north at Abu Roash. Built on a lofty spur of the desert plateau, and approached by a magnificent mile-long causeway, this pyramid was ambitiously sheathed in red granite rather than limestone. It is doubtful, though, that the monument was ever completed. At any rate, whatever work was done on the monument was undone in subsequent ages by unscrupulous rulers who systematically stripped the edifice of all of its fine granite blocks. Petrie states that in 1881, 300 camel loads a day were being removed from the site.

Although little is known of this obscure pharaoh, archaeologists were fortunate enough to have discovered

---

*Petrie discovered a few curved granite fragments in the trench of this pyramid which may have been part of an oval, granite sarcophagus similar to Eke's at Zawaiyet el-Aryan.

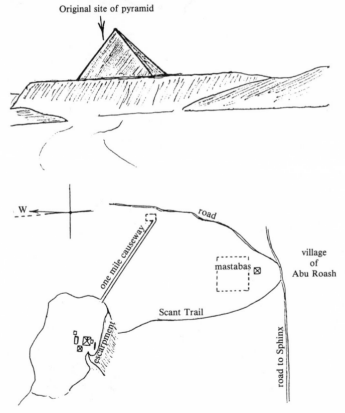

Top and center: *Mountain of Abu Roash — site of destroyed Pyramid of Rededef.* **Bottom:** *Pyramid of Rededef and surroundings, Abu Roash: Plan.* (J.P. LEPRE)

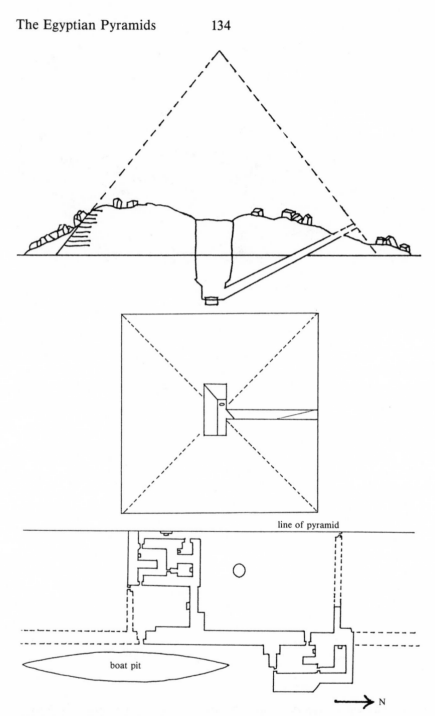

line of pyramid

boat pit

N

Pyramid of Rededef, Abu Roash. **Top:** *Cross-section.* **Center:** *Plan.* **Bottom:** *Plan of mortuary temple.* (J.P. LEPRE)

three beautiful statuette heads of the king buried beneath the rubble of a boat pit just east of the pyramid.

It was only several years ago that the remnants of this pharaoh's valley temple were accidentally discovered by a group of workmen from the town of Abu Roash. Excavation of this building is presently in progress.

Although Rededef was his Reed-and-Hornet name, his Hawk name was Kheper, "Creator." Aside from his pyramid and certain articles found at the site, few artifacts of his reign have survived. At his pyramid were discovered a large sandstone head of the king (now held by the Louvre Museum), ivory lions and other objects. There is also a small, green glazed plaque with his name recorded; but, more importantly, his hieroglyphic cartouche is inscribed on a block of stone at the site of the Pyramid of Eke, at Zawaiyet el-Aryan. The presence of his Fourth Dynasty name at a Third Dynasty site leads one to suspect that Rededef may have built the pyramid there, and that it did not belong to Eke. Although this train of thought is highly speculative, it is nevertheless supported by the fact that the rare oval sarcophagus of the Zawaiyet el-Aryan Pyramid is remarkably like that of King Khafra (post Rededef—Fourth Dynasty). Also, the Pyramid of Eke at Zawaiyet el-Aryan is similar to Rededef's at Abu Roash, in that both employed the trench rather than tunnel system of positioning the burial chamber and subterranean portions. The ambitious nature of the Zawaiyet el-Aryan pyramid, and the huge size of the granite blocks used therein, also point to a Fourth Dynasty conception. In light of these associations, Rededef may well have built the Unfinished Pyramid at Zawaiyet el-Aryan, which is currently assigned to Eke.

Although that pyramid has been temporarily assigned to Eke, Dynasty III, it may well have to be reassigned to Rededef, Dynasty IV, after a more thorough examination of both sites has been accomplished.

Pyramid: Rededef. *Name:* High One of Djedefre. *Number:* 3. *Exterior photos:* no. *Interior photos:* no. *Cross-sectional diagram:* yes. *Plan diagram:* yes. *Pyramid field:* Abu Roash (Abu Rawwash). *Field number:* II. *Length:* approx. 300 ft. *Height:* approx. 200 ft. *Angle:* ?. *Type:* true? *Materials:* granite casing, limestone core. *Location of entrance:* north. *Portcullises:* none. *Chambers:* one?.

Pyramid Complex: Rededef. *Main pyramid:* yes. *Satellite pyramid(s):* yes—one (pyramid no. 4) *Mortuary temple:* yes—fragments. *Valley temple:* yes—presently under excavation. *Offering shrine:* ?. *Mastaba(s):* yes—one. *Ship(s):* none. *Ship pit(s):* yes—one. *Causeway:* yes. *Temenos wall:* yes—fragments. *Canal:* destroyed. *Comments:* There are no published reports concerning Rededef's satellite pyramid.

Satellite Pyramid: Rededef. *Name:* Pyramid Queen Khentetenka. *Number:* 4. *Exterior photos:* no (sketch). *Interior photos:* no. *Cross-sectional diagram:* no. *Plan diagram:* no. *Pyramid field:* Abu Roash. *Field number:* II. *Length:* ?. *Height:* ?. *Angle:* ?. *Type:* true? *Materials:* limestone. *Location of entrance:* ?. *Portcullises:* ?. *Chambers:* one?. *Comments:* No record of investigation; author examined site 1/19/87. No trace of pyramid. Large mastaba to the west is visible.

PHARAOH 10: KHAFRA.
Position in dynasty: Third. *Portrait:* yes. *Length of reign:* 18 years. *Dates of reign:* 2758–2742 B.C. *Mummy:* not found. *Sarcophagus:*

Pharaoh Khafra and his cartouche. (CAIRO MUSEUM)

red granite. *Burial chamber:* yes?. *Treasure:* not found. *Hawk name:* Userib (Strong-Heart). *Vulture-and-Cobra name:* Rehotpe (Satisfaction of the Sun-God. *Set or Hawk-of-Nubi name:* Sekhem (Ruler). *Reed-and-Hornet name:* Khafra (The Sun-God in His Glory). *Son-of-the-Sun-God (Ra) name:* none. *Other names:* Chephre; Khefre; Hotpere; Suph; Userhati.

Although the pyramid of this pharaoh is of slightly smaller dimensions (15' shorter) than the adjacent pyramid of his brother, Khufu, it gives the illusion of being taller because it is built on higher ground.

The mortuary temple of this pharaoh (now razed) was a massive structure measuring 330' long by 150' wide. He is also credited with the construction of the Temple of the Sphinx (see pages 123–124) and of the Great Sphinx statue itself (it having been carved in his image). His is also the famed diorite statue (now in the Cairo Museum) found in a pit full of rubble in his valley temple.

An unusual, but not unique, feature found in this pharaoh's burial chamber is that the sarcophagus is sunk into the floor, not set upon it.

Immediately west of the pyramid lie the rock-cut barracks which once

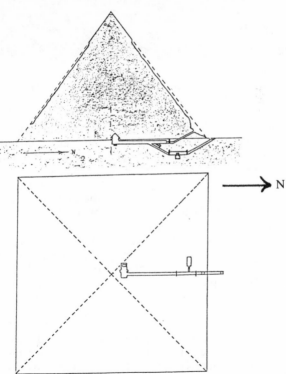

Pyramid of Khafra, Giza. **Top:** *Photo.* (A. FAKHRY) **Center:** *Cross-section.* (H. VYSE AND J. PERRING) **Bottom:** *Plan.* (J.P. LEPRE)

housed the pyramid workmen. Petrie tells us that they consisted of 91 spacious chambers capable of housing perhaps 4,000 men.

Khafra was this pharaoh's Reed-and-Hornet name, whereas his Hawk name was Userib (Userhati), "Strong-heart." His Hawk-of-Nubi name

Pyramid Khafra, Giza, showing packing blocks at lower end and remaining casing stones at top level. (J.P. LEPRE)

(unusually written with *three* hawks over the Nubi sign) was Sekhem, "Ruler," and his Vulture-and-Cobra name was Rehotpe, "Satisfaction of the Sun God."

The Turin Papyrus assigns him a reign of 18 years, and he legalized his accession to the throne by marrying Meritsenkh, Khufu's daughter and his own niece.

Besides Khafra's mortuary and valley temples—typical parts of a pyramid complex—he is credited with erecting two other temples as well. One is a much-ruined building at Bubastis and the other is the famous Temple of the Sphinx, adjacent to the King's Valley Temple. The latter has long been associated with King Khafra; but as has been pointed out in my discussion of this temple's relationship with that of the mortuary temple of Khufu, that long-accepted theory needs to be seriously questioned. (See pages 123–126.) The relationship of King Khafra to the

giant Sphinx statue itself is somewhat more obvious due to Khafra's close physical resemblance to the Sphinx, but any direct relationship between Khafra and the Temple of the Sphinx—other than their close proximity—is more doubtful.

Maceheads of Khafra were found at his mortuary temple; but aside from these and other scant remains (some scarab and cylinder seals and sealings), other artifacts are lacking. Indeed, the bulk of any physical remains which we have of this pharaoh—other than his pyramid and the temples themselves—are the numerous statues and statue-fragments which were discovered in the pyramid temples. More than 50 larger-than-life stone statues of Khafra were said to be housed there.

Historians tell us that Khafra was as detested in his time as was his brother Khufu, for the populace very much disliked the prolonged,

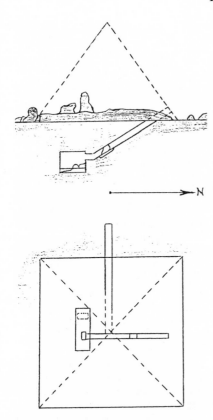

Subsidiary pyramid of Khafra, Giza:
Cross-section (top) and plan. (J.P.
LEPRE)

conscripted labor which existed at
the larger pyramid sites.

So often among historians Khufu
and Khafra are described as being
father and son, but the facts unreservedly point to them being
brothers. The hieroglyphic text cites
Menkara as stating that Khufu and
Khafra were his father and his uncle.
If they were father and son to one
another, then Menkara would have
described them as "my father and my
brother" or "my father and my
grandfather."

In respect to any apparent contradictions between the original hieroglyphic texts and the recordings of
both classical and modern historians,
I would unhesitatingly give more
credence to the former.

Pyramid: Khafra. *Name:* Khafra
is Great. *Number:* 9. *Exterior
photos:* yes. *Interior photos:* yes.
Cross-sectional diagram: yes. *Plan
diagram:* yes. *Pyramid field:* Giza.
Field number: III. *Length:* 707 ft.
Height: 471 ft. *Angle:* 52 degrees, 20
minutes. *Type:* true. *Materials:*
limestone core; limestone and granite
casing. *Location of entrance:* two —
one on north face; one on north
ground. *Portcullises:* three — one
upper corridor, vertical granite; two
lower corridor, vertical granite.
Chambers: two. *Comments:* Volume
= 78 million cu. ft.

Pyramid Complex: Khafra. *Main
pyramid:* yes. *Satellite pyramid(s):*
yes — one (pyramid no. 10). *Mortuary
temple:* yes — fragments. *Valley temple:* yes — well preserved. *Offering
shrine:* destroyed. *Mastaba(s):*
yes — scores. *Ship(s):* no. *Ship pit(s):*
yes — five. *Causeway:* yes. *Temenos
wall:* yes — fragments. *Canal:*
destroyed.

Satellite Pyramid: Khafra. *Name:*
Pyramid　Queen　Mertenkhes.
Number: 10. *Exterior photos:* yes
(aerial). *Interior photos:* no. *Cross-
sectional diagram:* yes. *Plan
diagram:* yes. *Pyramid field:* Giza.
Field number: III. *Length:* 65 ft.
Height: approx. 40 ft. (now razed).
Angle: 52 degrees. *Type:* true.
Materials: limestone. *Location of
entrance:* 2) north face and west
ground. *Portcullises:* none?. *Chambers:* one. *Comments:* Second
(western) entrance is not depicted in
diagram.

PHARAOH 11: SHERO.
No pyramid for this pharaoh.
Position in dynasty: Fourth. *Por-
trait:* no. *Length of reign:* 1 year.
Dates of reign: 2741–2740 B.C.

Mummy: not found. *Sarcophagus:* none. *Burial chamber:* not found. *Treasure:* not found. *Hawk name:* ?. *Vulture-and-Cobra name:* ?. *Set or Hawk-of-Nubi name:* Shero. *Reed-and-Hornet name:* ?. *Son-of-the-Sun-God (Ra) name:* none. *Other names:* Sheiru.

Cartouche of Pharaoh Shero.

Surprisingly enough, this pharaoh, son of the great Khafra, built neither a pyramid nor a mastaba worthy of any note. Although this may seem strange in a dynasty that produced the three great pyramids at Giza, it is not too difficult to understand in light of the fact that this pharaoh enjoyed a reign of only one year (hardly enough time to build a monument of any substantial size).

Very little is known of this king, except for an inscription at El-Kab, which gives his Hawk-of-Nubi title, Shero. He is assigned his position in the Fourth Dynasty because his short tenure seems to coincide with the reign of a pharaoh whose obliterated name appears during that era in the Turin Papyrus King List.

PHARAOH 12: MENKARA.
Position in dynasty: Fifth. *Portrait:* yes. *Length of reign:* 18 years. *Dates of reign:* 2739–2722 B.C. *Mummy:* fragments only found. *Sarcophagus:* yes — basalt. *Burial chamber:* yes. *Treasure:* not found. *Hawk name:* Kekhet (The Bull-God in the Flesh). *Vulture-and-Cobra name:* Ke (The Bull). *Set or Hawk-of-Nubi name:* ?. *Reed-and-Hornet name:* Menkeure (Menkara) (Establishing the Spirits of the Sun-God). *Son-of-the-Sun-God (Ra) name:* none. *Other names:* Menchere; Mykeri.

The son of Khufu and nephew of Khafra, this pharaoh's true worth lies not in the size of his pyramid (as its 9 million cubic feet of masonry is dwarfed by the neighboring pyramids of his father and uncle — 94 million and 78 million, respectively), but in the fact that he attempted the ambitious project of sheathing his monument, at least partially — and perhaps fully — in granite rather than limestone. Because he died prematurely, though, his causeway, valley and mortuary temples were finished in mud-brick rather than limestone by his son and successor, Shepseskaf.

Menkara's beautiful basalt sarcophagus, a drawing of which is included in this portfolio, was unfortunately lost at sea in a storm off the coast of England in 1837, while en route to the British Museum.

The pyramid of this pharaoh is noteworthy in having some of its *in situ* casing stones, on the north side of the monument, still equipped with the construction bosses or lugs left there by the quarriers at Aswan.

Although, officially, both Herodotus and Diodorus state that Menkara was the son of Khufu, this could well be yet another corruption of the true historical account. For while the physical resemblance of Menkara to Khufu is slight, his resemblance to Khafra is more familial. Could Menkara be the son of Khafra, then, and not of Khufu? If so, when Menkara spoke of these kings as being "my father and my uncle," he was referring to Khafra, then Khufu, and not to Khufu, then Khafra.

Pharaoh Menkara. (MUSEUM OF FINE ARTS, BOSTON)

For the present, though, as far as the records are concerned, we will allow Khufu, not Khafra, to be listed as the father of Menkara.

Menkara was known as a far more beneficient king than his two megalomaniac predecessors; and it was recorded that he reopened all of the temples in Egypt which Khufu had closed. In this regard, the ancient Egyptians praised him more than any other king. Indeed, the amount of work projects under his reign was only a fraction of what had previously occurred during the tenures of Khufu and Khafra. He was thereby known as a fair king with a mild disposition.

The Turin Papyrus gives him a reign of 18 years and 4 months, and this indicates further — given the particular era and the achievements of his predecessors — that he had ample time to construct a much larger pyramid, but declined to do so; so that he was, as he is so often described, of a less ambitious nature.

Several statue heads and triads have been found of Menkara in his pyramid temple. Among these was a little headless ivory figurine (Boston); a fine alabaster piece (Cairo Museum); the torso of a statue revealing fine craftsmanship; several unfinished statues found by Reisner; another statuette (University College, London); and four triads of Menkara with the province goddesses of Egypt.

Also found at the pyramid site were some scarabs, cylinder-seals and sealings, and a piece of a wand.

Pyramid: Menkara. *Name:* Divine is Menkara. *Number:* 12. *Exterior photos:* yes. *Interior photos:* yes. *Cross-sectional diagram:* yes. *Plan diagram:* yes. *Pyramid field:* Giza. *Field number:* III. *Length:* 356 ft. *Height:* 218 ft. *Angle:* 51 degrees. *Type:* true. *Materials:* limestone core; granite casing. *Location of*

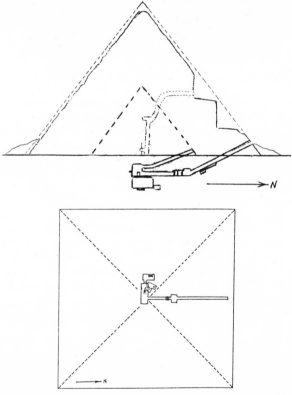

Pyramid of Menkara, Giza: **Top:** *Photo shows ruined mortuary temple to the left.* (A. FAKHRY) **Center:** *Cross-section.* (AUTHOR'S IMPROVEMENT ON H. VYSE AND J. PERRING) **Bottom:** *Plan.* (AUTHOR'S IMPROVEMENT ON H. VYSE AND J. PERRING)

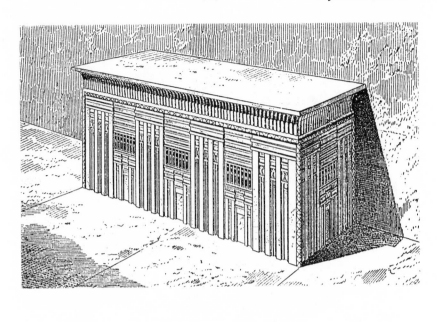

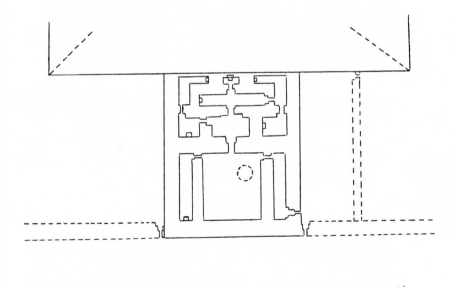

Top: *Basalt sarcophagus of Menkara, Dynasty IV.* (G. Perrot and C. Chipiez) **Bottom:** *Mortuary temple, Menkara's eastern satellite pyramid, Giza.* (J.P. Lepre)

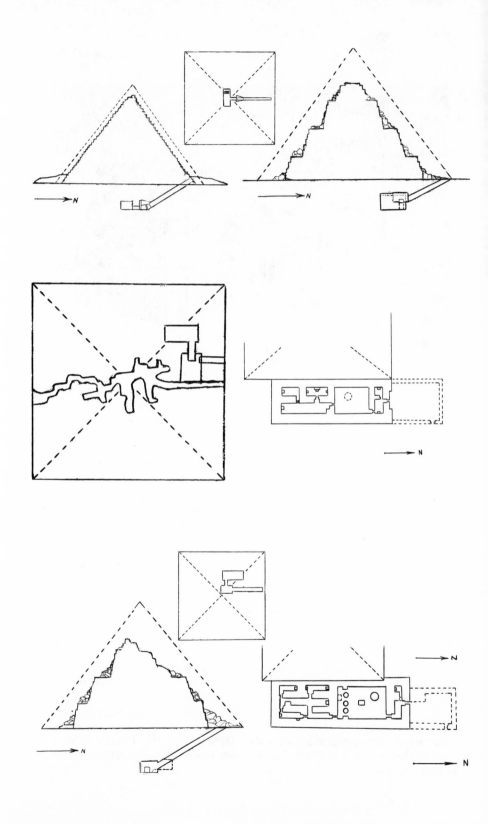

entrance: north face. *Portcullises:* three vertical, red granite. *Chambers:* three. *Comments:* Volume = 9 million cubic feet. **Pyramid Complex: Menkara.** *Main pyramid:* yes. *Satellite pyramid(s):* yes—three (pyramid nos. 13, 14 and 15). *Mortuary temple:* yes—fragments. *Valley temple:* yes—fragments. *Offering shrine:* destroyed. *Mastaba(s):* yes—several. *Ship(s):* none. *Ship pit(s):* none. *Causeway:* yes—fragments. *Temenos wall:* yes—fragments. *Canal:* destroyed.

Western Satellite Pyramid: Menkara. *Name:* Pyramid Princess?. *Number:* 13. *Exterior photos:* yes. *Interior photos:* no. *Cross-sectional diagram:* yes. *Plan diagram:* yes. *Pyramid field:* Giza. *Field number:* III. *Length:* 110 ft. *Height:* 65 ft.? (now 30 ft.) *Angle:* approx. 53 degrees. *Type:* true. *Materials:* limestone core, never cased. *Location of entrance:* north face. *Portcullises:* none. *Chambers:* two. *Comments:* This pyramid has a mortuary temple on its east side.

Central Satellite Pyramid: Menkara. *Name:* Pyramid Princess Maetkhe. *Number:* 14. *Exterior photos:* yes. *Interior photos:* no. *Cross-sectional diagram:* yes. *Plan diagram:* yes. *Pyramid field:* Giza. *Field number:* III. *Length:* 110 ft. *Height:* 65 ft.? (now 30 ft.) *Angle:* approx. 53 degrees. *Type:* true. *Materials:* limestone core, never cased. *Location of entrance:* north face. *Portcullises:* no. *Chambers:* two. *Comments:* Small red granite sarcophagus and skeleton of a young woman found in burial chamber; mortuary temple on east side of pyramid.

Eastern Satellite Pyramid: Menkara. *Name:* Pyramid Queen Khamerernebty II. *Number:* 15. *Exterior photos:* yes. *Interior photos:* no. *Cross-sectional diagram:* yes. *Plan diagram:* yes. *Pyramid field:* Giza. *Field number:* III. *Length:* 117 ft. *Height:* 75 ft.? (now 35 ft.) *Angle:* approx. 53 degrees. *Type:* true. *Materials:* limestone core, granite casing. *Location of entrance:* north face. *Portcullises:* no. *Chambers:* one. *Comments:* Red granite sarcophagus found in burial chamber; mortuary temple on east side of pyramid.

PHARAOH 13: SHEPSESKAF.
No pyramid for this pharaoh.
Position in dynasty: Sixth. *Portrait:* yes. *Length of reign:* 4 years. *Dates of reign:* 2721–2718 B.C. *Mummy:* not found. *Sarcophagus:* black basalt. *Burial chamber:* yes?. *Treasure:* not found. *Hawk name:* Shepses. *Vulture-and-Cobra name:* ?. *Set or Hawk-of-Nubi name:* ?. *Reed-and-Hornet name:* Shepseskaf. *Son-of-the-Sun-God (Ra) name:* none. *Other names:* Asychis; Seberchere; Sepercheres; Shepseskafra; Shepseskef; Shepseskefre.

This sixth pharaoh of the Fourth Dynasty, son of Menkara, deviated from building his tomb in the traditional pyramid style of that era, and constructed a mastaba of huge proportions. Yet this remarkable Mastabet Fara'un (Mastaba of the

Opposite: Satellite Pyramids of Menkara, Giza. **Top:** *Eastern satellite cross-section (inset: plan) at left; middle satellite cross-section at right.* **Center:** *Middle satellite plan (at left) and mortuary temple plan.* **Bottom:** *Western satellite cross-section (inset: plan) at left, and mortuary temple plan.* (MIDDLE MORTUARY TEMPLE PLAN, J.P. LEPRE; ALL OTHERS, AUTHOR'S IMPROVEMENT OF H. VYSE AND J. PERRING.)

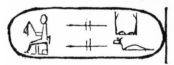

Top: *Pharaoh Shepseskaf and his cartouche.* (HEAD: MUSEUM OF FINE ARTS, BOSTON.) **Bottom:** *Mastaba of Shepseskaf (Mastabet Fara'un).* (C. LAGIER)

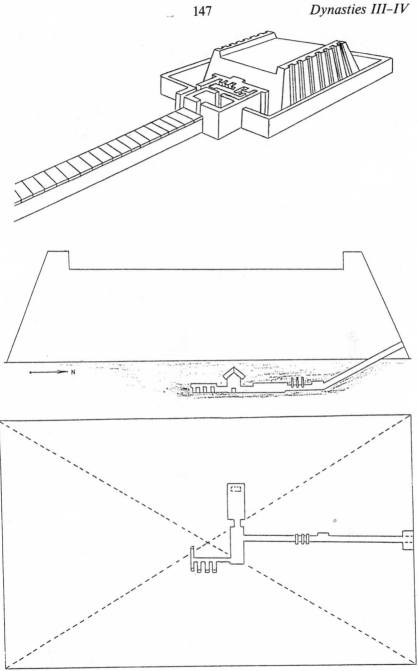

Mastaba of Shepseskaf (Mastabet Fara'un). **Top:** *Reconstructed drawing.*
Center: *Cross-section.* **Bottom:** *Plan.* (J.P. LEPRE)

Pharaoh), as it is called, was not a mastaba in the true sense, but was shaped rather in the form of an Old Kingdom sarcophagus, being 335' long and 235' wide. The internal arrangement, however, was quite similar to that of a pyramid, and for that reason, this curious-looking monument is included in this text.

The Palermo Stone tells us that in this king's first year two religious festivals were held. It also states that he selected the site for his pyramid at this time and entitled that future pyramid "The Place of Refreshment."

Although the heyday of great pyramid building was just toning down, the hieroglyphic records relate that during Shepseskaf's reign money was scarce and commerce curtailed. In this declining atmosphere, the practice was initiated whereby a person needing a substantial loan pledged his father's "body" (family tomb) as collateral.

Only a few statue heads have been found of Shepseskaf, along with a single scarab and sealing. It is evident by the scarcity of material from his reign that the strength of this great dynasty was rapidly waning.

Mastaba: Shepseskaf. *Name:* Qebh (Pure is Shepseskaf). *Number:* 60*. *Exterior photos:* yes. *Interior photos:* yes. *Cross-sectional diagram:* yes. *Plan diagram:* yes. *Pyramid field:* South Sakkara. *Field number:* VII. *Length:* rectangular 330 ft. by 235 ft. *Height:* 60 ft. *Angle:* 65 degrees. *Type:* sarcophagus shaped. *Materials:* limestone, with granite skirting. *Location of entrance:* north face. *Portcullises:* three vertical, red granite. *Chambers:* two.

*For the sake of simplicity, although it is not a pyramid per se, we have assigned this monument Pyramid no. 60.

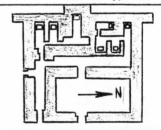

Mastaba of Shepseskaf (Mastabet Fara'un). **From the top:** *Antechamber; Burial chamber* (F. FIRTH); *Plan of mortuary temple* (J.P. LEPRE).

Pharaoh Imhotep (?) and his cartouche. (HEAD: FREER GALLERY OF ART).

Mastaba Complex: Shepseskaf. *Main mastaba:* yes. *Satellite pyramid(s):* no. *Mortuary temple:* yes—destroyed. *Valley temple:* yes—not yet excavated. *Offering shrine:* no. *Mastaba(s):* no. *Ship(s):* no. *Ship pit(s):* no. *Causeway:* yes. *Temenos wall:* yes—two. *Canal:* destroyed.

CHRONOLOGICAL RECKONING OF ANCIENT EGYPT. Although Cyril Aldred's chronology has been telescopically referred to as a source with which to define the position of the head of the Pharaoh Imhotep (Dy-

nasty IV), his over-all chronology differs considerably from my own. This difference is attributed to our having referred to separate sources for chronological reckoning. This supposed discrepancy can be explained, however, through the following quote from Sir E.A. Wallis Budge, contained in his text entitled *The Mummy* (1894). In his section on the Ancient Egyptian Chronology, Budge enlightens the reader to the fact that: "The chronology of Egypt has been, and must be for some time yet, a subject of difficulty and of variety of opinion. The fixed points in Egyptian history are so few and the gaps between them so great, that it is quite impossible to establish an accurate system of chronology: approximate dates are all that can be hoped for at present. Nearly every student of Egyptian chronology arrives at conclusions different from any of his predecessors, and how widely different they are is seen from the fact that the date given for Menes by Champollion-Figeac is 5867 B.C. by Bockh 5702, by Bunsen 3623, by Lepsius 3892, by Lieblein 3893, by Mariette 5004, and by Brugsch 4400."

For the reason just cited by Budge, my reckoning is quite different than that put forth by Aldred; and although Budge wrote this account nearly 100 years ago, the wide disparity of opinions from various authors and Egyptologists is as prominent as ever.

My own chronological account is based on that established by Sir Arthur Weigall. Throughout the entire length of his 600-page *History of the Pharaohs* (vols. I and II), he brilliantly and painstakingly addresses the entire chronology of ancient Egypt through his reconstruction and comparisons of the various king lists and numerous secondary sources. No other Egyptologist, to my knowledge, has ever devoted so much time and energy to such a comprehensive study of the entirety of the ancient chronology; and for this reason, I have chosen to adjust my dates to those of this exemplary scholar, whom I consider to be the authoritative source in this particular area of Egyptology.

PHARAOH 14: IMHOTEP.
No pyramid for this pharaoh.
Position in dynasty: Seventh (last).
Portrait: yes?*. *Length of reign:* 2 years. *Dates of reign:* 2717–2716 B.C. *Mummy:* not found. *Sarcophagus:* not found. *Burial chamber:* not found. *Treasure:* not found. *Hawk name:* ?. *Vulture-and-Cobra name:* ?. *Set or Hawk-of-Nubi name:* ?. *Reed-and-Hornet name:* Imhetep (Imhotep). *Son-of-the-Sun-God (Ra) name:* none. *Other names:* Djedef-Ptah (Thampthis); Hurdadef?; Iamphth; Iemhotpe.

Not to be confused with the Third Dynasty Imhotep, architect of the Step Pyramid of Djoser, this little-known last pharaoh of the Fourth Dynasty did not build a pyramid or a mastaba of any note, most likely because of his short (two-year) tenure on the throne. He may be the very same Hurdadef, a brother to Shepseskaf, his predecessor, but this

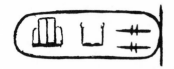

Cartouche of Queen Khentkawes.

identification cannot be ascertained until additional evidence is forthcoming. At any rate, however, in the words of A. Weigall (*History of the Pharaohs,* p. 189), "With his death the dynasty, which had begun in such splendour, collapsed in ignominy."

QUEEN: KHENTKAWES.
Position in dynasty: Not a pharaoh; contemporary with Seventh Pharaoh Imhotep. *Portrait:* no. *Length of reign, Dates of reign:* did not reign. *Mummy:* not found. *Sarcophagus:* not found. *Burial chamber:* yes. *Treasure:* not found. *Hawk name:* none. *Vulture-and-Cobra name:* none. *Set or Hawk-of-Nubi name:* none. *Reed-and-Hornet name:* none. *Son-of-the-Sun-God (Ra) name:* none. *Other names:* unknown.

It seems appropriate to mention the odd-shaped tomb of this queen in this text of pyramids, as it is often referred to as the Eleventh Pyramid at Giza (or the Fourth of Khufu, or the Fourth of Menkara). In reality, and for purposes of clarification, it

---

*Cyril Aldred, in his book, *Egyptian Art,* describes the head on page 149 as that of an "unknown king" and dates it at "c. 2525 B.C." He goes on to date the famous granite head of King Userkaf at "c. 2520 B.C." Now, as Userkaf is indisputably classified as the first pharaoh of the Fifth Dynasty, then the above-mentioned head of an "unknown king" (due to the exact chronological dates just cited) must represent that of the last pharaoh of the Fourth Dynasty. By this reckoning the head is therefore attributed to the Pharaoh Imhotep, who occupied that slot in the register of that dynasty. Even if the chronology cited by Aldred should prove to be slightly flexible, the head in question must still be attributed to Imhotep, for it certainly does not in any way resemble the known head of the pharaoh who preceded Imhotep (King Shepseskaf), King Userkaf, or the pharaoh who succeeded Userkaf (King Sahure). It rather has distinct facial features of its own, and no doubt represents yet another pharaoh, who again, according to Aldred's exact dating, can be none other than the obscure Imhotep.

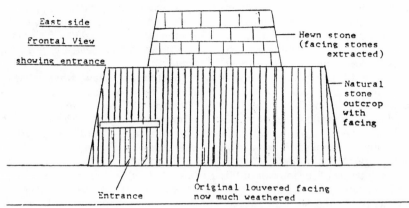

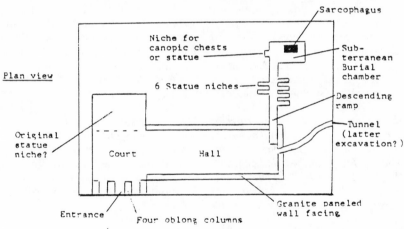

Tomb of Queen Khentkawes, Giza. (J.P. Lepre)

must be emphasized that it is not a pyramid per se, but merely in the shape of a ruined pyramid, due to its sheathing stones having been extracted. Originally, it was in the shape of an enormous sarcophagus, designed in much the same manner as the tomb of the Queen's brother, Shepseskaf, the pharaoh within whose reign this monument was built. The "palace facade" design, which was popular with some Old Kingdom sarcophagi, can still be seen on some of the remaining lower casing stones of this building (south side).

L. Cottrell, in *The Lost Pharaohs,* p. 98, makes the mistake of referring to this monument as a pyramid: "Not far from the row of Kheop's [Khufu's] Queen's pyramids was found the base of a 4th unfinished pyramid." He then speaks of "the 4 pyramids which Kheops built for his queens," (p. 102).

G.A. Reisner (in *Egyptian Architecture*, p. 101, by Smith) makes the very same mistake, stating that "southeast of the Pyramid of Menkara are the foundations of an unfinished pyramid." But Dr. Fakhry, in his book *The Pyramids*, p. 155, corrects this error by telling us that "Hassan calls her (Queen Khentkawes) tomb a pyramid, and terms it the 'fourth pyramid' (at Giza). . . . It is, however, impossible to call this building a pyramid—the word describes a specific geometrical form and cannot be applied to every royal tomb, regardless of its design." From an examination of the interior of this tomb, we can readily see that it is unlike any pyramid design and that the statement of Dr. Fakhry is entirely correct.

Quite recently (1984), a second monument of this queen—a true pyramid—was discovered at Abu Sir by a Czechoslovak expedition.

Pyramid: Queen Khentkawes. *Name:* Queen Khentkawes. *Number:* 24. *Exterior photos:* no. *Interior photos:* no. *Cross-sectional diagram:* no. *Plan diagram:* no. *Pyramid field:* Abu Sir. *Field number:* V. *Length:* ?. *Height:* ?. *Angle:* ?. *Type:* true?. *Materials:* limestone?. *Location of entrance:* ?. *Portcullises:* ?. *Cham-*

bers: ?. *Comments:* This pyramid is newly discovered (1984).

Pyramid Complex:* Queen Khentkawes. *Main pyramid:* yes?. *Satellite pyramid(s):* ?. *Mortuary temple:* ?. *Valley temple:* ?. *Offering shrine:* ?. *Mastaba(s):* ?. *Ship(s):* ?. *Ship pit(s):* ?. *Causeway:* ?. *Temenos wall:* ?. *Canal:* ?.

Mastaba: Queen Khentkawes. *Name:* Tomb of Queen Khentkawes. *Number:* 11. *Exterior photos:* no. *Interior photos:* no. *Cross-sectional diagram:* no—facade only. *Plan diagram:* yes. *Pyramid field:* Giza. *Field number:* III. *Length:* rectangular; 150 ft. long by 70 ft. wide. *Height:* 40 ft. *Angle:* 78 degrees. *Type:* sarcophagus-shaped. *Materials:* limestone. *Location of entrance:* east side; also with possible western entrance. *Portcullises:* none?. *Chambers:* one? Also interior court and hall.

Mastaba Complex: Queen Khentkawes. *Main mastaba:* yes. *Satellite pyramid(s):* no. *Mortuary temple:* yes—interior. *Valley temple:* yes—destroyed. *Offering shrine:* no?. *Mastaba(s):* no. *Ship(s):* yes—one southwest corner; now missing. *Ship pit(s):* yes—one southwest corner. *Causeway:* yes. *Temenos wall:* no. *Canal:* ?.

*Until more evidence is available concerning this newly discovered (1984) pyramid, we are in the dark as to the exact elements of its pyramid complex, or whether a complex existed at all.

VI. Dynasties V-XI/
(The Decline)

DYNASTY V

• *Duration:* 128 years (2715-2588 B.C.). *Pharaohs:* 1. Userkaf. 2. Sahure. 3. Neferefre. 4 Sisires. 5. Neferirkare. 6. Neuserre. 7. Menkeuhor. 8. Djedkare. 9. Unas.

While the principal pyramids of the middle to late Third Dynasty and early to middle Fourth Dynasty relied upon their awesome volume to thwart the efforts of tomb robbers, and the principal pyramids of the Twelfth and early Thirteenth Dynasty revival period relied upon the complexity of their internal arrangements to achieve that purpose, the pyramids of the Fifth, Sixth, Seventh and Eighth dynasties comprising the period of decline (excluding the aberrant Eleventh Dynasty "pyramid-temple" designs) were so simple in the plan of their passageways and chambers that few, if any, obstacles impeded the ambitious tomb plunderer.

With the older pyramids, the major problem confronting the would-be thief was to deduce exactly where the pharaonic burial chamber might have been located in a monument so vast (although these pyramids were also imbued with a certain complexity of design), while with the Middle Kingdom pyramids, the major problem was in deducing the correct avenue to follow when dealing with a labyrinth of sophisticated passageways, portcullis block-

ing systems, and the possibility of the entrance into the monument being located at any one of its four sides.

Yet with the post-Fourth Dynasty pyramids, there is neither awesome bulk nor complicated arrangement to deal with.

Unlike the earlier pyramids, these later models were quite small in size and, without exception, had their entrances situated on their north side, typically at ground level. Moreover, the plan almost always involved a descending passageway leading to a subterranean section, consisting of a vestibule, three vertical granite portcullises, and then an antechamber, with a three-niche serdab to the east and the burial chamber to the west.

Beginning with Unas, the last king of the Fifth Dynasty, and carrying over through the whole of the Sixth Dynasty, the basic plan just described is the same.

The advent of this extremely simple design immediately follows the period marked by the individuality of each of its pyramid tombs. One possible explanation of this apparent change in methods of design is that the oversimplified plans of these Fifth and Sixth Dynasty pyramids (with only two having been built in the Seventh Dynasty, and one in the Ninth) represent a mere formality of architectural endeavor—cenotaphs or dummy-tombs of a sort—and that the true burial chambers of these several pharaohs are located elsewhere

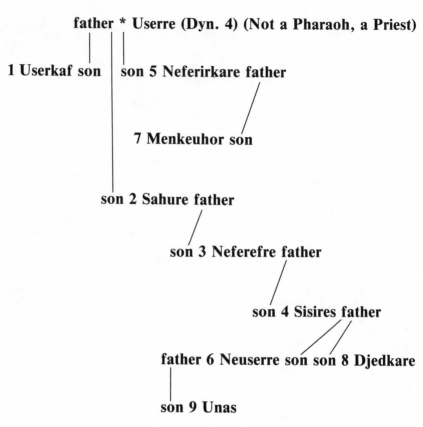

Dynasty V Genealogy

in the monuments, or in other places altogether. At least half of these kings are known to have constructed "sun temples" as well, at nearby Abu Gurab, all of which have since been razed and their foundations covered over by the shifting desert sands.

Could these Fifth and Sixth Dynasty pharaohs have been buried beneath these temples, rather than in their pyramids at Sakkara and Abu Sir? Then again, following the ingenuity and influence of earlier pyramids at Dahshur and Giza, perhaps these Fifth and Sixth Dynasty kings succeeded in devising a complexity in their pyramid plans which

has yet to be detected.

It is practically inconceivable, immediately following such a lengthy period of experimentation and sophistication of internal pyramid plans, that there would have been such a dramatic regression in the ability of the pyramid architects to foster a more ambitious design to stymie the efforts of tomb plunderers.

It is true that the pyramids of the Fifth and Sixth dynasties were much smaller than their predecessors, and this is partially understandable in light of the fact that the resources of these pharaohs were taxed by their additional construction of sun temples and quite large mortuary and valley temples, which were sumptuously decorated with wall reliefs of the highest artistic merit. Nevertheless, it seems inappropriate that the actual burial tombs—from which the entire complex derived its purpose—were so simple and repetitious as to have left little doubt where the burial chamber was located.

The theory that these pyramid pharaohs could have been buried in subterranean crypts connected with their sun temples, rather than in their pyramids, is not without merit. For example, it would appear from the reconstruction of the ground plan of Neferirkare's sun temple that a greater degree of animal sacrificing was done here than at his actual pyramid site; no fewer than ten huge sacrificial basins of alabaster were found situated at the inner court of that temple.

The Fifth and Sixth Dynasty pyramids were also of inferior workmanship compared to the earlier pyramids, with the core comprised of much smaller stones. (As a result, once the sheathing of fine Tura limestone was removed in later times, these pyramids were, for the most part, reduced to mere mounds of rubble and sand.) Much more time and much better materials were devoted to the sun temples and mortuary and valley temples. The carved reliefs comprising Sahure's pyramid complex alone are estimated to have covered over 80,000 square feet, all exquisitely carved and appropriated in subsequent dynasties for inclusion into other temple complexes and sundry building projects.

Reliefs of this kind usually consisted of wildlife scenes, date and palm-tree columns, captive slaves being led in procession, goldsmiths and silversmiths plying their trades, farmers gathering crops, servants bearing diverse provisions, hunting (deer, antelope, hippopotami, etc.), fowling in the marshes, fishing, and so on. All of the above scenes depicted the utopian life that the pharaoh would experience in the next world. The king is often shown trampling his enemies or at a sumptuous feast, where offerings of wine, beer, pigeons, ducks, geese, quail, bread, fruit and vegetables, etc., are in abundance. In the mortuary temple of Pepy II, 100 deities stand before the pharaoh, each carrying the hieroglyphic "ankh," the symbol for life.

Not only was much time and effort devoted to the artistic design of the various temples of these dynasties, but elaborate drainage systems were employed there as well. In Sahure's mortuary temple, rain falling from the roof ran off into stone spouts, while rain falling on the ground was collected by circular cavities, with both outlets directed to channels cut into the stone pavement. Several large stone basins containing lead plugs were located inside the temple for sacrificial purposes, whereby the applied liquid escaped through 1,000′ of copper pipes running beneath the temple floor.

The last of the Fifth and most of the Sixth Dynasty pyramids are popularly known for their pyramid texts which are inscribed into the limestone walls and sometimes highlighted by a blue pigment. Their main purpose was to secure a favorable afterlife for the deceased pharaoh. These texts were thought to contain the power to protect the king from all harm and to insure that he receive the proper nourishment for his daily sustenance. Not only was the king protected in this way, but emphasis was placed on the fact that he was worthy of such attention, so that the various texts represent a repetitious monologue of how fine was the character and benevolence of

Pharaoh Userkaf. **(Egyptian Museum, Cairo)**

Pharoah Userkaf cartouche.

this particular pharaoh in his dealings with his earthly subjects and with the gods of Egypt. The burial chambers of a few of these kings are also noteworthy for having tiny stars painted on their ceilings, symbolic of the pharaoh's association with the astral life.

Although the pyramids of this era—particularly those of the Sixth Dynasty—contained very many reliefs depicting the king in various daily and ceremonial scenes, only a few statues of these monarchs have

survived. Needless to say, the statues were the very first objects to have suffered at the hands of despoilers. That there was once a vast array of such statuary is not to be doubted, however. Not only were there the usual five or more Ka statues placed in the mortuary and valley temples, but likely there were three each in the eastern niches of the pyramids' subterranean galleries, with others having been set up within the vestibules of the various sun temples as well.

PHARAOH 15: USERKAF.
Position in dynasty: First. *Portrait:* yes. *Length of reign:* 7 years. *Dates of reign:* 2715-2709 B.C. *Mummy:* not found. *Sarcophagus:* basalt. *Burial chamber:* yes?.

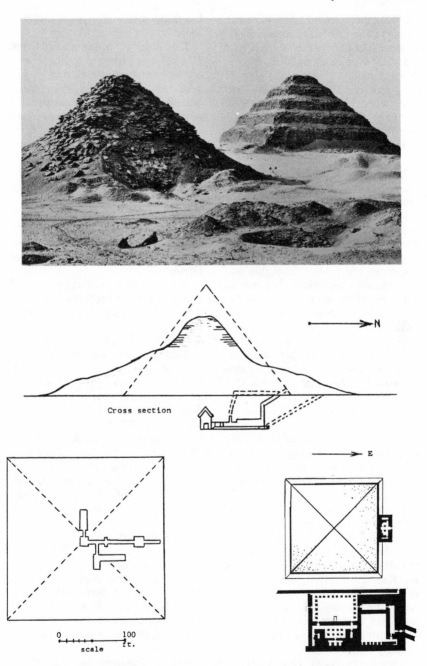

Pyramid Userkaf, North Sakkara. **Top:** *Userkaf in foreground, Pyramid Djoser in background.* (F. FIRTH) **Center:** *Cross-section.* (J.P. LEPRE) **Bottom left:** *Plan.* (J.P. LEPRE) **Bottom right:** *Plan of mortuary temple.* (J.P. LAUER)

Treasure: not found. *Hawk name:* Irimaet (The Truth is accomplished). *Vulture-and-Cobra name:* ?. *Set or Hawk-of-Nubi name:* ?. *Reed-and-Hornet name:* Userkaf (Mighty is His Spirit). *Son-of-the-Sun-God (Ra) name:* none. *Other names:* Nebkhey (The Good God, or Lord of the Ascension); Userchere; Userkef.

Besides building a pyramid at North Sakkara, this first pharaoh of the Fifth Dynasty also built a "sun temple" at Abu Gurab, one mile north of Abu Sir. Of this solar temple nothing now remains other than a large rectangular area of limestone chippings and rubble. That this was once the site of Userkaf's sun temple complex, mentioned in hieroglyphic inscriptions, is postulated from the unearthing here of an inscribed vase which refers to the solar temple of this kind, and from the fact that Neuserre, the sixth pharaoh of this dynasty, built his solar temple in this very same area.

Other than Userkaf and Neuserre, four other Fifth Dynasty kings built solar temples at Abu Gurab, but the remains of these buildings have yet to be discovered; apparently they were razed and covered over by the desert sands. These six Fifth Dynasty kings were the only pyramid pharaohs to build these sun temples.

Userkaf ascended the throne at age 50, after having been High Priest of On (Heliopolis), and introduced the Re (Ra) term for the pharaohs. With this, Re, the Sun-God of On, superseded the Hawk-God, Horus. Only later did the two become synonymous, used more or less interchangeably.

This king's Hawk name was Irimaet, which means "The Truth is Accomplished," and as Insi-Bya, or Reed-and-Hornet king, he was called Userkaf, meaning "Mighty is His Spirit."

The Palermo Stone records that Userkaf was generous in his priestly endowments and offered rich gifts of land, temples, shrines, sanctuaries and other provisions. He constructed new buildings in honor of the vulture goddess, Nekhbet, the cobra goddess, Utho, and the gods of the South Sanctuary, probably Elephantine or Hieraconpolis. For such charity he was rightly called the "Beloved of the Gods."

Further inscriptions indicate that Userkaf was a noble king, continuing to honor the mortuary endowments prescribed by King Menkara of Dynasty IV.

Aside from Userkaf's pyramid and temples, few artifacts remain of his reign—some cylinder seals and sealings.

Pyramid: Userkaf. *Name:* Pure Are the Places of Userkaf. *Number:* 35. *Exterior photos:* no. *Interior photos:* no. *Cross-sectional diagram:* yes. *Plan diagram:* yes. *Pyramid field:* North Sakkara. *Field number:* VI. *Length:* 231 ft. *Height:* approx. 145 ft. (now 105 ft.) *Angle:* approx. 49 degrees. *Type:* true. *Materials:* limestone. *Location of entrance:* north face. *Portcullises:* one vertical, granite. *Chambers:* three. *Comments:* Pyramid volume = 2½ million cu. ft.

Pyramid Complex: Userkaf. *Main pyramid:* yes. *Satellite pyramid(s):* yes—two (nos. 36 and 37). *Mortuary temple:* yes—destroyed. *Valley temple:* not found. *Offering shrine:* yes. *Mastaba(s):* no?. *Ship(s):* no. *Ship pit(s):* no. *Causeway:* yes. *Temenos wall:* yes—destroyed. *Canal:* destroyed.

Satellite Pyramid: Userkaf. *Name:* Pyramid Queen?. *Number:* 36. *Exterior photos:* no. *Interior photos:* no. *Cross-sectional diagram:* no.

Location of entrance: north. *Portcullises:* no. *Chambers:* one.

Satellite Pyramid: Userkaf. *Name:* Pyramid Princess?. *Number:* 37. *Exterior photos:* no. *Interior photos:* no. *Cross-sectional diagram:* no. *Plan diagram:* no. *Pyramid field:* North Sakkara. *Field number:* VI. *Length:* 55 ft. *Height:* ? (now 20 ft.) *Angle:* 50–55 degrees. *Type:* true. *Materials:* limestone. *Location of entrance:* north. *Portcullises:* no. *Chambers:* one.

MORTUARY TEMPLE OF USERKAF. The mortuary temple of this pharaoh is uniquely situated on the south side of his pyramid, a deviation from the standard placement of the mortuary temple to the east of the monument, as was the case in virtually every other pyramid complex. This departure from tradition was due either to: a) a brief change in the religious rituals performed in the temple, because of the new emphasis on sun worship, or b) to topographical considerations which made the placement of this temple to the east of the pyramid unsuitable for construction purposes.

Although little or nothing now remains of this mortuary temple, we are fortunate in that some fragments of its beautiful painted limestone reliefs have been unearthed (1928) and preserved (see photo, page 15). Also unearthed, was a huge granite head of this pharaoh, which was three times life size (Now in Cairo Museum) (see page 156).

Pharaoh Sahure and his cartouche. (STATUE: METROPOLITAN MUSEUM OF ART)

Plan diagram: no. *Pyramid field:* North Sakkara. *Field number:* VI. *Length:* 50 ft. *Height:* ?. *Angle:* ?. *Type:* true. *Materials:* limestone.

PHARAOH 16: SAHURE.
Position in dynasty: Second. *Portrait:* yes. *Length of reign:* 12 years. *Dates of reign:* 2708–2697 B.C. *Mummy:* not found. *Sarcophagus:* not found?. *Burial chamber:* yes?. *Treasure:* not found. *Hawk name:* Nebkheu (The Lord in His Ascension). *Vulture-and-Cobra name:* ?.

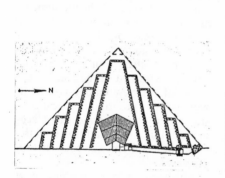

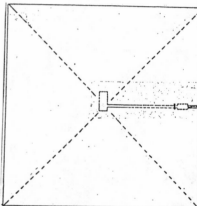

Top: *Pyramid field of Abu Sir, showing sun temples of Abu Gurab in the* *background.* (J. Breasted) Center: *Pyramid of Sahure, Abu Sir: Cross-section (left) and plan.* (Author's Improvement on L. Borchardt) Bottom: *Valley temple of Sahure, Abu Sir: Reconstruction.* (L. Borchardt)

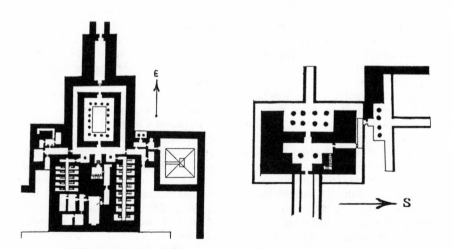

Top: *Ruined mortuary temple of Sahure, Abu Sir.* (H. SCHAFER AND W. ANDRADE) **Bottom left:** *Mortuary temple of Sahure, Abu Sir: Plan.* (L. BORCHARDT) **Bottom right:** *Valley temple of Sahure, Abu Sir: Plan.* (L. BORCHARDT)

Set or Hawk-of-Nubi name: ?. *Reed-and-Hornet name:* Sahu-Ra (Sahure) (The Possession of Ra). *Son-of-the-Sun-God (Ra) name:* none. *Other names:* Sephre.

Although reigning for only 12 years, this pharaoh was very active in initiating new building projects, among which were his pyramid and a solar temple.

During his reign, Sahure raided the Phoenician coast and the Bedouin tribes of Sinai. A tablet inscribed upon the rocks of Wady Maghara shows him smiting his enemies. Another rock inscription bearing Sahure's name has been discovered at Tomas, in Lower Nubia; a third at the First Cataract on Sehel Island; and a fourth at Nekheb (El Kab), the ancient city of the Hawks.

Other remains of Sahure's reign include some cylinder seals and sealings, and a well-cut diorite sculpture of the king with the goddess of Koptos. There is also an inscription (Cairo Museum) recording the pharaoh's Jubilee Ceremony.

Sahure, like his predecessor, Userkaf, made numerous endowments to the gods, donating estates and land to Hathor, Nekhbet, Utho and Re.

Other hieroglyphic records state that Sahure had a "false door" of stone fashioned for an offering shrine, placing the work under the direction of the two High Priests of Ptah at Memphis.

Yet another inscription makes mention of Sahure's queen, Nofrehotpes, and of the mortuary endowment set aside for her tomb.

This pharaoh, following the newly established and short-lived tradition of his brother Userkaf, also built a solar temple at Abu Gurab, in addition to his pyramid at Abu Sir. Unfortunately, though, while this sun

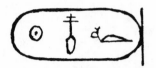

Cartouche of Pharaoh Neferefre.

temple is mentioned in the Palermo Stone Transcript, no trace of it has yet been found.

An interesting feature of this pharaoh's mortuary temple was its drainage system, which consisted of lion-headed gargoyles situated on the roof to carry off rain water to channels cut into the pavement. There was also an underground drainage system of copper pipes located under the temple, and which followed the line of the 750' causeway to an outlet at its eastern end.

Pyramid: Sahure. *Name:* The Soul of Sahure Shines. *Number:* 19. *Exterior photos:* no. *Interior photos:* no. *Cross-sectional diagram:* yes. *Plan diagram:* yes. *Pyramid field:* Abu Sir. *Field number:* V. *Length:* 257 ft. *Height:* 156 ft. *Angle:* 50 degrees, 36 minutes. *Type:* true. *Materials:* limestone, sand and rubble core; limestone casing. *Location of entrance:* north face — at ground level. *Portcullises:* one granite. *Chambers:* two. *Comments:* Volume = 3½ million cu. ft.

Pyramid Complex: Sahure. *Main pyramid:* yes. *Satellite pyramid(s):* yes — one (no. 20). *Mortuary temple:* yes — partially intact. *Valley temple:* yes — much ruined. *Offering shrine:* no. *Mastaba(s):* no?. *Ship(s):* no. *Ship pit(s):* no. *Causeway:* yes. *Temenos wall:* yes. *Canal:* destroyed.

Satellite Pyramid: Sahure. *Name:* Pyramid Queen?. *Number:* 20. *Exterior photos:* yes. *Interior photos:* no. *Cross-sectional diagram:* no. *Plan diagram:* no. *Pyramid field:*

Abu Sir. *Field number:* V. *Length:*
40 ft. *Height:* ?. *Angle:* ?. *Type:* true.
Materials: limestone. *Location of entrance:* north face. *Portcullises:* no.
Chambers: one?.

PHARAOH 17: NEFEREFRE.
Position in dynasty: Third. *Portrait:* no. *Length of reign:* 4 years.
Dates of reign: 2696–2693 B.C.
Mummy: not found. *Sarcophagus:*
not found?. *Burial chamber:* yes?.
Treasure: not found. *Hawk name:*
Nefer-Kheu. *Vulture-and-Cobra
name:* ?. *Set or Hawk-of-Nubi
name:* ?. *Reed-and-Hornet name:*
Neferefra (Neferefre). *Son-of-the-
Sun-God (Ra) name:* none. *Other
names:* Chere: Khere-nefer.

Very little is known of this third
pharaoh of the Fifth Dynasty, except
that he was probably the son of
Sahure and that he is mentioned in
the Abydos King List as having a
short reign of four years. Within that
confined time, though, he was able to
build himself, not only a pyramid at
Abu Sir, but also a solar temple at
Abu Gurab. No trace of the temple
has survived, and its exact location
remains a problem that future investigation may someday solve. We
are aware of its existence from inscriptions found in the private tombs
of that area.
    Pyramid: Neferefre. *Name:* The
Souls of Neferefre are Divine.
Number: 25. *Exterior photos:* no. *Interior photos:* no. *Cross-sectional
diagram:* no. *Plan diagram:* no.
Pyramid field: Abu Sir. *Field
number:* V. *Length:* 195 ft. *Height:*
approx. 125 ft. (now razed). *Angle:*
approx. 50 degrees. *Type:* true.
Materials: limestone. *Location of entrance:* north face. *Portcullises:*
none?. *Chambers:* one.
    Pyramid Complex: Neferefre.
Main pyramid: yes. *Satellite pyra-*

mid(s): yes – three (nos. 26, 27 and
28). *Mortuary temple:* never completed. *Valley temple:* never completed. *Offering shrine:* no.
Mastaba(s): no?. *Ship(s):* no. *Ship
pit(s):* no. *Causeway:* never completed. *Temenos wall:* no. *Canal:*
destroyed.
    Satellite Pyramid: Neferefre.
Name: Pyramid Queen?. *Number:*
26. *Exterior photos:* no. *Interior
photos:* no. *Cross-sectional diagram:*
no. *Plan diagram:* no. *Pyramid field:*
Abu Sir. *Field number:* V. *Length:* ?.
Height: ?. *Angle:* ?. *Type:* true.
Materials: limestone. *Location of entrance:* ?. *Portcullises:* ?. *Chambers:*
one?.
    Satellite Pyramid: Neferefre.
Name: Pyramid Queen?. *Number:*
27. *Exterior photos:* no. *Interior
photos:* no. *Cross-sectional diagram:*
no. *Plan diagram:* no. *Pyramid field:*
Abu Sir. *Field number:* V. *Length:* ?.
Height: ?. *Angle:* ?. *Type:* true.
Materials: limestone. *Location of entrance:* ?. *Portcullises:* ?. *Chambers:*
one?.
    Satellite Pyramid: Neferefre.
Name: Pyramid Princess?. *Number:*
28. *Exterior photos:* no. *Interior
photos:* no. *Cross-sectional diagram:*
no. *Plan diagram:* no. *Pyramid field:*
Abu Sir. *Field number:* V. *Length:* ?.
Height: ?. *Angle:* ?. *Type:* true.
Materials: limestone. *Location of entrance:* ?. *Portcullises:* ?. *Chambers:*
one?.

PHARAOH 18: SISIRES.
Position in dynasty: Fourth. *Portrait:* no. *Length of reign:* 7 years.
Dates of reign: 2692–2686 B.C.
Mummy: not found. *Sarcophagus:*
?. *Burial chamber:* yes?. *Treasure:*
not found. *Hawk name:* Sekhem-
Kheu (Ruler in His Ascension).
Vulture-and-Cobra name: ?. *Set or
Hawk-of-Nubi name:* ?. *Reed-
and-Hornet name:* Shepseskara

(Shepseskere). *Son-of-the-Sun-God (Ra) name:* none. *Other names:* Asa; Heruakau?; Isesi; Isi; Shepseskere Isesi; Sisi; Sisire. This pharaoh, the son of his predecessor, Neferefre, built a pyramid at Sakkara, which was not discovered until 1980. The only information published concerning this monument is that it has a base length of 180 feet and an elaborate subterranean system of passages and chambers. If this information is correct, then this pyramid constitutes an exception to a rule, as most of the pyramids of this era have a simple, rather than complex, subterranean design.

Until more information is forthcoming, it is not possible to draw cross-section or plan diagrams of this monument.

Less evidence is available concerning Sisires' other, more recently discovered pyramid (1984), at Abu Sir.

Very little archaeological evidence has been discovered and handed down to us concerning this king, although the last year of his reign is recorded on the Palermo Stone, and he is further mentioned under the name Shepseskere in the Sakkara King List.

Pyramid: Sisires. *Name:* Pyramid Sisires. *Number:* 45. *Exterior photos:* no. *Interior photos:* no. *Cross-sectional diagram:* no. *Plan diagram:* no. *Pyramid field:* South Sakkara. *Field number:* VII. *Length:* 180 ft. *Height:* approx. 115 ft. *Angle:* approx. 50 degrees. *Type:* true. *Materials:* limestone. *Location of entrance:* ?. *Portcullises:* ?. *Chambers:* one?.

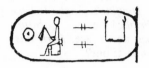

Cartouche of Pharaoh Sisires.

Pyramid Complex:* Sisires. *Main pyramid:* yes. *Satellite pyramid(s):* ?. *Mortuary temple:* ?. *Valley temple:* ?. *Offering shrine:* ?. *Mastaba(s):* ?. *Ship(s):* ?. *Ship pit(s):* ?. *Causeway:* ?. *Temenos wall:* ?. *Canal:* ?.

Pyramid: Sisires. *Name:* Pyramid Sisires. *Number:* 18. *Exterior photos:* no. *Interior photos:* no. *Cross-sectional diagram:* no. *Plan diagram:* no. *Pyramid field:* Abu Sir. *Field number:* V. *Length:* ?. *Height:* ?. *Angle:* ?. *Type:* true?. *Materials:* limestone?. *Location of entrance:* ?. *Portcullises:* ?. *Chambers:* ?. *Comments:* Recently discovered (1984).

Pyramid Complex:** Sisires. *Main pyramid:* yes. *Satellite pyramid(s):* ?. *Mortuary temple:* ?. *Valley temple:* ?. *Offering shrine:* ?. *Mastaba(s):* ?. *Ship(s):* ?. *Ship pit(s):* ?. *Causeway:* ?. *Temenos wall:* ?. *Canal:* ?.

PHARAOH 19: NEFERIRKARE.
Position in dynasty: Fifth. *Portrait:* yes?. *Length of reign:* 21 years. *Dates of reign:* 2685–2665 B.C. *Mummy:* not found. *Sarcophagus:* ?. *Burial chamber:* ?. *Treasure:* not found. *Hawk name:* Userkheu (Mighty in His Ascension). *Vulture-and-Cobra name:* Khemsekhemuneb (Ascending as the Lord of

---

*Until more material is published concerning this pyramid (found in 1980), we shall have to be in the dark as to which and how many elements comprised its pyramid complex.

**Until more material is published concerning this pyramid (found in 1984), we shall have to be in the dark as to which and how many elements comprised its pyramid complex.

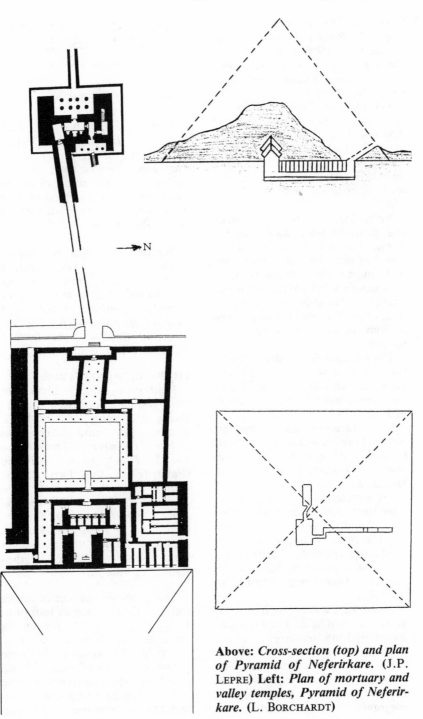

Above: *Cross-section (top) and plan of Pyramid of Neferirkare.* (J.P. LEPRE) **Left:** *Plan of mortuary and valley temples, Pyramid of Neferirkare.* (L. BORCHARDT)

Dominion. *Set or Hawk-of-Nubi name:* ?. *Reed-and-Hornet name:* Neferarikara (Neferirkare). *Son-of-the-Sun-God (Ra) name:* none. *Other names:* Keku; Neferirkare Kekei; Nepherchere.

This pharaoh, brother of Userkaf and Sahure, built a sun temple at Abu Gurab, and a pyramid at Abu Sir. The former has never been found. We know of its existence through inscriptions found in adjacent tombs in the area of his pyramid.

Neferirkare was the name taken by this pharaoh upon ascending the throne, but as Lord of the Vulture and the Cobra, he was called Khemsekhemuneb, "Ascending as the Lord of Dominions." His Hawk name was Userkheu, "Mighty in His Ascension," but he is referred to as Keku on some of the blocks used for his pyramid.

The Palermo Stone tells us that in his first year of rule, he donated much land and had a statue of electrum commissioned for the Temple of Hathor in Meret-Snofru.

In his fifteenth year as pharaoh, Neferirkare celebrated the mysterious "Ascension" or "Appearance" Festival as the Reed-and-Hornet King.

An inscription from this king's reign states how he ordered a splendid coffin of ebony wood to be made for his recently deceased Vizier, Weshptah, with Neferirkare showing great concern over the death of this subject and the proper execution of the coffin.

Neferirkare was approximately 87 years old when he died and was succeeded by King Neuserre.

Pyramid: Neferirkare. *Name:* Neferirkare Has Become a Soul. *Number:* 23. *Exterior photos:* yes. *Interior photos:* no. *Cross-sectional diagram:* yes. *Plan diagram:* yes.

Cartouche of Pharaoh Neferirkare.

Pyramid field: Abu Sir. *Field number:* V. *Length:* 360 ft. *Height:* 227 ft. *Angle:* 53 degrees. *Type:* true. *Materials:* limestone core; limestone casing, with lowest course of granite. *Location of entrance:* north face. Now clogged with sand—not visible. 1987. *Portcullises:* ?. *Chambers:* two?.

Pyramid Complex: Neferirkare. *Main pyramid:* yes. *Satellite pyramid(s):* none. *Mortuary temple:* yes—ruined. *Valley temple:* yes—ruined. *Offering shrine:* no?. *Mastaba(s):* no?. *Ship(s):* no. *Ship pit(s):* no. *Causeway:* yes. *Temenos wall:* no. *Canal:* destroyed.

PHARAOH 20: NEUSERRE.
Position in dynasty: Sixth. *Portrait:* yes. *Length of reign:* 11 years. *Dates of reign:* 2664–2654 B.C. *Mummy:* not found. *Sarcophagus:* ?. *Burial chamber:* ?. *Treasure:* not found. *Hawk name:* Istib-toui (Favorite in the Two Lands). *Vulture-and-Cobra name:* ?. *Set or Hawk-of-Nubi name:* ?. *Reed-and-Hornet name:* Userenra; Enuserra (Neuserre). *Son-of-the-Sun-God (Ra) name:* none. *Other names:* An; Anu; Neuserre Ratho (Retho); Ratho; Rathure.

This pharaoh, the son of Sisires, followed the tradition of four of his five predecessors and built a sun temple at Abu Gurab, as well as a pyramid at Abu Sir. Although the former is now in a state of ruin, it is still possible to trace out its ground plan.

This complex had a lower valley temple which gave rise to a causeway

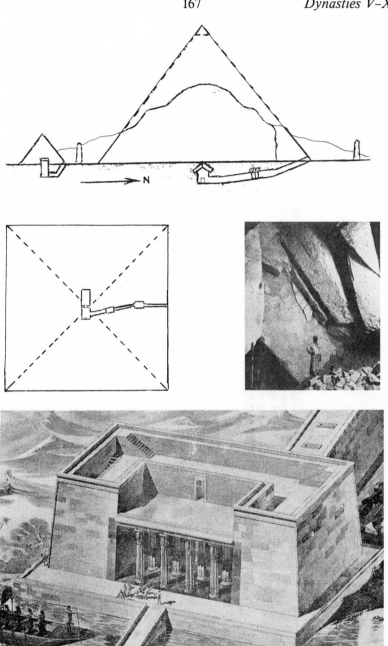

Top: *Pyramid of Neuserre and subsidiary pyramid: Cross-section.* (AUTHOR'S IMPROVEMENT ON L. BORCHARDT) **Center left:** *Pyramid of Neuserre: Plan.* (J.P. LEPRE) **Center right:** *Pyramid of Neuserre: Burial chamber.* (L. BORCHARDT) **Bottom:** *Valley temple of Neuserre: Reconstruction.* (J. CAPART)

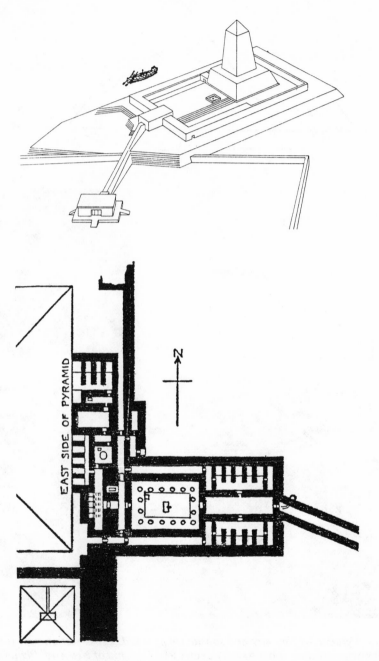

EAST SIDE OF PYRAMID

N

Top: *Solar temple of Neuserre, Abu Gurab: Reconstruction* (F.W. Bissing)
Bottom: *Mortuary temple of Neuserre, Abu Sir: Plan.* (L. Borchardt)

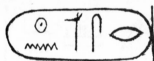

Pharaoh Neuserre and his cartouche.
(STATUE: BRITISH MUSEUM)

extending southwest to a 350′ by 260′ rectangular enclosure. Within this compound was a large 250′ square, open court, to the rear of which stood an imposing 110′ high obelisk, set on a massive 100′ high platform with a 500′ base perimeter.

Within the area of the courtyard, and immediately east of the obelisk, was an alabaster altar. This altar was the only surviving element of the entire complex, other than the remnants of a large, 100′ long brick-barque, located outside and south of the enclosure wall.

Neuserre is known to have celebrated a Jubilee Festival during his reign (commemorating a period of 30 years from his initiation as heir-apparent), and was said to have decorated his solar temple with reliefs depicting this celebration.

An inscription from this pharaoh's reign tells of how a priest in his service built his own tomb and did not appropriate the older tomb of another, and of how he was rewarded for his scruples by the Pharaoh Neuserre.

Further inscriptions name two of Neuserre's wives, Khenti-Kheus and Nubi; and two of his daughters, Khemerer-Nebti and Mertetes. A statue of him, which is dated to the Twelfth Dynasty, indicates that he was revered centuries after his death.

Pyramid: Neuserre. *Name:* Enduring Are the Places of Neuserre. *Number:* 21. *Exterior photos:* no. *Interior photos:* yes. *Cross-sectional diagram:* yes. *Plan diagram:* yes. *Pyramid field:* Abu Sir. *Field number:* V. *Length:* 274 ft. *Height:* 165 ft. *Angle:* 51 degrees, 50 minutes. *Type:* true. *Materials:* limestone, sand and rubble core; limestone casing. *Location of entrance:* north face—at ground level, now clogged with stones—1987. *Portcullises:* three vertical, granite. *Chambers:* two.

Pyramid Complex: Neuserre. *Main pyramid:* yes. *Satellite pyramid(s):* yes—one (no. 22). *Mortuary temple:* yes—ruined. *Valley temple:* no (utilized that of Neferirkare). *Offering shrine:* no?. *Mastaba(s):* no?. *Ship(s):* no. *Ship pit(s):* no. *Causeway:* yes. *Temenos wall:* no. *Canal:* destroyed.

Satellite Pyramid: Neuserre. *Name:* Pyramid Queen Khenti-Kheus. *Number:* 22. *Exterior* photos: no. *Interior photos:* no. *Cross-sectional diagram:* yes. *Plan diagram:* no. *Pyramid field:* Abu Sir. *Field number:* V. *Length:* 50 ft. *Height:* 34 ft. *Angle:* approx. 52 degrees. *Type:* true. *Materials:* limestone?. *Location of entrance:* north face—at ground level. *Portcullises:* no. *Chambers:* one.

PHARAOH 21: MENKEUHOR.
Position in dynasty: Seventh. *Portrait:* yes. *Length of reign:* 8 years. *Dates of reign:* 2653–2646 B.C. *Mummy:* not found. *Sarcophagus:* not found. *Burial chamber:* not found. *Treasure:* not found. *Hawk name:* Menkheu (Established in His Ascension). *Vulture-and-Cobra name:* ?. *Set or Hawk-of-Nubi name:* ?. *Reed-and-Hornet name:* Menkauheru (Menkeuhor). *Son-of-the-Sun-God (Ra) name:* none. *Other names:* Akau-Heru; Menchere; Menkeuhur; Menkeure; Menkeure Ikeure.

This king, son of Neferirkare, built both a pyramid and a solar-temple, but neither of these monuments has yet been found.

Menkeuhor, "Establishing the Spirits of the Sun-God," is the Reed-and-Hornet name of this pharaoh, while the royal names Iheure and Menkheu are also used. Although the king enjoyed only a short tenure on the throne, there is reference within the context of the latter of these names—"Established in His Ascension"—to his having celebrated his Jubilee Ceremony. It appears, then, that he enjoyed the status of heir-apparent for quite a few years prior to his reigning as pharaoh.

The various names of Menkeuhor's royal titulary are recorded on a rock in Sinai, and built into a wall of the Serapeum at Sakkara is a slab of

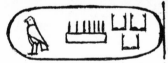

Pharaoh Menkeuhor and his cartouche. (PHOTO OF STATUE: J. VANDIER)

stone with his figure carved into it (Louvre).

Few other remains of his reign have been found. A stele inscribed with his name and an alabaster statue, both from Sakkara; a vase (now in Berlin); and a single cylinder-seal and sealing from Abu Sir are the only items that have come to light thus far.

Pyramid: Menkeuhor. *This pyramid recorded in Dahshur Charter,*

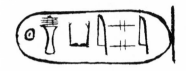

Cartouche of Pharaoh Djedkare.

but never found. Name: Divine Are the Places of Menkeuhor. *Number:* 67. *Exterior photos:* no. *Interior photos:* no. *Cross-sectional diagram:* no. *Plan diagram:* no. *Pyramid field:* Dahshur. *Field number:* VIII. *Length:* ?. *Height:* ?. *Angle:* ?. *Type:* true?. *Materials:* limestone?. *Location of entrance:* ?. *Portcullises:* ?. *Chambers:* ?.
Pyramid Complex: Menkeuhor. *Main pyramid:* yes?. *Satellite pyramid(s):* ?. *Mortuary temple:* ?. *Valley temple:* ?. *Offering shrine:* ?. *Mastaba(s):* ?. *Ship(s):* ?. *Ship pit(s):* ?. *Causeway:* ?. *Temenos wall:* ?. *Canal:* probably destroyed.

PHARAOH 22: DJEDKARE.
Position in dynasty: Eighth. *Portrait:* no. *Length of reign:* 28 years. *Dates of reign:* 2645–2618 B.C. *Mummy:* not found. *Sarcophagus:* ?. *Burial chamber:* ?. *Treasure:* not found. *Hawk name:* Tetkhau (Dadkheu) (Enduring in His Ascension or Appearance). *Vulture-and-Cobra name:* ?. *Set or Hawk-of-Nubi name:* Dad. *Reed-and-Hornet name:* Tetkara (Djedkare). *Son-of-the-Sun-God (Ra) name:* Assa (Isesi) (Sisi) (Issi). *Other names:* Dadkere; Djedkare-Isesi; Maatkara.

Djedkare, son of Sisires, is noted for having been the first pharaoh to use the royal Sa-Ra (Son-of-the-Sun-God) title before his name. He is also known to have written a book of maxims.

Djedkare, meaning "Enduring is the Spirit of Re," was this king's Reed-and-Hornet name, whereas his Hawk-of-Nubi name was Dad. His Hawk-name was Dadkheu, "Enduring in His Appearance."

The Sa-Ra (Se-Re) title which he initiated, and which was thereafter quite popular with the pharaohs, was instrumental in declaring his descendancy from the Sun-God, Ra (Re). Actually, practically every pharaoh thereafter unhesitatingly used this designation.

In certain inscriptions regarding Djedkare, names of his officials are revealed. Senethemib, the king's prime minister and "Master of the King's Secrets," being one of these privileged personages, describes how King Djedkare personally bestowed great honors upon him, and how Djedkare thanked him for successfully completing a building in the palace, and for being commissioned to plant a garden there also—1200 cubits long (2060′) by 221 cubits wide (379′). The building itself may well have been an addition to the existing national archives, for the issuing of the orders regarding this project had occurred in the Place of the Archives, and the prime minister, Senethemib, also enjoyed the title of chief scribe of the royal archives.

Inscriptions of Djedkare's name appear on an alabaster vase, where his Jubilee Ceremony is cited; at Wady Hammamat; and on rock tablets at Sinai, where he is shown in the traditional form of smiting an Asiatic enemy. Herein he is hailed as "The Smiter of all Countries." Even as far as Tomas, in Lower Nubia, his name was inscribed on a rock, indicating his military presence there.

Other objects of Djedkare's reign include several cylinders and scarabs, and an ink-slab.

Pyramid of Djedkare-Isesi, South Sakkara. (A. FAKHRY)

His book of maxims, by far the most important relic of his tenure, was edited by a royal prince, Ptah-hotpe, and contained the sayings of olden times. The object of the book is for the common man to receive wisdom from a wise, older figure. Some of Djedkare's advice contained in his book instructs the reader not to look for the best seat when invited to the palace, lest he take it and then be asked to move; and not to turn away from one's needy mother when she is old and infirmed, lest the gods be angered.

As Djedkare and every pharaoh who followed him ceased to build the solar-temples which were so popular with the earlier Fifth Dynasty kings, there may have been a dramatic decline in the influence of the Heliopolitan priesthood of Ra during his reign. Djedkare, then, represented the official break with this priestly lineage, a sequence which was further fractured by the reign of the next pharaoh, Unas.

Pyramid: Djedkare. *Name:* Djedkare-Isesi is Beautiful. *Number:* 48. *Exterior photos:* yes. *Interior photos:* no. *Cross-sectional diagram:* no. *Plan diagram:* no. *Pyramid field:* South Sakkara. *Field number:* VII. *Length:* 265 ft. *Height:* approx. 165 ft. (now 80 ft.) *Angle:* approx. 51 degrees. *Type:* true. *Materials:* limestone. *Location of entrance:* ?. *Portcullises:* ?. *Chambers:* ?.

Pyramid Complex: Djedkare. *Main pyramid:* yes. *Satellite pyramid(s):* yes—one (no. 47). *Mortuary temple:* yes—ruined. *Valley temple:* yes—ruined. *Offering shrine:* no. *Mastaba(s):* no?. *Ship(s):* no. *Ship pit(s):* no. *Causeway:* yes. *Temenos wall:* no. *Canal:* destroyed.

Satellite Pyramid: Djedkare. *Name:* Pyramid Queen?. *Number:*

Cartouche of Pharaoh Unas.

47. *Exterior photos:* yes. *Interior photos:* no. *Cross-sectional diagram:* no. *Plan diagram:* no. *Pyramid field:* South Sakkara. *Field number:* VII. *Length:* 125 ft. *Height:* ? (now 25 ft.) *Angle:* ?. *Type:* true. *Materials:* limestone. *Location of entrance:* ?. *Portcullises:* ?. *Chambers:* one?.

Note: The pyramids of the next seven pharaohs, Unas (Dyn. V), Teti (Dyn. VI), Ity (Dyn. VI), Pepy I (Dyn. VI), Merenre I (Dyn. VI), Pepy II (Dyn. VI), and Merenre II (Dyn. VI) have similar subterranean designs.

PHARAOH 23: UNAS.
Position in dynasty: Ninth (last). *Portrait:* no. *Length of reign:* 30 years. *Dates of reign:* 2617–2588 B.C. *Mummy:* right arm, fragments of skull, other bones. *Sarcophagus:* black basalt. *Burial chamber:* yes. *Treasure:* not found. *Hawk name:* Uthtoui (Flourishing in the Two Lands). *Vulture-and-Cobra name:* ?. *Set or Hawk-of-Nubi name:* Uth. *Reed-and-Hornet name:* Unas. *Son-of-the-Sun-God (Ra) name:* Unas. *Other names:* Onnos; Unis; Unnos; Wenus.

Unas, the last king of the Fifth Dynasty, and son of Neuserre, is most noted for his pyramid being the earliest to have its walls inscribed with Pyramid Texts. Though he is popular for the discovery of the texts and a beautiful basalt sarcophagus within his burial chamber, it is unfortunate that there are no known portraits of this king in existence. If such portraitures do exist, say in one or more of the great museums of the world, that fact is little published, and photographs are not in circulation.

While the personal name of this pharaoh was Unas, his Hawk name was Uthtoui, "Flourishing in the Two Lands," and his Hawk-of-Nubi name was Uth. According to the Turn Papyrus, his reign lasted 30 years, and he died at approximately age 70.

The pyramid texts which were found inscribed on the walls of his burial chamber assert that the king is not dead. "He is merely resting," the inscription reads, "and is now among the imperishable stars." The text goes on to describe Unas as a hawk, or a falcon, ascending the sky, on his journey to meet the gods. When he arrives on the heavenly plane, the heralds cry, "O Re, our hearts were not glad until you came to us."

The pyramid texts are composed of passages which appear to have been recorded from a remote age in Egyptian history, and depict pharaoh as a mighty hunter in the celestial sphere.

Unas' name has been found inscribed on several alabaster vases (British Museum and Florence), and on a rock at Elephantine. Another vase, also inscribed with Unas' name, was found at the ruins of the ancient temple at Byblos, in Syria.

Although Unas represents the last king of the Fifth Dynasty, there is no indication that this signaled a break in the royal line, for Unas was, in reality, more closely associated with the Sixth than with the Fifth Dynasty.

Actually, insofar as the religious aspect is concerned, the Fifth Dynasty more accurately ends with the previous pharaoh, Djedkare-Isesi; Unas, however, having left no heirs,

Pyramid of Unas, North Sakkara — showing entrance. (J. BREASTED)

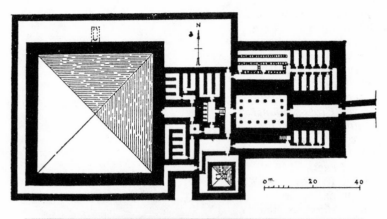

Top: *Mortuary temple of Unas, North Sakkara: Plan.* (L. BORCHARDT)
Bottom: *Pyramid of Unas: Sarcophagus in burial chamber.* (H. SCHAFER AND W. ANDRADE)

allowed a new genealogical family to ascend the throne, thus instituting a novel era of dynastic parentage.
Pyramid: Unas. *Name:* Nefer-Isut (Beautiful Abode). *Number:* 41. *Exterior photos:* yes. *Interior photos:* yes. *Cross-sectional diagram:* yes. *Plan diagram:* yes. *Pyramid field:* North Sakkara. *Field number:* VI. *Length:* 220 ft. *Height:* 143 ft. (now 62 ft.) *Angle:* approx. 51 degrees. *Type:* true. *Materials:* limestone. *Location of entrance:* north—ground level. Before this pyramid only four others (Djoser, Djoser-Tati, Khaba, and Khafra) had ground-level entrances; after this pyramid was built, only one other pyramid (Khui) had an above-ground entrance. *Portcullises:* three vertical—granite. *Chambers:* three. *Comments:* Two boat pits were found south of the western extremity of this pyramid's causeway.
Pyramid Complex: Unas. *Main pyramid:* yes. *Satellite pyramid(s):* yes—one (no. 42). *Mortuary temple:* yes. *Valley temple:* yes. *Offering shrine:* no?. *Mastaba(s):* no?. *Ship(s):* none?. *Ship pit(s):* yes—two. *Causeway:* yes. *Temenos wall:* no?. *Canal:* destroyed.
Satellite Pyramid: Unas. *Name:* Pyramid Queen?. *Number:* 42. *Exterior photos:* no. *Interior photos:* no. *Cross-sectional diagram:* no. *Plan diagram:* no. *Pyramid field:* North Sakkara. *Field number:* VI. *Length:* ?. *Height:* ?. *Angle:* ?. *Type:* true?. *Materials:* limestone?. *Location of entrance:* north. *Portcullises:* ?. *Chambers:* one?.

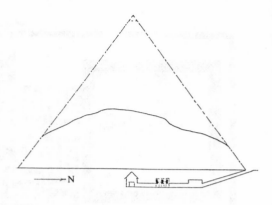

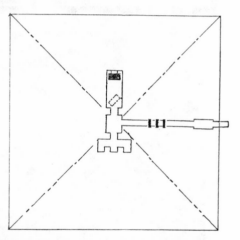

Pyramid of Unas, North Sakkara. **Top:** *Cross-section.* **Bottom:** *Plan.* (G. MASPERO)

DYNASTY VI

• *Duration:* **135 years (2587–2453 B.C.). Pharaohs: 1. Teti. 2. Ity. 3. Pepy I. 4 Merenre I. 5. Pepy II. 6. Merenre II. 7. Khui. 8. Merikare.**

PHARAOH 24: TETI.
Position in dynasty: First. *Portrait:* yes. *Length of reign:* 8 years. *Dates of reign:* 2587–2580 B.C. *Mummy:* arm and shoulder fragments only. *Sarcophagus:* black basalt. *Burial chamber:* yes?. *Treasure:* not found. *Hawk name:* Sehotpe-Toui (Contenting the Two Lands). *Vulture-and-Cobra name:* ?.

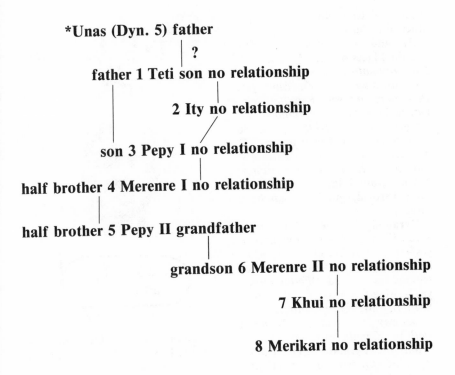

Unas (Dyn. 5) father
|
?
|
father 1 Teti son no relationship
|
2 Ity no relationship
|
son 3 Pepy I no relationship
|
half brother 4 Merenre I no relationship
|
half brother 5 Pepy II grandfather
|
grandson 6 Merenre II no relationship
|
7 Khui no relationship
|
8 Merikari no relationship

Dynasty VI Genealogy

Set or Hawk-of-Nubi name: ?. *Reed-and-Hornet name:* Teta; Tata. *Son-of-the-Sun-God (Ra) name:* ?. *Other names:* Atet; Othoe; Ototi; Thoe; Toti.

Although not directly connected to the previous pharaoh, Unas, Teti doubtless legalized his accession by a marriage to a princess of the old line, for a pharaoh who had no direct claim to the throne often legalized his claim to kingship through such a union.

Statuary depicting this king is quite rare, an indication that perhaps he died prematurely, before the statues for his mortuary and valley temple could be executed.

A hieroglyphic inscription explains how Teti unified the two posts

of High Priests of the god Ptah of Memphis into one office. The new sole priest, Sabu Thety, describes how nothing like this had ever been done before. Also noted is the fact that Teti now adds, "Beloved of Ptah" to his name. It seems, then, that the waning priesthood of Ra at On (Heliopolis) was gradually giving way to a revival of Ptah worship, and that this transition was instituted by Teti.

Not only royal statuary, but other objects of Teti's reign are scarce as well. Several inscribed vases are known, as are an inscription on a rock at Tomas, in Lower Nubia; an obliterated decree from Ebod (Abydos); and a door lintel from Memphis. At the youthful age of 30, Teti was supposedly murdered, an account given us by Manetho and other historians.

Pyramid: Teti. *Name:* Enduring Are the Places of Teti. *Number:* 33. *Exterior photos:* no. *Interior photos:* no. *Cross-sectional diagram:* yes. *Plan diagram:* yes. *Pyramid field:* North Sakkara. *Field number:* VI. *Length:* 210 ft. *Height:* approx. 130 ft. (now 65 ft.) *Angle:* approx. 51 degrees. *Type:* true. *Materials:* limestone. *Location of entrance:* north—ground level. *Portcullises:* three vertical, granite. *Chambers:* three.

Pyramid Complex: Teti. *Main pyramid:* yes. *Satellite pyramid(s):* yes—three (nos. 29, 30 and 34). *Mortuary temple:* yes—ruined. *Valley temple:* yes—ruined. *Offering shrine:* yes—ruined. *Mastaba(s):* no?. *Ship(s):* no?. *Ship pit(s):* no?. *Causeway:* yes—ruined. *Temenos wall:* no. *Canal:* destroyed.

Satellite Pyramid: Teti. *Name:* Pyramid Queen Iput I (Pepy's mother). *Number:* 29. *Exterior photos:* no. *Interior photos:* no. *Cross-sectional diagram:* no. *Plan diagram:* no. *Pyramid field:* North Sakkara. *Field number:* VI. *Length:* 50 ft. *Height:* ? (now 15 ft.) *Angle:* 65 degrees. *Type:* true. *Materials:* limestone?. *Location of entrance:* none—no shaft leading to burial chamber. *Portcullises:* none. *Chambers:* one. *Comments:* Limestone sarcophagus, cedar coffin, human bones, gold necklace and gold bracelet found in burial chamber; mortuary temple to east of pyramid; offering shrine on north side; one of the ten pyramids with pyramid texts.

Satellite Pyramid: Teti. *Name:* Pyramid Queen Khuit. *Number:* 30. *Exterior photos:* no. *Interior photos:* no. *Cross-sectional diagram:* no. *Plan diagram:* no. *Pyramid field:* North Sakkara. *Field number:* VI. *Length:* 50 ft. *Height:* ?. *Angle:* ?.

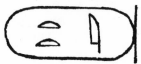

Pharaoh Teti and his cartouche. (HEAD: EGYPTIAN MUSEUM, CAIRO)

Type: true. *Materials:* limestone?. *Location of entrance:* north. *Portcullises:* none. *Chambers:* one. *Comments:* Mortuary temple on east side of pyramid.

Satellite Pyramid: Teti. *Name:* Pyramid Princess?. *Number:* 34. *Exterior photos:* no. *Interior photos:* no. *Cross-sectional diagram:* no. *Plan diagram:* no. *Pyramid field:* North Sakkara. *Field number:* VI. *Length:* 50 ft. *Height:* ? (now 13 ft.) *Angle:* ?. *Type:* true. *Materials:* limestone. *Location of entrance:* north. *Portcullises:* no. *Chambers:* one. *Comments:* This pyramid has its own mortuary temple on its east side.

PHARAOH 25: ITY.

Position in dynasty: Second. *Portrait:* no. *Length of reign:* 6 years. *Dates of reign:* 2579–2574 B.C. *Mummy:* not found. *Sarcophagus:*

Cartouche of Pharaoh Ity.

not found. *Burial chamber:* not found. *Treasure:* not found. *Hawk name:* Skhem-kha-u. *Vulture-and-Cobra name:* ?. *Set or Hawk-of-Nubi name:* ?. *Reed-and-Hornet name:* Ati (Ity). *Son-of-the-Sun-God (Ra) name:* ?. *Other names:* Akhe; Athuthi; Userkere; Userkere Athtuthi.

With the new pharaoh Ity, emphasis shifts back to Re from Ptah. In this vein, Ity receives the name Userkere, meaning, "Mighty is the Spirit of Re." It is possible, then, that the death of the previous king Teti was the result of a violent struggle between the two priesthoods of these gods. Indeed, even though the name Ity follows that of Teti in the Abydos King List, it is omitted in the Sakkara List, one which would have been written and controlled by the Ptah faction.

The ancient texts speak of the effort put into the building of the pyramid of Ity, but it was of small size and all traces of it have now vanished. It was called "Fame of Athuthi."

Pyramid: Ity. *Name:* Fame of Athuthi. *Number:* 44. *Exterior photos:* no. *Interior photos:* no. *Cross-sectional diagram:* no. *Plan diagram:* no. *Pyramid field:* Sakkara (south?). *Field number:* VII. *Length:* ?. *Height:* ?. *Angle:* ?. *Type:* true?. *Materials:* limestone?. *Location of entrance:* ?. *Portcullises:* ?. *Chambers:* ?.

Pyramid Complex: Ity. *Main pyramid:* yes?. *Satellite pyramid(s):* ?. *Mortuary temple:* ?. *Valley temple:* ?. *Offering shrine:* ?. *Mastaba(s):* ?. *Ship(s):* ?. *Ship pit(s):* ?. *Causeway:* ?. *Temenos wall:* ?. *Canal:* probably destroyed.

PHARAOH 26: PEPY I.
Position in dynasty: Third. *Portrait:* yes. *Length of reign:* 20 years. *Dates of reign:* 2573–2554 B.C. *Mummy:* a few fragments found. *Sarcophagus:* black basalt. *Burial chamber:* yes. *Treasure:* not found. *Hawk name:* Mery-toui (Beloved of the Two Lands). *Vulture-and-Cobra name:* Mery-khet (Beloved of the Community). *Set or Hawk-of-Nubi name:* ?. *Reed-and-Hornet name:* Meri-Ra (Beloved of Ra). *Son-of-the-Sun-God (Ra) name:* Pepi. *Other names:* Piop; Phiop; Pepy; Meryre.

The son of Teti, this pharaoh's claim to fame lies in the fact that his pyramid was the first to be *discovered* containing pyramid texts. (Chronologically, the pyramid of Unas, the last king of the Fifth Dynasty, was the earliest to be endowed with such inscriptions.) Until this discovery by Maspero in 1881, it was assumed that the interiors of the pyramids were not at all incised with hieroglyphic inscriptions.

Upon ascending the throne, Pepy took the Reed-and-Hornet name Meryre, "Beloved of Re," and added the Son-of-the-Sun-God (Re) before his name Pepy. His Hawk name was Mery-toui, "Beloved of the Two Lands," and his Vulture-and-Cobra name was Mery-khet, "Beloved of the Community."

Several queens of Pepy are mentioned in the texts: Imtes, who is referred to as "The Great Royal Wife," and Meryre-enkhnes (Piopenkhnes), with the latter probably having been wedded to him in the thirteenth or fourteenth year of his tenure, when she was 12 or 13 years of age. In ancient times, this was the usual age at which a girl was married. Shortly after giving birth to a son called Mehtiemsuf, Queen Meryreenkhnes died and Pepy married her twin sister, who had the same name. This lady gave birth to a son whom Pepy called Pepy II.

A 6'-tall copper statue of Pepy was found by Quibell at Hieraconpolis, with the eyes inlaid with obsidian and limestone.

Besides his pyramid at South Sakkara, numerous other building projects occurred during Pepy's reign. At Koptos he enlarged the temple of the god Min; at Abydos (Ebod) he rebuilt the temple; at Dendereh he rebuilt the temple of the goddess Hathor; at Tanis and Bubastis, in the Delta, he built temples and huge gateways; at On (Heliopolis) he erected an obelisk; and at Elephantine he built a granite shrine. There are also inscriptions dating to his reign at the alabaster quarries of Hetnub, near Tell el-Armana, in the Sinai copper and malachite quarries, and in the breccia quarries of Wady Hammamat. Rock inscriptions giving his name are also recorded on the island of Sehel, at Tomas, El Kab, Silsileh and Iebo.

The texts regarding Pepy make frequent mention of his most trusted friend, Uni, whom Pepy held in high esteem. It appears as if Uni was a master of organization who was made chief commander of the pharaoh's mighty army of "many tens of thousands."

Pepy's pyramid was called Mennofre, "The Well-established."

Other small relics of Pepy's reign have been found. These include several inscribed vases, scarabs and cylinder-seals.

Top: *Pepy I and his son, Merenre I.* (EGYPTIAN MUSEUM, CAIRO) Bottom: *Cartouche of Pepy I.*

Pharaoh Merenre I and his cartouche. (STATUE: EGYPTIAN MUSEUM, CAIRO)

Pepy died after a reign of 20 years, at age 40.

Pyramid: Pepy I. *Name:* Enduring is the Beauty of Pepi. *Number:* 46. *Exterior photos:* yes—one. *Interior photos:* no. *Cross-sectional diagram:* yes. *Plan diagram:* yes. *Pyramid field:* South Sakkara. *Field number:* VII. *Length:* 250 ft. *Height:* approx. 160 ft. (now 40 ft.) *Angle:* approx. 50 degrees. *Type:* true. *Materials:* limestone. *Location of entrance:* north—ground level. *Portcullises:* three vertical. *Chambers:* three. *Comments:* Granite canopic chest with three of the four alabaster vases was found in the burial chamber.

Pyramid Complex: Pepy I. *Main pyramid:* yes. *Satellite pyramid(s):*

no. *Mortuary temple:* yes—ruined (not yet excavated). *Valley temple:* yes—ruined (not yet excavated). *Offering shrine:* no?. *Mastaba(s):* yes. *Ship(s):* no. *Ship pit(s):* no. *Causeway:* yes. *Temenos wall:* no. *Canal:* destroyed.

PHARAOH 27: MERENRE I.
Position in dynasty: Fourth. *Portrait:* yes. *Length of reign:* 4 years. *Dates of reign:* 2553–2550 B.C. *Mummy:* not found. *Sarcophagus:* black granite. *Burial chamber:* yes?. *Treasure:* not found. *Hawk name:* Enkh-kheu (Living in His Ascension). *Vulture-and-Cobra name:* Enkh-kheu. *Set or Hawk-of-Nubi name:* ?. *Reed-and-Hornet name:* Merenra (Merenre). *Son-of-the-Sun-God (Ra) name:* Mehtiemsuf (The God Mehti is His Protection). *Other names:* Methusuph.

The mummy of this boy pharaoh (ascended to the throne at age 7, died at age 12), has never been found. There are misleading statements by some authors that Merenre's mummy was found in the burial chamber of his pyramid when it was first entered in modern times (1880), that it had been stripped of all its bandages, but was nevertheless in a fairly good state of preservation. It has since been proven, though, that the mummy found at that time (now in the Cairo Museum) was merely a latter-day intrusive interrment, and not the actual body of the king.

This pharaoh's monument was one of the ten found with Pyramid Texts in the burial chamber.

Merenre was this pharaoh's Reed-and-Hornet name, while his Son-of-the-Sun-God name was Mehtiemsuf. As Lord of the Vulture-and-Cobra and as Hawk-king he took the name Enkh-kheu, "Living in His Ascension."

Merenre's pyramid, referred to as "Merenre Shines and is Beautiful," was furnished with a sarcophagus, false door and pyramidion provided by the very same personage, Uni, who was so favored by the preceding pharaoh, Pepy I. Although Merenre was only seven years old, construction of his pyramid was begun immediately upon his accession to the throne. In carrying out this operation, or certain major parts of it, Uni employed a fleet of Nile ships, supporting strong hieroglyphic evidence that the heavy granite blocks used in the building of the pyramids were brought down river this way, via ship from the Aswan quarries, 500 miles upriver.

Uni also speaks of the alabaster quarries of Hetnub, and of transporting a great stone altar via a 60-cubit- (103'-) long ship of acacia wood. He notes, rather proudly, that although the ship was a large one, it was nevertheless constructed in only 17 days. Uni speaks of cargo boats, tow boats and even a warship to protect the fleet.

Besides Uni, another chief personage of Merenre's reign was a learned priest named Herkhuf. Like Uni, he undertook expeditions to the First Cataract and beyond for building purposes. As a result of these expeditions, it is recorded that the boy pharaoh Merenre also journeyed to the area, and here he recorded his visit, inscribing the occurrence on the rocks. Interestingly, it is noted that Merenre undertook this journey to the hot southland in late January, the best and coolest season for that area.

Other inscriptions of Merenre have been found at the Wady Hammamat quarries, Aswan, and the temple of Osiris at Abydos. Besides this, we have the black granite sarcophagus from his pyramid, the canopic burial jars, several vases and an ivory box. Merenre died at age 12.

Pyramid: Merenre I. *Name:* Merenre Shines and is Beautiful. *Number:* 49. *Exterior photos:* no. *Interior photos:* no. *Cross-sectional diagram:* yes. *Plan diagram:* yes. *Pyramid field:* South Sakkara. *Field number:* VII. *Length:* 310 ft. *Height:* approx. 200 ft. (now much less). *Angle:* approx. 50 degrees. *Type:* true. *Materials:* limestone. *Location of entrance:* north–ground level. *Portcullises:* three vertical. *Chambers:* three.

Pyramid Complex: Merenre I. *Main pyramid:* yes. *Satellite pyramid(s):* no. *Mortuary temple:* yes–ruined (not yet excavated). *Valley temple:* yes–ruined (not yet excavated). *Offering shrine:* no?. *Mastaba(s):* no?. *Ship(s):* no. *Ship pit(s):* no. *Causeway:* yes–ruined (not yet excavated). *Temenos wall:* no. *Canal:* destroyed.

PHARAOH 28: PEPY II.
Position in dynasty: Fifth. *Portrait:* yes. *Length of reign:* 90 years–the longest recorded reign in history. *Dates of reign:* 2640–2549 B.C. *Mummy:* mummy wrappings only, found in burial chamber. *Sarcophagus:* granite. *Burial chamber:* yes. *Treasure:* not found. *Hawk name:* Neter-Kheu (Divine in His Ascension). *Vulture-and-Cobra name:* Neter-kheu. *Set or Hawk-of-Nubi name:* Sekhem (Ruler). *Reed-and-Hornet name:* Neferkere (Beautiful is the Spirit of the Sun-God). *Son-of-the-Sun-God (Ra) name:* Pepi. *Other names:* Piop; Phiop; Pepy.

The half-brother of Merenre I, this pharaoh enjoyed the longest reign of any king ever to rule over Egypt or, for that matter, anywhere in the world–an incredibly lengthy

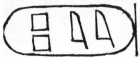

Top: *Pharaoh Pepy II with mother, Queen Ankhmes-Meri-Ra.* (Brooklyn Museum) **Bottom:** *Pharaoh Pepy II's cartouche.*

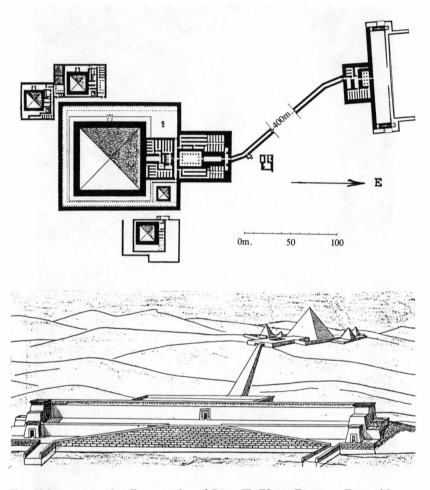

Top: *Mortuary and valley temples of Pepy II: Plans.* **Bottom:** *Pyramid complex of Pepy II: Reconstruction.* (G. JEQUIER)

kingship of 90 years! Pepy ascended the throne at six years of age, and lived to the ripe old age of 96.

His main pyramid, and three of his eight satellite pyramids (nos. 51, 53 and 58), were four of the ten pyramids found to contain Pyramid Texts in their burial chambers.

As Reed-and-Hornet king, Pepy II took the name Neferkere, "Beautiful is the Spirit of the Sun-God"; as Lord of the Vulture-and-Cobra and as Hawk-king he was called Neterkheu, "Divine in His Ascension"; as Son-of-the-Sun-God he used his personal name, Pepy; and as Hawk-of-Nubi he took the name Sekhem, "Ruler."

From the hieroglyphic inscriptions it appears as if Pepy II's mother acted as his mentor throughout the early years of his reign, and she is given many titles to make this relationship official.

An interesting royal letter from Pepy II's early period describes how an expedition of his, returning from the land of Yam in the deep interior of Lower Nubia, was bringing him a pygmy as a present. The child-king was apparently very much excited with this and sent a message to the expedition's leader to bring the pygmy with haste to the palace at Memphis.

Evidence points to a reasonably stable and peaceful reign for Pepy II. It was through the stability of the royal line at that time and the quiet conditions which prevailed that he was successfully able to gain and to hold his kingship at such a young age. In his more mature years Pepy II was known as an amiable ruler, but one who did not hesitate to enforce order among rebels whom his expeditionary forces encountered in their frequent journeys to southern Egypt and Nubia. In this respect, dealing with trade and strengthening the southern frontier, Pepy II was most aggressive. However, in the latter part of his unprecedented 90-year reign, his power and influence waned considerably.

From Nubia Pepy II's expeditions brought back ivory (in the form of elephant tusks), carob-wood chests, ointment and gold. A great number of prisoners were also brought out of Nubia at this time, to be used as slaves at Memphis.

The ancient texts refer to Pepy II's pyramid as "Neferkere (Pepy) Shines and Is Beautiful." Mention is also made of a pyramid city.

Pepy II's Prime Minister was Theu, the brother of his wife, the queen. The names of several princes are also known from this era, the most noteworthy being Ibi, Theu-Shemai, and another Theu.

For the burial of the latter, the records indicate that a wooden coffin, oil, perfume and 200 pieces of fine linen were used.

At Koptos (Qebt), Pepy II built a temple; at Abu Sir he made certain restorations in Pharaoh Neuserre's temple; at Elephantine the king's *second* Jubilee Festival is recorded on the rocks; at El Kab is yet another inscription of his reign; at Hieraconpolis the base of a royal statue of his was found; and at Hetnub, at the alabaster quarries, yet another inscription cites Pepy II's sixth year of tenure. Other objects of his reign also exist.

Pyramid: Pepy II. *Name:* Pepy Remains Living. *Number:* 55. *Exterior photos:* yes. *Interior photos:* yes. *Cross-sectional diagram:* yes. *Plan diagram:* yes. *Pyramid field:* South Sakkara. *Field number:* VII. *Length:* 255 ft. *Height:* 170 ft. (now much less). *Angle:* 53 degrees. *Type:* true. *Materials:* limestone. *Location of entrance:* north—ground level. *Portcullises:* three vertical, granite. *Chambers:* three. *Comments:* A gold ceremonial instrument, and broken alabaster and diorite vases were found in vestibule preceding burial chamber.

Pyramid Complex: Pepy II. *Main pyramid:* yes. *Satellite pyramid(s):* yes—eight (nos. 51, 52, 53, 54, 56, 57, 58, 59). *Mortuary temple:* yes—ruined. *Valley temple:* yes—ruined. *Offering shrine:* yes—now destroyed. *Mastaba(s):* yes. *Ship(s):* yes. *Ship pit(s):* yes. *Causeway:* yes—ruined. *Temenos wall:* yes. *Canal:* destroyed.

Satellite Pyramid: Pepy II. *Name:* Pyramid Queen Neit. *Number:* 51. *Exterior photos:* no. *Interior photos:* no. *Cross-sectional diagram:* no. *Plan diagram:* no. *Pyramid field:* South Sakkara. *Field number:* VII. *Length:* 79 ft. *Height:* 60 ft. (now 13 ft.) *Angle:* 60 degrees. *Type:* true. *Materials:* limestone. *Location of* *entrance:* north. *Portcullises:* one— vertical granite. *Chambers:* two. *Comments:* Granite sarcophagus and granite canopic chest found in burial chamber; mortuary temple on east side of pyramid, along with 16 wooden ships; pyramid texts on walls of burial chamber.

Satellite Pyramid: Pepy II. *Name:* Pyramid Queen Neit's Daughter. *Number:* 52. *Exterior photos:* no. *Interior photos:* no. *Cross-sectional diagram:* no. *Plan diagram:* no. *Pyramid field:* South Sakkara. *Field number:* VII. *Length:* 35 ft. *Height:* ? (now 8 ft.) *Angle:* 60 degrees. *Type:* true. *Materials:* limestone. *Location of entrance:* north. *Portcullises:* ?. *Chambers:* one?.

Satellite Pyramid: Pepy II. *Name:* Pyramid Queen Iput II. *Number:* 53. *Exterior photos:* no. *Interior photos:* no. *Cross-sectional diagram:* no. *Plan diagram:* no. *Pyramid field:* South Sakkara. *Field number:* VII. *Length:* 70 ft. *Height:* 50 ft. *Angle:* 55 degrees. *Type:* true. *Materials:* limestone. *Location of entrance:* north—ground. *Portcullises:* ?. *Chambers:* one. *Comments:* Mortuary temple on pyramids east side; pyramid texts found in burial chamber.

Satellite Pyramid: Pepy II. *Name:* Pyramid Queen Iput II's Daughter. *Number:* 54. *Exterior photos:* no. *Interior photos:* no. *Cross-sectional diagram:* no. *Plan diagram:* no. *Pyramid field:* South Sakkara. *Field number:* VII. *Length:* ?. *Height:* ?. *Angle:* ?. *Type:* true. *Materials:* limestone. *Location of entrance:* ?. *Portcullises:* ?. *Chambers:* one?.

Satellite Pyramid: Pepy II. *Name:* Pyramid Pepy II's Principal Queen?. *Number:* 56. *Exterior photos:* yes. *Interior photos:* no. *Cross-sectional diagram:* no. *Plan diagram:* no. *Pyramid field:* South Sakkara. *Field*

Cartouche of Pharaoh Merenre II.

number: VII. *Length:* ?. *Height:* ?. *Angle:* ?. *Type:* true. *Materials:* limestone. *Location of entrance:* north. *Portcullises:* ?. *Chambers:* one.

Satellite Pyramid: Pepy II. *Name:* Pyramid Queen?. *Number:* 57. *Exterior photos:* no. *Interior photos:* no. *Cross-sectional diagram:* no. *Plan diagram:* no. *Pyramid field:* South Sakkara. *Field number:* VII. *Length:* 50 ft. *Height:* ? (now 10 ft.) *Angle:* 52–55 degrees. *Type:* true. *Materials:* limestone. *Location of entrance:* ?. *Portcullises:* ?. *Chambers:* one.

Satellite Pyramid: Pepy II. *Name:* Pyramid Queen Udjebten. *Number:* 58. *Exterior photos:* no. *Interior photos:* no. *Cross-sectional diagram:* no. *Plan diagram:* no. *Pyramid field:* South Sakkara. *Field number:* VII. *Length:* 75 ft. *Height:* ?. *Angle:* 65 degrees. *Type:* true. *Materials:* limestone. *Location of entrance:* north. *Portcullises:* ?. *Chambers:* one. *Comments:* Pyramid texts were found in the burial chamber of this pyramid.

Satellite Pyramid: Pepy II. *Name:* Pyramid Queen Udjebten's Daughter. *Number:* 59. *Exterior photos:* no. *Interior photos:* no. *Cross-sectional diagram:* no. *Plan diagram:* no. *Pyramid field:* South Sakkara. *Field number:* VII. *Length:* ?. *Height:* ?. *Angle:* ?. *Type:* true. *Materials:* limestone. *Location of entrance:* north. *Portcullises:* ?. *Chambers:* one?.

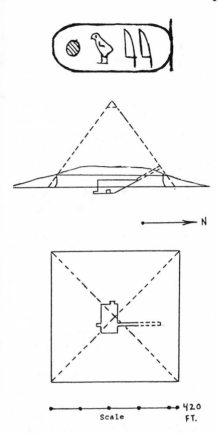

> N

Scale   420 FT.

Top: *Cartouche of Pharaoh Khui.*
Center and Bottom: *Pyramid of Khui, Dara: Cross-section (center) and plan.* (J.P. LEPRE)

PHARAOH 29: MERENRE II.
Position in dynasty: Sixth. *Portrait:* no. *Length of reign:* 1 year. *Dates of reign:* 2459–2458 B.C. *Mummy:* not found. *Sarcophagus:* ?. *Burial chamber:* ?. *Treasure:* ?. *Hawk name:* ?. *Vulture-and-Cobra name:* ?. *Set or Hawk-of-Nubi name:* ?. *Reed-and-Hornet name:* Merenra (Merenre). *Son-of-the-Sun-God (Ra) name:* Mehtiemsuf (The God Mehti is His Protection). *Other names:* Merenra-Mehtiemsuf; Methusuph.

The aged Pepy II, whose final years upon the throne weakened the country considerably, was, upon his death, succeeded by Merenre II, who was very likely his grandson.

On his accession, he took Merenre (II) as his Reed-and-Hornet name. The Abydos King List officially records him as the successor to Pepy II, but the Sakkara List omits his name. He is acknowledged in the Turin Papyrus, however, by his tenure of one year, although the name itself is obliterated. Beyond this nothing more is known of this king, but this is not at all unusual, in light of the exceptionally short duration of his reign.

Upon the death of Merenre II, the Sixth Dynasty was seriously weakened, and for some time there was no pharaoh on the throne. A period of anarchy was now ushered in, which in a six-year period witnessed the unstable reigns of two obscure pharaohs, Khui and Merikari.

Pyramid: Merenre II. *Name:* Pyramid Merenre II. *Number:* 31. *Exterior photos:* no. *Interior photos:* no. *Cross-sectional diagram:* no. *Plan diagram:* no. *Pyramid field:* North Sakkara. *Field number:* VI. *Length:* approx. 245 ft. *Height:* approx. 160 ft. (now 40 ft.) *Angle:* approx. 52 degrees. *Type:* true?. *Materials:* limestone?. *Location of entrance:* ?. *Portculisses:* three (vertical?). *Chambers:* three?.

Pyramid Complex: Merenre II. *Main pyramid:* yes?. *Satellite pyramid(s):* ?. *Mortuary temple:* ?. *Valley temple:* ?. *Offering shrine:* ?. *Mastaba(s):* ?. *Ship(s):* ?. *Ship pit(s):* ?. *Causeway:* ?. *Temenos wall:* ?. *Canal:* probably destroyed.

PHARAOH 30: KHUI.
Position in dynasty: Seventh. *Portrait:* no. *Length of reign:* 3 years. *Dates of reign:* 2458–2456 B.C. *Mummy:* not found. *Sarcophagus:*

?. Burial chamber: yes*?. Treasure:* not found. *Hawk name:* ?. *Vulture-and-Cobra name:* ?. *Set or Hawk-of-Nubi name:* ?. *Reed-and-Hornet name:* Khui. *Son-of-the-Sun-God (Ra) name:* ?.

After the period of anarchy following Merenre II's death, a provincial prince named Khui took the throne as the new pharaoh. Other than the fact that he built a substantial pyramid at Dara, near Menfalut, nothing at all is known of this obscure king. His name was found in a tomb at his pyramid site, but there is speculation that the site itself could date to the Seventh or even the Eighth Dynasty. Khui, then, is assigned to this period of the Sixth Dynasty only tentatively. The Abydos King List acknowledges him, but not the Turin Papyrus. His name space may well be one of those which has been obliterated due to the fragility of the aged papyrus.

Pyramid: Khui. *Name:* Pyramid Khui. *Number:* 94. *Exterior photos:* no. *Interior photos:* no. *Cross-sectional diagram:* yes. *Plan diagram:* yes. *Pyramid field:* Dara. *Field number:* XVI. *Length:* 420 ft. *Height:* approx. 250 ft. (now 15 ft.) *Angle:* approx. 52 degrees. *Type:* true. *Materials:* brick. *Location of entrance:* north face—the only pyramid from Unas on with an above-ground entrance. *Portcullises:* none?. *Chambers:* one?. *Comments:* There is a square depression cut into the floor of the burial chamber of this pyramid for a canopic chest.

Pyramid Complex: Khui. *Main pyramid:* yes. *Satellite pyramid(s):* no. *Mortuary temple:* yes — destroyed. *Valley temple:* no. *Offering shrine:* no. *Mastaba(s):* yes?. *Ship(s):* no. *Ship pit(s):* no. *Causeway:* no. *Temenos wall:* no. *Canal:* destroyed.

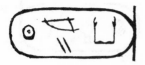

Cartouche of Pharaoh Merikari.

PHARAOH 31: MERIKARI. *Position in dynasty:* Eighth (last). *Portrait:* no. *Length of reign:* 3 years. *Dates of reign:* 2455–2453 B.C. *Mummy:* not found. *Sarcophagus:* ?. *Burial chamber:* ? shaft leading to ends in water. *Treasure:* not found. *Hawk name:* ?. *Vulture-and-Cobra name:* ?. *Set or Hawk-of-Nubi name:* ?. *Reed-and-Hornet name:* Merikara (Merikari) (Beloved of the Spirit of Ra). *Son-of-the-Sun-God (Ra) name:* ?.

Even less is known of this new pharaoh, Merikari, than was known of his predecessor, Khui. We have hieroglyphic evidence of his pyramid being built at North Sakkara, and it may well be the dilapidated structure which lies just north of Teti's pyramid. The lack of any evidence concerning this pharaoh and the previous one predicates the darksome era which significantly signals the end of the once-prosperous Sixth Dynasty.

Pyramid: Merikari. *Name:* Pyramid Merikari. *Number:* 32. *Exterior photos:* no. *Interior photos:* no. *Cross-sectional diagram:* no. *Plan diagram:* no. *Pyramid field:* North Sakkara. *Field number:* VI. *Length:* ?. *Height:* ?. *Angle:* ?. *Type:* true?. *Materials:* limestone. *Location of entrance:* ?. *Portcullises:* ?. *Chambers:* ?. *Comments:* The supposed pyramid of Merikari, lying just north of Teti's monument, has defied all attempts at investigation due to the presence of water at the bottom of its entrance shaft.

* 1 Neterkere　brother

|

2 sister　Nitorkris

3 Neferkere　foreigner

4 Neby　　　foreigner

5 Iby　　　foreigner

Dynasty VII Genealogy

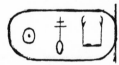

Cartouche of Pharaoh Neferkere.

Pyramid Complex: Merikari.
Main pyramid: yes?. *Satellite pyramid(s):* ?. *Mortuary temple:* ?. *Valley temple:* ?. *Offering shrine:* ?. *Mastaba(s):* ?. *Ship(s):* ?. *Ship pit(s):* ?. *Causeway:* ?. *Temenos wall:* ?. *Canal:* probably destroyed.

DYNASTY VII

• *Duration:* **75 years (2452–2378 B.C.).** *Pharaohs:* **1. Neterkere (no pyramid). 2. Nitokris (queen-pharaoh; no pyramid). 3. Neferkere. 4. Neby or Neferes (no pyramid). 5. Iby.**

PHARAOH 32: NEFERKERE.
Position in dynasty: Third. *Portrait:* no. *Length of reign:* 22 years.

Dates of reign: 2435–2414 B.C. *Mummy:* not found. *Sarcophagus:* ?. *Burial chamber:* ?. *Treasure:* not found. *Hawk name:* ?. *Vulture-and-Cobra name:* ?. *Set or Hawk-of-Nubi name:* ?. *Reed-and-Hornet name:* Neferkara (Neferkere). *Son-of-the-Sun-God (Ra) name:* ?. *Other names:* Murtaios.

The Seventh Dynasty, an obscurity in itself, was comprised of five rulers, with one of them being the Queen-Pharaoh, Nitokris. However, only two of these pharaohs built pyramidal tombs, namely, Neferkere and Iby.

Neferkere, the third pharaoh of this dynasty, built a pyramid at North Sakkara. The exact location, however, is not presently known. He ruled for 20 years.

Pyramid: Neferkere. *Name:* Pyramid Neferkere. *Number:* 43.

Exterior photos: no. *Interior photos:* no. *Cross-sectional diagram:* no. *Plan diagram:* no. *Pyramid field:* Sakkara (north?). *Field number:* VI. *Length:* ?. *Height:* ?. *Angle:* ?. *Type:* true?. *Materials:* limestone?. *Location of entrance:* ?. *Portcullises:* ?. *Chambers:* ?. *Comments:* This pyramid is recorded on the false door of Queen Ankhnes-pepi at Sakkara, but has never been found. **Pyramid Complex: Neferkere.** *Main pyramid:* yes?. *Satellite pyramid(s):* ?. *Mortuary temple:* ?. *Valley temple:* ?. *Offering shrine:* ?. *Mastaba(s):* ?. *Ship(s):* ?. *Ship pit(s):* ?. *Causeway:* ?. *Temenos wall:* ?. *Canal:* probably destroyed.

PHARAOH 33: IBY.
Position in dynasty: Fifth (last). *Portrait:* yes. *Length of reign:* 12 years. *Dates of reign:* 2389–2378 B.C. *Mummy:* not found. *Sarcophagus:* granite. *Burial chamber:* yes?. *Treasure:* not found. *Hawk name:* ?. *Vulture-and-Cobra name:* ?. *Set or Hawk-of-Nubi name:* ?. *Reed-and-Hornet name:* Ab (Ib) (Iby). *Son-of-the-Sun-God (Ra) name:* ?. *Other names:* Hakare-aba; Dedkeshemire Ib; Kakare-ibi; Dedkeshemire (The Sun-God in the Spirit of the Stranger).

Iby, the last pharaoh of this dynasty, built a pyramid with a sizeable mortuary temple at South Sakkara, just southeast of the valley temple of Pepy II. Although he reigned for 12 years, we know very little about him. The shemi portion of his Dedkeshemire or Dedkeshemire Ib name means "stranger" or "foreigner," and the addition of Ib is also foreign, indicating that he may have been of Asiatic origin.

This point is reinforced by the fact that during this unstable period of Egyptian history, there was an influx

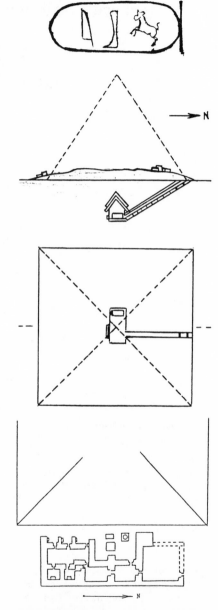

Top: *Cartouche of Pharaoh Iby.* **Second from top:** *Cross-section of Pyramid of Iby, South Sakkara.* **Third from top:** *Pyramid of Iby: Plan.* **Bottom:** *Mortuary temple of Iby.* (J.P. LEPRE)

*1) Akhtoy I father
|
     2) son Akhtoy II father
       |
         3) son Akhtoy III father
           |
           4) Akhtoy IV son

Dynasty IX Genealogy

of Asiatic foreigners into the country. Indeed, the name of the pharaoh preceding Iby, Neby or Neferes, is also of Asiatic strain.

With the death of Iby, the stormy Seventh Dynasty comes to a close, and the building of pyramids as royal tombs nearly ceases.

The only significance attached to this obscure pharaoh is the fact that Pyramid Texts were found in the burial chamber of his monument. **Pyramid: Iby.** *Name:* Pyramid Iby. *Number:* 50. *Exterior photos:* no. *Interior photos:* no. *Cross-sectional diagram:* no. *Plan diagram:* yes. *Pyramid field:* South Sakkara. *Field number:* VII. *Length:* 103 ft. *Height:* approx. 75 ft. *Angle:* approx. 60 degrees. *Type:* true. *Materials:* limestone. *Location of entrance:* north — ground. *Portcullises:* no?. *Chambers:* two. *Comments:* This pyramid had a *double casing* of limestone. **Pyramid Complex: Iby.** *Main pyramid:* yes. *Satellite pyramid(s):* no. *Mortuary temple:* yes — brick. *Valley temple:* no. *Offering shrine:* no. *Mastaba(s):* no?. *Ship(s):* no. *Ship pit(s):* no. *Causeway:* no. *Temenos wall:* no. *Canal:* destroyed.

DYNASTY VIII
- *Duration:* 106 years (2377–2272 B.C.). *Pharaohs:* 1. **Neferkere** (2377–? B.C.). 2. **Khuit.** 3. **Neferkere Khendui (Khendu).** 4. **Merenhur.** 5. **Neferhunihur (Hur).** 6. **Sneferke.** 7. **Nekere.** 8. **Terorol (Telolol)** (8 years). 9. **Neferkehur.** 10. **Piopsonb.** 11. **Sneferenkhre Piop (18 years).** 12. **Sneferke Ennu.** 13. . . .**keure.** 14. **Neferkeure.** 15. **Neferkeuhur (20 years).** 16. **Uthkere Sekherseny** (2281–2279 B.C.). 17. **Neferkhnumhur** (2278–2274 B.C.). 18. **Neferirkere** (2273–2272 B.C.).

Note: Many of these kings were foreign invaders who ruled Egypt during this era of instability. The exact relationship from one to the other is uncertain.

No pyramids were built during this dynasty.

DYNASTY IX

- *Duration:* 50 years (2271–2222 B.C.). *Pharaohs:* 1. **Akhtoy I** (Wahkere). 2271–2265 B.C. (No pyramid.) 2. **Akhtoy II** (Meryibre). 2264–2253 B.C. (No pyramid.) 3. **Akhtoy III** (Nebkeure). 2252–2228 B.C. (No pyramid.) 4. **Akhtoy IV** (Merykere). 2227-2222 B.C.

Note: This dynasty, ruling in the north, was contemporaneous with

the Eleventh Dynasty (2271–2122
B.C.), ruling in the south.
Only one pyramid was built during
this dynasty.

PHARAOH 34: AKHTOY IV.
Position in dynasty: Fourth (last).
Portrait: no. *Length of reign:* 6
years. *Dates of reign:* 2227–2222 B.C.
Mummy: not found. *Sarcophagus:*
?. *Burial chamber:* ?. *Treasure:* not
found. *Hawk name:* ?. *Vulture-and-
Cobra name:* ?. *Set or Hawk-of-
Nubi name:* ?. *Reed-and-Hornet
name:* Merikara (Merykere) (Beloved of the Spirit of Ra). *Son-of-
the-Sun-God (Ra) name:* ?. *Other
names:* Aa-kha-ra (Akhtoi) (Akhtoy).

Pyramid: Akhtoy IV. *Name:*
Pyramid Akhtoy. *Number:* 39. *Exterior photos:* no. *Interior photos:*
no. *Cross-sectional diagram:* no.
Plan diagram: no. *Pyramid field:*
North Sakkara. *Field number:* VI.
Length: 325 ft. *Height:* approx. 200
ft. *Angle:* ?. *Type:* true?. *Materials:*
limestone?. *Location of entrance:* ?.
Portcullises: ?. *Chambers:* one?.
Pyramid Complex: Akhtoy IV.
Main pyramid: yes. *Satellite
pyramid(s):* no. *Mortuary temple:*
no. *Valley temple:* no. *Offering
shrine:* no. *Mastaba(s):* no?. *Ship(s):*
no. *Ship pit(s):* no. *Causeway:* no.
Temenos wall: no. *Canal:* destroyed.
The Eighth Dynasty, like the
Seventh, was full of uncertainties
and factions. The Ninth Dynasty
was ruled by four kings, each having
the personal name Akhtoy. It was
the last of these pharaohs, Merykere Akhtoy, "Beloved of the Spirit
of Re," who, reigning for six years
only, managed to build a sizeable
pyramid at North Sakkara. Unfortunately, however, only fragments of
its long temenos wall now remain.
Another true pyramid would not be
built in Egypt until the Twelfth

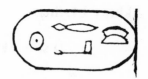

Cartouche of Pharaoh Akhtoy IV.

Dynasty revival period, over 100
years later.
At Akhtoy's pyramid site, a well-
executed statue of him was found
(Cairo Museum), and a palette found
at Assiout, and bearing his name, is
now in the Louvre.
There is a record of how Akhtoy
temporarily restored order in Egypt,
and how, in a show of confidence, he
traveled up and down the Nile River
with an enormous fleet, and was
hailed upon his return to the royal
palace.
Beside his pyramid, Akhtoy also
constructed quite a large temple at
Seut, which was dedicated to the god
Wepwet.
The rapid termination of the Ninth
Dynasty under Akhtoy indicates that
his reestablishment of peace and control throughout Egypt was short-
lived.
Considering the era of his reign,
then, it is not unreasonable to
assume either that he died without
leaving an official heir or that
another uprising brought about his
demise.

DYNASTY X

• *Duration:* **25 years (2221–2197**
B.C.**). *Pharaohs:* 1. Neferkere (no
pyramid). 2. Akhtoi (no pyramid). 3.
S...h (no pyramid). 4. ...? (no
pyramid). 5. Mer... (no pyramid).
6. Senti... (no pyramid). 7. H...
(no pyramid). 8. ...? (no pyramid).
9. ...? (no pyramid).**

*1) Intef I father
|
2) son Intef II brother
|
3) brother Mentuhotep I father
|
4) father Mentuhotep II son
|
5) father Mentuhotep III son
|
6) son Mentuhotep IV father
|
7) son Mentuhotep V

Dynasty XI Genealogy

Note: This dynasty is clouded in obscurity, and the relationships of these pharaohs (most of whose full names are not even known) is uncertain.

DYNASTY XI

• *Duration:* 160 years (2271–2112 B.C.). *Pharaohs:* 1. Intef (Wahenkh). 2271–2222 B.C. (No pyramid.) 2. Intef II (Nakht-Nebtepnefer). 2221–2212 B.C. (No pyramid.) 3. Mentuhotep I (Senkhibtoui). 2211–2197 B.C. (No pyramid.) 4. Mentuhotep II (Nebheptre). 2196–2172 B.C. (No pyramid.) 5. Mentuhotep III (Nebhapetre). 2271–2125 B.C. (No pyramid.) 6. Mentuhotep IV (Senkhkere). 2124–2115 B.C. (No pyramid.) 7. Mentuhotep V (Nebtouire). 2114–2112 B.C. (No pyramid.)

Note: No true pyramids were built during this dynasty. However, "pyramid temples" were erected. (See "Other Pyramids," pp. 231–232).

This dynasty, ruling in the south, was contemporaneous with the Ninth Dynasty (2271–2222 B.C.), ruling in the north.

VII. Dynasties XII–XIII (The Revival)

DYNASTY XII

- *Duration:* 212 years (2111–1899 B.C.). *Pharaohs:* 1. Amenemhat I. 2. Sunusert I. 3. Amenemhat II. 4. Senusert II. 5. Senusert III. 6. Amenemhat III. 7. Amenemhat IV. 8. Sebek-Neferu-Ra (Queen Pharaoh).

After the first great era of pyramid building and the decline which followed, Egypt experienced an unprecedented diffusion of its central authority, and anarchy ensued. During brief intervals of this age of lawlessness, semblances of order were partially restored, but much of the country continued to suffer the consequences of not having a ruler strong enough to unify the opposing factions and the various bands of renegades which had established themselves in certain quarters.

The line of Intefs, after having established the Eleventh Dynasty, met with a certain degree of success in this arena of conflict as did their successors, the Mentuhoteps; nevertheless, all failed in their attempt at total unification.

It was the destiny of the Twelfth Dynasty pharaohs, the Amenemhats, Senuserts and a queen pharaoh (Sebek-Neferu-Ra), finally to succeed where previous rulers had failed. This dramatic turn of events did not occur suddenly, with the rule of a single individual, but was a gradual undertaking which began with the establishment of this new dynasty by a former chief vizier, who ascended the throne as Amenemhat I.

Having been influenced by the pyramids of the late third and early fourth dynasties, this monarch constructed a sizeable pyramid at Lisht, surrounded by a complex complete with temenos wall, mortuary temple and over 100 royal mastabas.

Amenemhat's interest in the pyramid complexes of the Old Kingdom is exemplified by his assimilation of blocks of stone from those monuments into his own complex—primarily delicately carved reliefs—and also by his reproduction of those reliefs on fresh blocks cut at his own quarries.

Although the entrance passage of Amenemhat's pyramid was sealed with huge granite plugs when first completed, some effort has been made to reach and explore the burial chamber in modern times. A complete understanding of this crypt is lacking because that chamber is permanently flooded with Nile water. The only means of successfully exploring the submerged area would be through the use of scuba-diving equipment.

Amenemhat's successor, Senusert I, also built his pyramid at Lisht, and it, too, is permanently inaccessible because of the rise of the Nile at that pyramid field. This pharaoh also appears to have been influenced by the funerary architecture of the Old Kingdom, having built a mortuary

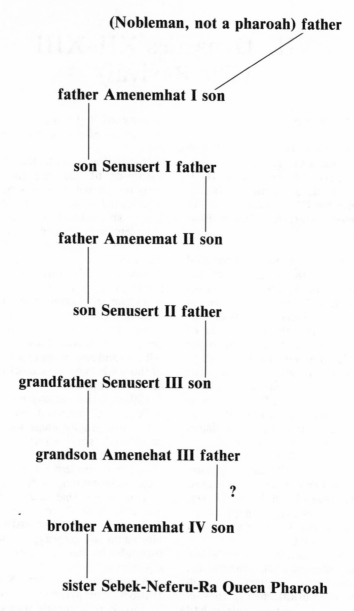

(Nobleman, not a pharoah) father

father Amenemhat I son

son Senusert I father

father Amenemat II son

son Senusert II father

grandfather Senusert III son

grandson Amenehat III father

?

brother Amenemhat IV son

sister Sebek-Neferu-Ra Queen Pharoah

Dynasty XII Genealogy

temple nearly identical in plan to that of Pepy II of Dynasty VI.

That the power and resources of this newfound dynasty were now on the rise is exemplified by the fact that Senusert I constructed not only his quite large parent pyramid, but ten smaller, satellite pyramids as well. Here we have not only a double temenos wall surrounding the entire complex, but additional ones built around each of the subsidiary pyramids as well.

The next pharaoh, Amenemhat II, chose to build his pyramid at Dahshur in the vicinity of Sneferu's three pyramids of the Third Dynasty. This pyramid did not have a complex internal design and was of a unimpressive length (265′); nevertheless it signaled a continuance in the stability of the blossoming Twelfth Dynasty.

The successor to Amenemhat II was Senusert II, who constructed a much larger pyramid (350′ long) at Lahun. This pyramid was especially notable for having a double entrance situated on the south, with both apertures at ground level. Also unorthodox was the devious course of the subterranean passageway leading to the burial chamber. This edifice, then marks the commencement of complex design for pyramids of this era.

The next pharaoh to rule in this dynasty, Senusert III, erected another 350′ pyramid at Dahshur, even more complex in design. It, too, was equipped with an unorthodox entrance, this time to the west, at ground level. The pyramid complex of this site is quite large, encompassing over 14 acres — the most extensive Twelfth Dynasty complex constructed up to that time.

This pharaoh, like the others of the Twelfth Dynasty, was also influenced by the architectural characteristics of the Old Kingdom, which is evidenced by the similarity of the outer design of his temenos or enclosure wall to that of Djoser's Step Pyramid at Sakkara — a design which is also evident on the sarcophagus found in the burial chamber of Senusert III.

With the ascendancy of the next pharaoh, Amenemhat III, the strength and influence of this dynasty reached its zenith. This king erected two pyramids, one at Dahshur and the other at Hawara. Both had unconventional entrances (the former, east ground, and the latter, south ground), and both were characterized, internally, by the most ingenious maze of corridors and chambers ever contrived in an Egyptian pyramid. The edifice at Dahshur was comprised of over 30 separate rooms or vestibules, with a labyrinth of corridors leading north, south, east and west; the one at Hawara occupied several subterranean levels.

The last two pyramids of the Twelfth Dynasty, those constructed by Pharaoh Amenemhat IV and Queen-Pharaoh Sebek-Neferu-Ra, also possessed complex internal designs. The former had an irregular entrance situated at its south side, at ground level. The latter, although entered from the north in modern times, has not yet revealed its original entrance. Massive portcullises were employed in both of these monuments, and resemblances to the internal structure of the pyramid of Amenemhat III at Hawara are evident.

The three pyramids of the Thirteenth Dynasty, those of the Pharaohs Ameny, Ay and Khendjer II, followed the characteristic internal plan favored by the previous pharaohs, with each monument having unorthodox entrances and a unique and intricate system of chambers and passages. Most notable is the pyramid of Ay, at South Sakkara, whose internal ingenuity rivals that of the two pyramids of Amenemhat III. Although this monument matches the length of the preceding pyramids of Dynasty XII, the others, of Ameny and Khendjer, are dramatically smaller (165′ and 170′, respectively), suggesting a decline in the power of the pharaohs at this time.

After the pyramid of Khendjer, another pyramid would not be built in Egypt for another hundred years (by the Seventeenth Dynasty Pharaoh, Sebekemsaf I), and that one would be much smaller and far less complex internally. The two great eras of pyramid building were now over, and would not be matched by the subsequent attempts of the Seventeenth, Eighteenth, Ptolemaic or Ethiopian dynasties.

PHARAOH 35: AMENEMHAT I.

Position in dynasty: First. *Portrait:* yes. *Length of reign:* 29 years. *Dates of reign:* 2111–2083 B.C. *Mummy:* not found. *Sarcophagus:* ?. *Burial chamber:* yes (now flooded). *Treasure:* not found. *Hawk name:* Nemmosut (Repeating the Story of Creation). *Vulture-and-Cobra name:* Nemmosut. *Set or Hawk-of-Nubi name:* Nemmosut. *Reed-and-Hornet name:* Sehotpeibre (Pacifying the Heart of the Sun-God). *Son-of-the-Sun-God (Ra) name:* Amenemhat (Ammenemhet) (The God Amen is Before Him). *Other names:* Amenemhet, Amen-emmes; Ameny.

This pharaoh, the founder of the Twelfth Dynasty and spearheader of the revival of pyramid building on a grand scale, is most noteworthy for a well-composed poem, which was addressed to his son, Senusert I, but was apparently intended for others as well. It was a highly regarded piece of literature in times past, and several fragments of it have been preserved.

Although there is no record of this pharaoh's sarcophagus having been found in his burial chamber, a hieroglyphic inscription cut into the rock of the desert quarry at Wady Hammamat describes how a flawless block of stone was cut and extracted there to make the sarcophagus.

Amenemhat I, meaning "The God Amen Is Before Him," was also known as Ameny, which is the shortened version of that name. He adopted the name Sehotpeibre, meaning "The Pacification of the Sun-God's Heart," as Reed-and-Hornet king, and the name Nemmosut as the Lord of the Vulture-and-Cobra, Hawk-king and Hawk-of-Nubi.

Amenemhat ruled Egypt with a strong hand, reestablishing law and order throughout the realm. Under him, the nation underwent a revitalization of prosperity, and great building projects were again resumed.

Amenemhat constructed and restored numerous temples at Bubastis, Crocodilopolis, Koptos, Denderah, Karnak, Tanis and other sites. He also established new landmarks and boundaries and expelled the Asiatics from Egypt, building a great barrier across the Wady Tumilat to keep them out. No trace of this wall exists, though, as it was probably built of mud-brick. Accounts of this wall indicate a project on the scale of the frontier wall of Britain, built by the Roman emperor Hadrian.

At some point in his reign, Amenemhat decided to transfer the royal residence from Thebes to a place near modern Lisht. Calling it Ithttoui, "The Control of the Two Lands," he ornamented it with gold and furnished it with doors of copper. In moving the capital from Thebes, where the previous Eleventh Dynasty monarchs resided, Amenemhat signaled a distinct break in both policy and genealogy, and set a precedent for other rulers of his line to follow.

Pharaoh Amenemhat I and his cartouche. (HEAD: EGYPTIAN MUSEUM, CAIRO)

Although Amenemhat's break with the Eleventh Dynasty established a new lineage of ascendancy to the throne, he was nevertheless of the old Theban order himself. It was evidently through his mother's branch of the family that the beginning of a rift with that order occurred, for she was of Nubian descent.

Amenemhat's pyramid was called Kenofre, "The Lofty and Beautiful," and mention of it and its mortuary temple endowment are recorded in the Kahun Papyrus. It is also noted at Aswan, in one of the granite quarries. Mention is also made in inscriptions at Hammanat of quarrying expeditions of Amenemhat being sent to that region in the cool November.

In the twenty-first year of his tenure there was an assassination attempt against Amenemhat, an event which he survived but which also left him bitter and untrusting. In his famous poem addressed to his son, Amenemhat counsels him to "trust no one." In the middle of the thirtieth year of his reign, Amenemhat passed away, leaving his son Senusert to succeed him. The Chronicle of Sinuhe notes that with the death of Amenemhat, the great double doors of the palace were closed, while the people sat with bowed heads and wept.

Pyramid: Amenemhat I. *Name:* Beautiful Height of Amenemhat. *Number:* 75. *Exterior photos:* no. *Interior photos:* no. *Cross-sectional diagram:* yes. *Plan diagram:* yes. *Pyramid field:* Lisht. *Field number:* X. *Length:* 275 ft. *Height:* 180 ft. (now 65 ft.) *Angle:* 54 degrees. *Type:* true. *Materials:* limestone. *Location of entrance:* north — ground. *Portcullises:* no. *Chambers:* two.

Pyramid Complex: Amenemhat I. *Main pyramid:* yes. *Satellite pyramid(s):* no. *Mortuary temple:* yes. *Valley temple:* probably exists, not yet unearthed. *Offering shrine:* yes — destroyed. *Mastaba(s):* yes. *Ship(s):* no. *Ship pit(s):* no. *Causeway:* yes. *Temenos wall:* yes. *Canal:* destroyed.

PHARAOH 36: SENUSERT I.
Position in dynasty: Second. *Portrait:* yes. *Length of reign:* 35 years. *Dates of reign:* 2082–2047 B.C. *Mummy:* not found. *Sarcophagus:* no. *Burial chamber:* yes?. *Treasure:* not found. *Hawk name:* Ankhmestu. *Vulture-and-Cobra name:* ?. *Set or Hawk-of-Nubi name:* ?. *Reed-and-Hornet name:* Kheperkara (Kheperkere). *Son-of-the-Sun-God (Ra) name:* Usertsen (Senusert). *Other names:* Enkhmosut; Sesostri; Sesostris; Sesusri.

The pyramid of this pharaoh, the son of Amenemhat I, employed the unusual feature of massive retaining walls, rather than accretion layers, as was the case with most other pyramids.

The burial chamber of this pyramid, like that of the previous pharaoh, is permanently flooded with Nile water. This phenomenon is due to the rise of the river at this pyramid site, and makes examination of the interior of the monument near impossible.

An interesting feature of this pha-

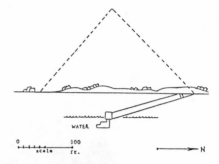

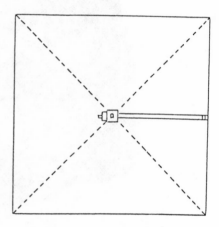

Pyramid of Amenemhat I, Lisht: Cross-section (top) *and plan.* (J.P. LEPRE)

raoh's pyramid complex is the existence of no fewer than ten satellite pyramids built for his favorite queens and princesses.

Ten limestone statues of this king, representing him seated on his throne, were discovered in his mortuary temple in 1894 (now in Cairo Museum). Thirteen stone altars dedicated to him by his priestesses were likewise found there.

The personal name of this pharaoh, Senusert, was employed for his Son-of-the-Sun-God title. His Hawk-of-Nubi, Hawk-king and Lord of the Vulture-and-Cobra names, however, were all Enkhmosut. As Reed-and-

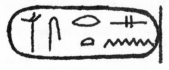

Pharaoh Senusert I and his cartouche. (HEAD: EGYPTIAN MUSEUM, CAIRO)

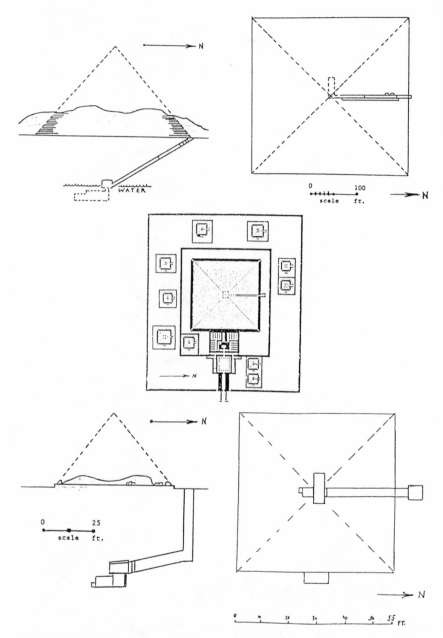

Top: *Pyramid of Senusert I, Lisht: Cross-section (left) and plan.* (J.P. LEPRE)
Center: *Pyramid complex of Senusert I, Lisht, showing plans of main and sub-sidiary pyramids.* (D. ARNOLD, IN I.E.S. EDWARDS) Bottom: *Principal sub-sidiary pyramid of Senusert I, Lisht: Cross-section (left) and plan.* (J.P. LEPRE)

Hornet king, he was crowned Kheperkere, "Existing by the Spirit of the Sun-God."

At Heliopolis (On), Senusert constructed a temple for this Sun-God, and inscriptions there tell of how the pharaoh called together his cabinet to announce this project. The text tells of numerous altars and offerings to the Sun-God, Harakhte, and of how Senusert entrusted the building of the temple to the steward of the treasury. Little remains of this great temple today, except for some inscribed stones and a 66'-high obelisk of pink granite. These inscriptions and the obelisk itself record the name of Senusert and indicate that the temple was built in order to commemorate his jubilee. One of the other inscriptions found mentions the presence of bronze, copper, silver and gold vases and censers.

Other remains of Senusert's reign are numerous. At Tanis, three fragmented statues of the king were found; near Tanis, a granite sphinx; from Bubastis, a temple wall; from Atouleh, a fragment of another temple; at Ebod, a door lintel and jamb; from Begig, a granite obelisk; and some small tablets of a foundation deposit from Abydos.

At the ancient capital of the Hawk-kings, Hieraconpolis, Senusert built a temple; at Elephantine, a second temple; and at Koptos, yet another temple to the local god, Min. At Philae, a stele of the king was found; at Nekheb, an altar; and another altar at Taud.

The granite quarries at the First Cataract, the breccia quarries at Wady Hammamat, the turquoise and copper mines at Sinai, the gold mines at El Kab, and other quarries and mines were used extensively during Senusert's reign.

In the winter of the eighteenth year of his reign, Senusert conducted a great military expedition to the Third Cataract, and mention is made of his having sailed through the Land of Kush (Cush).

Taken together, the numerous inscriptions ascribed to Senusert make mention of 20 years of his 35-year tenure.

Aside from the larger remains of his reign, such as pyramids (Senusert built 11 altogether: one major, his own, and ten smaller subsidiary models for his queens), temples, obelisks, statues, altars, and large, inscribed tablets of stone, much smaller artifacts as well have been discovered, including vases, weights, inscribed shells, scarabs, cylinder-seals, a copper axe, a lion of amethyst, and a carnelian statuette.

In the thirty-third year of his reign, Senusert, who was now 70 years of age, established a co-regency with his son, Amenemhat II. It was not long after this that Senusert ordered the sculpting of the ten limestone statues which were found in his pyramid mortuary temple at Lisht. These statues, however, although completed, failed to be set up inside the temple and were discovered lying on the ground outside. It appears as if the pharaoh met an untimely death at that time (in his thirty-fifth year of tenure) and the kingship was passed on to his son, Amenemhat II.

Pyramid: Senusert I. *Name:* Protected Place of Senusert or Senusert Surveying the Two Lands. *Number:* 76. *Exterior photos:* no. *Interior photos:* no. *Cross-sectional diagram:* yes. *Plan diagram:* yes. *Pyramid field:* Lisht. *Field number:* X. *Length:* 350 ft. *Height:* 190 ft. *Angle:* 49 degrees. *Type:* true. *Materials:* limestone. *Location of entrance:* north — ground level. *Portcullises:* none?. *Chambers:* one?.

Pyramid Complex: Senusert I.
Main pyramid: yes. *Satellite pyramid(s):* yes—ten (nos. 77-86). *Mortuary temple:* yes. *Valley temple:* probably existed—not yet found. *Offering shrine:* yes. *Mastaba(s):* yes. *Ship(s):* no. *Ship pit(s):* no. *Causeway:* yes. *Temenos wall:* yes—two (inner and outer). *Canal:* destroyed.

Satellite Pyramid: Senusert I.
Name: Pyramid Queen?. *Number:* 77. *Exterior photos:* no. *Interior photos:* no. *Cross-sectional diagram:* no. *Plan diagram:* yes. *Pyramid field:* Lisht. *Field number:* X. *Length:* 50 ft. *Height:* approx. 30 ft. *Angle:* approx. 51 degrees. *Type:* true. *Materials:* limestone. *Location of entrance:* north—ground. *Portcullises:* yes?. *Chambers:* one?. *Comments:* This satellite pyramid has its own mortuary temple, offering shrine and temenos wall.

Satellite Pyramid: Senusert I.
Name: Pyramid Queen?. *Number:* 78. *Exterior photos:* no. *Interior photos:* no. *Cross-sectional diagram:* no. *Plan diagram:* yes. *Pyramid field:* Lisht. *Field number:* X. *Length:* 50 ft. *Height:* approx. 30 ft. *Angle:* approx. 51 degrees. *Type:* true. *Materials:* limestone. *Location of entrance:* north—ground. *Portcullises:* yes?. *Chambers:* one?. *Comments:* This satellite pyramid has its own mortuary temple, offering shrine and temenos wall.

Satellite Pyramid: Senusert I.
Name: Pyramid Queen?. *Number:* 79. *Exterior photos:* no. *Interior photos:* no. *Cross-sectional diagram:* no. *Plan diagram:* yes. *Pyramid field:* Lisht. *Field number:* X. *Length:* 60 ft. *Height:* approx. 35 ft. *Angle:* approx. 51 degrees. *Type:* true. *Materials:* limestone. *Location of entrance:* north—ground. *Portcullises:* yes?. *Chambers:* one?. *Comments:* This satellite pyramid

has its own mortuary temple, offering shrine and temenos wall.

Satellite Pyramid: Senusert I.
Name: Pyramid Queen?. *Number:* 80. *Exterior photos:* no. *Interior photos:* no. *Cross-sectional diagram:* no. *Plan diagram:* yes. *Pyramid field:* Lisht. *Field number:* X. *Length:* 55 ft. *Height:* approx. 32 ft. *Angle:* approx. 51 degrees. *Type:* true. *Materials:* limestone. *Location of entrance:* north—ground. *Portcullises:* yes?. *Chambers:* one?. *Comments:* This satellite pyramid has its own mortuary temple, offering shrine and temenos wall.

Satellite Pyramid: Senusert I.
Name: Pyramid Princess?. *Number:* 81. *Exterior photos:* no. *Interior photos:* no. *Cross-sectional diagram:* no. *Plan diagram:* yes. *Pyramid field:* Lisht. *Field number:* X. *Length:* 50 ft. *Height:* approx. 30 ft. *Angle:* approx. 51 degrees. *Type:* true. *Materials:* limestone. *Location of entrance:* north—ground. *Portcullises:* ?. *Chambers:* one?. *Comments:* This satellite pyramid has its own mortuary temple, offering shrine and temenos wall.

Satellite Pyramid: Senusert I.
Name: Pyramid Princess?. *Number:* 82. *Exterior photos:* no. *Interior photos:* no. *Cross-sectional diagram:* no. *Plan diagram:* yes. *Pyramid field:* Lisht. *Field number:* X. *Length:* 55 ft. *Height:* approx. 32 ft. *Angle:* approx. 51 degrees. *Type:* true. *Materials:* limestone. *Location of entrance:* north—ground. *Portcullises:* yes?. *Chambers:* one?. *Comments:* This satellite pyramid has its own mortuary temple, offering shrine and temenos wall.

Satellite Pyramid: Senusert I.
Name: Pyramid Princess?. *Number:* 83. *Exterior photos:* no. *Interior photos:* yes. *Cross-sectional diagram:* yes. *Plan diagram:* yes. *Pyramid field:* Lisht. *Field number:* X.

Length: 55 ft. *Height:* approx. 32 ft. *Angle:* approx. 51 degrees. *Type:* true. *Materials:* limestone. *Location of entrance:* north – ground. *Portcullises:* yes?. *Chambers:* one?. *Comments:* This satellite pyramid has its own mortuary temple, offering shrine and temenos wall; and with two layers of casing stones.

Satellite Pyramid: Senusert I.
Name: Pyramid Princess?. *Number:* 84. *Exterior photos:* no. *Interior photos:* no. *Cross-sectional diagram:* no. *Plan diagram:* yes. *Pyramid field:* Lisht. *Field number:* X. *Length:* 55 ft. *Height:* approx. 32 ft. *Angle:* approx. 51 degrees. *Type:* true. *Materials:* limestone. *Location of entrance:* north – ground. *Portcullises:* yes?. *Chambers:* one?. *Comments:* This satellite pyramid has its own mortuary temple, offering shrine and temenos wall; quartzite sarcophagus and canopic chest found in burial chamber.

Satellite Pyramid: Senusert I.
Name: Pyramid Princess Itakayt. *Number:* 85. *Exterior photos:* no. *Interior photos:* no. *Cross-sectional diagram:* no. *Plan diagram:* yes. *Pyramid field:* Lisht. *Field number:* X. *Length:* 50 ft. *Height:* approx. 30 ft. *Angle:* approx. 51 degrees. *Type:* true. *Materials:* limestone. *Location of entrance:* north – ground. *Portcullises:* yes?. *Chambers:* one?. *Comments:* This satellite pyramid has its own mortuary temple, offering shrine and temenos wall.

Satellite Pyramid: Senusert I.
Name: Pyramid Senusert's principal Queen Neferu. *Number:* 86. *Exterior photos:* no. *Interior photos:* no. *Cross-sectional diagram:* no. *Plan diagram:* yes. *Pyramid field:* Lisht. *Field number:* X. *Length:* 70 ft. *Height:* approx. 40 ft. *Angle:* approx. 51 degrees. *Type:* true. *Materials:* limestone. *Location of entrance:* north – ground. *Portcullises:* yes?. *Chambers:* one?. *Comments:* This satellite pyramid has its own mortuary temple, offering shrine and temenos wall.

PHARAOH 37: AMENEMHAT II.
Position in dynasty: Third. *Portrait:* yes. *Length of reign:* 35 years. *Dates of reign:* 2046–2012 B.C. *Mummy:* not found. *Sarcophagus:* sandstone. *Burial chamber:* yes?. *Treasure:* not found. *Hawk name:* Hekenemmaet (The Worshipper in Truth). *Vulture-and-Cobra name:* Hekenemmaet. *Set or Hawk-of-Nubi name:* Maekheru (The True-Voiced). *Reed-and-Hornet name:* Nubkeure (The Golden One of the Spirits of the Sun-God). *Son-of-the-Sun-God (Ra) name:* Amenemhat (Ammenemhet). *Other names:* Amenemhet; Amenemmes; Amenu; Ameny.

The personal name Amenemhat was used by this pharaoh for his Son-of-the-Sun-God title. As Hawk-of-Nubi he was called Mekheru, "The True-Voiced"; and as Reed-and-Hornet king, Nubkeure, "The Golden One." As Lord of the Vulture-and-Cobra and as Hawk-king, he was called Hekenemmaet.

The texts cite the pyramid of Amenemhat II and work conducted on 16 of his statues which were placed there.

As with the previous pharaoh, Senusert I, Amenemhat made extensive use of the various granite, breccia, alabaster and sandstone quarries, and the copper mines of Sinai as well. Of the latter, two statuettes and several inscribed tablets were discovered.

In Amenemhat II's thirty-third year, at age 70, he officially sanctioned a co-regency with his son, Senusert II. Therefore, Amenemhat's thirty-third year corresponded to the first year of Senusert II. By this time,

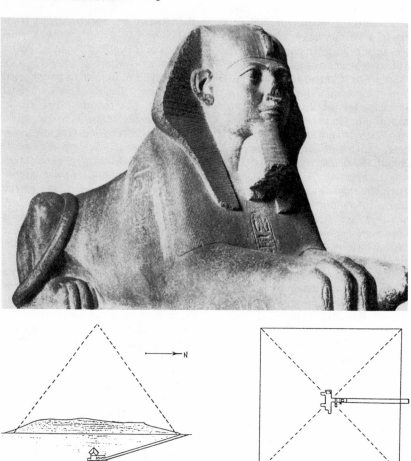

Top: *Pharaoh Amenemhat II (sphinx statue) and his cartouche.* (STATUE: METROPOLITAN MUSEUM OF ART, NEW YORK) **Bottom:** *Pyramid of Amenemhat II, Dahshur: Cross-section (left) and plan.* (J.P. LEPRE)

expeditions to the Land of Pount (Punt) were frequent. The noblemen Thethi and Khnumhotpe were recorded to have visited Pount 11 times.

An unusual (though not unique) feature found in this pharaoh's burial chamber was that his sandstone sarcophagus was sunk into the floor, rather than set upon it.

Outside the pyramid, on its east side, was found a magnificent grey-black granite pyramidion inscribed with the name of this pharaoh (now in the Cairo Museum). This capstone may have been removed from the apex or summit of the pyramid by latter-day despoilers, or it may never have been set into place.

Although neither this pharaoh nor any of his treasure has ever been found, it is worthy of mention that numerous gold items were discovered in the nearby tombs of his several queens and princesses. These included bracelets, pendants and chains.

As to the other artifacts of Amenemhat II's reign, an altar was discovered at Nebesheh, another altar of granite at Dehdemun, and a granite door lintel at Memphis.

In his thirty-ninth year of tenure on the throne, Amenemhat II, who at that time was 80 years old, was assassinated in his palace. The crown passed to his son, Senusert II.

Pyramid: Amenemhat II. *Name:* Dominion of Amenemhat. *Number:* 68. *Exterior photos:* no. *Interior photos:* no. *Cross-sectional diagram:* yes. *Plan diagram:* yes. *Pyramid field:* Dahshur. *Field number:* VIII. *Length:* 265 ft. *Height:* approx. 155 ft. *Angle:* ?. *Type:* true. *Materials:* limestone. *Location of entrance:* north – ground. *Portcullises:* two granite: one vertical; one transverse. *Chambers:* two.

Pyramid Complex: Amenemhat II. *Main pyramid:* yes. *Satellite pyramid(s):* yes – one (no. 69). *Mortuary temple:* yes. *Valley temple:* probably existed – not yet found. *Offering shrine:* no?. *Mastaba(s):* yes. *Ship(s):* no. *Ship pit(s):* no. *Causeway:* yes. *Temenos wall:* yes. *Canal:* destroyed.

Satellite Pyramid: Amenemhat II. *Name:* Pyramid Queen Keminub?. *Number:* 69. *Exterior photos:* no. *Interior photos:* no. *Cross-sectional diagram:* no. *Plan diagram:* no. *Pyramid field:* Dahshur. *Field number:* VIII. *Length:* ?. *Height:* ?. *Angle:* ?. *Type:* true?. *Materials:* limestone?. *Location of entrance:* ?. *Portcullises:* ?. *Chambers:* one?. *Comments:* This satellite pyramid has its own causeway on its east side.

PHARAOH 38: SENUSERT II.
Position in dynasty: Fourth. *Portrait:* yes. *Length of reign:* 13 years. *Dates of reign:* 2011–1999 B.C. *Mummy:* not found. *Sarcophagus:* red granite. *Burial chamber:* yes. *Treasure:* not found (but see next page). *Hawk name:* Seshemutoui (Administrator of the Two Lands). *Vulture-and-Cobra name:* Sekhemaet (He Who Causes the Truth to Shine). *Set or Hawk-of-Nubi name:* Neteruhotpe (Satisfaction of the Gods). *Reed-and-Hornet name:* Khekheperre (He Who Shines). *Son-of-the-Sun-God (Ra) name:* Usertsen (Senusert) (Sesusri). *Other names:* Sesostri; Sesostris.

The pyramid of this pharaoh, son of Amenemhat II, had an interesting peculiarity: the lower part was formed by a natural hillock, rather than the pyramid being set on level ground like other such monuments. It was unorthodox, too, in that its so-called "descending" passageway in this case actually ascended, to insure that the burial chamber would not become flooded with rainwater.

Senusert II also utilized the peculiar device of cross-walls for the core structure of his pyramid (as did his grandfather, Senusert I).

On the south, east and west sides of the monument were several groves of trees planted in rows of circular beds.

About a mile's distance east of the

pyramid the remains of a "pyramid town" were unearthed. This town consisted of over 2,000 separate rooms dispersed on 18 acres, and was unquestionably the living quarters of the pyramid workmen.

Another noteworthy feature is that this pyramid's lowest course is imbedded in the rock foundation as a precautionary measure to counter the outward thrust of the monument.

Of the treasure cache of Senusert II, only the gold cobra from the front of the royal crown was found in the burial chamber. Nevertheless, this is strong evidence that the entire treasure of this pharaoh, and his mummy, too, were once placed in this pyramid. Also found in the burial chamber was an alabaster offering table.

The Reed-and-Hornet king name of this new pharaoh was Khekheperre, meaning "He who Shines like the Sun." Neteruhotpe, "Satisfaction of the Gods," was his Hawk-of-Nubi name, and Seshemutoui, "Administrator of the Two Lands," was his Hawk name. His Lord of the Vulture-and-Cobra name was Sekhemaet, "He who causes the Truth to Shine."

According to the restored Turin Papyrus, Senusert II ruled for 19 years. His wife was Queen Nofret. The inscriptions ascribe to her the titles "Consort of *the* King" and "Daughter of *a* King," implying that she was Senusert's sister as well as his wife. Sister-brother marriages were customary practice within the royal families of ancient Egypt.

The names of two princesses are known from this reign: another Nofret, and Ateuhayt. A prince named Sesusisonb is also mentioned in the texts of this period.

Inscriptions from this reign mark the first three, the fifth, the sixth, and the thirteenth years of Senusert II.

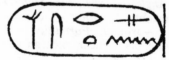

Above: *Pharaoh Senusert II and his cartouche.* (STATUE: EGYPTIAN MUSEUM OF CAIRO)

Opposite, Top: *Pyramid of Senusert II, Lahun.* (PHOTO: J. BREASTED) **Center:** *Cross-section (left) and plan.* (J.P. LEPRE) **Bottom:** *Drawing shows details of construction in exposed core of the pyramid.* (G. PERROT AND C. CHIPIEZ)

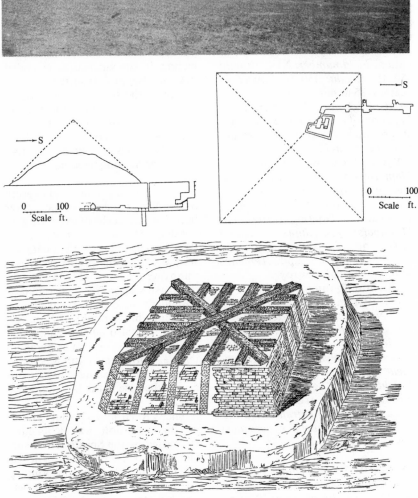

Beyond the two pyramids that were built by this pharaoh, he was also involved in other work projects. Most notable are a string of walls and fortifications in southern Egypt and Lower Nubia, the specific sites of the latter being Kubban, Koshtamneh and Anaybeh. This implies that the various tribes of the Sudan were hostile and in revolt, and the very real possibility of some sort of a foreign invasion was ever present during this pharaoh's reign.

Pyramid: Senusert II. *Name:* Senusert Appears. *Number:* 92. *Exterior photos:* yes. *Interior photos:* no. *Cross-sectional diagram:* yes. *Plan diagram:* yes. *Pyramid field:* Lahun. *Field number:* XIV. *Length:* 350 ft. *Height:* 150 ft. *Angle:* 42 degrees, 35 minutes. *Type:* true. *Materials:* brick core, limestone casing. *Location of entrance:* two on south, at ground level. *Portcullises:* no. *Chambers:* three.

Pyramid Complex: Senusert II. *Main pyramid:* yes. *Satellite pyramid(s):* yes — one (no. 91). *Mortuary temple:* yes — ruined. *Valley temple:* yes — ruined. *Offering shrine:* no. *Mastaba(s):* yes. *Ship(s):* no. *Ship pit(s):* no. *Causeway:* probably existed — not yet found. *Temenos wall:* yes. *Canal:* destroyed.

Satellite Pyramid: Senusert II. *Name:* Pyramid Princess Atmuneferu. *Number:* 91. *Exterior photos:* yes. *Interior photos:* no. *Cross-sectional diagram:* no. *Plan diagram:* no. *Pyramid field:* Lahun. *Field number:* XIV. *Length:* 85 ft. *Height:* 55 ft. *Angle:* 54 degrees, 15 minutes. *Type:* true. *Materials:* brick. *Location of entrance:* ?. *Portcullises:* ?. *Chambers:* no chamber has yet been found.

PHARAOH 39: SENUSERT III.
Position in dynasty: Fifth. *Portrait:* yes. *Length of reign:* 39 years.

Dates of reign: 1998–1960 B.C. *Mummy:* not found. *Sarcophagus:* red granite. *Burial chamber:* yes?. *Treasure:* not found. *Hawk name:* Neterkheperu (The God-Created). *Vulture-and-Cobra name:* Netermosut (The Divine-One of Births). *Set or Hawk-of-Nubi name:* Kheperu (The Created-One). *Reed-and-Hornet name:* Khekeura (Crowned by the Spirits of the Sun-God). *Son-of-the-Sun-God (Ra) name:* Usertsen (Senusert) (Sesusri). *Other names:* Khekeure; Lachares; Sesostri; Sesostris; Xachares.

Senusert III was one of the greatest pharaohs ever to rule over Egypt, engaging in activities that extended beyond Egypt's frontiers to the Sudan in the south, the Mediterranean region in the north, the Arabian Gulf in the east and as far as the districts of western Asia. He built great fortresses and spread Egyptian culture as he conquered nation after nation.

Although the mummy and treasure of this energetic monarch have never been found, a cache of exquisite gold jewelry was found by DeMorgan in the adjacent tombs of the pharaoh's several queens and princesses. These tombs were connected with the subterranean sections of the pyramid by an underground passageway.

Besides his pyramid of Dahshur, Senusert III also built a cenotaph at Abydos in the form of a pyramid-temple. Within this tomb was found an empty rose granite sarcophagus, as was the case in the Dahshur pyramid.

The Reed-and-Hornet name of this pharaoh was Khekeure, "Crowned by the Spirits of the Sun-God," while Netermosut, "The Divine-One of Births," was his Vulture-and-Cobra name and Neterkheperu was his Hawk name. As Hawk-of-

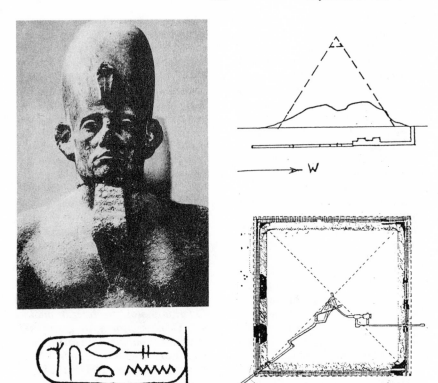

Left: *Pharaoh Senusert III and his cartouche.* (STATUE: EGYPTIAN MUSEUM, CAIRO) **Right:** *Pyramid of Senusert III, Dahshur: Cross-section (top) and plan.* (**Top:** J.P. LEPRE) (**Bottom:** J. DEMORGAN)

Nubi, he was called Kheperu, "The Created One," with his personal name being Sesusri, which he used for the Son-of-the-Sun-God title.

In keeping with previous pharaoh Senusert II's ambitious fortification campaign, Senusert III planned an invasion of the Sudan. It appears as if the threat of the hostile tribes there prompted him to deliver the first blow, lest he should be on the defensive with an invasion from that area. During Senusert III's eighth and twelfth years of reign, it is recorded that he journeyed upriver to overthrow the country of Kush. A third expedition was launched in the sixteenth year of this pharaoh's reign.

Several months after this expedition Senusert III proudly notes how he had recently extended his territory at the frontiers. The menace of Sudan, however, was only temporarily checked, for another inscription tells of the necessity of yet another expedition to the land of Kush by this pharaoh. This occurred three years later, in the nineteenth year of his reign. (It should be noted here that Kush [Cush], Pount [Punt], Sudan, and Lower Nubia are more or less used interchangeably.) At Kush, Senusert III was responsible for building numerous fortresses of unbaked bricks. The more popular ones were located at Semneh, Kummeh,

Matuga, Wady Halfa and the island of Uron Arti, with the latter being dubbed "Defeat of the Tribesmen."

Senusert III conducted another successful expedition to the Red Sea, near Somaliland, and Herodotus tells us that this king was the only pharaoh ever to conquer Ethiopia. Senusert III also led his forces to the borders of Syria. A nobleman called Khusobk records this event, mentioning an interior city therein, by the name of Sekmem.

In a letter, Senusert III directs his chief treasurer, Ikhernofret, to the tomb of Osiris so that he can present a gift of Nubian gold as an offering.

By return letter, Ikhernofret states how he faithfully executed the pharaoh's order and also established a shrine of gold, silver, lapis lazuli and carob wood there. Mention is also made of a "sacred ark (of the god)." The coffin itself Ikhernofret had inlaid with lapis lazuli, malachite, electrum and numerous costly stones.

Mention, too, is made by Ikhernofret of a sacred barque equipped with a chapel and of a highly religious ceremony which he enacted there, replete with procession and much decorum. Monthly and half-monthly feasts are also brought to our attention through this valuable chronicle.

Other objects of Senusert III's reign are a sphinx of diorite, an inscribed tablet from Koptos, and a gold ornament from Riqqeh. There are also several cylinder-seals and scarabs which were found at various sites.

In order to make passage through the First Cataract navigable, Senusert III had a huge canal dug at that point, just between the islands of Sehel and Elephantine. A certain master builder named Ronpetenenkh was entrusted with this task, and a wide, 250'-long channel was thereby cut. By using this channel, the barrier of the natural granite rock formation was circumvented. This event occurred in the eighth year of Senusert III's reign.

In his time, Senusert III was revered with fervor by the people. Lengthy passages describe his benevolence and wisdom, implying that "twice great" was anyone who happened to be blessed by him.

Toward the close of his tenure, Senusert III established a co-regency with the future pharaoh, Amenemhat III. The death of Senusert III, at nearly 70 years of age, brought to an end a tenure of dynamic energy and drive that may well have been one of the greatest eras in the Egyptian chronology.

Pyramid: Senusert III. *Name:* Senusert is at Peace. *Number:* 65. *Exterior photos:* no. *Interior photos:* no. *Cross-sectional diagram:* yes. *Plan diagram:* yes. *Pyramid field:* Dahshur. *Field number:* VIII. *Length:* 350 ft. *Height:* 255 ft. *Angle:* 56 degrees. *Type:* true. *Materials:* brick core, limestone casing. *Location of entrance:* west — ground. *Portcullises:* no?. *Chambers:* one.

Pyramid Complex: Senusert III. *Main pyramid:* yes. *Satellite pyramid(s):* no. *Mortuary temple:* yes — ruined. *Valley temple:* probably exists — not yet found. *Offering shrine:* no. *Mastaba(s):* yes. *Ship(s):* yes — eight. *Ship pit(s):* yes — eight. *Causeway:* yes — traces only. *Temenos wall:* yes. *Canal:* destroyed.

PHARAOH 40: AMENEMHAT III.
Position in dynasty: Sixth. *Portrait:* yes. *Length of reign:* 49 years. *Dates of reign:* 1959–1911 B.C. *Mummy:* charred bones only (Pyramid Hawara). *Sarcophagus:* two — one red granite, Pyramid Dahshur; one yellow quartzite, Pyramid Hawara. *Burial chamber:* yes. *Treasure:* not found. *Hawk*

name: Oebeu (Great-One of the Ancestral Spirits). *Vulture-and-Cobra name:* Ithetiueue (Grasping the Heritage of the Past). *Set or Hawk-of-Nubi name:* Wahenkh (Abundant is His Life). *Reed-and-Hornet name:* Nemaetre (Nemaere) (Possessing the Truth of the Sun-God). *Son-of-the-Sun-God (Ra) name:* Amenemhat (Ammenemhet). *Other names:* Amenemmes; Ameny; Ithetiuetoui (Grasping the Heritage of the Two Lands).

The grandson of the illustrious Senusert III, Amenemhat III was one of the mightiest pharaohs ever to rule over Egypt, having built two pyramids; the famous "Labyrinth," the largest of all Egyptian temples; and other special building projects of note.

The Reed-and-Hornet name of this king was Nemaetre, meaning "Possessing the Truth of the Sun-God." Amenemhat, his personal name, was also used with his Son-of-the-Sun-God title, while his Hawk-of-Nubi name was Wahenkh. His Hawk name was Oebeu, "Great-One of the Spirits." As Lord of the Vulture-and-Cobra, he was called Athetiueue, meaning "Grasping the Ancient Heritage," or Ithetiuetoui, "Grasping the Heritage of Upper and Lower Egypt."

Found on the ground outside the king's pyramid at Dahshur was the beautiful gray-granite pyramidion that once crowned the apex of the monument. This capstone was inscribed with the name of Amenemhat III, establishing him as the owner of this edifice. Also outside the pyramid, in the adjacent tombs of two of the pharaoh's princess daughters, Hathorhotpe and Nubhotpekherd, DeMorgan found beautiful gold jewelry (now in the Cairo Museum).

Of Amenemhat III's second pyramid, at Hawara, the author made the

Top: *Pharaoh Amenemhat III and his cartouche.* (HEAD: BERLIN MUSEUM, WEST BERLIN) **Center and Bottom:** *Pyramid of Amenemhat III, Dahshur: Cross-section* (J.P. LEPRE) *and plan.* (J. DEMORGAN)

following observations in March of 1987: "Now a shapeless heap ominously rising from the flat, desert terrain. Comprised of small, mud bricks (approximately 12″ long by 8″ wide by 4″ high). Situated at a considerable distance from the Nile, with an irrigation canal on its west side (modern or ancient?). No trace whatsoever of a limestone casing or of the south side entrance. However, area of its foundation can be discerned. Mortuary Temple completely gone with only a dozen or so sizeable fragments of granite blocks and columns remaining; one with the carving of Sobek, the Crocodile God (a quite popular god during this dynasty, and one from which an apparent daughter of Amenemhat III, Sobek – or Sebek – Neferu Ra partially derived her name)."

This pyramid at Hawara shows a good deal of ingenuity on the part of its architects. The core of this monument was built according to the design of the pyramids of Senusert I and Senusert II, having a series of criss-cross retaining walls rather than accretion layers, yet its uniqueness lay in the complexity of its subterranean sections.

The unusual plan of this pyramid begins with an unorthodox entrance on its south side, rather than on the customary north side. From here, a long, descending passageway with steps led to a vestibule constituting a dead end. At this point, hidden in the ceiling, was a twenty-ton movable stone which, when slid aside, revealed another vestibule. From here, a long, blind passageway, blocked with loosely packed stones and leading due north,

acted as a ploy to lure tomb robbers in that direction and away from a second corridor leading due east and, ultimately, to the burial chamber.

This second corridor led to a third vestibule, which constituted another dead end. Again, as with the first vestibule, a twenty-ton ceiling stone, when slid sideways, gave rise to a third level leading to another corridor system. At the end of this corridor was a fourth vestibule comprising yet another dead end, with yet another twenty-ton sliding ceiling stone. Finally, a short corridor led from here to a fifth, much larger vestibule, in which were set various other ingenious ploys to thwart the ambitious tomb robber.

As one enters this fifth vestibule, one notes that the wall to the left is built up of solid masonry, whereas the wall to the right is built of loosely packed blocks; the right wall was an additional ploy to lure tomb robbers away from the left wall, the general area of the hidden burial chamber. Shafts cut into the near and far ends of the floor of this vestibule were also intended to deceive robbers. Beneath the well-sealed center section of this floor was a short passage leading to the burial chamber.

The burial chamber of Amenemhat III was carved out of a single, 110-ton block of quartzite, and was roofed with three huge quartzite slabs weighing 45 tons each. The burial in this chamber is without parallel, in that two sarcophagi, rather than one, were found herein. These two quartzite chests were placed alongside one another, one belonging to Amenemhat III and the other to his favorite daughter, Ptah-Neferu. They

Opposite: *Pyramid of Amenemhat III, Dahshur.* **Top:** *Capstone.* (EGYPTIAN MUSEUM, CAIRO) **Center:** *Exterior view, showing Bent Pyramid of Sneferu in background.* (J. DEMORGAN) **Bottom:** *Tomb-chamber.* (PHOTO BY D. ARNOLD. METROPOLITAN MUSEUM OF ART)

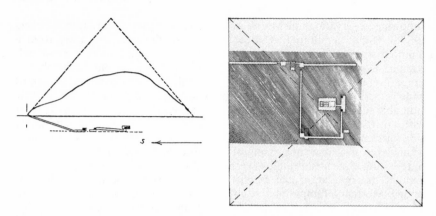

Pyramid Ammenemhet III − Hawara − Dyn. 12
3 Dimensional Plan

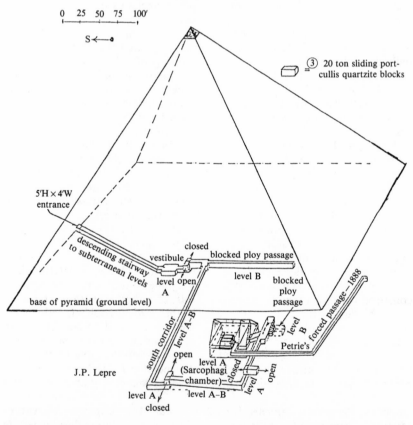

0 25 50 75 100'

S←o

③ 20 ton sliding port-
cullis quartzite blocks

5'H × 4'W
entrance

descending stairway
to subterranean levels

vestibule

closed

blocked ploy passage

level open
A

level B

blocked
ploy
passage

base of pyramid (ground level)

Petrie's forced passage − 1888

south corridor

level A-B

open

level A
(Sarcophagi
chamber)

closed

level A

open

J.P. Lepre

level A
closed

level A-B

level B

Pyramid of Amenemhat III, Hawara. **Top:** *Cross-section (left) and plan.*
(W.M.F. PETRIE) **Bottom:** *Three-dimensional plan.* (J.P. LEPRE)

contained the charred remains (probably burned by tomb robbers) of these two royal personages.

The pharaoh was almost always buried in his pyramid alone. There are instances where other members of royalty were also interred in the pharaoh's pyramid, but always in separate chambers from the king's. This is the only example which we have of someone actually being buried with the pharaoh in a single chamber. Not only this, but the two sarcophagi in Amenemhat's burial chamber were placed alongside one another, giving further testimony to the intimacy between this pharaoh and his special daughter.

An alabaster altar or offering table was also found in this burial chamber, along with two quartzite boxes for holding canopic jars, some alabaster bowls, an alabaster vessel, and a pharaonic beard of lapis lazuli. The alabaster altar and bowls were inscribed with the name Ptah-Neferu. The vessel bore the royal cartouche of Amenemhat III.

Although the treasure of this pharaoh and his daughter were never found in this pyramid, fragments of a treasure cache, including a beautiful gold necklace with precious stones, were discovered in a tomb lying southeast of the pyramid. Also within this tomb was a huge rose granite sarcophagus. This tomb has been identified as that of Amenemhat's daughter, Ptah-Neferu, the very same princess who was supposed to have been interred with Amenemhat in his pyramid at Hawara. One of these tombs with sarcophagi obviously acted as a cenotaph, while the other was the actual burial chamber. It is highly likely, though, that the burnt remains found in the sarcophagi of the Hawara pyramid were, in fact, those of Amenemhat and Ptah-Neferu.

Adjacent to, and south of, the pyramid are the remains of Amenemhat's mortuary temple, the famous "Labyrinth," so well described by Herodotus, Strabo and Pliny. It is unusually situated to the south, rather than to the east of the pyramid. The only other known example of a south side mortuary temple is that of the pyramid of Userkaf at North Sakkara. It should be noted that I.E.S. Edwards gives the figures of 1,000′ long by 800′ wide for this mortuary temple, whereas J.P. Lauer shows it as 950′ long by 650′ wide.

THE LABYRINTH. This colossal building was large enough to house the great temples of both Luxor and Karnak. It consisted of 3,000 chambers—1,500 above ground and 1,500 below. In addition to this, states Pliny, it contained "temples of all the gods of Egypt, columns of porphyry, statues of kings," etc., of which Petrie found numerous fragments in his investigation of the site in 1889. Weigall tell us, "In the Middle Ages the ruins were used as a quarry and the last remnants of the stone were removed by the workmen who built the Faiyum [Fayum] Railway in the nineteenth century."

Amenemhat III is also credited with the mighty engineering feat of constructing the irrigation canal now known as the Bahr Yusif, and of using this canal to regulate the flow of water from the Nile to Lake Fayum during the flood season. This water was held there by sluices, and later let out again, at will, back to the section of the Nile from Assyout down to the Mediterranean Sea, regulating the height of the river in that area during the dry season. This irrigation system was the prototype for the modern High Aswan Dam.

Although Amenemhat III was involved in several great engineering works, the Bahr Yusif endeavor is of special note. For here, two 20-mile long dykes—one straight and the other semicircular—were constructed so as to aid in the adjustment of the water level through the use of sluices, and to reclaim 20,000 acres of farmland by enriching the soil. Amenemhat III then built a commemorative temple at the site. A section of altar has been found there, and several fragments of an inscription written by the king, where he speaks of his association with the former pharaoh, Senusert III.

It is certain that the finished canal saved thousands of lives yearly; for prior to its being built, the entire country north of Assiout suffered from famines whenever the level of the Nile was low.

At Kummeh and Semneh inscriptions are cut at various levels, recording the Nile's fluctuating height. This was done in a total of 15 of the years of Amenemhat III's 48-year-reign. The recording does not average out to having occurred every third year, but seems rather to have been taken sporadically. For example, there is a recording every year from year four to year nine, excepting year eight, but then there is a sizeable gap of seven years between the recorded year 15 and year 22. At any rate, these records indicate that the Nile level was being studied at that time.

Amenemhat III was as vigorous as his active predecessors, if not even more so. He worked the copper mines at Sinai extensively, and inscriptions there record 23 years of his 48-year-reign. At the chief mine, Wady Maghara, another inscription relates how a treasury official of Amenemhat III arrived there with 734 men in the second year of this pharaoh's reign. Journey to these mines was by sea.

Other inscriptions of this king's tenure were found at the First Cataract, recording years 14, 15, 24 and 25 of Amenemhat III's reign; between the First and Second Cataracts, at Kubban, recording year 11; and at Dehmid, recording the eleventh year and fourth month. Inscriptions regarding Amenemhat III were also found at the Tura limestone quarries, on the east bank of the Nile, and at El Kab, with the latter telling of a defensive wall being built in this pharaoh's forty-fourth year.

At Tell el-Yahudiyeh Amenemhat III constructed a garrison, while at Memphis he enlarged the temple of the god Ptah.

Other traces of this pharaoh's reign are many. A large stele was discovered at Abydos. It describes the king as "being possessed of silver and gold ... a man of truth." Another stele (Boston) found by Reisner refers to this king's jubilees, indicating by the plural that he celebrated this event twice.

Numerous small articles of Amenemhat III's reign have also been discovered. They include jewelry, plaques, cylinder-seals and statuettes.

A good number of portrait statues of this king have been found, wonderfully illustrating the facial evolution of this pharaoh in the various years of his reign. One portrait, from Hawara, depicts him as a young man, whereas another (of obsidian) shows him several years later, where his face is notably more fixed and rigid. A serpentine head (Berlin) depicts him years later, care-worn, and with heavy eyes. Also belonging to his late years are the portrait-sphinxes discovered at Tanis (Cairo Museum), and a statuette head (Petrograd-Hermitage Museum). Also in Berlin is a full statue of this king with a stern look, and another statue from Karnak (Cairo Museum) shows him as a melancholy, older man. At Abydos, Petrie and Weigall found yet another head of Amenemhat III, a colossal granite one, depicting a very old man, expressing profound sorrow.

Amenemhat III was respected in his time, and his influence spread beyond Egypt and into the neighboring countries; as far as Bylos, on the coast of Syria, artifacts from tombs and temples have been found bearing his name.

It was not until his final year of tenure on the throne that Amenemhat III established a co-regency with his son and successor, Amenemhat IV. He died at about 70 years of age.

Dahshur Pyramid: Amenemhat III. *Name:* Amenemhat is Beautiful?. *Number:* 70. *Exterior photos:* yes. *Interior photos:* no. *Cross-sectional diagram:* yes. *Plan diagram:* yes. *Pyramid field:* Dahshur. *Field number:* VIII. *Length:* 342 ft. *Height:* 250 ft. *Angle:* 57 degrees, 20 minutes. *Type:* true. *Materials:* brick core; limestone casing. *Location of entrance:* east – ground. *Portcullises:* yes?. *Chambers:* one (also seven vestibules). *Comments:* Black granite pyramidion found near base of this pyramid.

Dahshur Pyramid Complex: Amenemhat III. *Main pyramid:* yes. *Satellite pyramid(s):* no. *Mortuary temple:* yes – destroyed. *Valley temple:* not yet found. *Offering shrine:* no. *Mastaba(s):* yes. *Ship(s):* no. *Ship pit(s):* no. *Causeway:* yes. *Temenos wall:* yes. *Canal:* destroyed.

Hawara Pyramid: Amenemhat III. *Name:* Amenemhat Lives. *Number:* 90. *Exterior photos:* yes. *Interior photos:* no. *Cross-sectional diagram:* yes. *Plan diagram:* yes.

Pyramid field: Hawara. *Field number:* XIII. *Length:* 335 ft. *Height:* 180 ft. *Angle:* 48 degrees, 45 minutes. *Type:* true. *Materials:* brick core; limestone casing. *Location of entrance:* south – ground. *Portcullises:* three (quartzite?). *Chambers:* one (also with five vestibules).

Hawara Pyramid Complex: Amenemhat III. *Main pyramid:* yes. *Satellite pyramid(s):* no. *Mortuary temple:* yes – the famous "Labyrinth" (see below). *Valley temple:* no. *Offering shrine:* no?. *Mastaba(s):* no. *Ship(s):* no. *Ship pit(s):* no. *Causeway:* no. *Temenos wall:* no?. *Canal:* destroyed.

The Mortuary temple (the "Labyrinth") was the largest temple ever built in the world – so enormous that it could have held eight other great Egyptian temples within its walls, as shown in the following chart:

Temple	Length (in ft.)	Width	Sq. Ft.
Amenemmes III at Hawara	950	650	= 617,500
1. Amon at Luxor (Thebes)	850	175	= 148,750
2. Amon at Karnak (Thebes)	700	275	= 192,500
3. Rameses II (Ramesseum) (Thebes)	550	175	= 96,250
4. Hathor at Dendera	300	100	= 30,000
5. Hatshepsut at Deir El Bahri	250	150	= 37,500
6. Horus at Tanis	250	100	= 25,000
7. Horus at Edfu	400	150	= 60,000
8. Sethos I (The Osireion) at Abydos	200	125	= 25,000
			615,000

PHARAOH 41: AMENEMHAT IV.

Position in dynasty: Seventh. *Portrait:* yes. *Length of reign:* 9 years. *Dates of reign:* 1910–1902 B.C. *Mummy:* not found. *Sarcophagus:* red granite. *Burial chamber:* yes?. *Treasure:* not found. *Hawk name:* Kheperkheperu (The Being of Beings). *Vulture-and-Cobra name:* ?. *Set or Hawk-of-Nubi name:* ?. *Reed-and-Hornet name:* Maekherure (Maekherura) (The Truth of the Voice of the Sun-God). *Son-of-the-Sun-God (Ra) name:* Amenemhat (Ammenemhet). *Other names:* Amenemmes; Ameny.

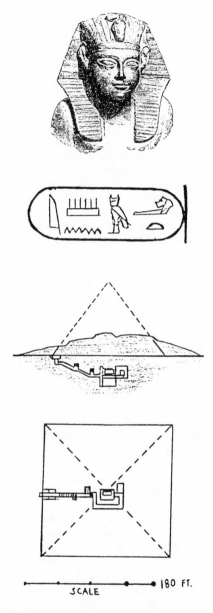

For his Reed-and-Hornet name, this king chose Maekherure, "The Truth of the Voice of the Sun-God." Amenemhat, his personal name, was also used for his Sun-of-the-Sun-God title, while as Hawk-king, he took the name Kheperkheperu, "The Being of Beings." Of this king's Vulture-and-Cobra and Hawk-of-Nubi names we have no record.

Traces of this pharaoh's reign are not as abundant as with his immediate predecessors. There is a fragment from a yellow quartzite sphinx from Abu Sir; a mortuary table of an official named Khuy; a green, glazed, schist plaque with the King's name inscribed (British Museum); papyri from Kahun, with the king's first, sixth and tenth years of tenure given; and four isolated scarabs.

He is recorded as having reigned precisely 9 years, 3 months and 27 days, according to the Turin Papyrus, which would end his reign on February 17, 1901 B.C.

During Amenemhat IV's reign, the policy of measuring the various levels of the Nile was continued, for at Kummeh, a rock inscription records the height of the river in year five of this king.

Top: *Pharaoh Amenemhat IV.* (G. MASPERO) **Second from top:** *His cartouche.* **Third from top:** *Cross-section of Pyramid of Amenemhat IV, Mazghuna.* (J.P. LEPRE) **Bottom:** *Plan of same pyramid.* (J.P. LEPRE)

Not far from Jebel Silsileh, in Upper Egypt, Amenemhat IV's name was found inscribed on the rocks of Shat-er-Rigal.

Additional inscriptions of this monarch's reign are to be found at Serabit and Wady Maghara, both in Sinai, where he actively worked the copper mines.

Pyramid: Amenemhat IV. *Name:* Southern Mazghuna Pyramid. *Number:* 74. *Exterior photos:* no. *Interior photos:* no. *Cross-sectional diagram:* yes. *Plan diagram:* yes. *Pyramid field:* Mazghuna. *Field number:* IX. *Length:* 180 ft. *Height:* approx. 115 ft. *Angle:* ?. *Type:* true. *Materials:* brick core; limestone casing. *Location of entrance:* south— ground. *Portcullises:* two transverse—red granite; 42 and 24 tons. *Chambers:* one. *Comments:* Square depression for canopic chest in burial chamber floor.

Pyramid Complex: Amenemhat IV. *Main pyramid:* yes. *Satellite pyramid(s):* no. *Mortuary temple:* yes. *Valley temple:* may have existed, not yet found. *Offering shrine:* no. *Mastaba(s):* no?. *Ship(s):* no. *Ship pit(s):* no. *Causeway:* may have existed, not yet found. *Temenos wall:* yes (wavy type). *Canal:* destroyed.

QUEEN PHARAOH 42:
SEBEK-NEFERU-RA.
Position in dynasty: Eighth (last). *Portrait:* yes.* *Length of reign:* 3 years. *Dates of reign:* 1901–1899 B.C. *Mummy:* not found. *Sarcophagus:* yellow quartzite. *Burial chamber:*

yes?. *Treasure:* not found. *Hawk name:* Merytre (Beloved of the Sun-God). *Vulture-and-Cobra name:* Sit-sekhem (Daughter of Dominion). *Set or Hawk-of-Nubi name:* Dedetkhe (Enduring in Her Ascension). *Reed-and-Hornet name:* Sobknofru (The Beauties of the God Sobk). *Son-of-the-Sun-God (Ra) name:* Sobknofru. *Other names:* Sebek-Neferu; Shedet-sobk-nofrura; Skemiophr; Sobken-ophr.

Sister of Amenemhat IV, this woman holds the distinguished honor of being the only queen-pharaoh of the pyramid age. Other pyramids were built for queens and princesses by the various pyramid pharaohs, but these women did not occupy the throne or build their own pyramids, as was the case with this female monarch.

Other than the fact that she built a large pyramid with an elaborate internal passage and chamber system, little is known of this queen-pharaoh.

Sebek-Neferu is interpreted as meaning "The Beauties of the God Sobk" (patron deity of the Fayum and Crocodile God). This she retained for her Reed-and-Hornet name, sometimes employing the longer version of Shedetsobkno-frure, meaning "Displaying the Beauties of Sobk and of the Sun-God."

Sebek-Neferu-Ra's Hawk name was Merytre, "Beloved of the Sun-God," while her Hawk-of-Nubi name was Dedetkhe, "Enduring in Her Ascension." As Lady of the

*This head, shown on page 222, is cited by numerous authors as being a royal head of Dynasty XII. More specifically, it must be that of the last ruler of that dynasty, Queen Sebek-Neferu-Ra. She was the only queen-pharaoh of that dynasty, the other (male) pharaohs being the three Senuserts and the four Amenemhats, and must, therefore, be the royal personage alluded to in the description of this pharaonic head. Not only this, but the royal cobra present on the forehead of this statue is reserved exclusively for the portrayal of a pharaoh. If Sebek-Neferu-Ra was in fact the only queen-pharaoh of Dynasty XII (which she was), and if the statue head in question is repeatedly ascribed to that dynasty (which it is), then the head must represent her.

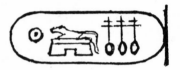

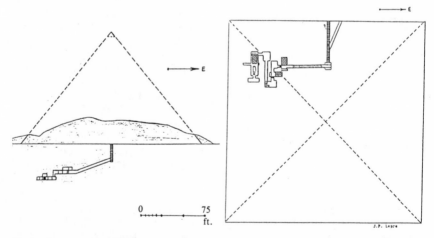

Top: *Queen-pharaoh Sebek-Neferu-Ra and her cartouche.* (HEAD: BROOKLYN MUSEUM) **Bottom:** *Pyramid of Sebek-Neferu-Ra, North Mazghuna: Cross-section (left) and plan.* (J.P. LEPRE)

Vulture-and-Cobra, she was called Sitsekhem, "Daughter of Dominion," and as daughter of the Sun-God, she employed her personal name, Sòbknofru.

Besides her sophisticated pyramid at Mazghuna, there are only a few remains of her reign. Her name is inscribed on several fragments at Amenemhat III's Labyrinth at Hawara, and she appears to have constructed or reworked a temple or a shrine there which remained relatively intact up until modern times.

Besides some scarabs and cylinder-seals, this queen's name is found inscribed on the architraves from the temple at Eheninsi, and partially obliterated on a stone sphinx discovered in the Delta at Khataaneh, close to ancient Tanis (Thoan).

In the month of September, after only a short reign of two years, Sebek-Neferu-Ra died, leaving no legitimate male or female heir. Thus the great Twelfth Dynasty comes to a close and we enter a more obscure period comprised of a host of pharaohs constituting the New Thirteenth Dynasty.

Pyramid: Sebek-Neferu-Ra. *Name:* Northern Mazghuna Pyramid. *Number:* 73. *Exterior photos:* no. *Interior photos:* no. *Cross-sectional diagram:* yes. *Plan diagram:* yes. *Pyramid field:* Mazghuna. *Field number:* IX. *Length:* rough approx. = 200 ft. *Height:* rough approx. = 120 ft. *Angle:* ?. *Type:* true. *Materials:* limestone. *Location of entrance:* latter passage on north side now used; true entrance not yet found. *Portcullises:* three transverse — quartzite. *Chambers:* one (five vestibules also).

Pyramid Complex: Sebek-Neferu-Ra. *Main pyramid:* yes. *Satellite pyramid(s):* no. *Mortuary temple:* no. *Valley temple:* no. *Offering shrine:* no. *Mastaba(s):* no?. *Ship(s):* no. *Ship pit(s):* no. *Causeway:* no. *Temenos wall:* no. *Canal:* destroyed.

DYNASTY XIII

• *Duration:* 153 years (1898–1745 B.C.). *Pharaohs:* 1. Khetouire Ugef. 1898–1896 B.C. (No pyramid.) 2. Sekhemkere... 1895–1890 B.C. (No pyramid.) 3. ...re Amenemhet.

1889–? B.C. (No pyramid.) 4. Sehotpeibre Amenemhet. (No pyramid.) 5. ...Iufni. (No pyramid.) 6. Ameny Intef Amenemhat. 1885–1883 B.C. 7. Smenkere... (No pyramid.) 8. Sehotpeibre... (No pyramid.) 9. Nothemkere... (No pyramid.) 10. Sekhemsmentouire Thuti. (No pyramid.) 11. ...Amenemhat. (No pyramid.) 12. Nothemibre... (No pyramid.) 13. Sobkhotpere. (No pyramid.) 14. ...Rensomb. 18?–1878 B.C. (No pyramid.) 15. Fuibre Herwet. 1877–1874 B.C. (No pyramid.) 16. Sethef...re... 1873–1871 B.C. (No pyramid.) 17. Sekhemkhetouire Amenemhat Sobkhotpe 1870–1869 B.C. (No pyramid.) 18. User...re... 1868–1867 B.C. (No pyramid.) 19. Smenkhkere Mermeshoi. 1866–1865 B.C. (No pyramid.) 20. Hotpekere. 1864–1863 B.C. (No pyramid.) 21. Kesetre Ren...seusr. 1862–1861 B.C. (No pyramid.) 22. Sekhemseuthtouire Sobkhotpe. 1860–1859 B.C. (No pyramid.) 23. Khesekhemre Neferhotpe. 1858–1854 B.C. (No pyramid.) 24. Sihathorre. 1853–1850 B.C. (No pyramid.) 25. Kheneferre Sobkhotpe. 1849–1841 B.C. (No pyramid.) 26. Kheenkhre Sobkhotpe. 1840–1839 B.C. (No pyramid.) 27. Menuthre... 1838–1837 B.C. (No pyramid.) 28. Neferenkhre... 1836–1835 B.C. (No pyramid.) 29. Khehotpere Sobkhotpe. 1834–1829 B.C. (No pyramid.) 30. Wahibre Ieuib. 1828–1821 B.C. (No pyramid.) 31. Merneferre Ay. 1820–1798 B.C. 32. Merhotpere Ini Sobkhotpe. 1797–1796 B.C. (No pyramid.) 33. Senkhenre Se...tu. 1795–1793 B.C. (No pyramid.) 34. Mersekhemre Int Neferhotpe. 1792–1791 B.C. (No pyramid.) 35. Seuthkere Heri. 1790–1789 B.C. (No pyramid.) 36. Mernothemre. 1788–1787 B.C. (No pyramid.) 37. Seuthkheure. 1786–17? B.C. (No pyramid.) 38. Sesekhemkere Amenemhetsonbf.

(No pyramid.) 39. Sekhemwahkere Rehotpe. (No pyramid.) 40. Menhotpere. (No pyramid.) 41. Merenkhre Mentuhotpe. (No pyramid.) 42. Seuthenre Mentuhotpe. (No pyramid.) 43. Sewahenre Sonbmiu. (No pyramid.) 44. Seneferibre Sesusri. (No pyramid.) 45. Merkheperre. (No pyramid.) 46. Khekere... (No pyramid.) 47. Seseusrtouire... (No pyramid.) 48. Seuthenre... (No pyramid.) 49. ... ...besu. (No pyramid.) 50. Nebmaetre Ibi. (No pyramid.) 51. ...ubenre. (No pyramid.) 52. Merkeure Sobkhotpe. 1763-1761 B.C. (No pyramid.) 53. Maetre Sobkhotpe. 1760-1759 B.C. (No pyramid.) 54. Nemaetenkhe Khendjer (Khendjer I). 1758-1751 B.C. (No pyramid.) 55. Usrkere Khendjer (Khendjer II). 1750-1749 B.C. 56. Menkheure Seshib. 1748-1747 B.C. (No pyramid.) 57. Sekhemibtouire.... 1746-? B.C. (No pyramid.) 58. Nehesire. (No pyramid.) 59. Khethire... (No pyramid.) 60. Nebfure ... ?-1745 B.C. (No pyramid.)

Note: This dynasty, ruling in the south, was contemporaneous with the Fourteenth Dynasty (1879-1745 B.C.), ruling in the north.

As was the case with the eighth and tenth dynasties, the exact relationships of these thirteenth dynasty pharaohs are uncertain. Therefore, an accurate genealogical table cannot be reconstructed. Only the relationship between the fifty-fourth pharaoh of this line (Khendjer I) and the fifty-fifth pharaoh (Khendjer II), father to son, is known. It is evident, nevertheless, that in light of the reoccurence of the names Sobkhotpe and Sekhem..., etc., that a familial strain of a sort characterized this dynasty.

PHARAOH 43: AMENY.
Position in dynasty: Sixth. *Portrait:* yes. *Length of reign:* 2 years. *Dates of reign:* 1885-1883 B.C. *Mummy:* not found. *Sarcophagus:* yes (quartzite?). *Burial chamber:* yes?. *Treasure:* not found. *Hawk name:* Sehertoui. *Vulture-and-Cobra name:* Sesekhemkheu. *Set or Hawk-of-Nubi name:* Heqmaethet. *Reed-and-Hornet name:* Senkhibre. *Son-of-the-Sun-God (Ra) name:* Ameny-Intef-Amenemhat. *Other names:* Ameny-Aamu (Ameny the Asiatic).

Although the Thirteenth Dynasty was comprised of 60 kings, only three of these built pyramids: Ameny, the sixth pharaoh of the line; Ay, the thirty-first; and Khendjer II, the fifty-fifth. It is possible that other kings of this dynasty also constructed pyramid tombs, but at present, there is no evidence to indicate that this was so.

The Reed-and-Hornet name of this king, which is Senkhibre, is interpreted as, "The Sun-God Reviving the Heart." As Hawk-king, he was named Sehertoui, "Contenting Upper and Lower Egypt," and as Hawk-of-Nubi, he was Heqmaethet, "The Eternal Prince of Truth." The Vulture-and-Cobra name of Ameny was Sesekhemkheu, while the triple-name Ameny-Intef-Amenemhat was adopted for his Son-of-the-Sun-God title.

Except for his pyramid at South Sakkara, a sarcophagus (quartzite?) and canopic jars found therein, a fine offering table found at Karnak, a single cylinder-seal, and a scarab bearing his name, nothing more has been handed down or is known to us concerning this pharaoh.

Pyramid: Ameny. *Name:* Pyramid Ameny. *Number:* 64. *Exterior photos:* no. *Interior photos:* no.

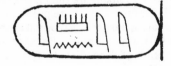

Pharaoh Ameny and his cartouche.
(HEAD: EGYPTIAN MUSEUM, CAIRO)

Cross-sectional diagram: no. *Plan diagram:* no. *Pyramid field:* South Sakkara. *Field number:* VII. *Length:* 165 ft. *Height:* approx. 105 ft. *Angle:* approx. 51 degrees. *Type:* true. *Materials:* limestone. *Location of entrance:* ?. *Portcullises:* ?. *Chambers:* one?.

Pyramid Complex: Ameny. *Main pyramid:* yes. *Satellite pyramid(s):* no. *Mortuary temple:* no. *Valley temple:* no. *Offering shrine:* no. *Mastaba(s):* no. *Ship(s):* no. *Ship pit(s):* no. *Causeway:* no. *Temenos wall:* no. *Canal:* probably destroyed.

PHARAOH 44: AY.
Position in dynasty: Thirty-first. *Portrait:* no. *Length of reign:* 23 years. *Dates of reign:* 1820–1798 B.C. *Mummy:* not found. *Sarcophagus:* yes — quartzite. *Burial chamber:* yes. *Treasure:* not found. *Hawk name:* ?. *Vulture-and-Cobra name:* ?. *Set or Hawk-of-Nubi name:* ?. *Reed-and-Hornet name:* Mernefer-Ra (Merneferre) (The Beloved and Beautiful-One of the Sun-God). *Son-of-the-Sun-God (Ra) name:* Ai (Ay). (The Proclaimed). *Other names:* Demaiu (?); Merneferre Ay; Timaio (?); Toutimai (?).

As Reed-and-Hornet king, this pharaoh took the name Merneferre, meaning "The Beloved and Beautiful one of the Sun-God." We have no knowledge of his Hawk, Hawk-of-Nubi, or Vulture-and-Cobra names, but his Son-of-the-Sun-God name was simply Ay. The Jewish historian, Josephus, renders the latter interpretation "Timaio," by association of the hieroglyphic Demaiu, meaning, "The Proclaimed."

It has been noted how Dynasties XIII and XIV were, in fact, contemporaneous. Actually, the latter part of Dynasty XIII even meshed with the beginning of Dynasty XV as well. In the case of Ay, his reign as pharaoh conflicted with that of the exceptionally aggressive first king of Dynasty XV, Apopi, with the result that Apopi stripped all power from Ay and reigned supreme. Yet although Apopi was the more powerful of the two rivals, he was, like Ay, a more or less insignificant monarch who left few traces of his reign.

Under such strain, the Pharaoh Ay still managed to undertake several building projects, most notably in the area of Memphis.

With so little evidence available, it

is the natural inclination of the archaeologist to make the most of what he has. A. Wigall points out that the five scarabs found which bear the name of Ay were discovered at the temple ruins of Koptos, Abydos and Lisht, and at Pebast and Tell-el-Yehudiyeh. Geographically, we can learn from this that Ay, although overshadowed by the Pharaoh Apopi of the Fifteenth Dynasty, nevertheless had temples in various parts of the land; for the first three locations are in Upper Egypt, while the latter two are in Lower Egypt (the Delta).

After Ay's power had been considerably reduced by Apopi, the remaining Thirteenth Dynasty monarchs continued to rule as nothing more than vassals before the new Hyksos influx. Of the 60 Dynasty XIII kings, the damaged Turin Papyrus only records 31, the other 29 names being obliterated.

At the entrance to Ay's unfinished pyramid, lying on the ground outside, were found two black granite pyramidions, one pointed and the other truncated, both unfinished and uninscribed. (They are now in the Cairo Museum.)

It is curious that two pyramidia would have been prepared for one pyramid. The reason is naturally open to much speculation. Perhaps the architects had ordered the truncated pyramidion fashioned at the pyramid site, and then later changed their minds in favor of the pointed model, or vice-versa; or perhaps there was a slight flaw in the angle of their first model, thus prompting the commission of the second. This is one problem which may forever remain unsolved.

With the exception of his pyramid at South Sakkara, and his recorded name on the Turin Papyrus, on the gateway at the temple of Karnak and

Cartouche of Pharaoh Ay.

on a few scarabs, nothing is known of this pharaoh.

An additional point worthy of mention is that the sarcophagus and canopic chest found in this pharaoh's burial chamber do not represent individual or separate pieces; at their lower sections, they form one piece with the floor, being fashioned from the very same stone.

It is also worth mentioning that there were two burial chambers in this pharaoh's pyramid, each containing a yellow quartzite sarcophagus. The second interment was likely that of Ay's favorite queen or princess, as there are no satellite pyramids accompanying the main pyramid. This somewhat rare presence of two sarcophagi and two burial chambers is repeated in the satellite pyramid of Khendjer II (Pyramid no. 61).

Pyramid: Ay. *Name:* Pyramid Ay. *Number:* 63. *Exterior photos:* no. *Interior photos:* no. *Cross-sectional diagram:* yes. *Plan diagram:* yes. *Pyramid field:* South Sakkara. *Field number:* VII. *Length:* 310 ft. *Height:* approx. 200 ft. (now 10 ft.) *Angle:* approx. 55 degrees. *Type:* true. *Materials:* brick core; limestone casing. *Location of entrance:* east – ground. *Portcullises:* three horizontal. *Chambers:* four.

Pyramid Complex: Ay. *Main pyramid:* yes. *Satellite pyramid(s):* no. *Mortuary temple:* yes – not yet unearthed. *Valley temple:* yes – not yet unearthed. *Offering shrine:* no. *Mastaba(s):* no?. *Ship(s):* no. *Ship pit(s):*

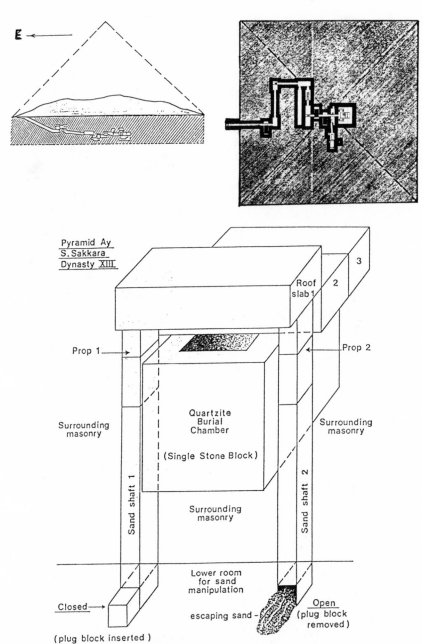

Pyramid of Ay, South Sakkara. **Top:** *Cross-section (left) and plan.* (G. JEQUIER) **Bottom:** *Unique method of sealing a burial chamber, showing how escaping sand from shafts enables roof slab to be lowered.* (J.P. LEPRE/K. MAYER)

no. *Causeway:* yes — not yet unearthed. *Temenos wall:* yes — wavy
type. *Canal:* probably destroyed.

PHARAOH 45: KHENDJER II.
Position in dynasty: Fifty-fifth.
Portrait: yes. *Length of reign:* 1
year. *Dates of reign:* 1750–1749 B.C.
Mummy: not found. *Sarcophagus:*
?. *Burial chamber:* yes?. *Treasure:*
not found. *Hawk name:* ?. *Vul-
ture-and-Cobra name:* ?. *Set or
Hawk-of-Nubi name:* ?. *Reed-and-
Hornet name:* Khent-her (Khendjer)
(Khenzer). *Son-of-the-Sun-God
(Ra) name:* ?. *Other names:* Usr-
kere.

Found near the north offering
shrine of this pharaoh's pyramid was
a polished granite pyramidion inscribed with hieroglyphs and decora-
tions.

The satellite pyramid of Khendjer
II, located northeast of the parent
pyramid, is unusual in that is has two
burial chambers, with each containing a quartzite sarcophagus. Both
lids for these sarcophagi had been
left resting on columns of masonry,
indicating that these chests had never
been occupied. In one of these
chambers was also found an empty
quartzite canopic chest. This
somewhat rare occurrence of two
sarcophagi and two burial chambers
is repeated in the pyramid of the
Pharaoh Ay. The twin burials in
Khendjer's satellite pyramid were
almost certainly for two of his
favorite wives or daughters, there being no instance whatsoever of a male

Top: *Pharaoh Khendjer II.* (EGYP-
TIAN MUSEUM, CAIRO) **Second from
top:** *Cartouche of Khendjer II.* **Third
from top:** *Cross-section of Pyramid
of Khendjer II, South Sakkara.* (J.P.
LEPRE) **Bottom:** *Plan of same
pyramid.* (G. JEQUIER)

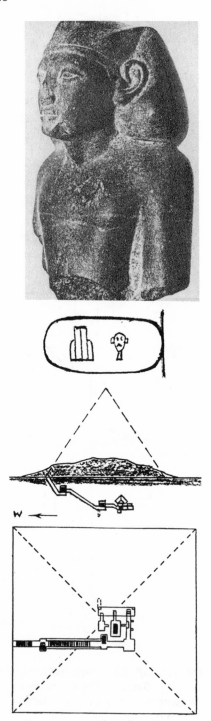

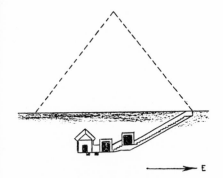

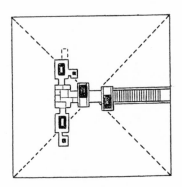

Satellite pyramid of Khendjer II, South Sakkara: Cross-section (left) and plan.
(J.P. LEPRE)

ever having been interred in a subsidiary pyramid.
Pyramid: Khendjer II. *Name:* Pyramid Khendjer. *Number:* 62. *Exterior photos:* no. *Interior photos:* no. *Cross-sectional diagram:* yes. *Plan diagram:* yes. *Pyramid field:* South Sakkara. *Field number:* VII. *Length:* 170 ft. *Height:* 120 ft. *Angle:* 55 degrees. *Type:* true. *Materials:* brick core; limestone casing. *Location of entrance:* west — ground. *Portcullises:* two. *Chambers:* two.
Pyramid Complex: Khendjer II. *Main pyramid:* yes. *Satellite pyramid(s):* yes — one (no. 61). *Mortuary temple:* yes. *Valley temple:* no.

Offering shrine: yes. *Mastaba(s):* no?. *Ship(s):* no. *Ship pit(s):* no. *Causeway:* no. *Temenos wall:* yes — two. *Canal:* destroyed.
Satellite Pyramid: Khendjer II. *Name:* Pyramid Queens? and?. *Number:* 61. *Exterior photos:* no. *Interior photos:* no. *Cross-sectional diagram:* yes. *Plan diagram:* yes. *Pyramid field:* South Sakkara. *Field number:* VII. *Length:* 80 ft. *Height:* approx. 50 ft. (now 20 ft.) *Angle:* 55 degrees. *Type:* true. *Materials:* brick core; limestone casing. *Location of entrance:* east — ground. *Portcullises:* two horizontal. *Chambers:* three.

VIII. Other Pyramids

In Dynasty XI and Dynasties XIV through XL, approximately 400 other pyramids were built in Egypt and neighboring Cush. These can hardly be compared with their predecessors, as they were of inferior scope and less complex design. Therefore, they will be only briefly discussed.

The first group of 100 Egyptian pyramids spanned approximately 1,000 years (2887–1800 B.C.), whereas the second group of 400 Egyptian and Cushitic pyramids spanned approximately 2,000 years (2150–150 B.C.).

Group 2, the late Egyptian and the Cushitic pyramids, ran thus:

The seven pharaohs comprising Dynasty XI—two of the Intef line, and five of the Mentuhotep—built "pyramid-temples" that consisted of chapels surmounted by small, steep-sided, brick pyramids. These pyramids did not house the mummies of the pharaohs; the actual burials were in the adjacent cliffs to the west.

There were no pyramids built in Dynasties XIV through XVI. In Dynasties XVII through XIX, at least seven pharaohs each built a small, steep-sided, degenerative brick pyramid. These eight (Pharaoh Amosis built two) or more pyramids were located at Thebes, Abydos and Deir El Medina. Their builders were as follows:

1. *Sebekemsaf I* (Dynasty XVII) reigned for 6 (?) years, from 1650–1644 B.C. (?). His Hawk name was Hetep-neteru; his Reed-and-Hornet name, Sekhem-Uotch-Khau-Ra; and his Son-of-the-Sun-God name, Sebekemsaf I. His Vulture-and-Cobra and Hawk-of-Nubi names are not known.

2. *Intef IX* (Dynasty XVII) reigned for 4 (?) years, from 1636–1632 B.C. (?). His Hawk name was Upuem-maat; his Reed-and-Hornet name, Seshesh-Ra, and his Son-of-the-Son-God name, Antef-Aa (Intef). His Hawk-of-Nubi and Vulture-and-Cobra names are not known.

3. *Intef X* (Dynasty XVII) reigned for 10 (?) years, from 1632–1621 B.C. (?). His Hawk name was Nefer-kheperu; his Son-of-the-Son-God name, Antef-Aa (Intef); and another obscure rendition being Nub-kheper-Ra. His Vulture-and-Cobra, Hawk-of-Nubi and Reed-and-Hornet names are not known.

4. *Tao* (Dynasty XVII) reigned for 3 (?) years, from 1596–1593 B.C. (?). His Reed-and-Hornet name was Seqenen-Ra; his Son-of-the-Son-God name, Tau-Aa (Tao); and a third, undetermined name, Senakhtenre. His Hawk name, Vulture-and-Cobra and Set (Hawk-of-Nubi) names are not precisely known.

5. *Taoo* (Dynasty XVII) reigned for 12 years (?), from 1592–1580 B.C. (?). His Reed-and-Hornet name was Seqenen-Ra, while as Son-of-the-Sun-God, he was known as Tau-Aa (Taoo). His Hawk name, Vulture-and-Cobra name and Hawk-of-Nubi names are not known.

6. *Kamose* (Dynasty XVII) reigned

for 3 years (?), from 1574–1571 B.C. (?). His Reed-and-Hornet, Vulture-and-Cobra, and Hawk-of-Nubi names are not known, but as Son-of-the-Sun-God, he was known as Kames Kamose, and as Hawk-king he took the name Setef-Tch-Tata. He is also sometimes called Uatch-Kheper-Ra.

7. *King Amosis I,* the first pharaoh of the illustrious Eighteenth Dynasty, may have built two pyramids—one for himself and a second for his grandmother, Tetisheri. These monuments, both presumably located at Abydos, were supposedly found to be empty when first entered. As Reed-and-Hornet king, Amosis took the name Nebpehti-Ra; as Son-of-the-Sun-God, he was called Aahmes (Amosis); and as Hawk-king, Uat Kheperu. His Vulture-and-Cobra and Hawk-of-Nubi names are not known.

There were no pyramids built in Dynasties XX through XXIV. In Dynasty XXV, over 350 small, steep-sided pyramids were built by the Cushite kings at Meroe (170 pyramids), Tankasi (40), Nuri (35), Kuru (25), Zuma (25), Gebel Barkal (25), Begraiviya (10), Napata (10), and Karanog (10)—all in the Sudan. A number of these contained subterranean burials. There were no burials in the superstructures of these monuments.

Lastly, 30 small pyramids of this type were also built during the Ptolemaic Period, although none have survived, all having since been razed.

The pyramids at Nuri were 60 to 100′ high, although that of the prominent King Taharqos was 150′ high. Nearly all of these pyramids had ritual deposits of vessels, etc., at each of their foundation corners. Each was also surrounded by its own temenos wall.

The Meroe pyramids were plastered and painted, and most contained burials, not only of the pharaohs, but also of their servants, horses and oxen.

KING TUTANKHAMEN

The author would here like to comment on the modern-day popularity of the boy-pharaoh, Tutankhamen. It seems that of the nearly 300 pharaohs that once ruled Egypt, the general public is aware of only this king. The reason for this awareness is that, of all these pharaohs, Tutankhamen was the sole one whose tomb was found intact. There is evidence that someone penetrated the crypt earlier, but little or nothing was taken by these intruders, who were apparently apprehended at the site by the tomb guardians.

Of the majority of pharaohs no traces remain. This is due to the fact that most of their tombs were penetrated, and everything, including the mummy, was stolen; and also because some of their tombs are yet to be discovered. Only a few dozen of these many pharaohs have been found, sans treasures or possessions, and are presently on display in the special mummy-room at the Cairo Museum.

The reader would do well to realize that Tutankhamen was an Eighteenth Dynasty pharaoh, and that in this time period the kings had lost much of their power to the priestly and political classes. Tut and other pharaohs of this era were fast becoming puppet kings. In the earlier dynasties, however, most especially the late third and early fourth (the hey day of pyramid building), the pharaoh was considered absolute monarch, and wielded a power and influence never again matched by any line of royalty in history.

An example of the wealth (and thereby the power) of the early pyramid pharaohs, as compared to that of King Tutankhamen, is evident, not only in the fact that Tutankhamen was not able to "afford" the expense of a monolithic pyramid, and had to be content with a small subterranean tomb, but also from comparisons of his funerary equipment with that of the third and fourth dynasty pharaohs. Consider, for example that the burial equipment of King Khufu of Dynasty IV included two 150'-long cedar-wood solar boats, whereas the solar boats of King Tutankhamen's burial equipment were a mere 3' long and constituted nothing more than models of the real thing.

The author does not mean to belittle the importance of the Tutankhamen find, but only wishes to stress the existence and significance of more important and colorful pharaohs than this one. This study of ancient Egypt is quite involved, and should not revolve around the single crypt of this boy-pharaoh.

IX. Methods of Pyramid Construction

Anyone who has ever heard of the Egyptian pyramids, or of ancient Egypt, has at some time probably asked himself the question: How did they do it? How did they move those massive blocks of stone and lift them to such great heights, all without the aid of modern tools or technology? There have been many theories regarding this question throughout the ages — some practical, some impractical — ranging from the simple use of wooden rollers and pulleys, to complex mind-over-matter techniques and anti-gravity machines.

Without attempting to list the numerous theories put forth by the various authors, or to be placed in the position of having to agree or disagree with them, this author prefers to systematically present the archaeological evidence — meager though it may appear to some — and let the truth of the matter reveal itself.

Such evidence does in fact exist, but most people are not at all aware of it. This evidence illustrates that the ancient builders did not employ complex or mysterious devices or techniques for their manipulation of heavy stone, but executed their grand task by use of the most simple and practical methods available to intelligent men.

Manipulation was the second of three major processes involving the stone for the pyramids. The first process was quarrying; the quarried stones were then manipulated (moved, raised, and set into place). The third process, sealing of the stones, did not take place in all cases.

Prior to these three processes, the pyramid builders had to deal with the problem of leveling and aligning the rock foundation in order to accommodate the base of the monument. Leveling was accomplished by enclosing the entire square foundation in water through the use of mud-brick walls. Within this area a network of troughs or trenches was fashioned, forming a gridiron pattern. Evidence of such a network is still intact at the north side of the Fourth Dynasty Pyramid of King Khafra at Giza. It was not necessary to level the entire foundation, but only those critical sections comprising the four base sides of the pyramid. Any natural mounds of rock which may have been located on the plateau were most likely left intact, not only to lessen the area to be worked, but to further act as points of reinforcement.

The squaring of the monument's base may well have been achieved by the use of measuring cords composed of flax-fiber or palm-fiber, while north, south, east and west orientation was probably accomplished through use of the astrolabe, the precursor of our modern sextant; the V-shaped bay; and the merkhet or plumb bob. All three of these instruments are mentioned in the hieroglyphic texts and were doubtless used in conjunction with the heavenly bodies, with an emphasis on the earth's sun and the pole star.

235

astrolabe   bay   merkhet

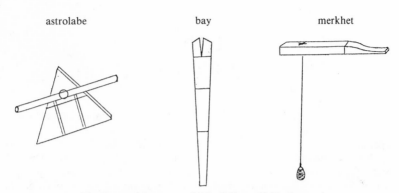

Tools used in pyramid building. (J.P. LEPRE)

Of the three major processes — the quarrying, manipulation and sealing of the stones — the first two, and most especially the second, will require most of our attention, as their context is far more involved than the third. Actually, the third process merely involves the use of gypsum mortar, a sulfate of lime. Colonel Howard Vyse, famed Egyptologist, tells us that "such is the tenacity of the cement . . . that a fragment of one casing [stone] that had been destroyed remained firmly fixed in its original position, notwithstanding the lapse of time, and the violence to which it had been exposed."

The first process, quarrying, involved (1) the extraction or cutting of the stone from the quarry, and then the (2) squaring, (3) dressing, and if necessary (4) polishing of the stone. Additionally, it sometimes included (5) the hollowing-out of the stone, as with the sarcophagi or canopic chests. Thus there were up to five stages involved in this first process.

The second process, manipulation, involved (1) the transportation of the stones from the quarry to the pyramid site; (2) the raising and (3) setting of the stones into place; and in certain instances — as with the portcullis or blocking systems — the (4) raising *and* lowering of blocks of stone. There was also the added stage of (5) leveling the stones. Thus the second process also had up to five stages.

The third process had only one stage. All told, then, we have three processes comprising up to eleven stages.

We will now, in step-by-step fashion, discuss the processes of quarrying and manipulating heavy stone, making mention of the several tools employed in the various stages. We commence with the first stage of the first process, the cutting or extraction of the blocks from the quarry. The chart entitled "Methods of Pyramid Building" (page 238) will aid the reader in understanding this discussion. The tools employed were copper chisels, dolerite hammers and mauls, soaked wooden wedges, and in some cases, dolerite ball pounders. Photos (page 237) of wedge slots cut into limestone and granite blocks at a building site and at the Aswan quarry show how the ancients were able, not only to extract the stones from the quarry without excessive expenditure of labor, but to shape said stones as well.

As to the copper cutting tools, it should be realized that as early as the First Dynasty (prepyramid) age, the Egyptian engineers were making extensive use of the copper mines at

Examples of stone-splitting process used by the ancient Egyptians. Notches or slots were chiseled into the limestone or granite. Wooden wedges were soaked in water, then inserted into the chiseled notches. When the wood expanded, it split the rock. (I.E.S. EDWARDS)

Sinai. This can be proved by numerous hieroglyphic inscriptions found at these sites.

As for dolerite tools, large numbers of dolerite pounders used for working hard stone have been found at the ancient stone quarries south of Aswan. These sites were the principal sources for rose granite and other hard stone.

At the quarries of Tura and Masara one can still see the red-ocher guidelines painted by the ancients to aid them in cutting the stone. Indeed, the references in hieroglyphic inscriptions to quarrying are numerous. One such inscription in the quarries of Wadi Hammamat, written during the reign of the Pharaoh Ity, Dynasty VI, relates that 200 soldiers and 200 workmen arrived there to carry out quarrying work in connection with the erection of the king's pyramid at Sakkara.

The second and third stages of the quarrying process, the squaring and dressing of the extracted stones, were performed with the aid of copper saws, fine copper chisels, dolerite hammers, wooden squares and wooden facing plates.

That copper saws were used to cut and square the stones is evident from examination of the sarcophagi of Khufu and Menkara, and of the back portion of the famous slate triads of Menkara. In each case, the saw marks are clearly discernible to the naked eye. Their length on Khufu's granite sarcophagus indicate that the saw used was at least 8' long.

An excellent example of a set-square was found at the pyramid site of Lisht. And Petrie tells of the use of facing-plates to test the smoothness of the blocks in the final stage of the squaring process.

Although it may seem irrelevant to the subject of Egyptian pyramid building, the author would like

Stone Blocks — Tools listed alphabetically

Column groups: **QUARRY** (Extract-Cut, Square, Polish, Hollow Out — Sarcophagi & Canopic Chests) · **MANIPULATE** (Transport: Roll on Causeway / Pull on Causeway; Raise Obliquely: Roll Up Inclined Ramp / Pull Up Inclined Ramp; Lower Obliquely: Roll Down Inclined Ramp / Slide Down Inclined Ramp; Portcullises: Raise Vertically / Lower Vertically / Close Horizontally; Level) · **SEAL** (Seal) · Orientation of Pyramid

Tool	Extract-Cut	Square	Polish	Hollow Out	Roll on Causeway	Pull on Causeway	Roll Up Incl. Ramp	Pull Up Incl. Ramp	Roll Down Incl. Ramp	Slide Down Incl. Ramp	Raise Vertically	Lower Vertically	Close Horizontally	Level	Seal	Orientation of Pyramid
ABRASIVES			•													
BALL POUNDER — DOLERITE	•															
BAY																•
BEAMS OR BAULKS							•	•	•	•		•				
BOSSES OR LUGS											•	•				
CAUSEWAY — STONE					•	•										
CHISELS — COPPER	•	•														
COUNTERWEIGHTS — LG. BLOCKS												•				
DRILLS — DOLERITE OR DIAMOND				•												
LEVERS — IRON BARS											•	•				
LUBRICANT — OIL						•		•		•						
MANPOWER — TEAM					•	•	•	•	•							
MAULS OR HAMMERS — DOLERITE	•	•														
MEASURING CORDS — FIBER		•														•
MORTAR — GYPSUM															•	
PLATES — IRON											•	•				
PLUMB BOB (MERKHET)														•		•
PROPS — SMALL BLOCKS											•	•		•		
RAMP OR INCLINED PLANE							•	•	•	•						
ROPES					•	•	•	•	•	•		•				
SAND														•		
SAWS — COPPER		•														
SAWS — STONE		•														
SLEDGES						•		•								
SET SQUARES AND WOODEN FACING PLATES		•														•
TROUGHS — MUD — BRICK														•		•
WEDGES — AS CHOCKS							•	•	•	•						
WEDGES — SOAKED	•															
WHEELS OR CRADLES					•		•		•							

Tools not used

Tool																
COMPASS (MAGNETIC)																
CRANES OR WINCHES																
PULLEYS																
ROLLERS — WOODEN																
SCREW																

Wall painting from Egyptian tomb shows stone-cutters finishing the dressing of limestone blocks. (A. ROSELLINI)

to mention, in passing, that the stones of the famed Solomon's Temple of the Jews were "hewn and sawed with *stone* saws" (I Kings 7:9). When considering the close proximity of that ancient civilization to the Egyptian (a mere 275 miles), it is perhaps not too far-fetched to assume that the builders of these civilizations were aware of each other's methods, and that the Egyptians may have employed stone as well as copper saws.

The fourth stage of the quarrying process, that of polishing some (but not all) of the stones, was accomplished by use of an abrasive in the form of powdered pumice stone. Such a procedure is used to this day by stone workers in modern Egypt.

As to the hollowing-out of the sarcophagi and canopic chests, there can be little doubt that dolerite, copper or even diamond drills were used.

Opposite: *Pyramid building methods.*

This is marvelously indicated in the sarcophagus of Khufu, where the drill used was slightly over 4″ in diameter, this being illustrated by two sections where it was allowed to run too deep. Also, Sir Petrie excavated a granite drill core, tubular drill hole and sawn piece of basalt.

The transportation of the blocks from the quarry to the pyramid site, constituted the first stage of the manipulation process. The elements needed for this operation were a smooth causeway leading up to the pyramid site; wooden sledges on which to place the blocks of stone to bring them up the causeway; manpower and ropes to pull these sledges; and lubricating oil to lessen the friction between sledge and causeway, facilitating the process.

The remains of a considerable number of causeways, generally between ¼ and 1 mile long, and oriented from the west bank of the Nile to the various pyramid sites, have

All Pyramids

Materials		Number of Pyramids	Pharaoh	Granite Casing	Dyn.
Inner Layer Core	**Outer Layer Casing**				
brick	brick	13			
brick	fine limestone	8			
coarse limestone & rubble	fine limestone	2			
coarse limestone	fine limestone	53			
coarse limestone	fine limestone & granite	2	1 Neferirkare 2 Khafra	1st coarse only 1st two courses only	5 4
coarse limestone	granite	3	1 Menkara's Queen Kham. II 2 Rededef 3 Menkara	at least partially at least 3 courses at least 16 courses	4 4 4
coarse limestone	plaster	1			
coarse limestone	not known	3			
not known	not known	15			

Total = 100

| | All Entrances | | | | | Unorthodox Entrances | | | |
| | Face | | Ground | | | | | | |
Location	Face	Probably Face	Ground	Probably Ground	Total		Pharaoh	Pyramid	Dynasty
North	22	4	24	8	58				
South	-	-	4	-	4	1	Senusert II	Lahun	12
						2	Senusert II	Lahun	12
						3	Amenemhat III	Hawara	12
						4	Amenemhat IV	Mazghuna	12
East	-	-	3	-	3	1	Amenemhat III	Dahshur	12
						2	Ay	South Sakkara	13
						3	Khendjer's Queen	South Sakkara	13
West	1	-	3	-	4	1	Senusert III	Dahshur	12
						2	Khendjer II	South Sakkara	13
						3	Sneferu / Face	Dahshur	3
						4	Khafra's Queen	Giza	4
None No Shaft Leading to Burial Chamber	-	-	-	-	2	1	Beby	Nagada	3
						2	Teti's Queen Iput	North Sakkara	6
Unknown	-	18	-	11	29				
	23	22	34	19	100				
	45		53						
	98		+2		100				

In actuality, there are 100 pyramids with 104 entrances; 4 pyramids have 2 entrances each.

Dyn.
1 Pyramid-Bent-Sneferu-N.&W.Face   3
2 Pyramid Khafra-N.Face&Ground   4
3 Pyramid Sesostris II-Both S.Ground   12
4 Pyramid Khafra's Queen-N.Face&W.G.   4

Comparison of locations of entrances on the various pyramids. (J.P. LEPRE)

been discovered and unearthed in modern times. (See photo, page 16.) It is apparent that before such causeways were used for the funerary cortege, they were employed for the transport of the heavy stone to the pyramid site. Although the majority of causeways were located on the east side of the pyramid and pointed east to the Nile, there are instances where they are built on the west side of the pyramid, pointing westward to the desert. These western causeways were used exclusively for construction purposes, for it was in the western desert where the majority of the stone used in building the pyramids was quarried. This stone was the core material; the material for the casing stones was at the Mokattan, Tura and Maura hills across the river, on the east bank. An exception

Opposite: *Materials of the 100 pyramids.* (J.P. LEPRE)

to this rule would be the pyramid of Huni at Maidum, where there are two causeways, both on the east side: one exclusively funerary and the other exclusively for construction.

Although western causeways must have been built for the majority of pyramids, only a few examples have survived to date and been excavated, probably because the western construction causeways were built of mud-brick and may even have been later dismantled by the builders themselves, in order to use the material elsewhere. The eastern funerary causeways on the other hand, were built of large stone blocks and were considered to be a permanent element of the pyramid complex.

Examples of construction causeways can be found at the pyramid site of Dahshur, at the North Stone Pyramid; there are two extending from the pyramid westward.

Many authors make the mistaken assertion that all of the stones used to build the pyramids were quarried across the river. They further claim that these stones were brought from the east to the west bank exclusively by raft or barge. There are several references to the use of such boats, but this does not imply that other means of crossing were not used.

It is possible that, besides being ferried across, the stone blocks were transported over a bridge constructed specifically for this purpose. Many bridges exist today over the Nile, and surely if the ancients were capable of building such enormous pyramids, they were capable of building at least one bridge.

When one reflects on the size and number of the more-or-less continuous building projects conducted on the west bank, and on the staggering number of stones that had to be taken across from the east bank quarries, it seems sensible to assume that a system of both barges and bridges was used — not as a matter of choice, but of necessity.

That the ancient Egyptians dragged wooden sledges loaded with blocks of stone up the causeway and to the pyramid site is reflected in the mural found in the Fifth Dynasty tomb of the Nobleman Mereruka at North Sakkara. This mural depicts a sixty-ton alabaster statue of this official being conveyed on a sledge from the workshop to the tomb. It shows no fewer than 166 men using ropes to pull the sledge. It also shows one man pouring lubricant before the sledge to minimize friction between sledge and causeway. Another man is rhythmically clapping his hands so that the men could pull in unison and with cadence, making the most of their efforts.

An illustration of this mural, and a photo of a wooden sledge used at the funeral of Senusert I and discovered at his pyramid site at Lisht, are on page 243, along with another mural discovered at the limestone quarries of Tura. That mural depicts six oxen driven by three men, pulling a sledge with a stone block.

As scenes such as the ones depicted on the following page are rarely found in Egypt, or in any of the other ancient civilizations, for that matter, I find it necessary here to insert a

Opposite: *Examples of sledges used by the ancients.* **From top:** *Mural from Fifth Dynasty tomb of nobleman Mereruka.* (E. SOLDI) *Wooden sledge from pyramid of Senusert I, Lisht.* (J. DEMORGAN) *Assyrian slaves towing barge along Tigris River (circa 700 B.C.) Note presence of overseers with clubs and that workmen are lashed together, indicating slave status.* (H. SCHAFER) **Bottom:** *Sledge transport, ancient Egypt.* (J. WILKINSON)

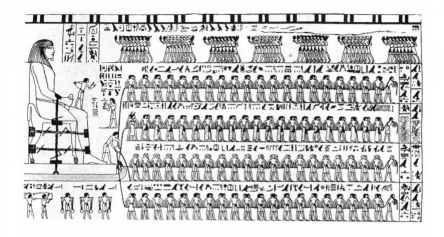

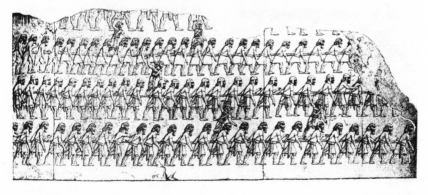

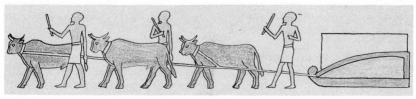

copy of a bas-relief found at the ancient site of Nineveh, the capital of the great Assyrian Empire, to illustrate that another civilization besides Egypt used gangs of workmen organized in files for heavy transport.

Whether the Egyptians employed oxen or other animals for these projects to any great degree is not known, but it is more likely that the majority of the sledge work was done by human laborers. Egypt has always enjoyed an overabundance of people, but farm animals were a less plentiful commodity and were likely, for the most part, confined to agricultural rather than construction tasks.

Larger wooden sledges than that found in the Pyramid of Senusert I were unearthed at the pyramid sites of Senusert II at Lahun and Senusert III at Dahshur. These were evidently used for the transport of the funerary ships to the sites. And indeed, one of the sacred boats used in shrines and religious processions is depicted in hieroglyphs placed on such a sledge:

In an ancient hieroglyphic inscription reference is made to this type of transport. The author, apparently a chief of engineers, relates how they "*dragged* two huge statues of white marble and alabaster" and placed them to the right and left of a false door set up for the pharaoh. Additionally, a hieroglyphic inscription dated to the reign of Pharaoh Mentuhotep V, the seventh king of the Eleventh Dynasty, records the completion of a building project and mentions that the four-ton lid of a sarcophagus "was *dragged* down to the Nile . . . as it came forth from the work of dressing."

Also, with the previously mentioned sixty-ton statue of Mereruka, the inscription describing the

transport of that statue states that "the way over which the statue had to come down from the quarries was very difficult . . . because of the rough stone of the ground [a poorly built road or causeway]. So I caused the young men of the recruits to come to make a new road [causeway] for it, together with gangs of necropolis stone-cutters and quarrymen. . . . The men of strong arm were there, together with the weak. Their courage rose, their arms grew strong, so that each one of them put forth the strength of a thousand men."

Further proof that the ancients employed sledges for the transport of stone can be seen in the hieroglyphic sign for a sledge carrying a stone, which is: , or a sledge without a stone, which is: . Also, in hieroglyphs, the word for sledge is written: (*aspt*) or (*unsh-t*). In both cases the determinative (key hieroglyphic sign) is the sign (meaning "wood"). Yet another way for writing the word sledge is: (*akhn*) , with the determinative here being the sign (meaning "to pull," or more specifically, "to haul").

And finally, we have the depiction in a hieroglyphic sign of a funerary chest set onto a sledge thus: .

There can be little doubt, then, that the ancients utilized sledges on an extensive basis for the transport of heavy stone.

We now arrive at the second stage of the manipulation process, that of raising the stones from the ground to their final resting places in the super-structure of the pyramid.

With the stones still resting on the sledges, the sledges were pulled up an inclined ramp that was generally situated on the east or north side of the monument. These ramps consisted primarily of mud and rubble (for ease of dismantling) faced with a pavement of smooth stones, and had a gradient of about 1 in 12.

Remains of such construction ramps have been discovered on the east face of the pyramid of Amenemhat I at Lisht; at the unfinished step pyramid of Djoser-Tati (Sekhemkhet) at North Sakkara; at the pyramid of Huni, Maidum; at Giza, near Khafra's pyramid; and at Queen Hatshepsut's funerary temple at Deir el Bahri.

They were also found at the unfinished mortuary temple of Menkara at Giza, and at the unfinished first pylon of the temple at Karnak.

The sledges were pulled up these inclined ramps in the same manner that they were dragged over the level causeway, the sole difference being the employment of wooden chocks or wedges to hold the sledges in position during rest intervals (required because of the more laborious task of pulling the sledge up an inclined ramp rather than on level ground) or pauses to adjust a loose block of stone, etc.

Wooden baulks or beams which were set into the ramps at intervals were probably used to hold the chocks in place. Examples of such baulks were found *in situ* in the ramps of the pyramid of Amenemhat I at Lisht.

Some authors have suggested that the ramp system was not confined to one side of the pyramid, but that it was extended to all four sides. Illustrations of two different types of single-ramp systems and one type of multi-ramp system are presented on page 246.

The third stage of the manipulation process, that of actually setting the stones into place once they had reached their relative positions in the superstructure, required the use of levers (in the form of iron crow bars — Fakhry speaks of large wooden crow bars) working in conjunction with rough-cut "bosses" (lugs or protuberances left on the blocks of stone at the quarries).

Conclusive proof that the pyramid builders were using iron at a very early date lies in the discovery of a piece of wrought iron imbedded in the masonry of the south air channel of the burial chamber of the pyramid of Khufu. This specimen, found by Colonel Howard Vyse, is probably the oldest piece of worked iron in existence, as the dating of this pyramid has been ascertained at circa 2770 B.C.

Some authors have been inclined to doubt the authenticity of this iron specimen, but Sir W.M.F. Petrie stated that "the vouchers for it are very precise; and it has a cast of a nummulite on the rust of it, proving it to have been buried for ages beside a block of nummulitic limestone . . . and therefore to be certainly ancient. No reasonable doubt can therefore exist about its being really a genuine piece used by pyramid masons."

Also, an examination of the nine monolithic ceiling beams in that same burial chamber indicates that they had been lifted into position by the use of leverage. On each of their undersides are vague, oblong outlines — the "tell-tale" signs of plates of sheet iron having once been used there to prevent the crowbars from biting into and defacing the finished stone surface.

Unfortunately, not a single picture

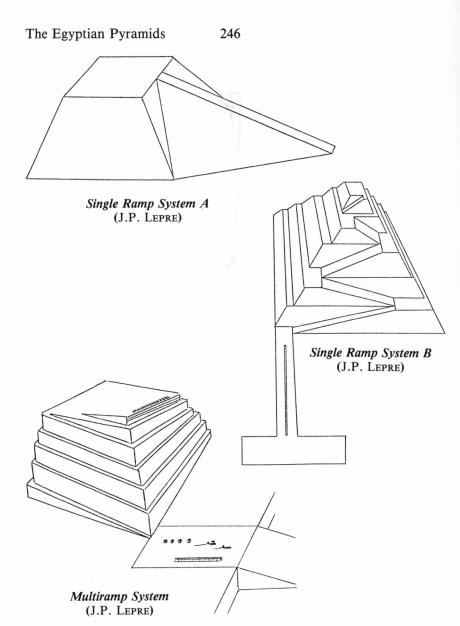

Single Ramp System A
(J.P. LEPRE)

Single Ramp System B
(J.P. LEPRE)

Multiramp System
(J.P. LEPRE)

depicting the ancient Egyptian builders using a lever in conjunction with a raised boss has been discovered to date. Either no such scenes were ever drawn, or they were drawn and have since been defaced by man or the natural elements. However, it is interesting to note that a bas-relief of just such a maneuver has been discovered at Kouyunjik, the site of the ancient city of Nineveh, capital of the once great Assyrian Empire. A copy of this bas-relief is shown above.

A second method of transporting blocks of heavy stone was adopted by Chersiphron, a Roman engineer. What he did was build wooden

Assyrians using a lever to manipulate a stone bull on a sledge. (H. SCHAFER)

"wheels" around stone columns and thereby roll, rather than drag them (as with a sledge) across open ground. This method consisted of wooden "quarter circles" lashed together to form a full circle. That the Egyptians may also have used this technique to transport heavy stone (and that Chersiphron borrowed this principle from them) is suggested by the fact that such quarter circles have been unearthed in Egypt.

Egyptologists have long thought that these quarter circles were used as "cradles" or "rockers" to gradually lift the blocks of stone from tier to tier, but it is more probable that they were used in the same manner as they were used by Chersiphron. To have used the quarter circles as rockers would have been both awkward and inefficient.

In December 1981, a Boston engineer, Mr. John Bush, gave an impressive demonstration of Chersiphron's method by successfully rolling a 2½-ton block of concrete *up* a loading ramp with the aid of six other men. It should be noted, however, that while Mr. Bush's experimental quarter-circles have holes drilled into them to accommodate the lashing of them together with ropes, the samples discovered in Egypt are devoid of such holes.

Regarding the method of rolling the stones up a ramp rather than placing them on sledges, it should be mentioned in passing that this technique was used to build the previously mentioned Solomon's Temple of the Jews. Ezra 5:8 states that "The house of the Great God . . . is being built with stones *rolled into place.*"

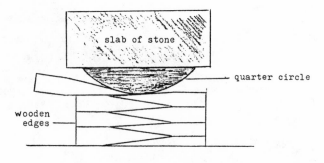

(as cradle or rocker to raise stone - unfeasible)

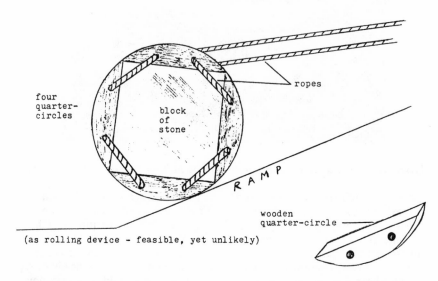

(as rolling device - feasible, yet unlikely)

Use of quarter-circles. **Top:** *As cradle or rocker.* **Bottom:** *As rolling devices.* (J.P. LEPRE)

Beyond the manipulation of the pyramid's core stones, backing (packing) and casing stones, there was also the raising *and* lowering of the portcullis blocking stones. This blocking system was usually located at the bottom of the descending passage leading to the subterranean burial chamber, or in an antechamber which lay slightly north of this chamber. These blocking stones were set in either vertical fashion (as in the pyramid of Khafra at Giza), horizontal fashion (as in the pyramid of Amenemhat III at Hawara) or oblique fashion (as in the Bent Pyramid of Sneferu at Dahshur).

The already-mentioned system of lever and boss was sometimes used with the portcullis arrangement, as is evident by the protruding boss on the granite counterweight in the antechamber of the Great Pyramid.

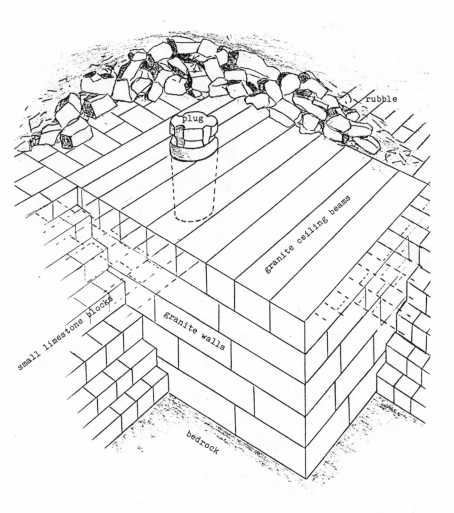

Step Pyramid of Djoser, North Sakkara. Drawing shows roof of granite burial chamber and three-ton plug stone with grooves for ropes. (Partially exposed view.) (J.P. LEPRE)

With these portcullis systems, though, ropes and beams were often used in conjunction with the levers and bosses. In the just-mentioned antechamber of Khufu's pyramid, cut-out semi-hollows are present on the upper portion of the west wainscot. These hollows were evidently intended to receive rounded wooden beams for the ropes to pass over in order to raise and lower the three huge portcullis blocking slabs which once fit into grooves cut in the east and west walls of this chamber.

In the Step Pyramid of Djoser at Sakkara, the three-ton granite plug stone set into the roof of the burial chamber has several notched grooves in its sides to receive ropes which were once used to lower the plug into

Pyramid of Khufu, Campbell's Chamber: Showing rock-cut basins.
(J.P. LEPRE)

place. A drawing of this feature is on the preceding page.

This method of using ropes and beams was employed in raising and lowering not only vertical portcullis slabs, but also sarcophagi.

In the burial chamber of the pyramid of Huni at Maidum, at least four sockets for cross-beams are visible in the wall sections.

One still contains the remnants of a cedar stump, undoubtedly contemporary with the pyramid, and likely used in connection with ropes to raise the stone sarcophagus to that point from the vestibule below.

Also, the inner sides of Pepy II's sarcophagus, in the burial chamber of his pyramid at South Sakkara, have hollowed channels, undoubtedly used for ropes to help lower the wooden coffin into it.

Sockets such as the ones found at Maidum are also present in the chamber immediately preceding the burial chamber of Menkara's pyramid at Giza. Here we have six large sockets, 1' in diameter and 8" deep, located three on the north wall and three on the south, in perfect alignment with one another across the span of the room, and situated so as to receive three huge beams to aid in lowering the coffin and sarcophagus into the burial chamber.

Another means used for lowering vertical portcullis slabs was small blocks of limestone, simultaneously set into place under said slabs to prop them up. Then, with the aid of the lever and boss, the blocks were taken out one by one until the slab was fully lowered.

Examples of this method can still be seen in a number of mastabas at Maidum, where the portcullises were never lowered and were found still propped up by these small stones.

As to the closing of horizontal blocking stones, it is evident from examination of the unfinished pyramid of the Pharaoh Ay at South Sakkara that the release of sand from shafts was used to dislodge quartzite props

Example of projecting boss, Pyramid Khufu.
(J.P. Lepre)

that held the twenty-ton portcullis in place.

The leveling of the various blocks after they had been placed in their positions was accomplished by the use of water troughs set up at selective intervals at each successive level of construction. Such troughs probably consisted of stone slabs with hollows or basins cut into them. Modern carpenter's levels represent a variation on a theme of this suggested water technique.

It is tempting to think that two stones of this description which were found inside one of the construction chambers in Khufu's pyramid once served such a purpose. A photo of these stones is on page 250.

Although the water level was undoubtedly checked at each succeeding tier, the reference point for the entire leveling process was in a trench located at ground zero which followed the line of the perimeter of the pyramid, completely encircling the base of the monument. It was through the use of this trench that the rock foundation of the pyramid was first leveled, then the pyramid platform and then the succeeding courses of masonry.

Evidence of such a trench system has been found at the pyramid of Senusert II at Lahun. Petrie seemed to think that it was used to absorb rainwater flowing off the faces of the pyramid, but in a virtually rainless country such as Egypt, this suggestion should be reconsidered.

Many people seem to have the notion that the pyramids were constructed under the most trying conditions by hordes of slaves driven to their task by the whip. Upon examination, we find that this was certainly not the case. I daresay the working conditions of the present day — regarding such large-scale building projects as dams, skyscrapers and the like — are inferior to those which existed for the pyramid workmen.

The illustration on page 243 shows a work gang pulling in unison. Instead of moving under the whip, they move in harmony through interaction with an individual (standing on the statue) whose job it is to clap his hands and establish a rhythm.

DeCamp, author of *The Ancient Engineers,* tells us that "the pyramids and other Egyptian monuments were not, as is often thought, built by hordes of slaves. Although Egypt was a land of class differences, slavery in the strictest sense never played much part in its history." DeCamp goes on to say that "the king conscripted tens of thousands of peasants to help with the heavy work [on the pyramids] during the season of the annual flooding of the Nile, when these farmers would otherwise have been idle. It was forced labor, but the laborers were conscripts, not slaves. They

The Egyptian Pyramids 252

were probably paid in food, because money did not yet exist. They were organized in gangs with such heartening names as 'Vigorous Gang' and 'Enduring Gang.' The kings also freely pressed their soldiers into service for work on such monuments." DeCamp further states, "It has been suggested that the pyramid workers labored willingly . . . and that . . . such an attitude is not impossible."

In support of the above, we here take into account Professor Petrie's calculation that "with approximately 36,000 workers 1,200 blocks could have been easily and cheerfully dragged into position in a few hours, without confusion and without any of that sweating and straining under the taskmaster's lash which is so often supposed to have been a painful feature of the work."

And Weigall, in his *History of the Pharaohs,* states that "the Great Pyramid has been regarded for so long as an expression of the vanity of a ruthless and slave-driving tyrant, that I hesitate to point out the fallacy of this view. Yet the pharaoh's motive was not vain, nor was the execution of the work tyrannical, though his government, it seems evident, was severe and the whole nation was keyed up to a very high degree of efficiency, and must have been organized in an astonishing and almost ruthless manner. He desired to build an everlasting monument which should be for all time the glory of his race, and which should strike awe into the hearts of kings and peoples . . . throughout the ages. . . . In carrying out this great project he trained his people in organization, discipline, and united effort, yet did not in anyway interfere with their productiveness for the nine months in each year during which agriculture was possible."

HERODOTUS' MACHINE

The popular record has it that modern man has no knowledge of how the Egyptian pyramids were built. However, as has been attested in the previous section of text, Egyptologists do in fact possess a fair amount of information about this controversial subject. A summary of that information covers seven major points: (1) *Q. Where did the stones come from?* A. From quarries. (2) *Q. How were the stones cut from their quarries?* A. With copper chisels, dolerite mallets and soaked wooden wedges. (3) *Q. How were the stones shaped?* A. With copper chisels, drills and saws, and dolerite mallets. (4) *Q. How were the stones transported from the quarries to the pyramid?* A. By the use of sledges, ropes and teams of men. (5) *Q. How were the stones lifted from the ground to the pyramid's superstructure?* A. By the use of ramps. (6) *Q. How were the stones maneuvered into place?* A. With iron bars and with bosses protruding from the stones. (7) *Q. How were the stones leveled?* A. By the use of water troughs.

With the seven points just cited the basics of pyramid building would seem to have been revealed. Yet it should be realized that, although we are familiar with the rudiments of pyramid construction, we are ignorant of its specifics.

Although these methods are widely accepted by Egyptologists, and although I tend to be in general agreement, I am nevertheless somewhat critical of point no. 5, which postulates the use of ramps for lifting heavy stone. It is therefore my intention to illustrate how point no. 5, though seemingly acceptable in broad terms, is seriously flawed; in more specific terms it can be seen that it would not have been a feasible way to raise the heavy stone blocks. In the Great Pyramid, those blocks averaged 2½ tons each.

This is to say, that in regard to that phase of pyramid building where a heavy stone had to be transferred from a lower to a higher level, a ramp was not employed throughout the whole of the procedure.

Earlier in this section I showed how three different types of ramp systems may have been employed for the raising of the heavy stone blocks. This does not necessarily represent a contradiction of the view I have just stated, but an alternative plan.

It is my contention that a ramp system was in fact used on the pyramids to transport stone to high levels, but that this ramp was used only for the first five courses. The remaining courses — 201 in the case of the Great Pyramid — were raised by the use of a wooden machine; a machine that, although simple in design, was sophisticated in technique and succeeded in lifting each stone from a lower to a higher level.

In a discussion of the ramp theory it will be opportune to use as a reference the Great Pyramid of Khufu at Giza, as it was the largest pyramid built. In this way we will be calculating the volume of the largest ramps the Egyptians would have had to construct, giving us the full scope of the problems inherent in the ramp theory.

The volume of a long, single ramp placed against the east face of the Great Pyramid would have been approximately 25 million cubic feet. After the completion of the pyramid this type of ramp had to be dismantled. Thus, the workers would have been charged with the manipulation of approximately 50 million cubic feet of earth, mud-brick and stone — more than half the volume of the Great Pyramid itself, and the exact volume of the massive Bent Pyramid at Dahshur. Not only this, but the length of that single ramp would have been well over 1,000'. Whether it had a gradient of 1 to 8 or of 1 to 12, it still had to present a long, hard haul for the laborers whose task it was to pull the blocks upward.

If a multi-ramp was used by the builders, one that zig-zagged up the east face of the pyramid, it would have been cut into the monument rather than external to it, and thus would not have required dismantling afterwards. But the total length of the connecting of a multi-ramp system — that is, the distance over which the stones would have to be dragged — would have been approximately 1,500' or 500' more than the length necessary in the single ramp theory. With this design, the topmost stone would have to be hauled well over ¼ mile up a steep gradient before being set into place.

Another multi-ramp design calls for ramps which are once again cut into the pyramid, but this time on all four sides in a circuitous pattern; the ramp begins at the east face of the pyramid, then turns to traverse the north face, then the west and finally the south. If only four individual yet connecting ramps were employed in this fundamental design, the total distance that each of the topmost stones would have to be transported is an incredible 3,000'. It is more than likely, however, that this ramp pattern would have encircled the pyramid twice in order for the gradient to be adequately reduced to a working level, thereby increasing the total haulage distance to an astonishing 6,000'. Would it really have been feasible for the ancient builders to pull heavy stones over a mile's distance up steep grades in order to achieve their purpose?

The ramp theories, at a casual glance, appear to be practical enough, but as one can clearly see, when certain elementary measures and computations are taken, major flaws are evident.

Could the ancient Egyptians, so brilliant and adept in the field of engineering, have resorted to brute labor to manipulate heavy stone? Although, as earlier stated, the average block of stone in the Great Pyramid weighed approximately 2½ tons, there were also much larger stones incorporated into the monument, fifty- to seventy-ton monoliths which also had to be raised into place. Was it practical for the builders to assign hundreds of men to pulling such weight up such a great distance?

On the other hand, it is not unreasonable to think that the ancient engineers would have employed a single ramp for constructing the first five courses of the pyramid. For here, the ramp would not have been that long or wide. It is only beyond the first five courses that the ramp theory begins to defeat itself. As the pyramid becomes higher, the stones become smaller, but the amount of effort in shoring up and increasing the ramp—even though the ramp is now being narrowed—requires a great deal more effort than the work which would have been done at the lowest levels. Unquestionably, it would have been advantageous for the engineers to adopt an alternative method for lifting heavy stone.

With the Great Pyramid, the first five courses roughly comprise 11 million cubic feet of masonry, as compared with the monument's total volume of 93 million cubic feet. Yet with these first five courses the stones were much heavier and larger than the average 2½-ton stone, and weighed approximately double this

amount. For example, the height of the stones of the first five courses of the pyramid are, respectively, 58″, 45″, 44″, 42″ and 40″. But from the sixth course on the stones are an average height of 36″, and gradually decrease to a 20″ height, after which the peak or pyramidian caps the edifice.

Thus, for the manipulation of the heavier stones at the lowest masonry courses, it was practical for a short ramp to be utilized, the maximum length of which would have been a mere 100–200′. Yet beyond the fifth course, and for the remaining pyramid courses, the ramp would not have been used.

Accepting this assertion, one then begins to search for an alternative method for lifting the remaining 88 percent of the pyramid stones from level five on up. Surely, the architect of the first built and last remaining of the Seven Wonders of the Ancient World was capable of devising a more sophisticated system than we give him credit for—one where heavy stone and minimal manpower is used to lift other, heavier stone. For an architect whose stamp of genius is so artfully contrived in the dimensions and symmetry of the Grand Gallery and King's Chamber complex, it would all be in the balance, rather than in the struggle. The ancients were fond of employing ropes and counterweights in their building projects.

In our search for an alternative method for lifting heavy stone, we come across the curious statement made by the Greek historian Herodotus (fifth century B.C.), informing us that the builders of the Great Pyramid "*lifted* the stones with *levers* made of *short timbers.*"

It is interesting to note that very few scholars have taken this statement for the truth. Every historian is

Shadoof (shaduf). (A. Erman)

aware of gross inaccuracies perpetrated by Herodotus. He was a storyteller extraordinaire, but at the same time he was a conscientious recorder of historical fact. Thus, the scholar is faced with a dilemma each time he is introduced to any statements made by Herodotus. For this reason the majority of researchers dismiss Herodotus' mention of some sort of wooden machine being used to build the Great Pyramid and regress to the popular ramp theory. With this ramp theory having been discussed, let us now examine Herodotus' theory, one that should not be so readily dismissed.

Herodotus speaks of levers. The lever, acting with a fulcrum, is the simplest machine known to man. Yet the lever principle, however simple it may be, is capable of lifting great weight if manipulated correctly.

Herodotus (who received his information from the Egyptian priests of the time) was uncertain whether a single machine was used, and then periodically transferred to higher levels, or whether there was a machine situated at every level of the pyramid. My experiments show that if a lever-type machine was employed by the ancients, then one such machine would have been at each level of the monument.

If we look back to the hieroglyphic records, we find no mention of any machine being used for the manipulation of heavy stone. Yet if we look to the Egyptian countryside and villages, and to the tomb paintings and murals depicting the ancient Egyptian way of life, we do find that a simple lever of a sort was being employed extensively throughout the land. For the ancient Egyptians employed a lever device for lifting water from a lower level to a higher one in order to facilitate the watering of their crops and fields using minimal manpower.

This archaic tool, which is still widely used throughout Egypt, is called the *shadoof*. It consists of a

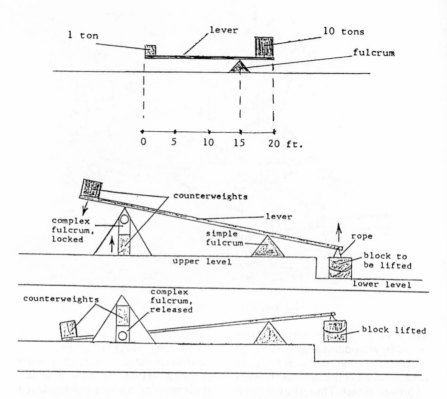

Top: *Simple lever and fulcrum machine.* Bottom: *Double-fulcrum counterweight system.* (J.P. LEPRE)

10'-long pole (lever) pivoted on a vertical stand (fulcrum), with a weight (counterweight) at its far end and a gourd attached by a rope for lifting water at its front end. The dictionary defines it as a counterpoised (or counterbalanced) sweep. This simple machine could have acted as the kernel of inspiration upon which the pyramid builders designed their more formidable machine to lift heavy stone rather than buckets of Nile water. The basic ingredients were a lever, a fulcrum, a counterweight and a rope manipulated by minimal manpower.

With the lever and the fulcrum the most basic design would be as shown on this page (top drawing). It must be stressed that the position of the lever on the fulcrum is critical to the manipulation of the weight desired to be lifted or balanced.

In employing the basic lever technique, it is probable that the pyramid builders would have used a somewhat more complex design in order to reduce the amount of raw manpower to be used, for here they were dealing with very heavy material. A lever system consistently used for heavy stone would have to contain a counterweight of a sort. If not, the energy of the workmen would be unnecessarily taxed. Therefore, a *double counterweight* along with a *double fulcrum* may well have been utilized by the Egyptians. This would elevate the nature of the machine from simple to complex. The principle would be the same, but the pattern would be more sophisticated, being, in a sense, parallel to the ability of modern machinery, where the machine does the actual lifting, with the manpower merely operating and maneuvering the machine.

The double fulcrum/counterweight system that may have been employed by the pyramid builders probably operated under the principle shown in the drawing on page 256, bottom.

Returning to the statement made by Herodotus concerning the "levers" and "short timbers," what historical evidence do we have that might possibly support such a description? We should look for reference, not only to levers and timbers in general, but also to a sizeable quantity, since if one machine were utilized at each of the Great Pyramid's 206 courses (eliminating the first five of these courses and the topmost course, as has been explained), then a considerable amount of wood must have been used. Yet Egypt has always been a country virtually devoid of trees or forests. The date palms, which are numerous in that country, could not have been considered for building timber, as they were too valuable as sources of food.

The hieroglyphic Palermo Stone text records the fact that the Pharaoh Sneferu sent a fleet of 40 ships to Lebanon to bring back cedar from that country. Short cedar beams or timbers were found in both the Maidum and Bent pyramids. Therefore, we can see where Sneferu had used several of these beams. But that would be but a fraction of 40 shiploads. We are aware that a great pharaoh such as Sneferu would have built several cedar pleasure and funerary ships, for his use in both the present and the afterlife. One such

cedar ship (cedar in the main, although many of the smaller sections are finished off with other types of wood) was found in a hewn pit immediately to the south of the Great Pyramid. But as yet, none have been discovered at either Maidum or Dahshur.

Even if Sneferu did construct a group of cedar ships with logs taken from his huge shipment, it is doubtful whether the amount needed would have equaled 40 shiploads. Surely, such a quantity of beams was to be employed for a massive building project. That quantity of beams would have been closer to the amount necessary if Herodotus' machines were constructed of cedar, and if each pyramid course required that one machine be set up there for the gradual transfer of the stones.

It should be noted that if such machines were used to elevate each successive pyramid course, it would only be for Sneferu's three large pyramids (that is, his two pyramids at Dahshur, and the one at Maidum, which he helped his father to build), Khufu's Great Pyramid, and perhaps Khafra's huge monument. For prior to the Huni/Sneferu Pyramid at Maidum, and post–Khafra, the pyramids were built on a much smaller scale, were composed of much smaller stones and could have been constructed using the ramp technique throughout.

While the story told by Herodotus may be pure fiction, it is a fact that the extended ramp theory is unfeasible. Some sort of machine must have been manipulated by the ancients. Whether my particular design is the one which was employed long ago is not all-important. What is important is that the reader be introduced to the idea of a system other than ramps being utilized by the builders of the pyramids.

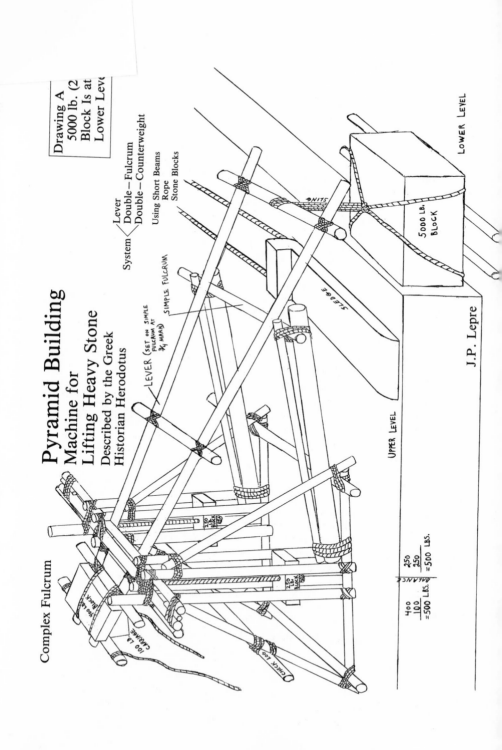

Pyramid Building
Machine for
Lifting Heavy Stone
Described by the Greek
Historian Herodotus

Complex Fulcrum

Drawing A
5000 lb. (2
Block Is at
Lower Leve

System $\left\{\begin{array}{l}\text{Lever}\\ \text{Double—Fulcrum}\\ \text{Double—Counterweight}\end{array}\right.$

Using Short Beams
Rope
Stone Blocks

LEVER (SET ON SIMPLE
FULCRUM AT
¾ MARK)

SIMPLE FULCRUM

SLING

SLEDGE

5000 LB.
BLOCK

LOWER LEVEL

UPPER LEVEL

CHECK LOG

100 LB.
CRADLE

250
LB.
BLOCK

250
LB.
BLOCK

400
100
=500 LBS.

250
250
=500 LBS.

BALANCE

J.P. Lepre

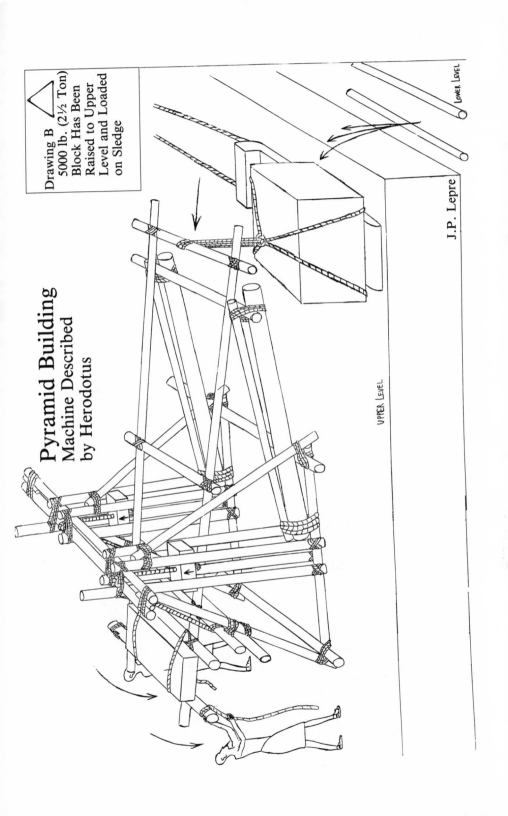

Pyramid Building
Machine Described
by Herodotus

Drawing B
5000 lb. (2½ Ton)
Block Has Been
Raised to Upper
Level and Loaded
on Sledge

UPPER LEVEL

LOWER LEVEL

J.P. Lepre

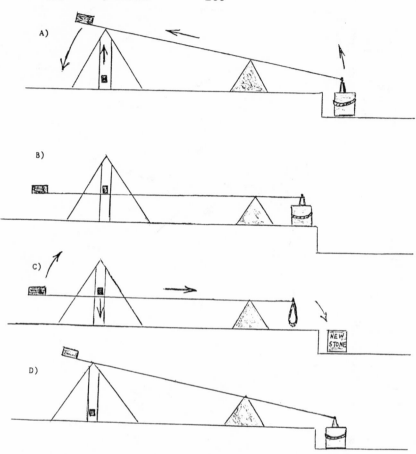

Herodotus' machine: Schematic mechanics. (J.P. LEPRE)

On pages 258 and 259 are drawings of a working model of a machine capable of lifting heavy stone from a lower level to a higher level using minimal manpower, the component parts of which include: *short timbers,* comprising a *double fulcrum* and a *lever; ropes,* for lashing assembly together and for use with *double counterweights;* and the three *stones* comprising those counterweights.

Other working models may be more appropriate. But for a lack of such I found it necessary to experiment with this particular design.

The Model. As can be appreciated by the illustrated rendition of Herodotus' "machine," a greater weight is being counterbalanced by a much lesser weight on a simple lever and fulcrum system. With this balance attained, it then becomes possible for two moderate-sized men to tip the balance to their advantage by pulling down on the lesser weight, raising the much heavier weight.

With the much heavier weight (5000 lb. block = 2½ tons) now raised, and the lesser weight (400 lb. block + 100 lb. carriage = ⅒ of a ton) now lowered, and after the

2½-ton block has been set on a sledge and the tension sling released, the ⅒ of a ton must now be raised to its initial position in order to be readied for the next stone to be lifted. The raising of this weight (or counterweight) is accomplished by balancing said weight with two smaller stones (250 lbs. each = 500 lbs.); counterweights to the counterweight. Thus we have a double-counterweight system.

As to the simple fulcrum, it merely — but all-importantly — supports the conglomerate weight stress directed to the ¾ mark of the lever. The other section of the double-fulcrum system, the complex fulcrum, has five basic purposes:

1. To lower and raise its counterweights, in order to gain the advantage over a 5,000-lb. block of stone, so as to lift it (upward and inward) to a higher level.

2. To check the 500-lb. counterweight system, so that, when being lowered, it does not regress beyond the "balance" point of the lever and simple fulcrum, or of the 250-lb. counter-counterweights.

3. To have its weight pulled back, so that the 5,000-lb. block which is being lifted will also be pulled in, as well as up. With this double maneuver, the block can be set upon the upper level. This is accomplished by the 45 degree rear-diagonal braces. They act as rails, so to speak, upon which the carriage rides up or down. Because these braces are angled, the carriage, when being lowered, begins to jut back. When it reaches its point of rest (on the horizontal "check" log) it is a full 5 feet from its original mark.

4. To be able to be reset (through the use of the counter-counterweights).

5. To minimize brute labor through the use of all of the above. It is obvious that the amount of stone to be lifted or manipulated is dictated by the size of the machine and the weight of its counterweights. For the lifting of the Great Pyramid's heaviest, seventy-ton stone, not only would the use of heavier counterweights (or of a larger machine) be recommended, but perhaps two, three or even four machines set side by side to one another. With so many variations of height, length, weight, lever-fulcrum distribution, etc., available to the scholar, it would be interesting to see what other type models could be conceived and then made to operate practically. Would they all obey the very same principles as this model, even though they were designed on a slightly different theme?

A final note is that, although I have depicted a sling (or double-sling) being used to fasten the 5,000-lb. block, I only did so to avoid confusing the reader with the particulars of another, alternative method. But as the reader has now been made aware of the work of the Herodotus model sans interruption, it should suffice to say that another, simpler method exists whereby a single sling is used. Thus:

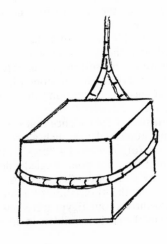

However, with the use of the single sling, a certain problem now arises. For although the majority of the pyramid stones were most likely of square or rectangular shape, the casing stones (of which there were 144,000 for the Great Pyramid) were slanted on their fronts. Thus:

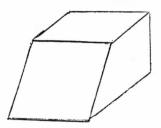

With the single sling set around this stone there would have been slippage due to its radical angle. If the sling were to be wrapped around another non-angled section of the stone, then that stone, when being set down, would be set on the wrong side and create an awkward situation overall. One might think to remedy the problem by using the double sling. Here though, an added responsibility and chore is created. For with the double sling, logs or timbers must be placed under the stone to be lifted in order for the sling to pass under that stone.

The double sling could be eliminated and the single sling used if there were some sort of protuberance on the face of the casing stone which would succeed in checking the rope slippage.

Is it then a coincidence that every casing stone had just such a protuberance (often termed a "boss") jutting out from its front, angled side? It is my contention that the bosses found on the thousands of casing stones throughout Egypt were hewn there by the ancient builders in order

to prevent slippage of the sling from the stone. This does not mean to say that the bosses were not used for other purposes also; they may very well have been. One thing is certain, though: the position of the bosses on the casing stones interacts admirably well with a single sling to prevent rope slippage. The true purpose of the raised bosses on the pyramid casing stones has never been adequately explained by any Egyptologist, historian or scholar. I, too, am guilty of stating how an iron bar may have interacted with the raised boss to aid in the manipulation of a stone. But I among others cannot as yet give a detailed description of the exact process involved. Perhaps the bosses were used in conjunction with a sling in the manner illustrated. Then again, they may have been used in an entirely different way and for an entirely different purpose.

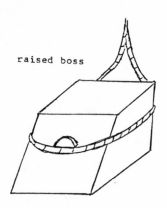

raised boss

Tools Used by the Ancient Builders

1. Abrasives
2. Astrolabe
3. Ballpounders (dolerite)
4. Bay
5. Beams or baulks
6. Bosses (lugs)
7. Causeway (stone)

8. Chisels (copper)
9. Counterweights (large blocks)
10. Drills (dolerite or diamond)
11. Levers (iron bars)
12. Lubricant (oil)
13. Manpower (team)
14. Mauls or hammers (dolerite)
15. Measuring cords (fiber)
16. Mortar (gypsum)
17. Plates (iron)
18. Plumb bobs (merkhets)
19. Props (small blocks)
20. Ramp (inclined plane)
21. Ropes
22. Sand
23. Saws (copper)
24. Saws (stone)
25. Sledges
26. Set squares and facing plates (wooden)
27. Troughs (mud-brick)
28. Wedges (as chocks)
29. Wedges (soaked)
30. Wheel (cradle)

Stones Used by the Ancients

Hard

1. Basalt **(B,S)**
2. Diorite **(S)**
3. Dolerite **(B)**
4. Granite **(B,S)**
5. Porphyry **(B,S)**

Soft

1. Alabaster **(B,S)**
2. Breccia **(S)**
3. Dolomite **(V)**
4. Limestone **(B,S)**
5. Quartzite **(B,S)**
6. Sandstone **(S)**
7. Schist **(S)**
8. Serpentine **(S)**
9. Slate **(S)**

B = building
S = statuary
V = vases

X. Secret Chambers

The pyramids of Egypt were built over a lengthy period of time by 42 pharaohs. Most notable of these monuments, and often the only ones mentioned by scholars and laymen alike, were those of the Fourth Dynasty monarchs Khufu, Khafra and Menkara. On the plain of Giza, close to the famed Sphinx, these three kings erected their massive tombs.

It is interesting to note that 500 pyramids were actually built along the Nile: 100 in Egypt proper by the Old and Middle Kingdom pharaohs, 50 in later dynasties, and 350 in the neighboring Sudan by the Twenty-fifth Dynasty Ethiopian kings. Of the first group, many were small or medium in size; but there were others which were of quite impressive dimensions and thereby capable of housing thousands of chambers within their massive volumes. Very few of these edifices have been thoroughly investigated throughout the centuries, and there is, therefore, very little doubt that undiscovered secret burial chambers exist in their extensive inner reaches.

Discovering one of these hidden chambers is not an easy task and few excavators or archaeologists have ever succeeded in this endeavor. Even in our present age of technology, the investigation of a pyramid is no easy task. To begin with, many of the Egyptian pyramids are quite inaccessible from the main or even secondary road systems, and are located, for the most part, on the outer fringes, and sometimes interior regions, of the desert. This makes the setting up of a camp or research base all the more difficult.

As if this natural barrier were not enough to frustrate the would-be-researcher, a good number of the pyramid sites are off-limits to curious investigators due to government and military restrictions. The site of the famed Bent or Blunted Pyramid of the Third Dynasty Pharaoh Sneferu (father of Khufu), located at Dahshur, is off-limits to practically all investigators due to the fact that it is on a permanent military base. The same is true of its sister monument, the Northern Pyramid at Dahshur, and of the Third Dynasty Pyramids of Eke and Khaba located on the army base at Zawaiyet el-Aryan. Only the most influential and affluent research teams can hope to obtain permission for access to these and other fields where the Egyptian military has established permanent bases of operation.

Beyond this, it is the mistaken belief of many archaeologists that all of the pyramids were penetrated in times past, the burial chambers discovered, and the mummies of the pharaohs defiled and tossed out into the desert. Yet while this is a widespread assumption in the archaeological and Egyptological community, there is absolutely no validity to it. It is, rather, a belief founded upon the inability to deal with the tremendous task at hand, fueled by the almost total ignorance and negligent research of pyramid construction and history.

The ancient architects were quite adept at hiding the bodies and treasures of their powerful pharaohs from any possible intruders into the sacred burial tombs. That very few tangible remains have ever been found concerning these pyramid pharaohs (see "Pyramid Pharaohs' Mummy Remains" and "Pyramid Queens' and Princesses' Mummy Remains," page 288) can be credited, not to the fact that they were dug up long ago, but to the genius of their architects. The cache of kings and members of royalty—including King Tutankhamen—that was discovered in the Valley of the Kings was the result of sheer accident! (An accident that did not occur until the 1920s at that.)

It is easy enough for the majority of archaeologists to treat the pyramids as simplified monuments which have long since yielded up their dead to past excavators and tomb plunderers, but it is another, more challenging avenue to research these monuments thoroughly, to travel to Egypt with a well-equipped expedition, and to deal with systematically searching for the hidden burial chambers of pharaohs entombed in complex, massive pyramids, the very sizes of which tend to boggle the mind and frustrate the most ingenious of investigators.

The mistaken belief that the pyramids have been fully explored, coupled with the harshness of the terrain, the inaccessible geographical position of some of the monuments and their respective fields, and the frustrating and time-consuming rendezvous with, and delays and inconsistencies of, government officials and military personnel, plus miles of red tape, make the investigation of a pyramid an almost impossible task.

There is a very strong belief among knowledgeable Egyptologists that each of the pyramid pharaohs had *two* tombs, northern and southern. This concept at first appears puzzling, but is actually quite acceptable in light of ancient Egyptian history and the fact that one of the five titles of the royal titulary of these pharaohs was King of *Upper* and *Lower* Egypt, Lord of the *Two* Lands.

That the separate kingdoms of Upper and Lower Egypt were first united under the first pharaoh of the First Dynasty, Menes, is a fact of history. All subsequent pharaohs held the dual title. It was for this reason that the most famous by far of all Old Kingdom cities was Memphis, the seat of power of the early pyramid pharaohs, founded by Menes and representing the duality of Egypt meshed into a single geographical locale.

Memphis was in fact situated at the border of Upper and Lower Egypt, at an area where the pharaoh could have maximum control over the dual kingdom. Located quite close to the Great Pyramid of Giza, Memphis lies at that point where the long Nile Valley (comprising Upper Egypt) meets with the Delta (comprising Lower Egypt). Thus, the pharaoh wore two separate crowns: the White (for Upper Egypt) and the Red (for Lower Egypt). He also wore a combined (double crown) depicting his power and sway over both of these kingdoms simultaneously.

Thus, the duality of the ancient kingdom of Egypt is established, and that of the pyramid pharaohs as well. With this thought in mind we will now consider the fact that there is sufficient evidence in the archaeological record to indicate that although the Old Kingdom pyramid pharaohs (and also some Middle and New Kingdom pharaohs, for that matter) were

Two granite sarcophagi from Giza mastabas — Dynasty IV. (W.M.F. Petrie, E. Mackay, and G. Wainwright)

actually interred in a tomb within the jurisdiction of either the northern or southern kingdom, they also had a second tomb (a cenotaph or "dummy" tomb) within the jurisdiction of the other kingdom. This being the case, we can then expect there to be, not 42 sarcophagi for 42 pharaohs, but 84 sarcophagi in all for 84 separate tombs. The first 42 would necessarily contain the actual burials and the other 42 would be mere receptacles, symbolical of the pharaohs' dual jurisdiction. Any or all of these tombs (both real and decoy) could well have been located in pyramids, mastabas or simple crypts cut out of the rock.

In light of this additional information the question then arises: Where were the pyramid pharaohs actually buried? In their northern or their southern tombs? This is indeed a difficult question to answer due to the fact that the remains of very few of these kings have ever been found. If, for example, most of their mummies were found in the north, then we could assume that their cenotaphs were situated in the south. But the fact is that the mummy remains are scant.

It will suffice at this time to list what little evidence we have for the actual existence of northern and southern tombs for the pyramid pharaohs. The hieroglyphic texts, in a number of instances, strongly allude to the existence of dual tombs, yet concrete proof is sorely lacking.

Just south of the famed Third Dynasty Stepped Pyramid of Djoser at North Sakkara, and located within its huge, walled courtyard, is a mastaba tomb with Djoser's cartouche or royal name inscribed on its false doors. It contains an empty granite sarcophagus, whereas the pyramid contained none.

The Third Dynasty Pharaoh Huni built a sizeable pyramid at Maidum, but it did not contain a sarcophagus. Yet a quite large mastaba located 275 miles to the south at Bet Khallaf did in fact contain a granite sarcophagus, within which were the total skeletal remains of a large man. This mastaba contained the royal name of Huni.

Sneferu, Huni's son, built two pyramids at Dahshur, a northern one and a southern one. No sarcophagus was found in either tomb. The latter, however, shows strong signs of containing a hidden burial chamber.

Amenemhat III, Dynasty XII, built two pyramids: one at Dahshur, with a granite sarcophagus, and the other 33 miles to the south at Hawara. This pyramid contained a quartzite sarcophagus, within which were found the fragments of charred bones.

Increasing the difficulty of deducing where the pyramid pharaohs are actually buried is the fact that the majority of the main pyramids have one or more smaller, subsidiary pyramids located immediately south of them. At first thought, one might surmise that these satellite pyramids are in fact the southern tombs of the pharaohs. Yet the deterrent to this theory is the fact that many of these tombs were inscribed with the names of queens or princesses of the pharaohs, and not of the pharaohs themselves.

An interesting point in this investigation is that before Memphis was established by Menes in Dynasty I, the previous seat of the pharaohs was the ancient city of Thinis, approximately 300 miles south of Giza. It was here that the earliest pharaohs, the Hawk kings, held sway over the south. Actually, Narmer was the last of these Hawk kings, and then Menes, his successor, made the giant step forward by conquering the north and uniting the two kingdoms. (As explained earlier in this book, contrary to popular belief, Narmer and Menes were not the same personage but separate individuals.)

Thus although the pyramid pharaohs had their seat of power at Memphis, through lineage, they had a close affinity to the city of Thinis. Thinis, then, acted as a huge cemetery for practically all of the old Hawk kings and Egyptian royalty, and the tradition may well have been carried on by later generations of pharaohs. Now, even though Thinis was in earliest times the center of government and the chief burial site of that age, there were great temples set up at Abydos, situated very close by. This is the location where the only known statue of the great Pharaoh Khufu was discovered by Professor Petrie. It seems odd that this 3″ high ivory statuette would be found here, so far to the south, when his Great Pyramid and those of his three queens were located in the north.

It is tempting, then, to speculate that perhaps the area of Thinis or Abydos may contain a cache of royal tombs of these pyramid pharaohs similar to that which was discovered in the early 1920s in the Valley of the Kings, wherein the child pharaoh Tutankhamen was interred. In the necropolis of that area were found a total of 60 royal tombs dating to the New Kingdom.

As to the relationship between Thinis (Theni) and Abydos (Ebod), they were within such close proximity that they were with good cause called the "Twin Cities." Khufu and the other pyramid pharaohs, realizing the affinity, of Thinis and Abydos, and also being aware of the fact that Thinis, even at the early age of the Fourth Dynasty, was recognized as a depository for the remains of

royalty, could likely have chosen Abydos for their southern tombs. Thus they would have been interred within the jurisdiciton of the old capital Thinis but outside its nucleus, thwarting the most ambitious of tomb robbers.

Of the 42 pyramid pharaohs cited in this text, the fragmentary mummy remains of only eight (including that in the mastaba of Huni) have been found. And of the 84 stone sarcophagi that should exist for these monarchs, only 23 have thus far been discovered (counting the two found in Djoser's and Huni's mastabas).

That there is still a great deal to be found in the pyramids is evident from the data above, as well as the following considerations: First, the fact that a sarcophagus was found in a pyramid does not necessarily imply that the pharaoh was ever interred there. This statement goes beyond the assumption that the sarcophagus may have been part of the arrangement of a mere cenotaph. Consider the example of the granite sarcophagus of Eke found at his pyramid at Zawaiyet el-Aryan. Although the sarcophagus was discovered there with its lid or cover slab, this "pyramid" constitutes nothing more than an open trench, with the sarcophagus literally exposed to the open sky rather than it being housed or protected in a burial chamber per se. This pyramid was never completed, with the pit being left open and the superstructure never having been executed above a few courses at the monument's outside perimeter. It is therefore obvious that although the sarcophagus is present, Eke could never have been interred in it.

With the pharaoh Amenemhat III, we have the discovery of not one, but two sarcophagi, as he built two pyramids. One such granite sarcophagus was found in his pyramid at

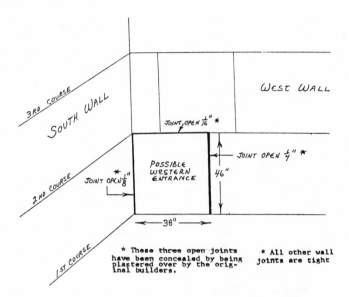

Drawing of King's chamber, Great Pyramid of Khufu, shows possible western entrance. This is but one small example of promising areas still to be explored in the pyramids of Egypt. (J.P. LEPRE)

Dahshur and the other, of quartzite, in his pyramid at Hawara. The mere fact, then, that two sarcophagi were discovered cannot imply that two burials had actually taken place; one body cannot fill two receptacles.

So then, the fact that 23 sarcophagi have been discovered by no means indicates we can account for 23 burials.

Surprisingly enough, there are still whole pyramids buried beneath the desert sands, pyramids that were either never finished or whose superstructures were long ago razed by latter-day rulers who used the already cut-and-squared blocks for new building projects. With the superstructures razed, and with the influence of the constantly shifting desert sands, we have the disappearance of pyramids of substantial size.

There are four such pyramids recorded in several hieroglyphic papyri

that have yet to be discovered. These are the pyramids of the pharaohs Menkeuhor, Dynasty V; Ity, Dynasty VI; Merikare, Dynasty VI; and Neferkere, Dynasty VII. Concerning Merikare, there is the possibility that the foundation of a small pyramid lying immediately north of the pyramid of the pharaoh Teti at North Sakkara may belong to him.

Such a phenomenon as the existence of a "lost pyramid" has been confirmed on several occasions throughout the twentieth century. As recently as 1980 the recorded pyramid of the fourth pharaoh of the Fifth Dynasty, Sisires, was discovered at Sakkara. The so-called "Buried Pyramid" of Djoser-Tati, the third pharaoh of Dynasty III, was not detected at North Sakkara by Dr. Zakaria Ghoneim until 1954. The "Unfinished Pyramid" of Eke, the fifth pharaoh of Dynasty III, was not discovered at Zawaiyet el-Aryan by

Alexander Barsanti of the Antiquities Dept. of the Egyptian Government until 1900. The Pyramid of Queen Khentkawes, Dynasty IV, and a second pyramid of Pharaoh Sisires, Dynasty V, were recently discovered (1984) at Abu Sir by a Czechoslavak expedition.

Additionally, although not a pyramid, the famous tomb of the mother of the great pharaoh Khufu, Queen Hetepheres, was not found until 1925, her crypt being located at the bottom of a 100′ vertical shaft on the east side of his Great Pyramid.

In addition to the mummies, burial chambers and whole pyramids of some of the pyramid pharaohs that have yet to be discovered, other elements of the pyramid complexes remain hidden as well, as suggested by the fact that the valley temple of Rededef at Abu Roash, Dynasty IV, was not discovered until August 1979; the second (ground) entrance to the pyramid of Khafra at Giza, Dynasty IV, until 1837; the 143′-long cedar funerary ship of Khufu, Dynasty IV (as well as seven ship pits) until 1954; and three funerary ships (and eight ship pits) belonging to Senusert III, Dynasty XII, until 1923.

There are also several pyramids which have never been investigated, or which have not been investigated scientifically in recent times. With monuments such as these there is always the hope, however slim, that a pharaoh's intact interment might possibly be found there. These pyramids number six and are: Dynasty III, pyramids at Athribis, Abu Roash and Ombos, possibly belonging to the pharaoh Beby; the Third Dynasty satellite pyramid of Huni at Maidum; the Fourth Dynasty satellite pyramid of Rededef at Abu Roash; and the Third Dynasty Pyramid at Seila, which may also

have been built by Beby, and which has definitely not yet been explored.

Then again, there are other pyramids which have been investigated, but which have defied all efforts to discover an entrance, descending passage or burial chamber. These are: Dynasty III, pyramids at Zawaiyet El Amwat (Zawaiyet El Mayatim); Nagada; and El Kola.

There are three other pyramids whose entrances and descending shafts have been discovered, but whose subterranean portions are permanently inaccessible, being flooded with Nile water. This flooding is the result of a change in the direction of the Nile River through the ages. These monuments are: Dynasty VI, pyramid of Merikare at North Sakkara; and the Dynasty XII, pyramids of Amenemhat I and Senusert I, both at Lisht.

It may interest the reader to know that it was the general practice in pyramid building for the burial chamber to be oriented slightly west of the north-south center line of the monument (just as the pyramid itself lay on the west bank of the Nile River). This arrangement was due to the religious belief of the ancient Egyptians that the pharaoh would journey from east to west in his ascent to the heavens which lay beyond. For this reason, the Egyptologist can well expect the crypt of the pharaoh to be situated west of the pyramid's center line.

There are a few pyramids that have been penetrated but have failed to yield a burial chamber in that location in the pyramid. Understandably, there may be a few pyramids that could have constituted exceptions to this rule, but of the 11 pyramids which we are about to list, it seems clear that at least some of them contain burials west of the center line which have not yet been discovered. These pyramids are: Dynasty III, pyramid Djoser, North Sakkara; pyramid Djoser-Tati, North Sakkara; pyramid Khaba, Zawaiyet el-Aryan; pyramid Huni, Maidum; and Bent pyramid of Sneferu, Dahshur; Dynasty VI, pyramid Khui, Dara; Dynasty XII, pyramid Amenemhat I, Lisht; pyramid Senusert I, Lisht; pyramid Senusert II, Lahun; and pyramid Amenemhat III, Dahshur; and Dynasty XIII, pyramid Khendjer II, South Sakkara.

Actually, with the above-mentioned pyramid of Amenemhat III at Dahshur, two queens' chambers were discovered there quite recently (1983), both located where expected, west of the north-south center line. Information on this find has not yet been published.

Additionally, a twelfth pyramid of this type, the satellite pyramid of a queen of Senusert II, Twelfth Dynasty, at Lahun, not only displays no burial chamber west of center, but has yet to reveal any chamber whatsoever either in its sub- or superstructure.

In some pyramids a burial chamber was discovered, but only as the result of a good deal of random excavation by the explorer. This is to say, that the monument was devoid of an entrance or descending passageway. In this rare occurrence, a vertical shaft was dug into the rock foundation at the center region of the pyramid's square base, a burial chamber constructed at its lower end, the mummy interred, the shaft plugged up and then the superstructure of the pyramid built over it.

This simple but ingenious method was employed in the pyramid of Queen Iput I at North Sakkara, Dynasty VI and may well be the method exercised in some of the already mentioned problem pyramids that have defied the archaeologists' efforts to penetrate a burial chamber.

MYSTERIES

The following unsolved mysteries are just a few examples of the sort of tantalizing evidence that continues to suggest further secrets to be uncovered in the tombs of the pharaohs.

Mystery of the Water. (Pyramid of Eke). In dealing with the Unfinished Pyramid of Eke at Zawaiyet el-Aryan, it is interesting to note the experience of pyramid explorer Alessandro Barsanti. This gentleman was convinced that, although the work on Eke's pyramid was never completed, and although it lacked a superstructure and a substructure proper, the area beneath the granite pavement of the open trench contained a hidden burial chamber. He therefore began removing the granite pavement stones and tunneled through the limestone blocks that had been set beneath them.

The reason for his hypothesis of a hidden burial chamber is that, in March of 1905, the trench was flooded with 10' of water from a violent rainstorm. At midnight, though, the water rapidly sank to a level of only 3'. The sudden disappearance of 7' of water (estimated at 14,000 cubic feet) prompted Barsanti to speculate that this water had passed into an underground burial chamber.

If this is so, then the estimated 14,000 cubic feet would account for a chamber approximately 35' by 23' wide by 17' high. Curiously enough, this is quite similar in size to the measurements of typical burial chambers. For example, the burial chamber in the Great Pyramid of Khufu measures 34' long by 17' wide by 19' high (11,000 cubic feet).

It has been surmised by some that the drained water could have found its way into a natural cavity in the rock foundation. At first thought this appears to be the only other plausible explanation for the loss of such volume. Yet, upon serious reflection, this theory is not without its flaws. For in order for the water to have disappeared so suddenly—the time element is all-important here—the hypothetical natural cavity in question would have to be immediately adjacent to the squared blocks of stone lying at the bottom of the pit, or have been fed by an extraordinarily large crevice or cleft. For if the assumed natural cavity were at any distance from the squared stone blocks, only a quite wide crevice would have been capable of funneling the water to that point at such speed.

It seems unlikely, though, with the pit having been dug and squared as well as it was—for the existing, visible sections of its high walls indicate that this squaring was executed to a remarkable degree of accuracy—that the builders would have been content with an adjacent natural cavity or cleft of large size not having been shored up with packing blocks previous to the laying of the squared limestone blocks, and then the granite ones over them. The builders may have been satisfied with passing over a much smaller adjacent cavity in the rock foundation in their bid to layer the bottom of the trench, but certainly not one of the size necessary to accept so much water so abruptly.

It is not so much the disappearance of the water, but its *sudden* disappearance which is most puzzling. A small to medium-size cleft would not have been able to carry off the water so swiftly. Can anything other than a deliberately hewn chamber have been allowed to exist adjacent

to or in the midst of such meticulous workmanship and accurate planning? The master builders of ancient Egypt were no doubt more astute and cunning than most modern scholars have given them credit for, and their ingenuity should not be underestimated.

Barsanti died during the excavation of this pyramid. Just previous to his demise, he had stated that he was only "two fingers" from finding the secret burial chamber. Sir W.M.F. Petrie suggested that the site be reexamined, but no one has excavated there since.

Mystery of the Wind. (Bent Pyramid of Sneferu). Dr. Ahmed Fakhry, late professor of Ancient History at Cairo University, conducted extensive research at the Bent or Blunted Pyramid at Dahshur and was convinced that there was an as yet undiscovered chamber located somewhere in this monument. He believed this to be true, not only from his own experiences while working in the pyramid, but from the experiences of two intrepid nineteenth century explorers—the esteemed Colonel Howard Vyse, and his protégé, Mr. Perring. To better understand this line of reasoning I will here introduce an account taken from Dr. Fakhry's book *The Pyramids* (p. 93).

This account is about work done at the Bent Pyramid by these two men, and it reads: "In the account of their operations, Perring and Vyse relate an incident which suggests a tantalizing train of speculation. They mention that while their men were working on the clearance of one of the passages, they suffered greatly from the heat and lack of air. On October 15, 1839, conditions were such that they could hardly continue the work. By that time the men had forced an entrance into one of the chambers. Suddenly a strong, cold wind began to blow from the interior of the pyramid outward. This current of cool air was so strong that it was only with difficulty that the men could keep their lamps lit. The wind blew strong for two days and then stopped as mysteriously as it had started; no one could explain from whence it came. Perring expressed the opinion that the chambers of the pyramid must have had some other connection with the outside. This could not have been the western entrance, because it was opened for the first time in 1951."

In the next paragraph, Dr. Fakhry states, "While working inside this pyramid in recent years, I have noticed that, on some windy days, a noise can be heard, especially in the horizontal corridor between the two portcullises at the end of the ramp leading to the western entrance. This noise sometimes continues for almost ten seconds and has occurred many times. The only explanation for it is that there is still an undiscovered part of the interior which leads to the outside. The problem must be settled in future investigations."

We can well see from this evidence that Dr. Fakhry had good reason to believe there was another chamber within this pyramid. Further evidence of this is that the two existing chambers in the Bent Pyramid are devoid of any stone sarcophagi.

The Mystery of the Smoke. (Great Pyramid of Khufu). Both the burial chamber (King's Chamber) and serdab chamber (Queen's Chamber) of the Great Pyramid are equipped with air channels. Until the discovery of these channels in the Queen's Chamber in 1872, the walls of this chamber appeared to be quite solid and the hidden air channels remained undetected. But a certain pyramid ex-

plorer, Mr. Waynman Dixon, while investigating this chamber "perceived a crack" in the south wall and inserted a small, thin rod into it for a good number of feet. When the rod disappeared, he proceeded to break into the wall at this point and discovered that only 5″ beyond the face of the wall was an air channel similar to those in the King's Chamber. He immediately surmised that there could be a like air channel within the north wall, and upon investigating, found this to be true.

An intriguing point here is that Dixon then lit a fire within the chamber, at the south air vent. The smoke went up the channel and disappeared. Bewildered assistants, waiting on the outside of the pyramid, could not detect smoke exiting from the pyramid. Perhaps there is another chamber in this monument into which the smoke went. Only future investigation will tell.

Trap Doors. In some instances of pyramid exploration a good deal of excavation is necessary in order to gain access to the burial chamber; but in other instances the opposite is true. Petrie, in his *Ten Years Digging in Egypt,* explains how entry into the burial chamber of the pyramid at Hawara was gained through huge sliding ceiling stones in the pyramid's passage system. He tells us that "the roof consisted of a sliding trap-door" and that the opening of this sliding stone lead to "another chamber with a trap-door roof." Dr. Edwards, also referring to these same trap-doors, notes that one of them "was a block of stone *twenty tons* in weight which slid sideways." At the pyramid of Queen Sebek-Neferu-Ra, such stones weighed in excess of 42 tons.

Mysterious Cavities. (Great Pyramid of Khufu). Although the mortuary temple of the Pharaoh Khufu is now destroyed, with only sections of its basalt pavement intact and a few fragments of granite columns lying here and there, there exists at the point where its inner sanctuary once stood a huge cavity cut into the rock foundation. It could not have been a natural chasm, present at the time of the construction of the Great Pyramid, or it would have been filled with squared blocks of stone throughout by the builders. It has been cemented over with a roof or cover of a sort in modern times and has an iron grating at its entrance which is rusted shut and obviously has not been opened for quite a long period of time. (Such are the hindrances with which the curious explorer is confronted when wishing to examine the various pyramid sites.) It is not unreasonable to assume that this cavity, because of its unique location beneath what was once the tabernacle of the mortuary temple, where the offering table and "false door" were positioned, may have represented an access route into the subterranean sections of the pyramid. The site should be opened and thoroughly examined. It is doubtful that this has already been done in the past, or at least one writer would have given his account of this operation. That no one has made mention of the presence of this cavity is somewhat puzzling; yet it is covered over rather inconspicuously, and the presence of the sealed iron grating is enough to dissuade and frustrate even the more adventurous investigators.

On the north side of the Great Pyramid, at its midpoint (which is in line with its only entrance), is a like cavity, although much smaller. This is situated precisely where the north offering shrine would have been built. Here, however, the cavity has been completely filled in and is now totally inaccessible. The only indication of its presence is from photographs taken of that site over 75 years ago by the brothers John and Mortan Edgar. It is incomprehensible that this cavity should have been filled in and left in its sealed condition up to this day. For the entrances to many of the subsequent Fifth Dynasty pyramids were located under the floorstones of the north offering shrines. Could the Great Pyramid have had a similar pattern which actually set the stage for the consistency of such entrances in those later pyramids? Indeed, the other giant pyramid at Giza, that of the Pharaoh Khafra, was equipped with two northern entrances, the lower of which was situated in the immediate area of its north offering shrine. If at all possible, this filled-in cavity on the north side of the Great Pyramid should be reexcavated and left open for any investigator who wishes to try his hand at locating a second entrance that may well give rise to a subterranean crypt or storage chambers which may exist therein.

It would not be at all unusual if both of the cavities just mentioned were mere depositories for the daily offerings which would have been needed at both temples for the worship of the deceased pharaoh, but we cannot accept that assumption with certainty. Every area where there exists even the slightest possibility of discovering a hidden chamber, entrance or passageway should be cleared of existing rubble and man-made fetters, and be made available for all serious-minded scholars and investigators to explore.

Possible Camouflaged Shaft. (Great Pyramid of Khufu). In an earlier discussion of the Queen's Chamber Horizontal Passageway

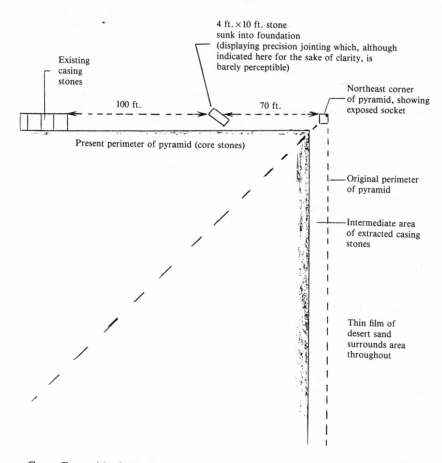

Pyramid surrounded by and set onto solid rock foundation

4 ft. × 10 ft. stone
sunk into foundation
(displaying precision jointing which, although
indicated here for the sake of clarity, is
barely perceptible)

Existing
casing
stones

Northeast corner
of pyramid, showing
exposed socket

100 ft.   70 ft.

Present perimeter of pyramid (core stones)

Original perimeter
of pyramid

Intermediate area
of extracted casing
stones

Thin film of
desert sand
surrounds area
throughout

Great Pyramid of Khufu: Possible camouflaged shaft in rock foundation.
(J.P. LEPRE)

inside the Great Pyramid, I emphasize that one of the keys to pyramid exploration is the discernment of the particular jointing patterns; for wherever stones were set into place, regardless of how precise the workmanship, the jointing pattern is there for the discriminating eye to behold. Study of the jointing patterns in the foundation of the Great Pyramid of Khufu suggests yet another tantalizing mystery.

In December of 1977, while scrutinizing the rock foundation on the north side of the Great Pyramid, I happened upon the most curious configuration. Precisely 70′ west of the pyramid's northeast corner marker (a modern brass pinion pounded into the solid rock at that point), and traversing the imaginary line of the face of the once-existing casing stones of that section, was a thin, almost imperceptible, continuous rectangular joint, marking the perimeter of a 4' wide by 10'-long stone sunk into the foundation at that point. This jointing did not represent a haphazard or crooked natural fracture in the rock foundation,* but was straight and true throughout, the obvious result of fine, precision workmanship on the scale of a surgeon's incision.

Why would the ancient builders sink a stone of this size into an otherwise seamless rock foundation unless to conceal something of value? The 4' by 10' rectangle would be the ideally sized cavity through which to lower a stone sarcophagus, while allowing tolerance for rope manipulation. For example, the granite sarcophagus in the burial chamber of the Pyramid of Khufu is 3'3" wide by 7½' long. The tolerance for lowering that particular chest into a 4' by 10' cavity would be 4½" at each side and 15" at each end, an ideal tolerance ratio.

Interestingly, the burial chamber of King Khufu's mother, Queen Hetepheres, was located just east of the Great Pyramid's northeast corner. The rectantular stone which we are now concerned with is located just west of that corner. Also, the hidden burial chamber of Queen Hetepheres was approached by a 100'-deep shaft cut into the rock foundation and blocked throughout its length with limestone plugs.

Could this 4' by 10' stone possibly lead to another royal burial?

While the jointing which defines this 4' by 10' stone sunk into the rock foundation is now visible to the investigative eye, it must be realized that when the Great Pyramid was completed, this jointing would have been camouflaged by the now-missing pavement and casing stones which were situated at that locale. Thus, not only was the jointing extremely fine, but it would have been covered over as well. Even with the pavement and sheathing stones now removed from this section of the pyramid's perimeter, the jointing can only be spotted if one is looking for it. A casual glance in that direction will, at most, register in the mind an insignificant crack or hairline in the foundation, a truth which is supported by the fact that countless tourists have undoubtedly passed over that point without every paying any attention whatsoever to it. Indeed, even pyramid investigators, whose purpose is to conduct intensive searches of the monument, apply themselves in virtually every instance to the interior of the Great Pyramid, entirely dismissing scrutiny of the barren and seemingly uninteresting rock foundation.

The author is certain that if the Egyptian Government were to investigate this phenomenon, they would

---

*The foundation area surrounding the Great Pyramid is riddled with numerous cutouts which were fashioned by the ancient builders to accommodate the placement, stability and interlocking of the pavement stones. In addition to these manmade geometrical lines (which are not seams or joints but rather rough ridges), traversing the area here and there are natural fractures ranging in width from minute to upwards of an inch or more, some representing the result of past earthquake activity. Beyond this, there are present irregular manmade fractures which were created by the extraction of those pavement stones in later times. All of these imperfections, coupled with the natural weathering of the foundation since that extraction process, present a marred appearance, which has made it all the more difficult for the casual observer to have recognized the precision jointing of the 4' by 10' stone. This jointing represents the only true seams in the entire foundation network just described. The approximate weight of this limestone block, if its depth is equal to its width (4'), would be ten tons.

authorize an exploratory probe of this site. Their present policy is to sternly discourage any excavations directed at disturbing the existing pyramids or surrounding temples. Enough haphazard probing has already been conducted in that country, and, admirably, the officials in charge of such things are at this point emphasizing restoration rather than demolition. Too much of the latter has already been responsible for ravaging the ancient monuments of Egypt. In this particular case, however, with the site in question being located outside of and at a short distance from the pyramid, it would only be a matter of tunneling through the rock foundation itself, a similar excavation to that which was conducted at the vertical shaft which led to the tomb of Queen Hetepheres. This phenomenon is there for all who visit the Great Pyramid complex to see, and now that the exact location has been duly cited, let us hope that the information will encourage the Egyptian Exploration Society to investigate and to conduct the necessary excavation of that site.

WHERE WAS KHUFU BURIED?

For many years the mysteries spoken of in the previous section have been all but ignored, while at the same time a question that seems quite solvable has been the subject of a great deal of attention and speculation. The question is whether Khufu was actually buried in the sarcophagus found in the "King's Chamber" of the Great Pyramid. The answer, or at least a reasonable conclusion, seems clear enough on close examination of the monument.

In this examination we should consider exactly how the Great Pyramid fits the description of an actual tomb—how the manipulation and orientation of blocks of stone at the entrance, in the passage system, and in the chambers point to tomb characteristics which must be addressed. We begin with the entrance to the monument.

In ancient times, in its original state, the entrance to the Great Pyramid was plugged by a block of stone weighing approximately two to five tons. This is the swivel stone spoken of by Strabo. (A similar stone was used at the entrance to the Bent Pyramid of Khufu's father, Senferu, at Dahshur.) These stones may well have operated in conjunction with some sort of a locking system or device, but in itself the force needed to push the stone open, even though it operated on a swivel-basis, would have been imposing. For even if the plug stone was devoid of any ingenious locking assembly, how did the pyramid builders exert enough force to push the stone *inwards*—outwards would be even more difficult—while situated on the outside of the monument where the finished, sheer limestone sides would not have provided even enough stepping room for a very small tenacious man? Difficult enough for the builders, who may have been aided by some ingenious device for swinging the door into place; all the more difficult for an intruder. Thus the plug-stone represents the first sign of a true tomb: a blocked entrance.

Proceeding from the entrance to the interior of the pyramid, one has free access to a descending corridor which culminates in a subterranean chamber. Whether it was a burial chamber is doubtful. There is no portcullis blocking the entrance—although an unfinished niche in the side wall of the corridor was intended to house at least one portcullis slab, had that area been finished — and, more importantly, there was no stone sarcophagus.

Here it must be noted that, when a pharaoh's tomb was plundered, everything in the burial chamber was taken away, for everything was of great value. The only item that was usually left behind was the stone sarcophagus. The inner coffins were much lighter than the sarcophagus, and were made of wood, not stone. Many times they were inlaid with gold and precious stones and were thereby taken out of the pyramid whole, or broken into pieces which were inevitably appropriated by tourists and souvenir-seekers, or burned — as were the coffins of Amenemhat III and his daughter. All of the other burial items received much the same fate.

But the sarcophagus was different, mainly in the fact that, typically, it would have weighed from three to six tons! Therefore, it was usually left behind as a stark, solitary reminder of the ingenuity — or luck — of the professional tomb plunderer. In rare instances, sarcophagi have in fact been broken up, or at least an attempt was made to do so, perhaps out of the thieves' rage over the high cost and laborious effort they had had to expend before gaining access to the treasure cache. Again, there is no sarcophagus in the Great Pyramid's subterranean chamber.

This chamber was ideally situated to act as a ploy, to make the unsuspecting mind believe that a pharaoh had once been buried here, but that it was so long ago that the room had since been stripped of mummy, treasure, and even sarcophagus and blocking stones. At any rate, thus far our journey through the pyramid provides no actual proof of a burial.

In the stone ceiling of the descending corridor which leads to the subterranean chamber just mentioned, there was a moveable stone which, when taken out, revealed the lower end of a five-ton granite plug stone ascending at a 26-degree angle. Behind this were two other similar granite plugs. They blocked access to a secret ascending corridor. Were it not for the camouflage ceiling stone accidentally being worked loose and dropping out of its slot during a ninth century excavation, these three plug stones and the ascending corridor which lay beyond them would never have been known to exist. Historically, it was not ingenuity that enabled modern man to penetrate this far into the Great Pyramid, but sheer luck.

We can see, then, that another blocking system has been confronted at the interior of the great pyramid.

Continuing on, we pass through the newly found ascending passageway after having gone around the plug stones; for here a rough parallel passage was forged by the intruders through the limestone in order to avoid having to cut through the much harder granite blocks.

At the termination of the ascending corridor one gains entrance into the long, lofty Grand Gallery, a high tunnel-like hall that leads, at its topmost end, to a great 3'-high stone step followed by a short, low horizontal passage. The ascent of the Grand Gallery is unimpeded, but after passing through the short passage beyond it, one is confronted with a third blocking system, this time 3 two-ton slabs of granite standing upright. They were set into grooves in the east and west walls and presented a formidable barrier.

These slabs have now entirely disappeared, having been broken asunder ages ago, so that access to the chamber which lay beyond might be gained. The obliterated grooves into which they were once set testifies to the force by which they were extracted.

Up to this point we have encountered three major obstacles to thwart penetration into the heart of the pyramid. Surely, something of great value was being guarded.

Passing freely through the small chamber (antechamber) where the granite portcullises were once housed, we traverse another short, low passage, and then arrive at a high, quite large room built entirely of rose granite.

Here there are no more passageways or corridors, no other entrances or exits. We have arrived at a stately apartment which for all practical purposes would qualify to be a chamber fit for the burial of a king. The design is simple, but majestic; five layers of granite blocks walled all the way around, with granite floor stones and huge, fifty-ton granite ceiling stones. The room is utterly empty but for a marred, lidless, dark-colored sarcophagus. It is of a sullen, chocolate tone, but only from the accumulated grime of thousands of years. Originally the sarcophagus, and the entire chamber too, were of a beautiful pink-red variegated hue; this high-grade granite was quarried and shipped from Aswan. The sarcophagus is 7½' long by 3'3" wide by 3½' high, the ideal size in which to house three large wooden coffins, with one set into the other, and the pharaoh's mummy. Was this a burial sarcophagus used to house the several wooden coffins and the mummy of King Khufu? Or does it represent a symbol of a sort? It is at any rate quite empty, having been deprived of its contents ages ago.

Scrutinizing the sarcophagus, one can discern that its top edge on three of its sides is beveled, indicating that a lid was originally meant to slide through the beveled grooves in order to seal the sarcophagus. This lid has been estimated to have weighed approximately 2¼ tons (with the rectangular sarcophagus itself weighing 3¾ tons). We can certainly regard a lid weighing over 4,000 pounds as a fourth obstacle in reaching the contents of the sarcophagus. Even if the precision of workmanship was so excellent (which it was) as to permit a smooth and well-balanced sliding of the lid to the closed position, a considerable effort still would have had to be made, both for sliding it shut or trying to slide it open.

Yet if this were not enough to discourage the dedicated plunderer, yet another sealing device was employed to lock the lid in place, so that it would not be slid backward. For the sarcophagus, on its flat, unbeveled, top edge has three almost imperceptible circles, each the size of a quarter, finely inscribed into it. These three circles, upon even closer scrutinization, prove to be drill holes which have broken granite pinions, or bolts, firmly embedded into them; and these granite bolts prove that the lid of the sarcophagus was sealed not only by being slid into the beveled grooves of the sarcophagus and shut tight, but also by this additional locking device, which brings to five the number of barriers imposed by the builders so as to protect whatever was inside the sarcophagus or stone chest.

What could have been of such great value in ancient Egypt? Two things come to mind: a great treasure, and a great pharaoh's remains. The former was protected inside the sealed burial chamber, and the latter inside the sealed sarcophagus.

As to the final sealing, that of the three pinions, they were first passed through three holes set just inside the front, long edge of the lid and then into the three lower sarcophagus holes. After being firmly set into place, their tops, and that of the sarcophagus lid itself at these points, would have been smoothed down, so as to leave no evidence of their being there.

Besides the presence of the snapped pinions lodged in the rim of the sarcophagus, there is further evidence to show that the sarcophagus was sealed. For with the sarcophagus having been successfully sealed, anyone wishing to open it would have been confronted with a virtually solid chest. What alternative would that despoiler have had than to smash into it from a corner? And in this context it obviously would be a top corner (for much easier maneuverability), rather than a bottom one; and a front corner, which is located at the open section of the chamber, rather than a rear corner, which stands close to the wall. Thus, in order to break into the well-sealed chest, either the top front corner to the north or the top front corner to the south would have to be assaulted.

Is it a coincidence, then, that although the granite sarcophagus of Khufu is marred and chipped to a minimal degree here and there, it has one extraordinary gash running from its top front corner at its south side, downward, to its approximate mid-height? This gash actually represents the absence of the entire corner of the sarcophagus at that point.

Once a sizeable hole was made in the corner of the sarcophagus, thieves could better view its contents. If the sarcophagus were empty, then the intruders would have left us a sarcophagus that, despite a gaping hole in one of its top corners, would still have had its lid relatively intact. Only the corner of the lid would have been

chiseled away. But because the lid was removed — at great additional cost — we can only assume that when the tomb robbers looked through the gaping hole they had made, they saw the outer wooden coffin of Khufu with the gold mask, and from this vantage point, they gained the needed position and leverage with which to pry off or extract the lid of the sarcophagus.

All of the tangible evidence suggests that Khufu may well have been interred within his Great Pyramid in the granite sarcophagus of the burial chamber. Historians say that this chamber has been misnamed the "King's Chamber," but perhaps that description is best after all. For why would anyone go to such great lengths to first build and then seal a great tomb if no one was to occupy it?

When this chamber was first penetrated in 820 A.D. by the Arab Caliph Al Mamoun, writers spoke of a great treasure being found there. The story, however, has been dismissed by more sober Egyptologists as being too fantastic, with mention of a large ruby on Khufu's head, as large as an egg.

Even if this story is exaggerated, it could perhaps possess a kernel of truth; but then again, it would not be an exaggeration to say that Khufu would be the one man capable of possessing such an immense ruby, he being the wealthiest and most powerful man in the world at that time.

In support of the theory of Khufu's sarcophagus being well-sealed without him having been placed in it, certain Egyptologists will point to the fact that the tomb of his mother, Hetepheres, also located on the Giza plateau, was located at the bottom of a 100' shaft sealed with plug stones, and that the closed sarcophagus found therein, when opened, proved to be empty. It could well be, though, that because the chamber within which the sarcophagus was housed was quite small, it acted as a mere separate depository for certain miscellaneous, minor grave goods and for a sarcophgus which was initially cut for this queen but then replaced by another, which was located in a larger tomb, wherein the queen was really interred.

A similar situation exists with the sarcophagus of Djoser-Tati (Sekhem-khet) found inside his pyramid at North Sakkara. Here too was a sealed pyramid and a closed sarcophagus which, when opened, prove to be empty.

With this particular case, though, the sealing of the pyramid itself was not that well done, and appears to represent the abrupt termination of an abandoned project rather than the professional sealing of a great crypt. This pyramid appears to have been in its rudimentary stages of construction when production was stopped, and the sarcophagus found there was merely placed in the main chambers in anticipation of a burial which never came to pass.

It should also be noted that the "natural inclination" of this sarcophagus is to be closed, unless manipulated to be opened, whereas with most other sarcophagus designs, the opposite is true. The closing of most Egyptian sarcophagi involved a lid which slid along the top of the sarcophagus, but with the unique sarcophagus of Djoser-Tati, the sarcophagus "lid" was not horizontal, but vertical. It was, in fact, a vertical gate of a sort, situated at one end of the sarcophagus. It opened and closed like a guillotine blade is made to go up and down. Gravity made the closed position the more natural one.

Another example where a sarcophagus was found sealed but empty exists with the pyramid of Eke at Zawaiyet el-Aryan. There too, the oval granite sarcophagus was closed when found; but that was only for convenience's sake. The sarcophagus and lid having been placed there quite early in the pyramid-construction process, it was more advantageous for them to be in one unit while the chamber was being built up. The exposure of the burial "chamber" to the open air — where an actual burial could never have taken place — shows that the object of closing the lid of the sarcophagus was not for an immediate burial.

Of the several cases just cited it should also be noted that, although these several sarcophagi were *closed,* only the Khufu sarcophagus was *sealed.*

In comparison to the other accounts just given, Khufu's pyramid, was large enough, majestic enough, and well enough sealed to have accommodated a monarch of his stature and influence. Is it not logical, in light of this evidence, to conclude that Khufu was in fact buried in his pyramid, and that his body and treasure were stolen at the time of the ninth century Arab penetration?

Some may refer to the fact that the Queen's Chamber of the Great Pyramid was also sealed off, and yet it contained no burial or sarcophagus. Yet with the Queen's Chamber the obstruction was not so much to seal off the chamber itself, but to seal it off *at an angle,* so that its blockage actually represented a ramp or bridging of a sort by which members of Khufu's funerary cortege might pass from the first ascending corridor to the slightly higher foot-level of the Grand Gallery.

Elsewhere in the text I have mentioned that a pyramid was usually for the burial of the pharaoh alone. The unusual exception to this rule is the twin burial of Amenemhat III and his daughter Ptah-Nefereu at Hawara. Yet one must be aware that, although two or more burials of royalty could have been possible in some pyramids (Khafra, Menkara, Amenemhat IV, Sebek-Neferu-Ra, Khendjer II, etc.), these were at no time mass graves. The only indication of anything like the Amenemhat III case would be the situations which exist for the pyramids of Djoser, Djoser-Tati and Khaba, who, interestingly, reigned in this exact sequence.

At first one is led to believe that the several apartments located in the subterranean portions of these three pyramids are mere store rooms of a sort; but the discovery of several sarcophagi in certain of these chambers in the pyramid of Djoser at Sakkara begs a reconsideration of this hypothesis. Was mass pyramid-burial practiced in the earlier dynasties?

The irritating fact remains that the events we are dealing with happened so very long ago as to make a fair clarification of the matter a tricky task at best. So much evidence has been lost or corrupted that any reasonable degree of understanding of the exact nature of royal burials is often clouded over by a cross-section of contradictions and additional, more demanding, questions.

A wooden coffin discovered in the burial chamber of Menkara's pyramid and inscribed with his royal cartouche ultimately proved to be a latter-day Saite incursion. The mummified foot presumed to be Djoser's (found in his pyramid), or the right arm presumed to be of Unis (found in his), or the cache of gold jewelry found in the pyramid of Djoser-Tati, may someday be discovered to have had a similar origin.

If we can be certain of one thing, however, it is not where the pharaohs were buried within their pyramids, or with whom or how many others of royalty they were buried, but that they were in fact buried there, in either the subterranean portion or the superstructure, and that the pyramids were in fact meant to be their eternal tombs.

THE THIRD DYNASTY PYRAMIDS

Thus far, only a generalized summation has been given of the possible whereabouts of the pyramid pharaohs. In dealing with the majority of the pyramids we have not considered anything specific regarding exact areas within these monuments that would be likely to contain the royal burial of a pharaoh. We do know that, in the Old Kingdom at least, the entrance to the pyramid would be on its north side, either at ground level or somewhere on its face. The only exception to this rule is a second, western, entrance found at the Bent Pyramid of Sneferu at Dahshur.

We are additionally aware of two other principles. The first is that the burial chamber would be located just west of the north-south centerline, and the second is that it would most probably be in the subterranean portions of the monument. Concerning the former principle, it is doubtful whether there were any exceptions to this rule. In the case of the few pyramids in which no burial chamber was found west of the north-south centerline, it is most likely that the true burial crypt has yet to be discovered. Regarding the latter principle, the Great Pyramid and a few other pyramids do in fact represent exceptions to the rule, and the unorthodox method employed by their architects should not lead us astray from the fact that any future investigation should, by the sheer established odds, concentrate on those subterranean sections more than on the superstructures of any of the monuments.

Thus we have the possibilities of secret chambers being discovered west of the north-south centerlines of pyramids and below ground level, in their subterranean sections—having gained access therein via a descending passage and outside entrance leading in from the north of the monument.

Aside from these established rules of pyramid burial, it is really anyone's guess as to where the pyramid pharaohs might be interred in these edifices. And, as many of these monuments are so very large, we are back to the point of looking for the proverbial needle in the haystack.

Therefore, unless a more thorough investigation of these pyramids is conducted—comparing certain specific techniques employed in some with those employed in others—the subject can never take on more than a generalized air of fanciful assumptions, the likes of which will never lead us to discover any of the secret chambers unless the elements of sheer luck or blind fate should miraculously happen to figure into the picture.

It is, then, the purpose of this essay to bring certain information to light, in the hope of better pinpointing the possible sites of any secret crypts. In order to achieve a semblance of order and logic in this respect, the author has chosen to focus on a specific period of pyramid building involving several monuments which tend to display similar "tell-tale" characteristics with regard to their interior designs, in the hope of establishing a correlation between said characteristics to the point of

more readily deducing where undiscovered chambers may be located.

The pyramids in question comprise four of the total of seven major ones which were built by six of the seven pharaohs of the Third Dynasty. Thus we have:

Pharaoh	Major Pyramids	Minor Pyramids
1. Beby		10
2. Djoser	1	
3. Djoser-Tati	1	
4. Khaba	1	
5. Eke	1	
6. Huni	1	1
7. Sneferu	2	1
	7	12

The four major pyramids which we will concentrate on are those of Djoser, Eke, Huni, and one of Sneferu's two. The twelve much smaller pyramids, ten of which have tentatively been attributed to Beby and one each of which belong to Huni and Sneferu, will not be discussed here.

Concerning the pyramid of Djoser at North Sakkara, the entrance is on the north at ground level. This opens into a descending passage, at the end of which is located a subterranean burial chamber set into the ground, with its roof exposed. Above this is a shaft, 60' long. The curious thing here is that the roof of the granite burial chamber accommodates a three-ton plug stone having grooves for ropes cut into its sides. (See illustration, page 249.) It seems obvious, then, that after the deceased pharaoh was interred in the chamber the plug stone was lowered with ropes, sealing off this apartment.

This arrangement presents certain problems, however, For the question naturally arises: If the roof and plug stone were exposed in ancient times, as they are now, then wouldn't the

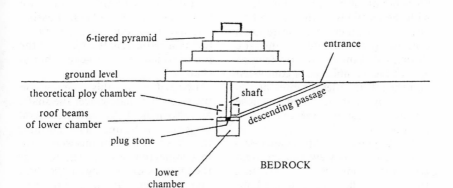

Theoretical arrangement of Pyramid of Djoser, North Sakkara (not to scale).

location of the burial chamber—and consequently, the whereabouts of the pharaoh—have been obvious to anyone gaining access into the pyramid after the interment? Furthermore, there is no evidence of overhead beam work, which would have been necessary for the manipulation of the ropes in the lowering of the granite plug stone.

From this picture, we can assume two things: First, that the burial chamber roof and plug stone were originally camouflaged or covered over; and second, that there once existed a framework of a sort with which beams worked in conjunction with ropes to lower said plug stone. From this, the author suggests that: (a) another, decoy, chamber once existed at ground level to the descending passage terminus, the floor of which would have hidden the roof beams and plug stone of the burial chamber beneath it; and (b) the beam and rope system was located in the shaft above. The ropes and beams were removed by the original builders after they had served their purpose, and the decoy chamber was dismantled by latter-day intruders, who used the squared and polished

granite blocks of the walls and ceiling for their own building purposes. In its original state, then, the true burial chamber would have been located **under the floor** of the decoy or "ploy" chamber, and **beneath a shaft** housing **ropes and beams.** (See illustration above.)

Asking the reader to keep the above boldface points in mind, we will now discuss the peculiarities of the second pyramid in question, that of the Pharaoh Eke, located at Zawaiyet el-Aryan.

The entrance to this monument is also on the north at ground level and follows a descending passage which culminates in a subterranean chamber. However, only the floor of this so-called chamber is intact, as the interior of the pyramid represents nothing more than a huge 73' deep by 82' long by 46' wide chasm cut out of the living rock, wherein the floor and sunken sarcophagus of the chamber are exposed to the open sky. The reason for this bizarre arrangement is that the pyramid was never completed beyond this point of construction, the site having been mysteriously abandoned.

The exposed floor of this subterranean chamber, although located in the depth of the pit, is at ground level with the terminus of the descending passage. It is, therefore, the author's opinion that this floor, and the theoretical chamber itself (which was either never completed, or completed and then dismantled), represented a mere ploy chamber, under whose massive floorstones the real burial chamber lay.

The Egyptologist Alessandro Barsanti shared this view and, at great cost and labor, began extracting these ten-ton floorstones in the hope of revealing the actual burial chamber which he was convinced lay beneath them. As is mentioned in the section of this chapter entitled "The Mystery of the Water," Barsanti died before he could complete his task, and the site was completely abandoned since that time (1905). The huge trench now serves as a garbage pit for the Egyptian Army. The water mystery, whereby 14,000 cubic feet of water suddenly disappeared under the existing floorstones after a rainstorm, is what prompted Barsanti to speculate that the true burial chamber was located beneath those granite stones.

It is the author's contention that the system employed here was the same as that which was present at the Pyramid of Djoser, and that the open trench not only once housed the granite walls and ceiling beams—as well as the existing **floor**—of the uppermost ploy chamber, but a system of **ropes and wooden beams** which would have been located in a **shaft** that could easily have been accommodated by the volume of the existing trench.

Regarding the third pyramid in question, that of the Pharaoh Huni, at Maidum, there is a similar situation of the monument's entrance being located on its north side, where it

opens into a descending passageway. At the bottom of this corridor are two small antechambers. Passing through these, one reaches the bottom of a vertical shaft 20′ high, at the top of which lies the so-called burial chamber.

Located within this chamber, in the area immediately over the shaft, and also in the shaft itself, are several large cedar beams. The popular theory is that these beams were used, in conjunction with ropes, to raise the mummy of the king up the shaft and into the chamber. However, given the evidence gleaned from the two pyramids just discussed, and also given the fact that no stone sarcophagus was ever discovered in this chamber, the author surmises that the **beamwork** found in this chamber and in the vertical shaft, acting with ropes, was *not* used to raise the mummy, but to *lower* it to the true, hidden burial chamber which lay **under the floor** of the **shaft**. And there, it is hypothesized, the great Pharaoh Huni still rests undisturbed, just as King Eke does in his unfinished pyramid.

In light of the information thus far presented, the curious internal arrangement of the fourth monument in question, the southern, Bent or Rhomboidal Pyramid of Sneferu at Dahshur, appears to fit quite well into the reconstructed picture. For in this pyramid the north entrance gives access to a descending passage, at the bottom of which lie two subterranean chambers. The southeast corner of the second compartment strangely contains a 42′ blind vertical shaft which apparently leads to nowhere, but which houses, at its upper end, two blocks of stone set into recesses in the masonry. These stones were undoubtedly meant to be transferred from their recesses into the shaft itself. But certainly they were not intended to block the shaft, for it led to nowhere. They must have been intended, then, to be *lowered* down the shaft to act as plugstones at the base of the shaft—at floor level— to camouflage a hidden chamber which must have been situated beneath that floor. Indeed, the investigative work of A. Hussein in 1946 did in fact reveal a hidden cavity **under the floor** at the base of the **shaft.** When this cavity was discovered, however, it was found to be empty. Apparently the pyramid architects had planned on using it for burial, and then, changing their minds, filled it in with stone blocks, leaving the now-useless plug stones in their original recesses at the upper end of the vertical shaft.

But if the site of the true burial chamber of Sneferu had now been altered, the question arises: Where was he interred in this monument? The author believes that the answer to this may lie in an investigation of a third existing chamber located higher up in the masonry of this pyramid. This third chamber contains, at its northern end, several huge **cedar beams** set into its walls which span the chamber from east to west. And as the walls of this compartment are constructed using the corbel technique—where the span of that compartment grows narrower as it progresses in height—then a **shaft** of a sort is consequently formed out of that arrangement in the area located immediately above the cedar beams. Could **ropes** have been used in conjunction with the beams to lower the mummy of King Sneferu into a secret crypt which lies **beneath the floor** of the existing chamber? For the fact that the true burial chamber of this mighty pharaoh still exists somewhere within the bowels of this colossal edifice is reinforced by the fact that the stone sarcoph-

agus, which would have been crucial to the burial, has yet to be discovered.

A great deal more can be said concerning the presence of **cedar beams** which were undoubtedly used in conjunction with **ropes** inside **vertical shafts** of other Old Kingdom pyramids, but it will suffice at this time to reflect on the information already given and to reserve further speculation for future essays on the subject. The interior designs of many third and fourth dynasty pyramids are quite complicated and give evidence of the determination and ingenuity of the ancient architects, whose principal purpose was to thwart the efforts of those who would endeavor to disturb the sacred mummies of their pharaohs. It is not surprising, then, that so little of these kings has ever been found. The very best minds of ancient Egypt were given the task of designing these complicated monuments; and it is this intelligence and this challenge which we are up against if we ever hope to penetrate the secret crypts of those pharaohs.

SUMMARY

The reader should now be able to appreciate the fact that the pyramids have not revealed all of their many secrets. There is still an impressive amount of investigation and exploration to be done concerning these edifices, both in the field and in library research.

When considering pyramid exploration, the reader should also be aware of the size of these structures. The Great Pyramid alone, the largest stone structure ever built on the Earth, is equal to an incredible 94 million cubic feet of masonry— enough volume to accommodate nearly 9,000 additional burial chambers! The calculation is simple: the Great Pyramid's volume (94,000,000 cubic feet) divided by the size of an average burial chamber (11,000 cubic feet, as in the case of Khufu's pyramid) equals 8,545.

The pharaohs who built these gigantic tombs were, by far, the greatest that ever ruled over Egypt. For the heyday of Egyptian history is synonymous with the heyday of pyramid building.

And somewhere within at least one of these mighty monuments lies the mummy of at least one of these great kings. That much, at least, we can fairly well assume.

King Tut is famous for being the only Egyptian pharaoh whose tomb was ever found intact, but Tut did not have a great pyramid. A greater find awaits mankind. Only future investigation will discern whether the world will ever have the opportunity to witness it.

PYRAMID PHARAOHS' MUMMY REMAINS

Dynasty III: Djoser
A mummified foot.
Dynasty III: Huni
Full skeleton. (Found in a mastaba, not pyramid.)
Dynasty III: Sneferu
A skeleton found in North (Red) Pyramid (possibly a post–Dynasty III interment).
Dynasty IV: Menkara
Mummy fragments (likely a Dynasty XXVI interment).
Dynasty V: Unas
Right arm, fragments of skull, other bones.
Dynasty VI: Teti
An arm and a shoulder.
Dynasty VI: Pepy I
Fragments of body.

Dynasty VI: Pepy II
Mummy wrappings only.
Dynasty XII: Amenemhat III
Charred bones.

Though it seems difficult to believe, this list of mummy remains constitutes all that has ever been found of the pyramid pharaohs. The only exceptions to finding anything else besides the bodies are:
Dynasty III: Djoser-Tati
Cache of gold jewelry.
Dynasty VI: Pepy I
Fragments of wooden coffin.
Dynasty XII: Senusert II
Gold cobra from front of royal pharaonic crown or funerary mask.
Dynasty XII: Amenemhat III
Pharaonic "false beard" of lapis lazuli, alabaster vessel and bowls.
Dynasty VI: Pepy II
Gold ceremonial instrument, broken alabaster and diorite vases.

This record is truly amazing when one takes into account the fact that each of the pyramid pharaohs was undoubtedly interred with numerous possessions, including the wooden and gold coffins and gold funerary mask.

PYRAMID QUEENS' AND PRINCESSES' MUMMY REMAINS

Dynasty III: Menkara's Queen
Fragments of skeleton.
Dynasty VI: Teti's Queen
Human bones, cedar coffin.
Dynasty XII: Amenemhat III's princess-daughter Ptah-Neferu
Charred bones.

PYRAMID PHARAOHS— SARCOPHAGI FOUND

Dynasty III: Djoser-Tati
Alabaster.

Dynasty III: Eke
Granite.
Dynasty IV: Khufu
Granite.
Dynasty IV: Khafra
Granite.
Dynasty IV: Menkara
Basalt.
Dynasty IV: Menkara's Princess Maetkhe
Granite.
Dynasty IV: Menkara's Queen Khamerernebty II
Granite.
Dynasty IV: Menkara's Queen?*
Granite.
Dynasty V: Userkaf
Basalt.
Dynasty V: Unas
Basalt.
Dynasty VI: Teti
Basalt.
Dynasty VI: Pepy I
Basalt.
Dynasty VI: Merenre I
Granite.
Dynasty VI: Pepy II
Granite.
Dynasty VII: Iby
Granite.
Dynasty XII: Amenemhat II
Sandstone.
Dynasty XII: Senusert II
Granite.
Dynasty XII: Senusert III
Granite.
Dynasty XII: Amenemhat III
Granite.
Dynasty XII: Amenemhat III
Quartzite.
Dynasty XII: Amenemhat IV
Granite.
Dynasty XII: Sebek-Neferu-Ra
Quartzite.
Dynasty XIII: Ameny
Unknown.
Dynasty XIII: Ay
Quartzite.

*Maspero, p. 194.

PYRAMID QUEENS AND PRINCESSES — SARCOPHAGI FOUND

Dynasty III: Sneferu's Queen Hetepheres
Alabaster.
Dynasty VI: Pepy I's Queen Iput I
Limestone.
Dynasty VI: Pepy II's Queen
Granite.
Dynasty XII: Senusert I's Princess
Quartzite.
Dynasty XII: Amenemhat III's Princess-Daughter
Quartzite.
Dynasty XIII: Ay's Queen
Quartzite.
Dynasty XIII: Khendjer II's Queen 1
Quartzite.
Dynasty XIII: Khendjer II's Queen 2
Quartzite.

MATERIALS OF VARIOUS SARCOPHAGI

Pyramid Pharaohs

  1 Alabaster
  3 Quartzite
  5 Basalt
  1 Sandstone
10 Granite
  1 Unknown
21

(The 21 sarcophagi for the pharaohs do not take into account the two granite sarcophagi found in the already-mentioned mastabas of Djoser and Huni, but only those found in pyramids.)

Pyramid Queens and Princesses

1 Alabaster
1 Limestone
5 Quartzite
4 Granite
11

**Pyramid Pharaohs, Queens
and Princesses**

    2 Alabaster — white
    1 Limestone — white and yellow
    8 Quartzite — yellow
    5 Basalt — black
    1 Sandstone — sandy
  14 Granite — rose (pink)
  <u> 1</u> Unknown
  32

Appendix A
Pharaohs of Dynasty I and Dynasty II

DYNASTY I

1. Mene (Menes) (Meni) .... 3407–3346 B.C.
2. Athothi (Khenti Athuthi) .... 3345–3289 B.C.
3. Kenken (Utho Khenkhen Athuthi) .... 3288–3260 B.C.
4. Uenneph (Ueneph) (Henneit Ato) *queen pharaoh ...... 3259–3234 B.C.
5. Usaphai (Udi Hesapti) .... 3233–3194 B.C.
6. Miebi (Othib Merbi) .... 3193–3181 B.C.
7. Semempse (Merkhet Shememsu) .... 3180–3172 B.C.
8. Binenth (Bienech) (Behu Bineth) .... 3171–3144 B.C.

DYNASTY II

1. Boetho (Neterbaiu) (Neterbeu Butho) .... 3143–3097 B.C.
2. Kaiecho (Kechou) (Kakau) (Nebre Kekeu) .... 3096–3058 B.C.
3. Binothr (Bineter) (Baenneter) .... 3057–3020 B.C.
4. Otlas (Uotnes) (Sekhemib Uothnes) .... 3019–3003 B.C.
5. Sethen (Sendi) (Senta) .... 3002–2966 B.C.
6. Nepherchere (Neferkere) .... 2965–2934 B.C.
7. Sesochr (Neferkara) (Neferkesokar) .... 2933–2926 B.C.
8. Chaire (Huthefi Kere) .... 2925–2915 B.C.
9. Thethi Kheneri (Chennere) .... 2914–2888 B.C.

Appendix B
The Flap-doors to the Pyramids of Sneferu and Khufu

Although the Greek geographer Strabo gave an account of how there was once a flap-door concealing the entrance to the Great Pyramid of King Khufu, Sir William F. Petrie is the only person who has drawn a rendition of this flap-door, and another of the flap-door which once existed at the entrance to the Bent (Rhomboidal) Pyramid of Khufu's father, King Sneferu. Petrie's designs for these doors were drawn according to information gleaned from his inspection of the entrance to the Bent Pyramid, where the obvious remnants of a ball-and-socket mechanism still exist. Petrie's designs, however, show serious defects.

With Petrie's renditions of the flap-door closed, an unsightly gap would necessarily exist at the top of that door where it meets the pyramid's casing stones.

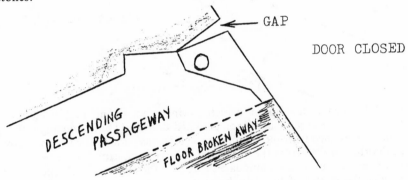

For if the gap were nonexistent when the door was closed,

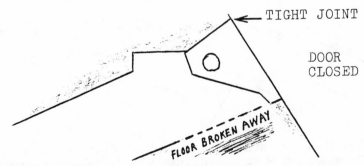

the door would be unable to swing open, as Petrie depicts it, for the top would already be tight against the existing casings.

In reverse then, if that gap were nonexistent with the door open then it would certainly exist with the door closed. The existence of this unsightly gap situated above the flap-door, where it obviously would have signaled the entrance to the pyramid, would not have been tolerated by the ancient architects.

The problem then, does not lie in the truth of Petrie's accurate drawing of the ball-and-socket joint and roof line of the descending passageway at the point of the entrance to the Bent Pyramid of Sneferu, but with Petrie mistakenly depicting the flap-door opening outward, and not inward. For with Petrie's design of the door swinging outward, not only is there the telltale gap left at the top of that door, but the inexplicable presence of a cut-out in the roof of the passageway (which serves no useful purpose for a flap-door swinging outward), and the additional fact that the floor of the passage at that point has been mysteriously broken away.

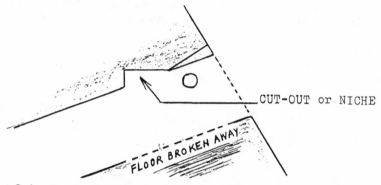

Only when the flap-door is depicted swinging in, and not out, do all of the elements fit perfectly. A flap-door designed differently and swinging inward along a redesigned floorline eliminates the existence of an unsightly gap above the doorline as seen from the outside of the pyramid, explains the reason for the ceiling cut-out (to accommodate the rear of this type of door), and further explains the matter of the floor being broken away at that locale (to allow passage into the pyramid by the high priests once the door was swung open).

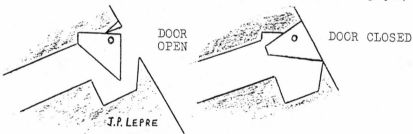

Thus, the floorline at this point was not "broken away" in later times, but was an intrinsic part of the original design. With the flap-door now missing, and a wide aperture now existing at the pyramids entrance, the floor cavity was filled in modern times in order to eliminate one having to step into the large floor hole, and thereby allowing easier access to the descending passage. The floor being haphazardly filled in is what gives it the "broken away" appearance.

With Petrie's design of a outward swinging door, other serious flaws reveal themselves. If the door was swung outward, then how could this be accomplished by the priests outside the pyramid who wished to enter the monument? How would anyone be able to apply enough pulling pressure to execute this task? Pulling such weight is vastly more difficult than pushing it. Where would the priest grip when pulling the door outward and confronted with a perfectly smooth and seamless surface? With the design of an inward swinging door, however, the priests would only have to push their combined weight against the smooth flap-door in order to open it. Once opened in this fashion, any sort of prop or wedge placed at the bottom of the door would suffice to check it.

Although finely balanced, the door would be inclined to close of its own weight due to the fact that the rear of the door which fit into the ceiling cut-out when the door was in the open position, was slightly heavier than the door's front section.

In conclusion, Petrie's error of depicting an outward, rather than an inward, swinging flap-door was based on the premise of Strabo's statement: "A stone may be taken out, which being raised up, there is a sloping passage." Although Petrie interpreted "taken out" and "raised up" as the flap-door being pulled outward, "raised up" could also refer to the rear of the door being raised up into the cut-out section of the ceiling, as is depicted with the inward-swinging version. As Strabo's original account was written in Greek and subsequently translated into English, it would be interesting to see what exact wording a second translation would reveal.

Appendix C
Hieroglyphics

The ancient Egyptians wrote using a hieroglyphic language, employing as many as 2,000 basic signs or symbols in varying combinations. Sir Alan Gardiner tells us that the earliest inscriptions go back to the First Dynasty, circa 3000 B.C., but Sir Arthur Weigall points out that the Egyptians may have begun their hieroglyphic writing at least 500 years before that time. In any event, hieroglyphs were synonomous with Egypt throughout her lengthy ancient history, until the last of them were written at Philae in A.D. 394.

There can be little doubt that this hieroglyphic language is related to the Semitic tongues (Hebrew and Arabic), yet, although Egypt is in Africa, the relationship of the hieroglyphs to the Hamitic (African) family is doubtful.

The hieroglyphic language passed through several marked stages in its development: Beginning as Old Egyptian (Dynasties I–VIII), it became Middle Egyptian (Dynasties IX–XVII), a vernacular form, and then Late (New) Egyptian (Dynasties XVIII–XXIV), yet another vernacular form.

Beyond Dynasty XXIV, at the advent of the post–Kingdom era (712 B.C.), the hieroglyphics developed into a sort of shorthand version. This corrupted form was called *Hieratic.* With the advent of time this language underwent a further corruption, whereby the writing was quite rapid, and was now known as *Demotic.* A final spoiling, which rendered it practically unrelated to the original script, became known as *Coptic,* and the pollution of the ancient tongue was complete.

The Egyptian hieroglyphs represent a sort of pictorial language, using phonograms (sound-signs) and ideograms (sense-signs). The language had vowels, but they were not written. In this sense, it is like the ancient Hebrew.

The term hieroglyphic is derived from the fact that these symbols were originally utilized for sacred sculpturings; sacred being the Greek *hieros,* and sculpturings (sculptured) the Greek *glupho* (*glyphics*).

Hieroglyphics were first deciphered in 1822 by Jean François Champollion, a brilliant linguist and scholar who at the age of 18 was a professor at Grenoble University in France. This deciphering was the result of the now famous Rosetta Stone having been discovered by Napleon's men on Egypt's northern coast in 1799. It was the Rosetta Stone that Champollion deciphered, using the royal name Cleopatra and an inscription in Greek as the keys. It is only fair to mention that the great scholar Thomas Young may well have found the "Cleopatra key" before Champollion, but Champollion was apparently the first to have his papers recognized and published. Champollion's motives might be questioned on this account, as he is said to have had knowledge of Young working with the Cleopatra cartouche (royal name); perhaps he had access to and utilized the details of that knowledge to make his own breakthrough, but

297

mentioned nothing of this in his presentation of his hieroglyphic treatise. Exactly ten years after Champollion's announcement of his deciphering, he died in Paris in his forty-first year.

Beyond these pioneers, the work of deciphering continued through the superlative effort of numerous linguists, historians and Egyptologists, the most noteworthy being Lepsius, Birch, de Rouge, Maspero, Mariette, Petrie, Sethe, Gunn, Gardiner, and Weigall.

The earliest body of hieroglyphic writings is the religious Pyramid Texts, which were inscribed on burial chamber walls (Old Kingdom). These eventually developed into the Coffin Texts which were written on burial coffins (Middle Kingdom), and then to the Book of Coming Forth by Day, where the texts were written on papyrus sheets (New Kingdom). All of this material together constituted the Book of the Dead, an assemblage of funerary spells, which were to aid the deceased in his journey to heaven.

Beyond the hieroglyphic religious texts — which were by far the most important — there were medical, lexicographical, court and administrative papyri, and private letters and historical records as well.

The direction of the hieroglyphic writing could start from the right or left, so long as the symbols faced into the reading in one uniform direction. One could also read or write the hieroglyphics from top to bottom, but not from bottom to top. The most common form, though, was from right to left, which is similar to ancient Hebrew. Yet because our modern languages are written and read from left to right, we adopt this form in the printing of the original material.

The hieroglyphic alphabet consisted primarily of 24 basic letters, but there were several more which served as alternatives or substitutes as the need arose. Actually, there are "doubles" for the letters A, D, K, S, T and four of the letter H. The alphabet possessed no C, E, J, L or O and mere inklings of Q, U, V, X and Z.

The hieroglyphic order was: (1) verb; (2) subject; (3) object; and (4) adverb or adverbial phrase.

SPELLING AND PRONUNCIATION OF ANCIENT EGYPTIAN PHARAONIC AND GEOGRAPHICAL PLACE NAMES

In dealing with the pyramid pharaohs we are constantly referring not only to their names and titles but also to the specific locations of their pyramids and other areas where their artifacts have been found. Spelling of those names and locations, however, can be quite inconsistent. Because the ancient Egyptians did not write out their vowels, we are at a loss as to exactly which ones we should use between the various consonants. With the absence of proper vocalization, a definitive transcription cannot be made.

As an example, consider the simple word [hieroglyph], meaning "that" (referring to yonder), and spelled P-F ([hieroglyph] = P, [hieroglyph] = F). It could have been pronounced in at least 20 different ways:

PAF	PEF	PIF	POF	PUF
P̄AF	P̄EF	P̄IF	P̄OF	P̄UF
PĀF	PĒF	PĪF	PŌF	PŪF
PĂF	PĔF	PĬF	PŎF	PŬF

With the word ![glyph], a geographical location spelled T-F-N-T

(◠ = T, ![glyph] = F, ○ = N, ◠ = T), could have been

pronounced:

TAFANAT	TEFENET	TIFINIT	TOFONOT	TUFUNUT
T̄ĀFĀNĀT	T̄ĒFĒNĒT	T̄ĪFĪNĪT	T̄ŌFŌNŌT	T̄ŪFŪNŪT
TĀFĀNĀT	TĒFĒNĒT	TĪFĪNĪT	TŌFŌNŌT	TŪFŪNŪT
TĂFĂNĂT	TĔFĔNĔT	TĬFĬNĬT	TŎFŎNŎT	TŬFŬNŬT

OR: T̄ĀFĂNĂT   T̄ĒFĔNĔT   T̄ĪFĬNĬT   T̄ŌFŎNŎT   T̄ŪFŬNŬT

OR: TAFĔNĪT   ETC.

OR: TŎFĒNĀT   ETC.

OR SIMPLY: TAFNAT   TEFNET   TIFNIT   TOFNOT   TUFNUT

OR: TĪFNŌT   TŌFNŬT   TIFNŬT   TŬFNĬT   TŪFNŌT

... nearly *ad infinitum*. The problem multiplies with the use of much larger words, and becomes hopeless when Greek corruptions are involved. For example, with the just-mentioned word, the popular transcription reads Tefnut, but the Greek usage is Thphenis.

To partially establish some sort of order, the rule has been established that, lacking the knowledge of which vowels were actually employed, the vowel E is inserted. This, however, only succeeds in establishing a slight degree of organization – one which, unfortunately, has no linguistic basis. The Egyptian Alphabet, although possessing some vowels, does not possess an E. The choice of a standard vowel insertion, then, would more appropriately have been an I, for the Egyptian alphabet contained an I, an A and a weak U (W).

The same situation holds true with the pharaonic names. For example,

with the royal name ![cartouche glyph], this is spelled IMNHTP

(![glyph] = I, ![glyph] = M, ⋀⋀⋀ = N, ![glyph] = H, ◠ = T, ▢ = P).

![glyph] ![glyph] – ![glyph] = IMN-HTP.

Here we have a situation where the full pronunciation could be:

IMAN-HATAP

IMEN-HETEP

IMIN-HITIP

IMON-HOTOP

IMUN-HUTOP

IMĀN-HĀTEP

IMĔN-HŎTIP

IMĪN-HĬTŎP

... etc., as in the previous examples.

Following the rules of inserting an "e" where there is no vowel, this transcription should be read IMEN-HETEP; yet the popularized transcription is Amenhotep. To complicate the matter even further the popularized Greek transcription reads Amenophis.

Thus a situation is created whereby certain pharaohs are referred to by several different names transcribed from the original hieroglyphs. What makes matters even worse is the fact that each pharaoh had five distinct names as part of his royal titulary, with renderings flowing in abundance from the pens of busy historians and Egyptologists.

Such is the complexity which unfolded with the absence of written vowels.

Appendix D
The Sphinx

Although this book is about Egyptian pyramids it would somehow not be complete were we not to mention this supreme, awe-inspiring statue—the face of a man with the body of a crouching lion.

This colossus is 240′ long, 65′ high and, contrary to popular belief, is not fashioned from individual blocks of stone, but is a single piece of solid sandstone, which in times past formed a protruding knoll in the barren desert. The idea of the Sphinx having been built of blocks stems from the many close-up photographs of this statue showing the latter-day Roman forearms of the lion; they were constructed of small limestone blocks, the originals having long since been destroyed.

Pliny the elder, Roman historian, tells us that the face of the Sphinx "was originally painted with red-ocher" (the color most often used by the ancients for depicting the complexion of male Egyptians). The eyes appear to have been painted black, and the headdress white.

That the Sphinx is in the image of a pharaoh is clear from its pharaonic (Royal Nemes) headdress, with the cobra symbol (the head of which is now broken off) and traces of a prop for a "false beard" still discernible at the area of its chest. This beard and headdress were worn only by these kings. A portion of the plaited beard has been preserved and is currently on display at the British Museum in London.

The question then arises: Which pharaoh does the Sphinx represent? Indeed, the so-called "Riddle of the Sphinx" is the riddle of its personage, not its age, as some have claimed. For we cannot begin to discern its age without first discerning in whose image it is hewn. This would not be so much of a problem, were it not for the fact that the nose of the statue was shot off with cannon in A.D. 1380 by a fanatical sheik. (This nose was carved from a separate piece of stone and fixed in a socket, still visible, between the eyebrows.) The face was further disfigured by the eighteenth century A.D. rulers of Egypt, the Marmalukes.

The sandstone nose is on display at the British Museum. If it were to be returned to its original position on the face of the statue, we might be better able to discern which king the Sphinx represents.

From the available evidence, however, it is reasonable to assert that the Sphinx is carved in the image of the Pharaoh Khafra, the builder of the second pyramid at Giza. This assumption is based on the fact that the statue is situated quite close to this pharaoh's pyramid, even closer to his valley temple and at the eastern end of his pyramid causeway.

Additionally, during the Eighteenth Dynasty, a certain pharaoh (Thutmosis IV) set up a granite stele between the paws of the Sphinx in reference to its

restoration. Part of the inscription on this stele refers to the Pharaoh Khafra, though the exact context is lost. From this, we may fairly well presume that Khafra was the builder of this famous statue. And finally, we cannot dismiss the fact that the image of the Sphinx bears a considerable resemblance to King Khafra, as the portrait of this pharaoh on page 302 demonstrates.

The author has experimented by adding the nose from a picture of King Khafra to a picture of the Sphinx, and by adding the missing cobra atop the headdress of the Sphinx, tress section of that headdress, and false pharaonic beard, in the hope of better understanding who this statue actually represents. And as the right side of the Sphinx's upper lip is also missing — having been shot off by cannon — a final adjustment has been made by shading in this area. This reconstructed drawing is also on page 302.

Opposite, Top: *Great Sphinx at Giza.* (J. BREASTED) **Bottom left:** *Pharaoh Khafra.* (MUSEUM OF FINE ARTS, BOSTON) **Bottom right:** *Reconstructed image of the Sphinx.* (PHOTO, A. FAKHRY; RECONSTRUCTION, J.P. LEPRE)

Appendix E
Some Principal Gods and Goddesses
of Ancient Egypt

Gods

1. Amen
2. Amset
3. Anubis (Anpu)
4. Asar (Ser)
5. Beb (Bebti)
6. Hapi (Hepr)
7. Hehu
8. Hep
9. Heru (Horus)
10. Hu
11. Keb
12. Kekui
13. Kerh
14. Khensu
15. Khepra
16. Khnemu
17. Menu (Amsi)
18. Nefer-Temu
19. Nu
20. Ptah
21. Qebhsenuf
22. Ra (Re)
23. Saa
24. Sebak
25. Set
26. Shai
27. Shu
28. Tem (Atmu)
29. Thoth (Tehuti)
30. Tuamutef
31. Up-uat
32. Osiris

Goddesses

1. Anqet
2. Ast
3. Bast
4. Hathor (Het-heru)
5. Hehut
6. Kekuit
7. Kerhet
8. Maat
9. Meht-urt
10. Meskhenet
11. Mut
12. Nebt-het (Nephthys)
13. Neheb-ka
14. Nekhebit
15. Net (Neith)
16. Nut
17. Renenet
18. Sati
19. Sekhmet
20. Taurt (Apt)
21. Isis

Appendix F
Pyramid Fields

Field no.	Field	Number of Pyramids	Pyramid Numbers
1	Athribis	1	1
2	Abu Roash	3	2-4
3	Giza	11	5-15
4	Zawaiyet el-Aryan	2	16-17
5	Abu Sir	11	18-28
6	North Sakkara	15	29-43
7	South Sakkara	21	44-64
8	Dahshur	8	65-72
9	Mazghuna	2	73-74
10	Lisht	12	75-86
11	Maidum	2	87-88
12	Seila	1	89
13	Hawara	1	90
14	Lahun	2	91-92
15	Zawaiyet el-Amwat	1	93
16	Dara	1	94
17	Abydos	1	95
18	Ombos	1	96
19	Nagada	1	97
20	El Kola	1	98
21	Edfu	1	99
22	Elephantine	1	100
		100	

LENGTH OF PYRAMIDS

Number of Pyramids	Approximate Length (in Feet)
5	600-765
1	450-600
14	300-450
18	150-300
40	35-150
22	Unknown
100	

Appendix G
Mathematical Notes on the Pyramids

**BASE-TO-HEIGHT RATIOS
OF 16 PYRAMIDS (IN METERS)**

	Pharaoh	Pyramid Field	Base	Height	Ratio
1.	Sesostris III	Dahshur	104.90	77.76	9.38/7
2.	Khendjer II	S. Sakkara	55	37.37	10.29/7
3.	Userkaf	N. Sakkara	70	44.5	10.50/7
4.	Pepy II	S. Sakkara	78	52	10.50/7
5.	Khafra	Giza	215.5	143.5	10.50/7
6.	Neferirkare	Abu Sir	106	70	10.57/7
7.	Neuserre	Abu Sir	80	52	10.71/7
8.	Sneferu	Maidum	144	92	10.92/7
9.	Khufu	Giza	232.5	148	11/7 or 7/11 = Pi (π)
10.	Sahure	Abu Sir	78	48	11.34/7
11.	Menkara	Giza	108.5	66.5	11.41/7
12.	Sesostris I	Lisht	105	61	11.90/7
13.	Ammenemes III	Hawara	100	58	12.40/7
14.	Unis	N. Sakkara	67	44	13.66/7
15.	Sesostris II	Lahun	106	48	15.40/7
16.	Sneferu	Dahshur	220	99	15.54/7

VOLUMES OF THE FIVE LARGEST EGYPTIAN PYRAMIDS

	Pyramid	Cubic ft. (in Millions)	
1.	Khufu	94	
2.	Khafra	78	
3.	Sneferu (Northern)	55	
4.	Sneferu (Bent)	50	
5.	Eke	35	(projected volume only; pyramid never completed)

Note: The largest pyramid in the world is the truncated Pyramid of Quetzalcoatl, at Cholula, 63 miles S.E. of Mexico City, Mexico. Its measurements are as follows:

309

Volume = 133 million cubic feet
Height = 177'
Length = 1,500'
Base = 45 acres

However, this pyramid is not of solid stone throughout, as is the case with the Great Pyramid of Egypt. It is built of a sand and rubble core sheathed with outer stones.

THE FIVE ANGLES OF A PYRAMID

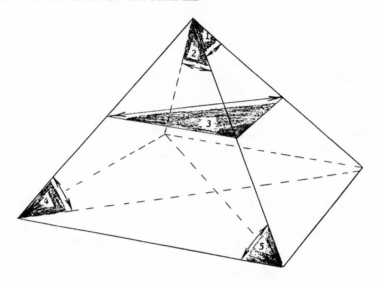

Example—Great Pyramid Khufu

1. Apex (interfacial) = 76° 17' 32" 2. Apex (edge to edge) = 96° 3. Dihedrael (face to face edge) = 112° 25' 39" 4. _____ (edge to level ground) = 41° 59' 50" 5. Base (base to level ground) = 51° 51' 14.3"

CALCULATING THE VOLUME OF A PYRAMID

$$V = \frac{Ah}{3}$$

A = Area of base
H = height

Example: Northern Pyramid of Sneferu, Dahshur

base = 720'
height = 320'
A (Area of base) = 720' × 720'
= 518,400 square feet

518,400 × 320' (height) = 165,888,000

165,888,000 ÷ 3 = 55,296,000 cubic feet

Pyramid Volume = 55 million cubic feet

CALCULATING THE AREA OF THE SIDES OF PYRAMIDS
(CALCULATING THE AREA OF A TRIANGLE)

By Hero — Geometrician of Alexandria

A = area

$A = \sqrt{S(S-A)(S-B)(S-C)}$

$S = 1/2(A+B+C)$

Example: A = 4 feet
        B = 5 feet
        C = 7 feet

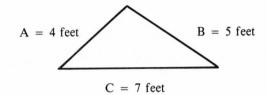

A = 4 feet   B = 5 feet

C = 7 feet

$S = 1/2(4+5+7) = 8$

$A = \sqrt{8(8-4)(8-5)(8-7)}$

$A = \sqrt{8 \times 4 \times 3 \times 1}$

$A = \sqrt{96}$

$A = 4\sqrt{6}$

A = 9.8 square feet

Appendix H
Comparison of Egyptian to Aztec and Mayan Pyramids

It seems to be a common belief of some groups of people that Egyptian, Aztec and Mayan pyramids were built on similar plans and were engineered by civilizations that communicated with one another down through the ages. This assumption is not in line with the truth; one can see through analysis that there are few similarities and many dissimilarities between the Egyptian models on the one hand, and the Aztec and Mayan on the other.

First, the Aztec and Mayan pyramids both had temples and altars of sacrifice built upon their summit platforms. These summits were, in all cases, flat-topped; whereas the summits of the Egyptian pyramids rose to a true peak and were thereby devoid of temples or altars of any kind.

Secondly, Aztec and Mayan pyramids (with one exception) were absent of any passageways or chambers within their superstructures or substructures; whereas Egyptian pyramids had numerous passages and burial chambers built into these areas.

Thirdly, the cores or main bodies of the Aztec and Mayan models were poorly constructed of loose rubble and debris; while the Egyptian models (with a few exceptions) were built of solid stone throughout.

A fourth point is that the Aztec and Mayan monuments had a staircase on one or more of their sides to accommodate the priests who would perform sacrificial rites at the summit temple; but the true Egyptian monuments, once finished, had sheer sides that were impossible to ascend.

And finally, Aztec and Mayan pyramids had their staircases decorated with figures of several of the gods, which looked much like the gargoyles or renaissance sculptures of early European cathedrals. Egyptian pyramids were devoid of any figures or images of this sort.

Appendix I
Notable Pyramid Authors and Explorers

Name	Approx. Date of Activity	Name	Approx. Date of Activity
1. Baikie, J.	1923	38. Gunn, B.	1924–1927
2. Barber	1930?	39. Hassan, S.	1932–1955
3. Barsanti, A.	1899–1907	40. Hayter, A.	1910–1911
4. Batrawi, A.	1948	41. Helck, W.	1956
5. Belzoni, G.	1818	42. Holscher, U.	1912
6. Borchardt, L.	1892–1932	43. Husseim, M.	1951
7. Bratton	1965	44. Jequier, G.	1928–1940
8. Breasted, J.	1924	45. Junker, H.	1928–1949
9. Brugsch, K.	1875–1879	46. Lansing, A.	1920–1934
10. Brunton, G.	1913–1921	47. Lauer, J. P.	1936–1966
11. Budge, E.A.	1893–1924	48. Lepsius, K.	1842–1884
12. Campbell, P.	1837	49. Loat, W.	1903–1913
13. Capart, J.	1930	50. Loftie, W.	1884
14. Caviglia, G.	1816–1836	51. Lucas, A.	1938–1948
15. Cerny, J.	1955–1958	52. Lythgoe, A.	1915–1919
16. Cottrell, L.	1956	53. Mace, A.	1914–1922
17. Covington, L.	1902–1910	54. Maragioglio, V.	1962
18. Daninos, A.	1871	55. Mariette, A.	1850–1881
19. Davies, N.	1905	56. Maspero, G.	1902–1906
20. Davison, N.	1765	57. Maystre, C.	1935
21. DeCamp, L.	1960–1974	58. Mencken	1935?
22. DeMorgan, J.	1895	59. Mendelssohn, K.	1974
23. Dixon, W.	1872	60. Moret, A.	1925
24. Donaldson, T.	1865	61. Morgan, J.	1895–1903
25. Drach, S.	1860	62. Mustapha, H.	1954
26. Drioton, E.	1939–1943	63. Newberry, P.	1943
27. Dunham, D.	1956	64. Niebuhr, K.	1774–1778
28. Edgar, M. and J.	1925–1926	65. Perring, J.	1835–1842
29. Edwards, I.E.S.	1947–1986	66. Petrie, W.M.F.	1883–1931
30. Engelbach, R.	1919	67. Pochan, A.	1934
31. Fakhry, A.	1951–1961	68. Quibell, J.	1900–1910
32. Firchow, O.	1942–1957	69. Raphael, M.	1937
33. Firth, C.	1923–1936	70. Reisner, G.	1905–1955
34. Gautier, J.	1902	71. Ricke, H.	1954–1957
35. Goneim, M.Z.	1956–1957	72. Rinaldi, C.	1962
36. Greaves, J.	1646	73. Rowe, A.	1929–1931
37. Grinsell, L.	1942–1945	74. Schmidt, V.	1910

Name	Approx. Date of Activity	Name	Approx. Date of Activity
75. Shaw, L.	1977	82. Varille, A.	1947
76. Smyth, C.	1864–1867	83. Vyse, R.	1835–1842
77. Spencer, P.	1721	84. Weigall, A.	1925
78. Spurrell, F.	1860	85. Wheeler, N.	1935
79. Strabo	10 A.D.	86. Winlock. H.	1906
80. Thomas, E.	1953	87. Yeates, T.	1833
81. Tompkins, P.	1972		

AUTHORS AND EXPLORERS
ASSOCIATED WITH PYRAMID INVESTIGATION

No.	Pyramid Field (listed N. to S.)	Person
I	Athribis	—
II	Abu Roash	Perring, Maragioglio
III	Giza	Belzoni, Borchardt, Campbell, Caviglia, Covington, Davies, Davison, Dixon, Drach, Holscher, Hassan, Helck, Junker, Perring, Petrie, Pochan, Quibell, Reisner, Shaw, Smyth, Thomas, Vyse
IV	Zawaiyet el-Aryan	Barsanti, Cerny, Lauer, Maspero
V	Abu Sir	Borchardt, Ricke
VI	North Sakkara	Barsanti, Droiton, Firth, Goneim,
VII	South Sakkara	Gunn, Hassan, Hayter, Jequier, Lauer, Quibell
VIII	Dahshur	Batrawi, Borchardt, DeMorgan, Fakhry, Maspero, Morgan, Ricke, Varille
IX	Mazghuna	Petrie
X	Lisht	Gautier, Jequier, Lansing, Lythgoe, Mace, Winlock
XI	Maidum	Borchardt, Daninos, Loftie, Mariette, Rowe
XII	Seila	Borchardt
XIII	Hawara	Hayter, Petrie
XIV	Lahun	Brunton, Engelbach, Lythgoe, Petrie, Winlock
XV	Zawaiyet el-Amwat	—
XVI	Dara	—
XVII	Abydos	Hall, Mace, Petrie
XVIII	Ombos	—

No.	Pyramid Field (listed N. to S.)	Person
XIX	Nagada	Petrie, Quibell, Spurrel
XX	El Kola	–
XXI	Edfu	–
XXII	Elephantine	–
*	Abu Gurab (Sun Temples)	Engelbach, Loat, Petrie

Bibliography

The following abbreviations have been used in this bibliography:

Ann. Serv.	*Annales du Service des Antiquités de l'Égypte.*
Bull. Inst. d'Ég.	*Bulletin de l'Institut d'Égypte.*
Bull Inst. fr.	*Bulletin de l'Institut Français d'Archéologie Orientale.*
Bull. M.M.A.	*Bulletin of the Metropolitan Museum of Art, New York.*
J.E.A.	*Journal of Egyptian Archaeology.*
M.D.A.I.K.	*Mitteilungen des deutschen archäologischen Institut, Abteilung Kairo.*
P.R.S.H.S.	*Proceedings of the Royal Society of Historical Studies, Cairo.*
Z.A.S.	*Zeitschrift für ägyptische Sprache und Altertumskunde.*

Aldred, C. *Ancient Egyptian Art.* London, 1965.
_____. *Art in Ancient Egypt.* London, 1969.
_____. *Egyptian Art.* London, 1980.
_____. *Egypt to the End of the Old Kingdom.* New York, 1965.
Baikie, J. *Ancient Egypt.* London, 1920.
Barber. *The Mechanical Triumphs of the Early Egyptians.* 1981.
Barsanti, A. "Ouverture de la pyramide de Zaouiet el-Aryan." *Ann. Serv.* II (1901), pp. 92–94.
_____. "Fouilles de Zaouiet el-Aryan (1904–06)." *Ann. Serv.* VIII (1907), pp. 201–210.
_____, and Maspero, G. *Fouilles autour de la Pyramide d'Ounas, 1900–1904.* Cairo.
Batrawi, A. "A Small Mummy from the Pyramid at Dahshur." *Ann. Serv.* XLVIII (1948), pp. 585–90.
Bissing, F.W. *Das Re-Heiligtum des Königs Ne-Woser-Re.* Berlin, 1905.
Bissing, F.W. and Kees, H. *Rathures.* Munich, 1922.
Bisson de la Roque, F. *Abou Roasch.* Cairo, 1924 and 1925.
Borchardt, L. "Die Pyramide von Silah." *Ann. Serv.* I (1900), pp. 211–214.
_____. "Ein Königserlass aus Dahschur." *Z.A.S.* XLII (1905), pp. 1–11.
_____. *Das Grabdenkmal des Königs Ne-Woser-re.* Leipzig, 1907.
_____. *Neuserre.* Leipzig, 1907.
_____. "Die Totentempel der Pyramiden." *Zeitschrift für Geschichte der Architektur* III, Heidelberg, 1907.
_____. *Nefer-ir-ke-re.* Leipzig, 1909.

_____. *Sahure*. Leipzig, 1910.

_____. *Das Grabdenkmal des Königs Sahure*. 2 vols. Leipzig, 1910-1913.

_____. *Die Pyramide, ihre Enstehung und Entwicklung*. Berlin, 1911.

_____. *Gegen die Zahlenmystik an der grossen Pyramide de Gise*. Berlin, 1922.

_____. *Langen und Richtungen der vier Grundkanten der grossen Pyramide bei Gise*. Berlin, 1926.

_____. *Die Entstehung der Pyramide an Baugeschichte der Pyramide bei Meidum nachgeweisen*. Berlin, 1928.

_____. *Eineges zur dritten Bauperiode der grossen Pyramide bei Gise*. Berlin, 1932; Cairo, 1937.

_____, and Sethe, K. *Zur Geschichte der Pyramiden*. Z.A.S. 30 (1892), pp. 83-106.

Bratton, F.G. *The Pyramids*. London, 1981.

Breasted, J. *History of Egypt*. New York, 1905.

_____. *History of Egypt (The Pyramid Builders)*. London, 1924.

_____. *The Dawn of Conscience*. New York, 1933.

Bruckmann, F. *Art of Ancient Egypt*. Vienna and London, 1936.

Brunton, G. *Lahun I: The Treasure*. London, 1920.

Budge, E.A. *An Egyptian Hieroglyphic Dictionary*. New York, 1978.

Budge, E.A. Wallis. *The Mummy*. Mass., 1894.

_____. *A Guide to the Egyptian Collections in the British Museum*. London, 1909.

Bush, J. *How Were the Pyramids Built?* Boston, 1981.

Busink, T.A. *Het Ontstaan der Pyramide*. Batavia, 1934.

Cambridge Ancient History. *The Pyramid Dynasties*. Mass., 1926.

Capart, J. *L'Art Egyptien*. Brussels, 1909.

_____. *Monuments Egyptiens*. Brussels, 1905.

_____. *Lectures on Egyptian Art*. North Carolina, 1928.

_____, and Werbrouck, M. *Memphis à l'ombre des Pyramides*. Brussels, 1930.

Cerny, J. "Name of the King of the Unfinished Pyramid at Zawaiyet el-Aryan." *M.D.A.I.K.* XVI (1958), pp. 25-29.

Clarke and Engelbach. *Ancient Egyptian Masonry*. London, 1930.

Cottrell, L. *The Mountains of Pharaoh*. London, 1956.

Davidson, D. *The Great Pyramid*. London, 1927.

Dawson, W. *Who Was Who in Egyptology*. London, 1951.

DeCamp, L. *The Ancient Engineers*. Mass., 1979.

DeMorgan, J. *Fouilles à Dachour*. Vienna, 1895-1903.

Drioton, E. *Le Sphinx et les Pyramides de Gizeh*. Service des Antiquités, Cairo, 1939.

_____, and Lauer, J.P. *Sakkara, the Monuments of Zoser*. Institut Francais d'Archéologie Orientale, Cairo, 1939.

Dunham, D. "Building an Egyptian Pyramid." *Archaeology* 9 (1956), no. 3, pp. 159-165.

Edgar, J. and M. *Great Pyramid Passages*. Vol. I. London, 1912.

Edgar, M. and J. *Great Pyramid Passages*. Glasgow, 1926.

Edwards, I.E.S. *The Pyramids of Egypt*. Middlesex, 1981.

_____. *The Pyramids of Egypt*. New York and London, 1985.

Emery, W. B. *Great Tombs of the First Dynasty*. Cairo, 1949.

Erman, A. *Life in Ancient Egypt.* New York, 1894.
Fakhry, A. *Sept Tombeaux à Gizeh.* Institut Français d'Archéologie Orientale, Cairo, 1935.
————. "The Southern Pyramid of Sneferu." *Ann. Serv.* LI (1951), pp. 509–522.
————. "The Excavation of Sneferu's Monuments at Dahshur, Second Preliminary Report." *Ann. Serv.* LII (1954), pp. 563–594.
————. *The Monuments of Sneferu at Dahshur.* Vol. I, *The Bent Pyramid.* Vol. II, *The Valley Temple.* Cairo, 1959–1961.
————. *The Pyramids.* Chicago: University of Chicago Press, 1974.
————. *The Pharaohs.* Chicago: University of Chicago Press, 1981.
Fechheimer, H. *Die Plastik der Ägypter.* Berlin, 1923.
Firchow, O. *Studien zu den Pyramidenlagen der 12. Dynastie.* Gottingen, 1942.
Firth, C. "Excavations of the Department of Antiquities at Sakkara (1928–1929). *Ann. Serv.* XXXIX (1929), pp. 64–70.
————, and Gunn, B. *The Teti Pyramid Cemeteries.* Cairo, 1926.
————; Quibell, J.; and Lauer, J.P. *The Step Pyramid.* Cairo, 1935.
Firth, F. *Ancient Egypt.* London, 1858.
Gardiner, A. *Egyptian Grammar.* Oxford, 1927.
————. *Egyptian Grammar.* Oxford, 1982.
Garstang, J. *The Third Egyptian Dynasty.* Westminster, 1904.
Gautier, J., and Jequier, G. *Fouilles de Licht.* Cairo, 1902.
Ghoneim, M.Z. *The Buried Pyramid.* London, 1956.
————. *Horus-Sekhem-khet, The Unfinished Step Pyramid at Sakkara.* Vol. I. Cairo, 1957.
Grinsell, L. *Egyptian Pyramids.* Gloucester, 1947.
Gunn, B. "The Name of the Pyramid-Town of Sesostris II." *J.E.A.* 31 (1945), pp. 106–7.
Hassan, S. *Excavations at Giza.* 8 Vols. Oxford and Cairo, 1932–1953.
————. *Excavations at Sakkara (1937–1938).* Cairo, 1938.
————. "The Causeway of Unis at Sakkara." *Z.A.S.* 80 (1955), pp. 136–144.
Hayes, W. *The Scepter of Egypt.* Cambridge, Mass., 1953.
Helck, W. "Zur Entstehung des Westfriedhofs an der Cheops-Pyramide." *Z.A.S.* 81 (1956), pp. 62–65.
Holscher, U. *Das Grabdenkmal des Königs Chephren.* Leipzig, 1912.
Hussein, M. "Pyramids Study Project." *P.R.S.H.S.* I (1951), pp. 27–40.
Jequier, G. *Le Mastabat Faraoun.* Cairo, 1928.
————. *La Pyramide d'Oudjebten.* Cairo, 1928.
————. *Les Pyramides des reines Neit et Apouit.* Cairo, 1933.
————. *La Pyramide d'Aba.* Cairo, 1935.
————. *Le Monument funéraire de Pepi II.* Cairo, 1936–1940.
————. *Deux pyramides du Moyen Empire.* Cairo, 1933 and 1938.
Junker, H. *Grabungen auf dem Friedhof des Alten Reiches bei den Pyramiden von Giza.* Vols. 1–12. Vienna, 1929–1955.
Kayler, F., and Roloff, E.M. *Ägyptien einft eind jekt.* Berlin, 1908.
Lagier, C. *Le Égypte Monumentale & Pittoresque.* Paris, 1922.
Lange, K., and Hirmer, M. *Egyptian Architecture, Sculpture & Painting in Three Thousand Years.* New York, 1966.
Lansing, A. "The Museum's Excavations at Lisht." *Bull. M.M.A.* XV (1920), pp. 3–11; XXI (1926), Section 2, pp. 33–40; XXIX (1934), Section 2, pp. 4–9.

Lauer, J.P. *La Pyramide à degrés.* 3 Vols. Cairo, 1936–1939.

————. "Le Temple funéraire de Kheops à la grande pyramide de Guizeh." *Ann. Serv.* XLVI (1947), pp. 245–259.

————. *Études complémentaires sur les monuments du roi Zoser à Saqqarah.* Cairo, 1948.

————. *Le Problème des Pyramides d'Égypte.* Paris, 1948.

————. "Les Grandes Pyramides étaient-elles pientes?" *Bull. Inst. d'Eg.* XXXV (1953), pp. 123–37.

————. "Comment furent construites les pyramides." *Historia* (1954), no. 86, (1954) pp. 57–66.

————. "Le Temple haut de la pyramide du roi Ouserkaf à Saqqarah." *Ann. Serv.* LIII (1955), pp. 119–33.

————. "Évolution de la tombe royale égyptienne jusqu'à la pyramide à degrés." *M.D.A.I.K.* XV (1957), pp. 148–165.

————. *Observations sur les Pyramides.* Cairo, 1960.

————. *Histoire monumentale des Pyramides d'Égypte.* Vol. I. Cairo, 1962.

————. "Sur l'age et l'attribution possible de l'excavation monumentale de Zaouiet el-Aryan." *Revue d'Egyptologie* 14 (1962), pp. 21–36.

————. *Le Mystère des Pyramids.* Paris, 1974.

Lucas, A. *Ancient Egyptian Materials and Industries.* Third edition. London, 1948.

Lythgoe, A. "Excavations at the South Pyramid of Lisht in 1914." *Ancient Egypt* (1915), pp. 145–53.

————. "The Treasure of Lahun." *Bull. M.M.A.* (Dec. 1919), Part 2.

Mace, A. "Excavations at North Pyramid of Lisht." *Bull. M.M.A.* IX (1914), p. 220.

————. "Excavations at Lisht." *Bull M.M.A.* (Nov. 1921), Part 2, pp. 5–19; (Dec. 1922), Part 2, pp. 4–18.

Maragioglio, V., and Rinaldi, C. *Notizie sulle Piramidi di Zedefra, Zedkara Isesi, Teti.* Turin, 1962.

Mariette, A. *The Monuments of Upper Egypt.* Boston, 1890.

Maspero, G. *Lectures Historiques.* Paris, 1890.

————. *Egypt and Assyria.* London, 1892.

————. *Les Monuments funéraires de l'Égypte ancienne.* Paris, 1899.

————. *Dawn of Civilization (Egypt and Chaldea).* London, 1901.

————. "Note sur le pyramidion d'Amenemhait III à Dahchour." *Ann. Serv.* III (1902), pp. 206–208.

————. *Recueil des Travaux.* Cairo, 1902.

————. *History of Egypt.* Vols. I–VIII. London, 1903.

————. *The Memphite Empire.* Paris, 1906.

————. *New Light on Ancient Egypt.* London, 1908.

————. *Egypt.* Paris and Cairo, 1912.

————. *Art in Egypt.* New York, 1921.

————, and Barsanti, A. "Fouilles de Zaouiet el-Aryan (1904–5)." *Ann. Serv.* VII (1906), pp. 257–86.

Maystre, C. "Les Dates des pyramides de Snefrou." *Bull. Inst. fr.* XXXV (1935), pp. 89–98.

Mendelssohn, K. *Riddle of the Pyramids.* New York, 1974.

Metropolitan Museum of Art. *Bull. M.M.A.* Part III. 1920.

Mitchell, L.M. *History of Ancient Sculpture.* New York, 1883.

Moret, A. *Au Temps des Pharaohs.* Paris, 1908.

_____. *The Nile and Egyptian Civilization.* London, 1927.

Moustapha, H. "The Bent Pyramid." *Ann. Serv.* LII (1954).

Museum of Fine Arts, Boston. *Treasures of Egyptian Art from the Cairo Museum.* Boston and London, 1970.

Nagel. *Encyclopedic Guide to Egypt (The Pyramids).* Geneva, 1978.

Newberry, P. "The Co-regencies of Ammenemes III, IV and Sebeknofru." *J.E.A.* 29 (1943), pp. 74–75.

Oppel, K. *Das alte Wunderland der Pyramidien.* Leipzig, 1906.

Perring, J. *On the Engineering of the Ancient Egyptians.* London, 1835.

_____. *Gizeh.* London, 1837–1840.

_____. *Gizeh III.* London, 1842.

Perrot, G., and Chipiez, C. *A History of Ancient Art in Egypt.* London, 1883.

Petrie, W.M.F. *The Pyramids and Temples of Gizeh.* London, 1883.

_____. "Mechanical Methods of the Ancient Egyptians." *Jour. Z.A.S.* XIII (1884).

_____. *Illahun, Kahun and Gurob.* London, 1890.

_____. *Kahun, Gurob and Hawara.* London, 1890.

_____. *Medum.* London, 1892.

_____. *Ten Years Digging in Egypt.* London, 1892.

_____. *History of Egypt.* London, 1895.

_____. *Naqada and Ballas.* London, 1896.

_____. *Hawara, Biahmu and Arsinoe.* London, 1899.

_____. *Royal Tombs of the 1st and 2nd Dynasties.* London, 1901–1902.

_____. *Excavations at Sinai.* London, 1906.

_____. *Lahun I, the Treasure.* London, 1920.

_____. *History of Egypt.* 1924.

_____. "The Building of a Pyramid." *Ancient Egypt* (1930), Part II, pp. 33–39.

_____. *Seventy Years in Archaeology.* London, 1932.

_____. *Egyptian Architecture.* London, 1938.

_____. *Ten Years Digging in Egypt.* Chicago, 1976.

_____; Brunton, G.; and Murray, M. *Lahun II.* London, 1923.

_____; Mackay, E.; and Wainwright, G. *Meydum and Memphis III.* London, 1910.

_____; _____; and _____. *The Labyrinth, Gerzeh and Mazghuneh.* London, 1912.

Pochan, A. "Observations relatives au revêtement des deux grandes pyramides de Giza." *Bull. Inst. d'Eg.* XVI (1934), pp. 214–20.

Quibell, J. *Saqqara.* Vol. III. Cairo, 1907–1908.

Raphael, M. "Nouveau nom d'une Pyramide d'un Amenemhet." *Ann. Serv.* XXXVII (1937), pp. 79–80.

Rawlinson, G. *History of Ancient Egypt.* Vol. I. New York, 1880.

Reisner, G. "Hetepheres, mother of Cheops." *Bull. of the Museum of Fine Arts, Boston,* 25, 26, and 30 (1927–1932).

_____. *Mycerinus. The Temples of the Third Pyramid at Giza.* Cambridge, Mass., 1931.

_____. *The Development of the Egyptian Tomb Down to the Accession of Cheops.* Cambridge, Mass., 1936.

_____. *A History of the Giza Necropolis.* Vols. I and II. Cambridge, Mass., 1955.

Ricke, H. "Baugeschichtlicher Vorbericht über die Kultanlagen der südlichen Pyramide des Snofru in Dahschur." *Ann. Serv.* LII (1954), pp. 603–623.

_____. "Erster Grabungsbericht über das Sonnenheiligtum des Königs Userkaf bei Abusir." *Ann. Serv.* LIV (1956–1957), pp. 75–82.

_____. "Zweiter Grabungsbericht über das Sonnenheiligtum des Königs Userkaf bei Abusir." *Ann. Serv.* LIV (1956–1957), pp. 305–316.

_____. "Dritter Grabungsbericht über das Sonnenheiligtum des Königs Userkaf bei Abusir." *Ann. Serv.* LV (1958), pp. 73–77.

Rosellini, A. *Monumenti Civili.* Paris, 1892.

Rowe, A. "Excavations of the Eckley B. Coxe, Jr., Expedition at Meydum, Egypt, 1929–30." *Museum Journal,* Philadelphia, Penn., March, 1931.

Schafer, H. *Von Egyptischer-Kunst.* Berlin, 1922.

_____, and Andrade, W. *Die Kunst des Alten Orients.* Propyläen Verlag, Berlin, 1925.

Schmidt, V. *Egyptian Sarcophagi.* Kobenhavn, 1910.

Shaw, L. *The Abode of an Unknown God.* New York, 1981.

Smith, W.S. *Art and Architecture of Ancient Egypt.* New York and Philadelphia, 1981.

Smyth, P. *Life and Words at the Great Pyramid.* Edinburgh, 1867.

_____. *Our Inheritance in the Great Pyramid.* New York, 1890.

_____. *Ancient Egypt.* Boston, 1961.

Soldi, E. *La Sculpture Egyptienne.* Paris, 1876.

Steindorff, G. *A Royal Head from Ancient Egypt.* Baltimore, 1913.

Stienon, J. "El Kolah." *Chronique d'Égypte.* Brussels, 1950.

Strabo. *Geographia.* ca. 10 A.D.

Thomas, E. "Air Channels in the Great Pyramid." *J.E.A.* 39 (1953), p. 113.

Tompkins, P. *Secrets of the Great Pyramid.* New York, 1972.

Vandier, J. *La Statuaire l'égyptienne.* Paris, 1958.

Varille, A. *À propos des pyramides de Sneferu.* Cairo, 1947.

Vyse, H., and Perring, J. *Operations Carried Out on the Pyramids of Gizeh.* 3 Vols. London, 1840–1842.

Ward, J. *The Sacred Beetle.* London, 1902 and 1906.

Weigall, A. *Ancient Egyptian Works of Art.* London, 1924.

_____. *The Glory of the Pharaohs.* New York, 1925.

_____. *History of the Pharaohs.* Vol. I. New York, 1925.

Wheeler, N. "Pyramids and Their Purpose." *Antiquity* IX (1935), pp. 172–185.

Wilkinson, J. *The Ancient Egyptians.* Vol. II. London, 1854.

Winlock, H. *The Treasure of Lahun.* New York, 1934.

Woldering, I. *God, Men & Pharaohs.* New York, 1967.

Worringer, W. *Egyptian Art.* New York, 1928.

List of Illustrations

325

Sources of Illustrations

Annales du Service des Antiquités de l'Égypte, *Catalogue General des Antiquités Égyptiennes,* Vol. 77 (Cairo, 1925): p. 213. A. Barsanti, "Fouilles de Zaouiet el-Aryan (1904–06)," *Annales du Service des Antiquités de l'Égypte* VIII (1907), pp. 201–210: p. 44 (author's improvement), p. 44 (author's improvement). Berlin Museum (West Berlin): p. 213 (Annales du Service des Antiquités de l'Égypte, *Catalogue Général des Antiquités Égyptiennes,* Vol. 77 [Cairo, 1925]). F.W. Bissing, *Das Re-Heiligtum des Königs Ne-Woser-Re* (Berlin 1905): p. 168. L. Borchardt, *Die Pyramide, ihre Enstehung und Entwicklung* (Berlin, 1911): p. 15. L. Borchardt, *Nefer-ir-ke-re* (1909): p. 165. L. Borchardt, *Das Grabdenkmal des Königs Sahure,* 2 vols. (1910–1913): p. 160 (author's improvement), p. 161, p. 161. L. Borchardt, *Das Grabdenkmal des Königs Ne-woser-Re* (1907): p. 167 (author's improvements), p. 168, p. 168, p. 175. J. Breasted, *History of Egypt* (New York, 1905): p. 48, p. 160, p. 174, p. 68 (photo by L.D. Covington), p. 180, p. 181, p. 209, p. 298. J. Breasted, *The Dawn of Conscience* (New York: 1933), p. 63 (photo by R. Hawthorne; reprinted with permission from the Oriental Museum, University of Chicago). Brooklyn Museum: p. 47, p. 183, p. 222 (head of Huni [?], red granite, Fourth Dynasty [ca. 2837–2814 B.C.], The Brooklyn Museum, 46.167, Charles Edwin Wilbour Fund). E.A. Wallis Budge, *Guide to the Egyptian Collection in the British Museum* (London, 1909): p. 169 J. Capart, *L'Art Égyptien* (Brussels, 1909): p. 45, p. 94, p. 167. J. DeMorgan, *Fouilles à Dachour* (Vienna, 1895–1903): p. 211 (bottom), p. 213, p. 214 (bottom), p. 243 (bottom). J. and M. Edgar, *Great Pyramid Passages,* Vol. I (London, 1912): p. 63, p. 76 (bottom), p. 80, p. 93, p. 118. I.E.S. Edwards, *The Pyramids of Egypt* (New York and London, 1985): p. 202, p. 237. Freer Gallery of Art, Washington, D.C.: p. 149. Egyptian Museum, Cairo: p. 31 (H. Schafer and W. Andrade, *Die Kunst des Alten Orients,* Propyläen Verlag, Berlin, 1925); p. 37 (L.M. Mitchell, *History of Ancient Sculpture,* New York, 1883); p. 156 (C. Aldred, *Egypt to the End of the Old Kingdom,* New York, 1965); p. 178 (J. Quibell, *Saqqara,* Vol. III, 1907–1908; p. 180 (J. Breasted, *History of Egypt,* New York, 1905); p. 181 (J. Breasted, *History of Egypt*); p. 201 (H. Fechhmeir, *Die Plastik der Ägypter,* Berlin, 1923); p. 208 (C. Aldred, *Art in Ancient Egypt,* London, 1969); p. 211 (F. Bruckmann, *Art of Ancient Egypt,* Vienna and London, 1936); p. 214 (J. Breasted, *History of Egypt*); p. 225 (J. Capart, *Monuments Égyptiens,* Brussels, 1905); p. 199 (J. Vandier, *La Statuaire l'Égyptienne,* Paris, 1958). A Erman, *Life in Ancient Egypt* (New York, 1894): p. 255. A Fakhry, *The Pyramids* (Chicago: University of Chicago Press, 1974): p. 15, p. 50 (Egyptian Museum, Cairo), p. 55 (author's improvement), p. 58, p. 60, p. 137, p. 142, p. 172, p. 298 (with author's reconstructions); with permission from the University of Chicago Press. F. Firth, *Ancient Egypt* (1858): p. 148, p. 157. J Garstang, *The Third Egyptian Dynasty* (Westminster, 1904): p. 8. G. Jequier,

Le Monument funéraire de Pepi II (Cairo, 1936–1940): p. 184, 184. G. Jequier, *Deux pyramides du Moyen Empire* (Cairo, 1938): p. 227, p. 228. C. Lagier, *L'Égypte Monumentale & Pittoresque* (Paris, 1932): p. 146. J.P. Lauer, *Le Mystere des Pyramids* (Paris, 1974): p. 39 (plate 10B in source), p. 45 (plate 14a in source), p. 45 (plate 14B in source), with permission from J.P. Lauer. J.P. Lauer, *La Pyramide à degrés*, 3 vols. (Cairo: 1936–1939): p. 34 (plate XIX in source), p. 33 (plate IV in source; photo and reconstructed model by J.P. Lauer), with permission from J.P. Lauer. J.P. Lauer, "Le Temple haut de la pyramide du roi Ouserkaf à Saqqarah," *Annales du Service des Antiquités de l'Égypte* LIII (1955), p. 119–33: p. 157 (plate III in source), with permission from J.P. Lauer. Louvre Museum: p. 29 (J. Vandier, *La Statuaire l'Égyptienne,* Paris, 1958), p. 132 (A. Weigall, *Ancient Egyptian Works of Art,* London, 1924). A. Mariette, *The Monuments of Upper Egypt* (Boston, 1890): p. 33. G. Maspero, *History of Egypt,* Vols. I–VIII (London, 1903): p. 20, p. 56. G. Maspero, *Recueil des Travaux* (Cairo, 1902): p. 176, p. 176. G. Maspero, *Art in Egypt* (Cairo, 1921): p. 220. Metropolitan Museum of Art, New York: p. 159 (C. Aldred, *Egypt to the End of the Old Kingdom,* New York, 1965); p. 206 (I.E.S. Edwards, *The Pyramids of Egypt,* New York and London, 1985); p. 214 (I.E.S. Edwards, *Pyramids of Egypt*); with permission from the Metropolitan Museum of Art and Dieter Arnold. Museum of Fine Arts, Boston: p. 15, p. 16, p. 41, p. 62, p. 131, p. 141, p. 146, p. 298. K. Oppel, *Das Alte Wunderland der Pyramidien* (Leipzig, 1906): p. 52. G. Perrot and C. Chipiez, *A History of Ancient Art in Egypt* (London, 1883): p. 7, p. 16, p. 56, p. 125, p. 143, p. 209. W.M.F. Petrie, *Ten Years Digging in Egypt* (London, 1892): p. 50. W.M.F. Petrie, *Medum* (London, 1892): p. 52. G. Rawlinson, *A History of Ancient Egypt,* Vol. I (New York, 1880): p. 72. A. Rosellini, *Monumenti Civili* (1892): p. 239. H. Schafer, *Von Egyptischer Kunst* (Berlin, 1922): p. 243, p. 247. H. Schafer and W. Andrade, *Die Kunst des Alten Orients* (Propyläen Verlag, Berlin, 1925): p. 161, p. 175. P. Smyth, *Our Inheritance in the Great Pyramid* (New York, 1890): p. 112, p. 129. Soldi, E., *La Sculpture Égyptienne* (Paris, 1876): p. 243 (top). Stienon, J. "El Kolah," *Chronique d'Égypte* (Brussels, 1950): p. 30. J. Vandier, *La Statuaire l'Égyptienne* (Paris, 1958): p. 42, p. 170. H. Vyse and J. Perring, *Operations Carried on at the Great Pyramid of Giza,* Vol. III (London, 1837): p. 53, p. 53 (author's improvements), p. 130 (author's improvements), p. 130 (author's improvements), p. 137, p. 142 (author's improvements), p. 130, (author's improvements), p. 144, (author's improvements), p. 144 (author's improvements), p. 144 (author's improvements). A. Weigall, *Ancient Egyptian Works of Art* (London, 1924): p. 132 (courtesy of Louvre Museum). J. Wilkinson, *The Ancient Egyptians,* Vol. II (London, 1854): p. 243. Remaining illustrations by author.

Index

Although this index covers the entire text, it omits the summary accounts for each pyramid pharaoh, where information concerning their alternative names, individual sarcophagi and pyramid complexes, etc., are listed. Refer to these personalized pharaoh sections when seeking these data.